The Encyclopedia of Old Fishing Lures Made in North America

Volume 13

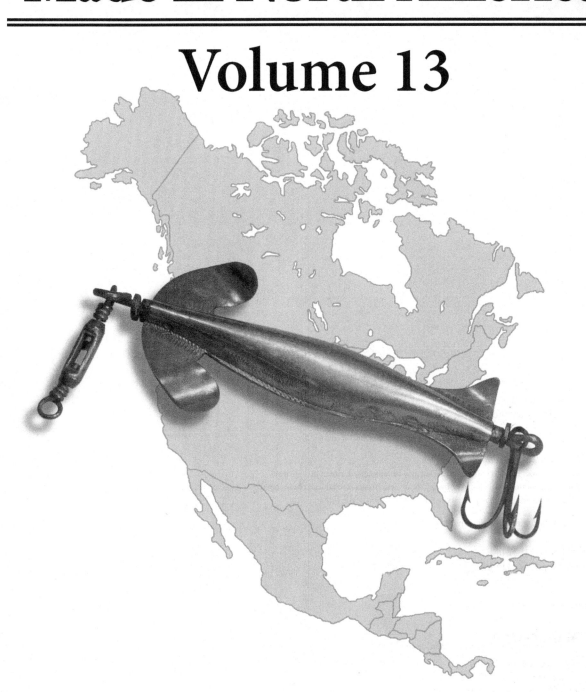

Order this book online at www.trafford.com
or email orders@trafford.com

Most Trafford titles are also available at major online book retailers.

Printed in the United States of America.

ISBN: 978-1-4251-5246-8 (sc)
ISBN: 978-1-4251-5247-5 (e)

Trafford rev. 11/16/2011

 www.trafford.com

North America & international
toll-free: 1 888 232 4444 (USA & Canada)
phone: 250 383 6864 ♦ fax: 812 355 4082

*Dedicated in loving memory to
Tony Nata III.*

A percentage of the proceeds of the sale
of this encyclopedia will be donated to

Tony's Room
FOUNDATION

Providing Kids with Leukemia a Room to Grow and a Chance to Survive

 **Tony's Room Foundation** is focused on building "clean room" environments in the homes of children battling Leukemia. Tony's Room Foundation was formed to build hope for families of children with Leukemia as a way to honor the memory of a courageous little boy from Slidell, Louisiana who really loved to fish — Anthony J. "Tony" Nata III.

To make a 100% tax-deductible donation and for more information, please visit www.tonysroom.org.

CONTENTS

ACKNOWLEDGMENTS

Writing a series of books on this scale took me over a nine-year path of research and photography. However, even with that, it would not have been possible for me to have completed this project without the assistance of hundreds of contributing people. Consequently, these books are the result of the collective efforts and contributions of the following people and many others too numerous to mention.

First of all, I would like to extend special thanks to Dan Basore of Warrenville, Illinois. I spent nearly a month at Dan's home as an invited guest on two separate visits to do research and photography. We spent countless hours pouring over the Richard Walton files alone. (Richard Walton is without a doubt this country's first intensive lure collector. He started shortly after the turn of the twentieth century and collected and kept meticulous records of his finds for another 50 years.)

Other major contributors included the following: Alan Bakke (MN), Adrien Delbasty (LA), Dennis Giese (WI), Billy Gregory (WI), Steve O'Hern (MN), Doug Lenicheck (WI), Gary Ludwig (IN), Dean A. Murphy (MO), Robert "Robbie" Pavey (GA), Virgil Potvin (WI), Joe Stagnitti (NY), Larry & Pat Sundal (IA), Al Tumas (WI), and Matt Wickham (KY).

There were many collectors and non-collectors who contributed serious time and effort into these books: Philip Allen (MN), Laurie Bingham (NY), Eric Borgerding (WI) David Budd (IN), Robert Bulkley (IN), Doug Carpenter (OH), Arlan Carter (WI), John Conlin (MN), Craig Farver (CO), the late Art Hansen (WI), Peter Heid (NY), Tom Jacomet (AZ), Jack Leslie (IN), Randy Nelson (IN), the late Richard Nissley (MI), the late George Richie (MI), Dale Roberts (MI), William Robinson (IN), Ray Rodgers (AK), Richard Rounds (Canada), Tom Schofield (WI), Travis Slater (NY), Chris Slusar (WI), Arne Soland (OR), Colby Sorrells (TX), David Spengler (WI), Mike Thompson (OK), John Workman (Canada), and the late Clarence Zahn (MI).

Other contributors to these books included the following: Bill Bailey (TX), Hollis Bosley (IL), Tom Clayton (NJ), Randall Cobb (CO), John Collen (WI), Curt Conner (IA), Gary Cripps (WI), Wayne Dionne (TX), William Earl (MI), Mike Echols (FL), Lindy Egan (OH), Mike Estep (TN), Jim Frazier (FL), Ron Fritz (FL), Dave Gusted (CA), Walter Geib (WI), Mike Hampton (CA), Ron Hanley (GA), Eddie Hobbs (IL), Dave Hoover (OH), Tom Jacomet (AZ), the late Art Kimball (WI), John Kolbeck (MN), Robert & Sue Kutchera (WI), John Laimon (WI), Bob Lehmkuhl (WI), Joe McCarthy (WI), Dennis McNulty (VA), John Muma (MS), Joe Muzynoski (WI), Mike Potthier (WI), Bill Stuart (FL), and Joe Yates (FL).

Edited by: Jessica & William Lehmann (WI)
Layout by: Robert Lehmann (WI)

ABOUT THE AUTHOR

Meeting Bob Slade for the first time was a shocking experience to me. It was December, 1988 that another collector introduced me to Bob, who at the time was completing research for his book, The History & Collectible Fishing Tackle of Wisconsin. Here was this big guy talking non-stop with unbelievable passion about Wisconsin fishing lures. Most impressive was his knowledge of the history of each lure and its inventor or manufacturer. To me, this is what sets Bob apart from many other lure collectors in this compulsive and rewarding hobby of ours. It helps that Bob is blessed with a wonderful memory that supplements his passion for collecting fishing tackle and the history of fishing lures. Bob trained himself in the art of photography to enhance his stories of lure history and lure identification.

Bob was born in 1938 in Charlotte, Michigan and grew up on the family farm. He was an avid fisherman and hunter and ran a trap line while in high school. Bob spent four years in the United States Air Force and graduated from Michigan State University. Bob worked in the insurance industry for over thirty years in both management and sales. Since his retirement, Bob has concentrated on fishing-lure collecting.

I have fished with Bob in the Northwest Territories at a lake at which he has fished for many years. The "fishing hole" is 140 miles north of Yellowknife and has yielded many monster pike and lake trout to Bob including a 35-pound pike that he boated. At home in Wisconsin, Bob is a fanatical bass fisherman.

All this fishing fits nicely into his passion for lure collecting. Before I met Bob, his lure collection had numbered over 12,000 lures – one of the largest collections in the United States – which he sold for health reasons. However, Bob could not be stopped for long and soon started collecting again. When he finished his book on Wisconsin lures, Bob sold his second collection of many thousands of lures.

Today, Bob is still very busy buying and selling lures for research of the history. This task could go on and on forever and never be finished. Bob is quickly recognized at lure shows carrying his camera, interviewing collectors, and taking photos of both new finds and different variations of known lures. (Many collectors have never known the history of some lures prior to Bob writing up their story.) He greatly enjoys the "hunt" part of collecting, and I think he is on a mission to provide all of us with a guide to tackle identification and to tell the stories of fishing lure history.

Bob is blessed with a wonderful wife, who graciously puts up with all of this "lure stuff" and also does the hard work of packaging and shipping his lures.

Thank you, Bob, for this encyclopedia of fishing lures.

DOUG LENICHECK

INTRODUCTION

When I started doing research and writing on this current book project in the fall of 1999, I had no idea that it would take nine years to complete. I have traveled to eleven states and three Canadian providences doing research and have taken well over 10,000 pictures.

I have been invited into dozens of homes to do photography and have spent many days in museums and libraries researching old archives. During these nine years, my normal fishing time has been cut in half, and our home has become a warehouse of boxes of papers and pictures.

I originally began the project with the intention of covering only a few Great Lakes States, and, in fact, the original title of the books was going to be, "Lures of The Great Lakes States." However, the undertaking kept growing and growing until finally it was covering all of the United States and parts of Canada. I'm not professing that these books cover every lure maker that existed in this country and Canada, but it covers only those that I became aware of in my 49 years of collecting or recent research. I have realized that it would take more than one lifetime to cover the entire subject of fishing-tackle makers.

Therefore, the first thing I decided was to not include the big six lure makers – Creek Chub, Heddon, Moonlight/Paw Paw, Pflueger, Shakespeare, and South Bend – to save space in my books and because there are countless books available that cover these important lure makers.

I also decided to not cover bobbers, fly rod lures, ice fishing decoys, rods, reels, and other miscellaneous fishing tackle. However, for reasons you will understand, there are exceptions to these statements found throughout the books.

A task of this magnitude meant that I had to accept help from many other people and didn't always do the photography. Consequently, there are some pictures in these books that are not of the quality I would like, as everyone does not own top-of-the-line camera equipment--so it is what it is. There are examples where only patent drawings could be shown, as the lures were too rare to come by.

The next issue was publication. I interviewed with over 35 different publishers. Some wanted to retain copy rights and pay only a token royalty that would not come close to covering my research cost. Some wanted close to $400,000 before they would print the first book, and others wanted to sell the set for over $1,000. I settled on Trafford Publishing because they print on demand, I do not have a book storage problem, and the books are reasonably priced. However, to accomplish this, I had to go with a soft cover and black-and-white pictures but with either a CD of color pictures in each book or a website with color pictures.

I am very fortunate to have my wife, Tess, who has put up with all this madness for these ten years.

MY PERSONAL FAVORITE LURE
EAST COAST BOSTON WHALER

Due to the vast numbers of lures that I have had in my collection over the years I have frequently been asked what my favorite lure was. There is no question in my mind that it was the pictured 4-1/2" IVORY MINNOW. Extensive research has revealed that this late 1800's solid ivory minnow was hand carved by a east coast Boston Whaler of an unknown name. The lure has a 1" long oval shaped solid silver in-lay just behind the eyes. The indented eyes have a deep set silver in-lay as well. Even the hand forged hook is silver plated. The intricate checker-scale pattern was all painstakingly done by hand. The long line tie is real leather that goes through the lure to the tail hook. I no longer own this lure, but the present owner, John Conlin of Maple Plain, Minnesota has graciously provided me with the attached pictures of this beautiful piece of art. John says the lure is the centerpiece of his collection and in his opinion… it is priceless.

Estimated trade value is $5,000

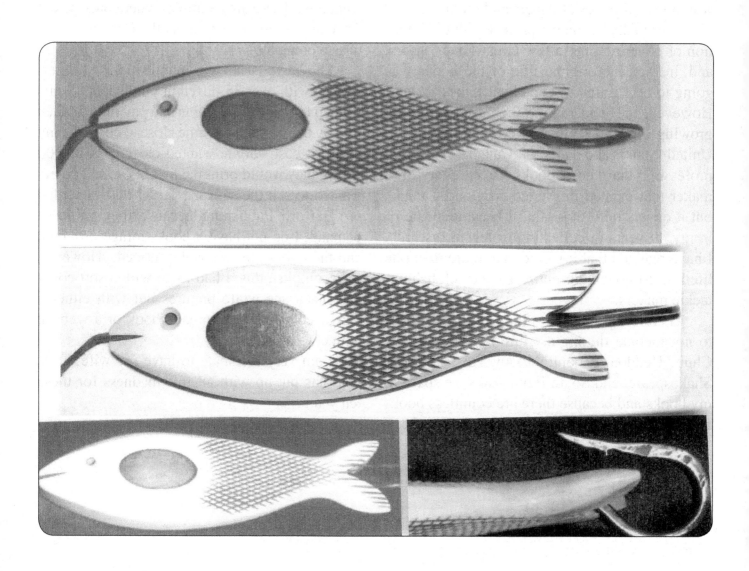

NORTH & SOUTH COAST MINNOWS
HENRY CLAY ROYER
TERMINAL ISLAND, CALIFORNIA

WILLIAM HOEGEE & COMPANY
LEO ALBERT BONNER
OKEECHOBEE, FLORIDA

The original **SOUTH COAST METAL MINNOW** was patented on January 2, 1912, under Patent No. 1,031,149 by Dr. Henry Clay Royer, who was located at Terminal Island, California. The flat, metal minnow had a single tail hook and a hole for an eye and was made in four sizes of 4", 3-1/4", 2-1/4", and 1" long. The reason the single hook was not placed in the center of the tail of the metal minnow was because, in the lower position, the hook kept the minnow upright on retrieve or the troll. Royer also distributed this minnow made of wood with glass eyes and a U-shaped tail prop and a single tail hook. I don't know if Royer was just a distributor of this wooden version, or if he had actually made the wooden version first, but I suspect that he did. A 4" example is pictured in a green-gray back blending into a pale gold.

Dr. Royer started his operation out of 335 Wilson in Los Angeles, California, and had moved his factory to Terminal Island by 1912. Around 1913, he sold the rights to his lures to Heddon, who made their version of the Coast Minnow, starting in 1914. However, neither the Heddon version nor the later 1925 Pflueger version had the little knob on the tail like the one pictured on the Royer and Hoegee versions. Sometime in the early 1900's, William Hoegee made these same lures as his famous **NORTH COAST MINNOW**. Hoegee made his cigar-shaped wooden minnow without a tail prop in the 2-5/8" size, like the green with white belly lure pictured. His larger 3" size had the folded-over, swept-back-wings tail prop. However, when Pflueger bought the rights to his lure and introduced their lures in 1925, their two sizes were 4" and 2-1/2", with the swept-back tail props on the larger ones and no props on the smaller ones. The Hoegee versions had inserted glass eyes, a wire through to the single tail hook, and a little baseball bat knob at the tail. The Hoegee minnows were finished in two colors, with darker backs and light color bellies.

Another Florida man made the exact copy of the 3" size of the Hoegee minnow in Florida. The **BONNER'S BASS BAIT**, introduced in 1934 out of Padgetts Tackle Shop in Okeechobee, Florida, was a 3"-long, wooden minnow-shaped lure with a knob at the tail and a wire through to a single tail hook. The lure had glass eyes and a swept-back single tail prop, or, in other words, it was the exact copy of Hoegee's North Coast Minnow. The lure maker was a retired lawyer from Ohio named Leo A. Bonner. We do not know if Bonner knew of the North Coast Minnow design and if his design was a coincidental or intentional copy.

The pictured Hoegee lure is courtesy of the Doug Bucha collection via John Muma. Other pictures are courtesy of the Joe Stagnitti collection.

The Dr. Royer metal South Coast Minnows trade in the $75 to $125 range and his wooden versions in the $250 to $300 range. The Hoegee North Coast Minnows trade in the $250 to $300 range, and the Heddon versions trade in the $300 to $500 range and were even higher at one time. Pflueger versions trade in the $175 to $225 range. The Bonner's versions are quite rare, and I have not seen an established trade value on them.

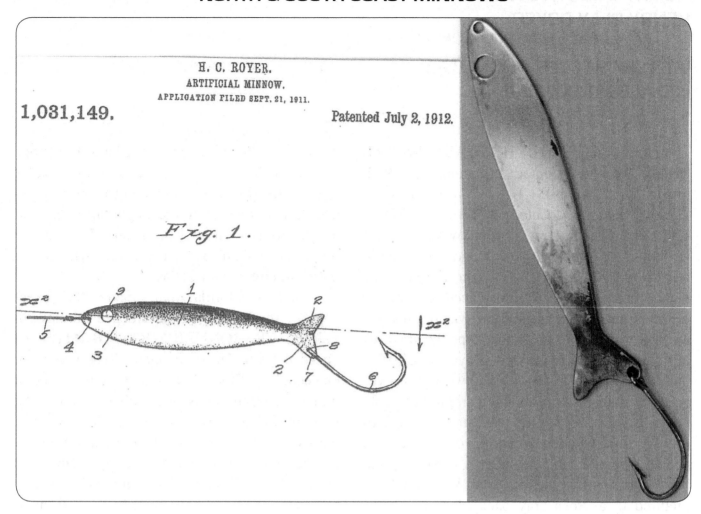

H. C. ROYER.
ARTIFICIAL MINNOW.
APPLICATION FILED SEPT. 21, 1911.

1,031,149.

Patented July 2, 1912.

Fig. 1.

H. C. ROYER.
ARTIFICIAL MINNOW.
APPLICATION FILED SEPT. 21, 1911.

1,031,149.

Patented July 2, 1912.

Fig. 1.

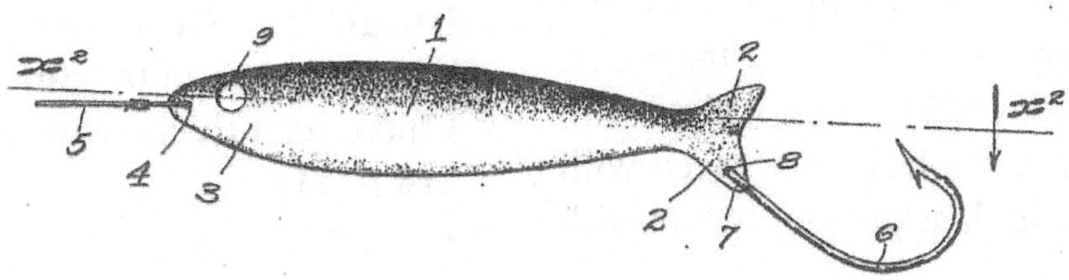

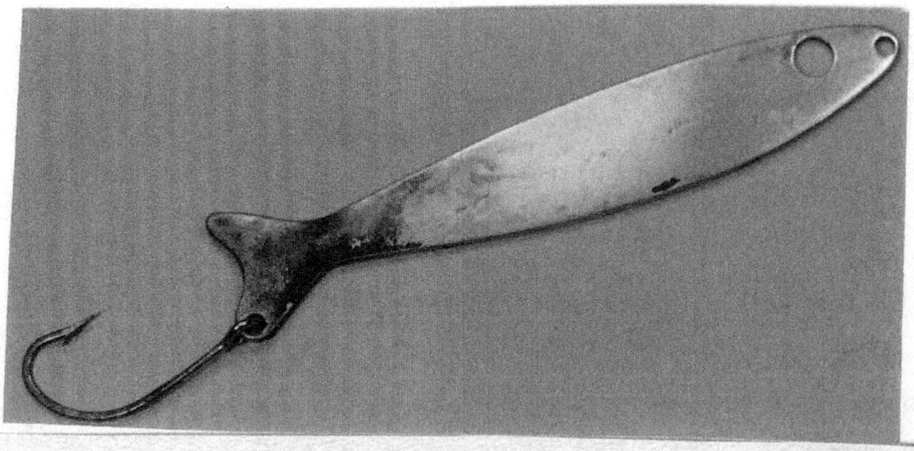

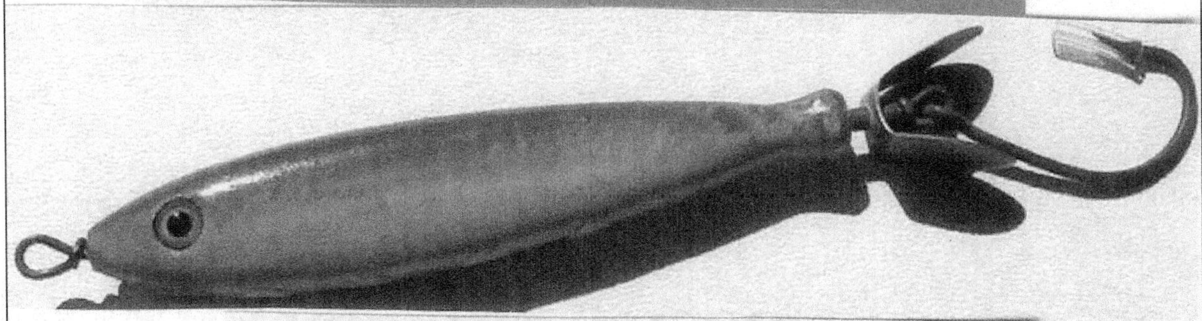

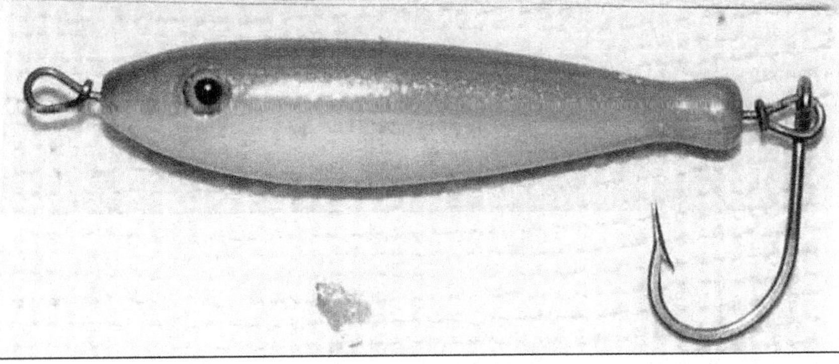

NORTH AMERICAN PRODUCTION COMPANY
WAYNE, MICHIGAN

Just after World War II, in the summer of 1946, the Van Hee Brothers of Detroit contracted with the North American Products Company of Wayne, Michigan, to make their **GURGLING JOE LARGE MOUTH CHUB** lure. It was 2-3/4", one-piece molded plastic lure with a wide, rather flat nose lip and had four angled hollow tube channels in the body. These channels were always painted in a contrasting color to the lure body itself. Some of the colors were amber with dark green chutes, yellow with brown chutes, clear with black chutes, red with yellow chutes, red with black chutes, white with blue chutes, and at least four other colors. The lure was sold in a red two-piece cardboard tube with a sleeve to slide the two parts together. The label was silver with blue print and had the brothers' names, manufacturer name, and address. The brothers, Achiel B. and William A. Van Hee, received Patent No. 2,467,244 on April 12, 1949, for their Gurgling Joe lure.

Gurgling Joe lures in their red tubes with labels trade $25 to $30. Without the label, I have seen the lure in tube trade down to $10 to $15.

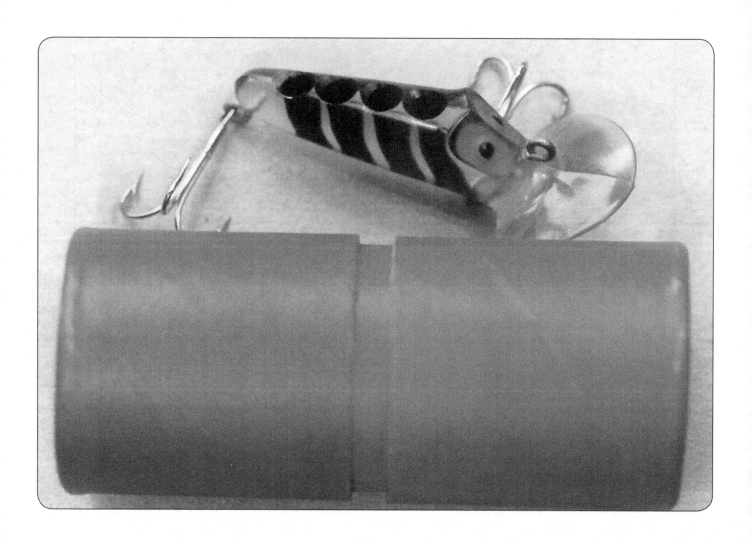

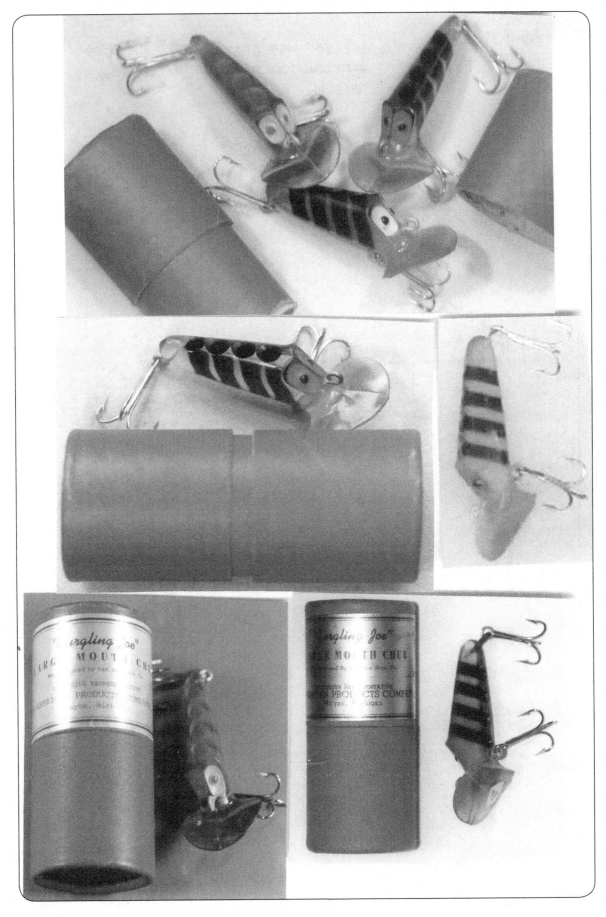

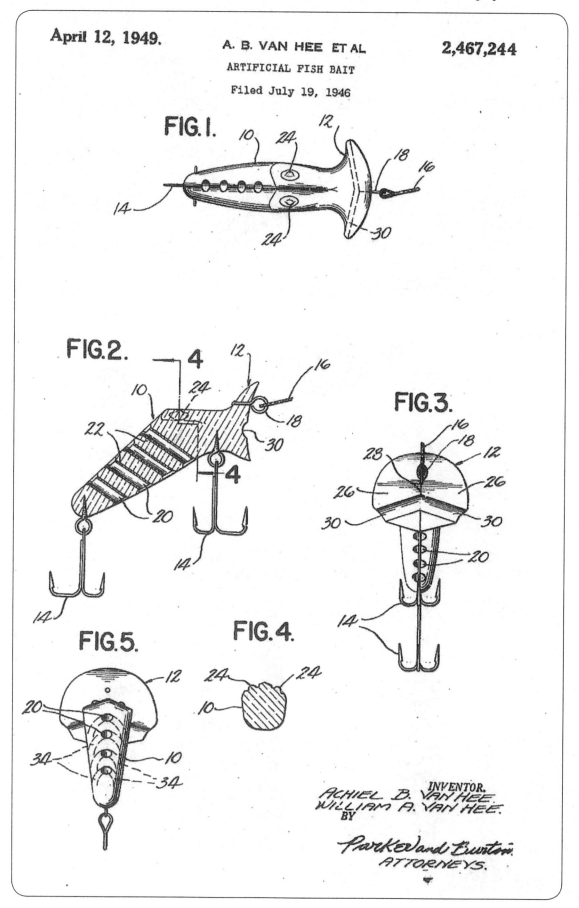

April 12, 1949.

A. B. VAN HEE ET AL

2,467,244

ARTIFICIAL FISH BAIT

Filed July 19, 1946

FIG.1.

FIG.2.

FIG.3.

FIG.5.

FIG.4.

INVENTOR.
ACHIEL B. VAN HEE
WILLIAM A. VAN HEE.
BY

Parker and Burton
ATTORNEYS.

NORTH AMERICAN TACKLE COMPANY
ROYAL OAK, MICHIGAN

The **TORPEDO RAY LURE** probably hooked as many fishermen as it did fish. It was a mean-looking lure with four single hooks that were tooled with screw shanks and placed on the sides of the lure and with another one at the tail. These outward-slanting hooks would have hooked anything that touched them. The 3-3/4"-long wooden lure was patented December 1, 1943, by John L. Bell, under Patent No. 2,437,803. The lure colors were red head with yellow with black and red spots, silver-black scale, and frog. The lure had a unique metal nose piece that was flat and placed in a slot cut in the nose of the lure. This flat piece was secured by a pin-axis through the lure's head. The metal piece side wing extensions would cause it to swing side to side, giving the lure an erratic wobbling action. The lure is quite scarce, and the original two-piece cardboard lure picture box is rare.

Many years later, in Minnesota, Larry McCartney carved a 10" wooden lure with rubber feet that he called the **CRITTER MUSKY LURE**. The lure was made with the same side-mounted multiple-single-hook concept, except the side hooks were secured with a staple system, and the tail hook was a double hook.

Boxed Torpedo Ray (rare combo) trades $150 and up. Lure alone in excellent condition (The lures had a tendency to develop chips in the paint mid-body.) trades $75 to $100 and with minor chipping $50. McCartney's Critter lure trades in the $10 to $15 range.

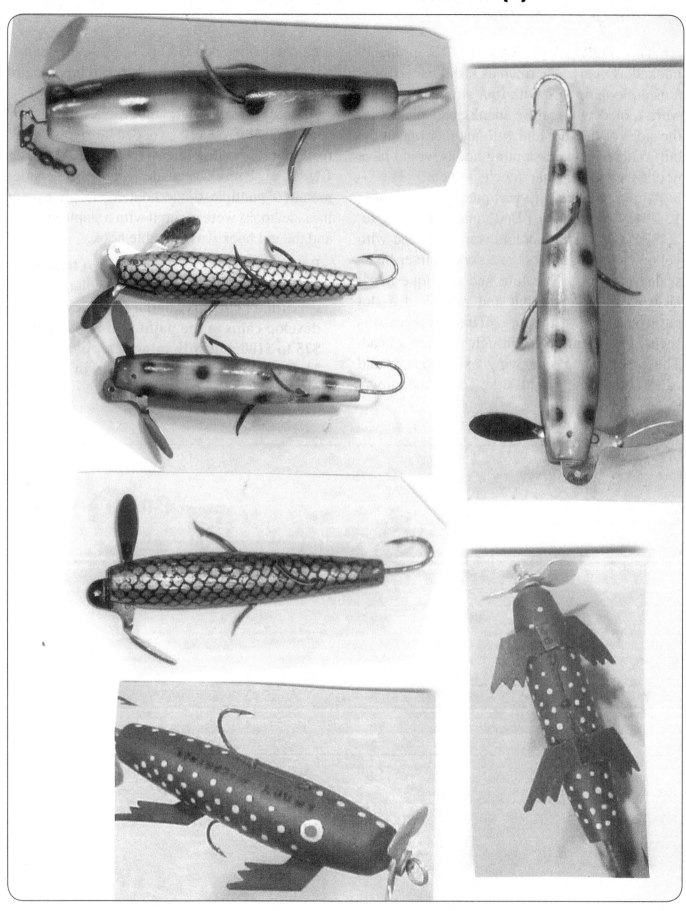

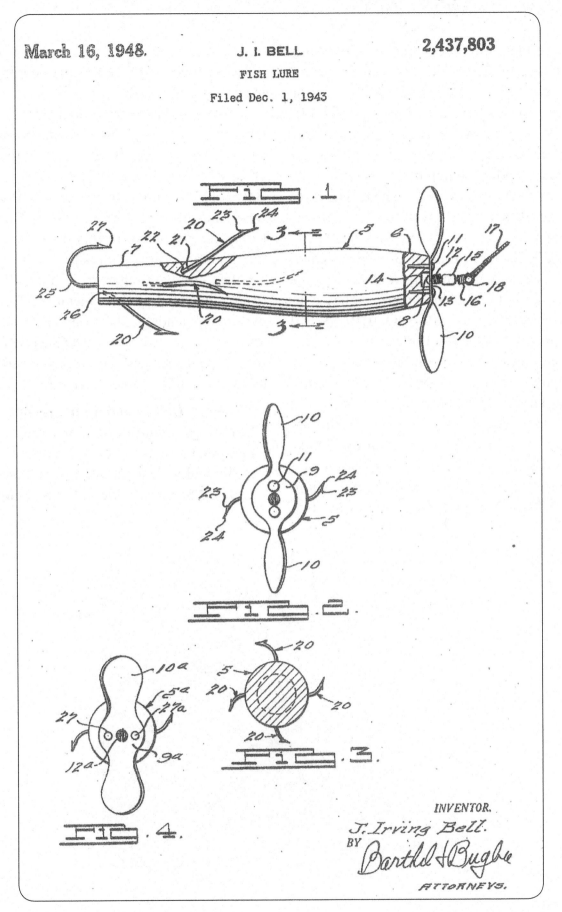

March 16, 1948.

J. I. BELL

FISH LURE

Filed Dec. 1, 1943

2,437,803

FIG. 1.

FIG. 2.

FIG. 3.

FIG. 4.

INVENTOR.

J. Irving Bell.

BY

Barthel H Bughe

ATTORNEYS.

NORTHERN BAIT
HEARST, ONTARIO, CANADA

The Holden Line Company of Cleveland, Ohio, claimed in their box papers that they dated to 1937 with their "CIRCLE H LURES". The real unique thing about their lures was the fact that the lure colors were on the inside of the clear plastic bodies. There never was any danger of the colors fading, chipping, or scraping, no matter how roughly they were fished. The lures had plastic eyes with a tiny H for each of the eye's pupils.

In 1955, Northern Bait, of Box 486, Hearst, Ontario, bought the company and moved the entire operation to northern Ontario. They continued to make the surface 3" **SOURPUSS** and the sinking 2-3/4" **BUTCH** for less than one year after they acquired the rights to these lures. They did stamp the metal dive lip with an "H" initially and then with an "F". Each lure was sold in a one-piece red cardboard box with a plastic top. They sold the two different lures in both sinking and floating models and in colors of red and white, perch, shad, spotty rainbow, and shore minnow. These six different colors in the two basic model types made a total offering of twelve different **FISHMASTERS**, the new trade name for these productions.

In 1956, after a very short distribution period, the company went bankrupt, and all remaining stock of approximately 500 boxed lures was purchased by the Hudson Bay Company. Hudson Bay sold the lures unchanged until inventory was depleted. See the story of the Holden Line Company elsewhere in this book for more history and more lure pictures.)

The company also made a 2-3/4" lure cut from a flat piece of sheet metal and formed with two major bends, a short one at the nose and a long one at the tail. The **SPAZAM SPOON** was sold in a plastic sack with a card insert that pictured a fish at the top of the card.

Northern Bait boxed Sourpuss or Butch lures, sold under the trade name Fishmaster, are somewhat scarce and trade in the $20 to $30 range. Carded and sacked Spazam Spoons trade in the $5 range.

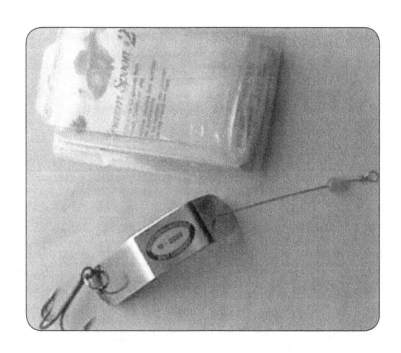

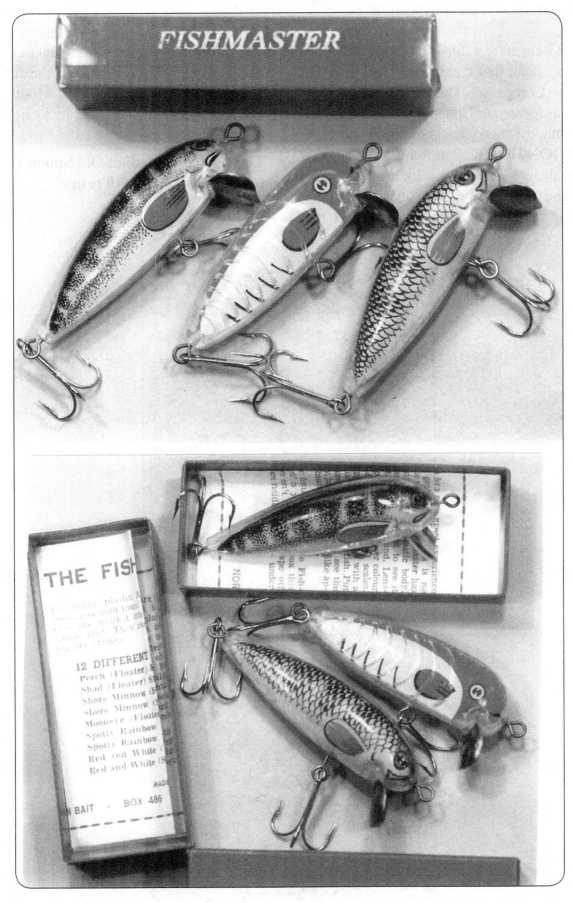

NORTHERN SPECIALTIES COMPANY
DODGE CENTER, MINNESOTA

There were at least three companies that I can think of off hand that were named the Northern Specialties Company. This one, from the late 1960's, was located in Dodge Center, Minnesota, and they made a musky bucktail spoon called the **OLD SPOON HOOK**. The 8-1/2"-overall-long red bucktail lure was made with a fluted nickel spinner and was just another bucktail spinner, except for the neat graphics on the card that made the combo impressive. It pictured a large down-jumping northern pike in the foreground with a red uniformed Canadian Mountie in the background standing on shore rocks fighting this hooked fish.

The carded Canadian Old Spoon Hook trades in the $5 to $10 range.

NORTHERN SPECIALTY COMPANY
WHITEHALL, NEW YORK

A former employee of the Buel Company, Nelson G. Fagan, teamed up with William E. Koch in 1912, and, together, they formed the Northern Specialty Company. The company was in business for over 50 years, even after Fagan retired in 1958, when the business was continued when employee, Ruth Jackson, bought the company. Over the years, the company made nearly 600 different types and sizes of metal lures. Some of their lures were willow leaf-, kidney-, oval-, Colorado-, and even Buel-type-shaped. They were rigged with fixed hooks, swing hooks, weedless hooks in single blades, and tandem double blades.

Some early lures included the **INDIAN LAKES WOBBLER**, with two sizes of egg-shaped hammered spoon-blades, and the **PARADOX WOBBLER**, made in three sizes and designed for lake trout. The **FISHER BAIT** was a Buel "Arrowhead" look-a-like, made in five sizes from 1" to 4-1/2" long. The **LAKE PLACID SPECIAL** was one of the company's more popular trolling lures made with a long teardrop spinner blade. An off-shoot of this lure was the **PISECO BAIT**, which took the spinner blade and added a single fixed hook and made it into a casting lure.

A 1948 ad statement made by Nelson G. Fagan himself said, "The biggest crank in the world is a fisherman. He knows what he wants and will not stop until he gets it. This is where we come into the picture. It is our business to make a bait that will meet with his approval in every way."

Northern Specialty lures trade in the $15 to $20 range

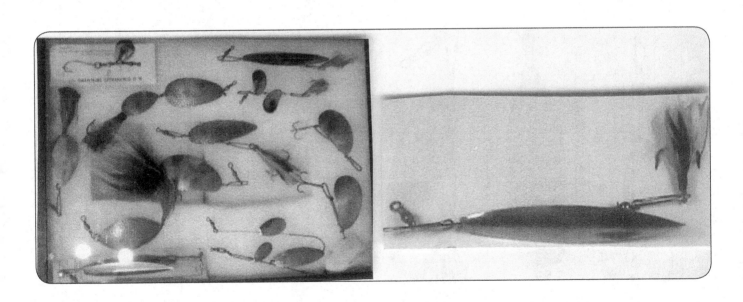

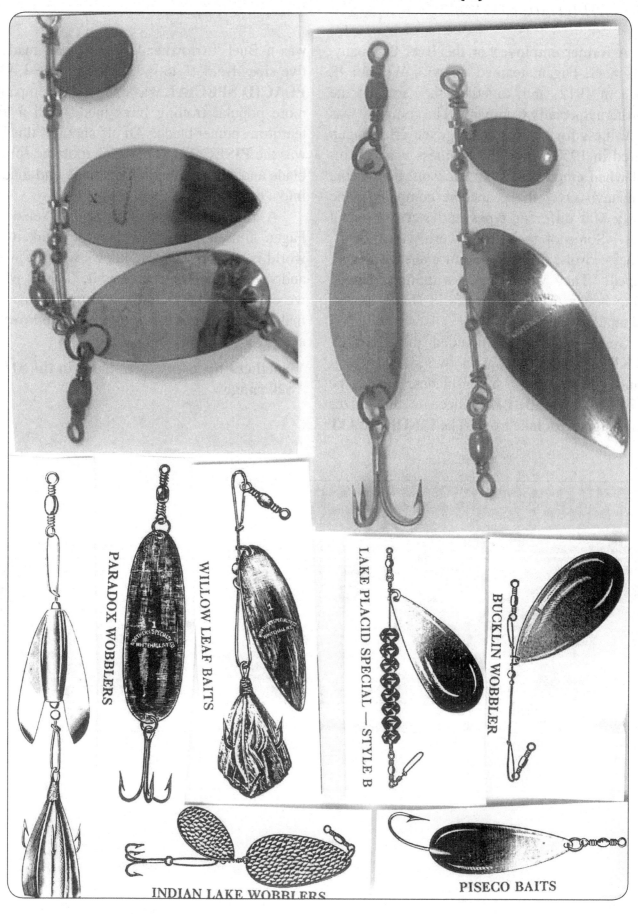

PARADOX WOBBLERS

WILLOW LEAF BAITS

LAKE PLACID SPECIAL — STYLE B

BUCKLIN WOBBLER

INDIAN LAKE WOBBLERS

PISECO BAITS

Northern **S**pecialty **C**ompany

R. WALTON

Received June 21, 1948.

FLY SPOONS
SPINNERS
WOBBLERS
LEADERS

WHITEHALL
NEW YORK

MAKERS OF HIGH CLASS BAIT SINCE 1912

FACTS CONCERNING OUR BAITS

We could go on and on and tell you what our baits will do, but we leave everything up to the fisherman himself. We will let him be the judge. He is the man who is going to use them.

As we all know, different waters require different style baits. Consequently the fisherman has to have a few different styles and sizes to try out. At the same time, how many times has a fisherman bought a bait, went out and tried it, and had no success. Right then and there, he was ready to condemn the bait. The very next day he could take the same bait, cover the same territory, and catch his limit in a short time. Believe it or not.

We do not wish to say that we are the only manufacturer making baits that will catch fish. There are many others. However, we do say, with our line of baits, we have had the ideas and suggestions of some of the best guides and fishermen, and through their generosity we have passed them on to you. We are always open to any suggestion or criticism you may suggest. That is what makes a perfect bait.

The biggest crank in the world is a fisherman. He knows what he wants and will not stop until he gets it. This is where we come into the picture. It is our business to make a bait that will meet with his approval in every way.

In the manufacture of our baits, we put into each one the very best of materials and the best of workmanship. If one should be found defective in any way, we will gladly replace it free of charge.

In the description of each bait mentioned in this catalog, we could mention what each bait could be used for, but from our experience, we have left that out. What one fisherman would use a bait for, the next one would use it to fish for a different kind of fish. We will let the man who uses it tell his own story.

We have found in our experience, some fishermen prefer the snap at bottom of wire and some prefer the sliding sleeve. We make them both ways on the smaller type spinners.

From the large assortment of metals we use, it gives the fisherman a good choice from which to select.

The wire used in making up our baits is tinned piano wire. We use the very best grade of swivels and our hooks are Mustad nickel plated hooks. Our feathered hooks are tied by experienced tiers and french nazura feathers are used.

With our 26 years' experience, we are always open to suggestions, so if you have an idea of a good bait, send it in and we will gladly go over it with you.

Yours for better fishing,

NORTHERN SPECIALTY COMPANY, Whitehall, N. Y.

NORTHERN TACKLE COMPANY
SUDBURY, ONTARIO, CANADA

Starting sometime in the 1940's, in Sudbury, Ontario, the Northern Tackle Company produced a 4" (5-1/2" overall) plastic lure called the **FLASH TAIL LURE**. The 1943-patented, fish-shaped lure had a nose spinner and a revolving tail with flashy brass inserts all mounted on a wire-through shaft to a barrel swivel in between the joints. The lures were finished in natural minnow colors of green or brownish-gold with red trim. However, by 1950, there were a total of six color finishes offered. The lure was packaged in a two-piece green cardboard box that read, "FLASH TAIL...The bait that breathes." This statement was based on the water-intake hole in the nose with two in-body channels to exit ports just behind the side fins. The resulting water discharge both created bubbles for attraction and helped cause water flow to spin the tail section. The box papers claimed that the FLASH TAIL was the "Best Imitation of Live Bait in the World."

There were two models. The early one had glass eyes, and the later had painted eyes. One model had a sagging belly "pregnant guppy" look and the other a more streamlined minnow-shaped body. Both models had double hooks secured on the undersides of each section and wide, thick, flared fishtail shapes. The forward in-line metal spinner blade was similar to a combination of the Al Foss "Regular and Adam" blades together. With the two side, extended fins, from a belly view, the lures looked like the underside of a shark.

A smelter at the International Nickel Company of Canada, Vaino Lehto, had invented the lure. Lehto was awarded Patent No. 2,317,781 on April 27, 1943, in the United States, and, later, on October 5, 1943, Patent No. 415,690 for a Canadian patent was granted. World War II was in its early stages at the time of these patents, and lure-making materials were scarce, so I believe, actual lure production was started in the later 1940's.

In the early 1950's, Vaino Lehto introduced another lure, a "flatfish" shaped one named the **NORTHERN MINNOW**. The lure was advertised as "the lure that breathes" because the water flowed through a hole in the head and then out below the bottom fins.

Vaino Lehto passed away in 1982 at the age of 76. He was born in 1906 in Finland and then immigrated to Canada in 1926. I assume that is why the Flash Tail had that European look about it.

The rare boxed Flash Tail lures trade in the $150 to $250 range, and the lures alone trade at half that level. For some reason, the younger Northern Minnow is even rarer, trading in the $50 and higher range.

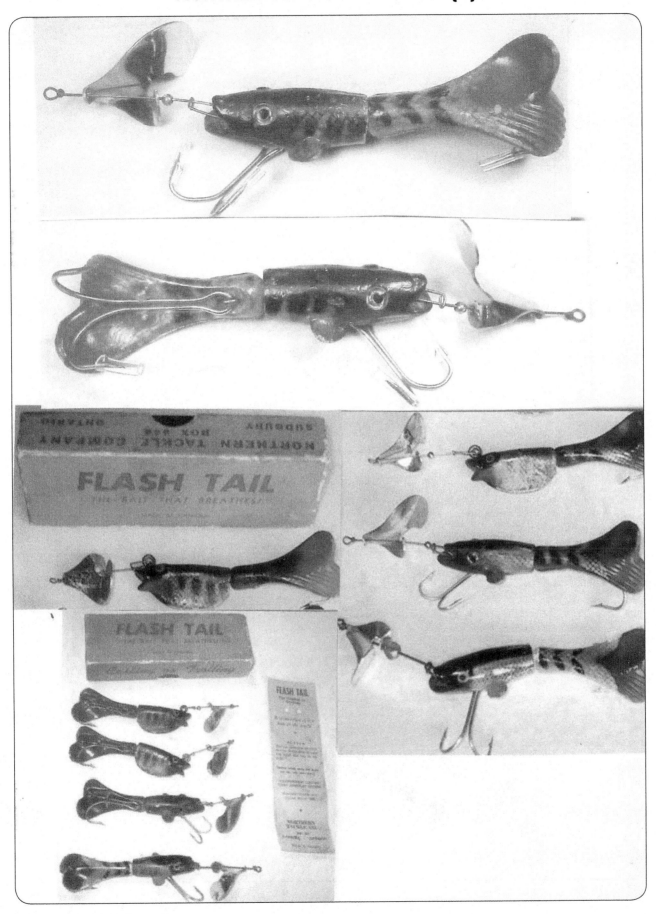

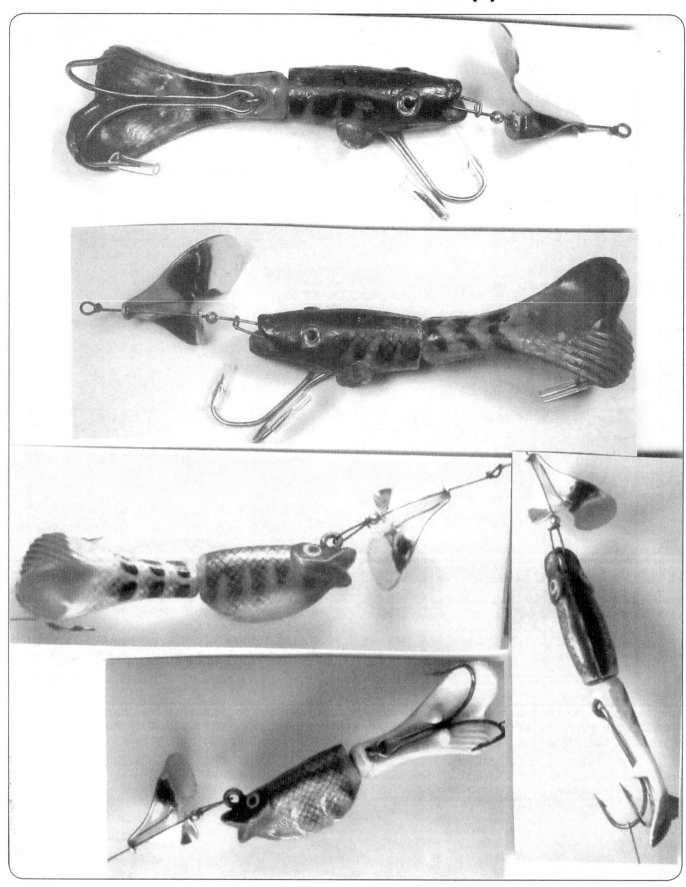

NORTHERN TACKLE COMPANY
CHICAGO, ILLINOIS & TREVOR, WISCONSIN

In 1948, Curtis F. Mellin started the Northern Tackle Company at 2544 Hutchinson Street in Chicago with the making of his metal **CASTING PORKY WEEDLESS MINNOW**. The stainless steel lures were made in the two sizes of 1-3/4" and 3-3/4" long. Mellin filed for a patent on March 18, 1948, and Patent No, 2,619,764 was granted to him on December 2, 1952. The lure was usually stamped, "PORKY...Trade Mark," and was designed to be fished with pork rind strips or Uncle Josh type "Pork Frog" trailers. The fixed-single-hook spoons were spearhead shaped with either bucktail tufts either side of the tail hook or little Colorado style spinner blades. The bucktails were made in natural deer hair or dyed black, yellow, white, or red.

By the early 1950's, the company had moved to P.O. Box 37, Trevor, Wisconsin. Unlike other companies who made a major relocation, this company did not change ownership with this move; Curtis F. Mullin remained the owner. In Wisconsin, new sizes were added, including a giant musky size at 5-1/2" long.

The lures were sold in one-piece yellow cardboard boxes with plastic covers. In red print, the side of the box stated, "CASTING PORKY WEEDLESS MINNOW...Cast into lily pads or weeds...Use with pollywog, port chunk, or frog...Reel slowly."

A copy of a 1953 store flyer is pictured, courtesy of the Dan Basore collection.

Boxed Porky spoons trade in the $15 to $20 range and to $25 for the musky size.

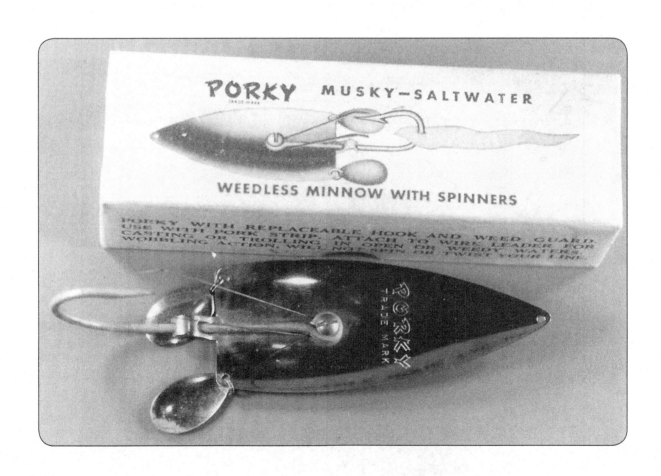

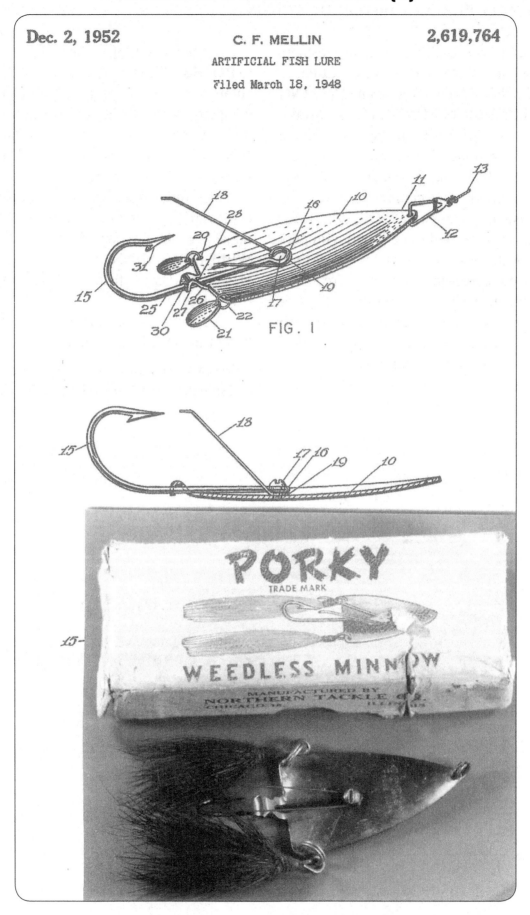

Dec. 2, 1952

C. F. MELLIN

ARTIFICIAL FISH LURE

Filed March 18, 1948

2,619,764

FIG. 1

PORKY
TRADE MARK

WEEDLESS MINNOW

MANUFACTURED BY
NORTHERN TACKLE CO.
CHICAGO 18   ILLINOIS

NORTHERN TACKLE CO.
Manufacturers of Fishing Tackle

P.O. Box 37

Trevor, Wis.

February 14, 1953

Mr. R. Walton
2301 Franklin St. North
Wilmington 2, Delaware

Dear Mr. Walton:

We were pleased to get your letter, and are
enclosing a catalog insert giving further
descriptions of our line of Porky Weedless
Minnows.

Since the grant of our patent in December, we
are now making the spinning and casting sizes
of Porkys, with a screw and tailpiece, as
shown for the Musky size. Therefore, the smaller
Porkys now have replaceable weedguards and hooks,
as do the Musky sizes.

Fishermen who use the Porky for saltwater
fishing, remove the weedguards.

We are proud of our perfect weedless bait, and
hope that you will give it a thorough tryout.
We should appreciate hearing from you about your
own experiences with the Porky.

Sincerely yours,

Curtis F. Mellin

cfm:al
enc:catalog insert

Curtis F. Mellin
NORTHERN TACKLE COMPANY

PORKY *catches fish*

FAMOUS
PORKY
T. M. REG. U. S. PAT. OFF.

WEEDLESS MINNOWS

NO. 2S BASS OR PIKE SIZE WITH SPINNERS

Received Feb. 1953

NG - 1/4 oz.
1F 1/2 oz.

WEEDLESS MINNOW

CUT IS ABOUT ONE-HALF ACTUAL SIZE.
PORK FROG IS SHOWN ATTACHED.

Mr. Fisherman, do you want a lure that will catch the big ones? Then get yourself a Porky Weedless Minnow and cast it far into the thickest of Lily Pads and weed beds and watch them go for Porky. It will not foul or get snagged while being retrieved. Its two flexible wire weed guards make it perfect for this type of fishing. Combine the distinctive action you get from Porky, the flash of bright shiny metal, with twin nickel spinners attached, going through the water with a pork chunk, pollywog or frog on the hook, and how can a fish resist it.

Individually boxed. 1 dozen to carton.

Porky is made of stainless steel, highly polished and there is no plating to wear off.

List for $1.00 each

NO. 2B BASS OR PIKE SIZE WITH BUCKTAILS

Here is the most famous and popular weedless lure. A killer on Bass and Pike. It has twin bucktail streamers attached that make it colorful and very flashy. Will not spin or twist your line and when a fish hits, he's hooked to stay.

No. 2-B - Casting - 1/2 oz.
1-B - Spinning 1/4 oz.

Made the same as No. 2-S in stainless steel and has the same distinctive action that you get only from Porky. Most effective when used with pork chunk or pollywog. Ideal for casting or trolling.

Bucktail can be had in the following colors: Red, Yellow, Black and Natural.

List $1.35 each

Individually boxed. 1 dozen to carton.

WEEDLESS MINNOW

OVERALL LENGTH IS 4 INCHES.

MUSKY SIZE PORKY WEEDLESS MINNOW

Has a fast wiggling action. Will not spin or twist your line. A killer on Big Northerns or Muscallonge, when used with pork strip.

Made of stainless steel, highly polished to bright finish. No plating to wear off.

Has replaceable hook and weed-guard. Hook is securely fastened to the spoon with a stainless steel screw. The two flexible wire weed-guards make this lure absolutely weedless—so you can cast into the weedy spots for the Big Ones. Ideal for trolling in open or weedy waters. Cannot lose your hook or fish when you get a strike.

No. 3-S

With Twin Nickel

Spinners attached.

List $1.60 each

No. 3-B

With twin Streamer Bucktails.

Comes in Red, Black, White, Orange, Yellow and Natural.

List $2.00 each

WEEDLESS MINNOW WITH SPINNERS

CUT IS ABOUT ONE-HALF ACTUAL SIZE.
Individually boxed. 1 dozen to carton.

Additional Streamer Bucktails for No. 2B........25c each
" " " " No. 3B........35c each
" " " " No. 3BSW ..35c each

NORTHERN TACKLE CO.

POST OFFICE BOX 37

(Over)

TREVOR, WISCONSI

NORTHERN TACKLE CO.

Manufacturers of Fishing Tackle

2544 HUTCHINSON ST.   »   »   CHICAGO 18, ILL.
P.O. Box 37   Trevor, Wis.

February 14, 1953

Mr. R. Walton
2301 Franklin St. North
Wilmington 2, Delaware

NORTHERN WATERS BAIT COMPANY
BOBCAYGEON, ONTARIO, CANADA

Two brothers P. and E. Hobson of Ontario, Canada, formed their small Northern Waters Bait Company and made a metal lure they named the **SPAZAM SPOON**. It was a simple lure cut from a flat piece of sheet metal in a rectangular shape with a rounded nose and tail tip and had the nose bent down and the tail also bent down. The 2-3/4" brass, nickel-plated lure was 7" long overall including the wire leader and split-ring held tail hook. It was a multi-purpose lure, as it could be trolled, cast, jigged, or used in ice fishing. It was advertised to have six light-reflecting surfaces and that it would swim like a wounded minnow making a clicking noise underwater. The lure was sold in a plastic sack with yellow paper ID and "use" instructional papers and, later, in a hinged blister pack with a yellow card insert. The metal lure was also distributed by the Northern Bait Company out of Hearst, Ontario, Canada in the same time period.

The Spazam Spoon trades in the $5 range or less at this time.

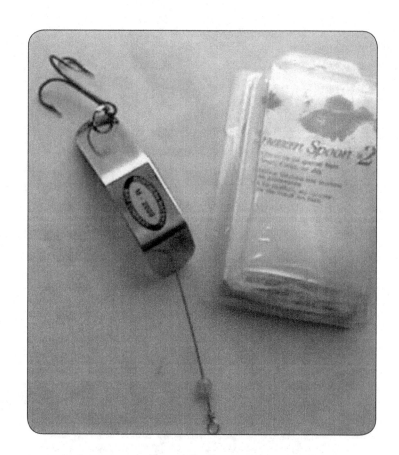

NORTHERN WISCONSIN BUCKTAIL MUSKY LURE MAKERS

These four men deserve recognition in these books. Pictured upper left is a **DAN BERSTROM BUCK TAIL** of Neenah, Wisconsin (1950's), who fished the Manitowish Waters, Buttermore, and Winnebago Lakes. Upper right is a **MICKEY SINGER BUCK TAIL** of Three Lakes, Wisconsin, (1950's), who fished the Three-Lake Chain. Lower Left is a **R. JOLIN FLUTTED BUCK TAIL** of Gresham, Wisconsin (1950's - 60's). Lower right is a **BILL TUTT BUCK TAIL** of Mercer, Wisconsin (1950's - 70's). These muskie bucktails are popular collectibles with Wisconsin collectors, particularly with those who fished muskies over the years.

Trade values range from $35 to over $100.

NORTHPORT INDUSTRIES, INC.
NORTHPORT, MICHIGAN

MAGNA-DYNE PRODUCTS COMPANY
HOLLAND, MICHIGAN

Northport, Michigan, is located in Leelanau County west of Travis Bay in the finger-like peninsula north of Travis City Michigan. Holland, Michigan, is many miles to the south of Grand Rapids on the shoreline of Lake Michigan. Yet, somehow these two companies are connected by either a buy-out by Magna-Dyne or a merger.

In any event, in the late 1960's, the earlier Northport Industries specialized in the manufacture of Homer LeBlanc's plastic **SWIM WHIZZ** lures after Homer stopped making them and before Drifter Tackle started making them as their Believers. Pictured is a scarce size 4"-long Swim Whizz by Northport on their bubble-topped card. They manufactured the Swim Whizz in four sizes and many colors.

The Magna-Dyne Products Company was located at 17024 Brockwood in Holland, and they specialized in salmon spoons in the 1970's. Pictured is the company's 3-1/2"-long, white-with-green-flash-trim **DR. HOOKS SPOON** (Prescription Salmon Spoon) and their 3-1/4"-long, green-with-green-yellow-flash **NORTHPORT NAILER SPOON**. Both of these were very lightweight flutter spoons that could be fished alone, but were primarily designed to be fished behind a Dodger for coho, chinook, lakers, atlantics, browns, and steel head in the Great Lakes and the Pacific Northwest. The Northport Nailer Spoon was a winner in the 1981 American Salmon Derby. Each of this company's lures was sold on a white card with a drawing of a swimming salmon and their trademark of a red head with white fish symbol with the tail formed into an "M" and the head into a "D."

Carded Northport Swim Whizz lures trade in the $15 to $25 range. Carded Magna-Dyne Spoons trade in the $5 range or less.

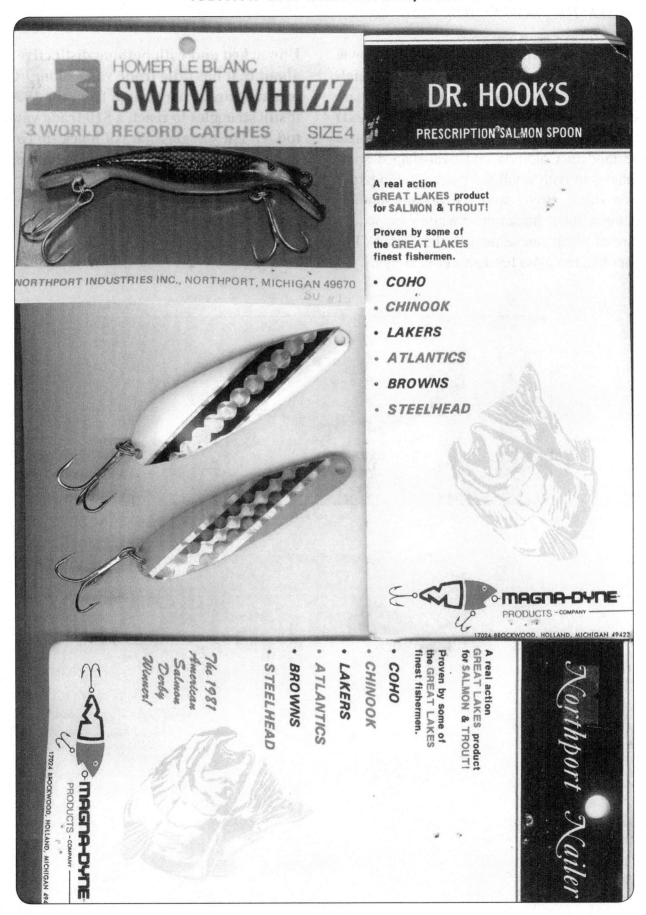

NORTHWAY PRODUCTS
SEATTLE, WASHINGTON

The Seattle, Washington-based Fey Boyle and his Northway Products Company specialized in salmon and trout fishing tackle. His main product line was glass jars of **TVEE BRAND** red prepared salmon eggs. His company also made tandem Colorado and oval-shaped spinner blades in both small trout sizes and in larger salmon sizes. Boyle sold his forward spinner-attractor without hooks on a white card with a picture of a fall-run salmon in the center. The spinner had red glass bead spacer-bearings.

Unmarked and with nothing distinctive about it, it has little trade value alone. On original card, even though from the 1920's, it still struggles to reach a $10 trade value today. The old glass jars of black tin cover Tvee Salmon Eggs, actually trade higher, in the $20 to $25 range.

NORTHWEST SILVERSMITHS COMPANY
PORTLAND, OREGON

Another company starting just after World War II in 1946 was the Northwest Silversmiths Company of 118 N. E. 24th Avenue, Portland, Oregon. They made a number of unique spinning lures, but all of them incorporated the name **VIBR-O-LITE** in the lures' names. These spinners and spoons were either gold or silver plated and involved horizontal flutes running from the head of the spoon or blade to the tail. Pictured are the **VIBR-O-LITE TROLL** and the **VIBR-O-LITE WOBBLER** that were made in sizes from 2" to 4-1/2" long. The company also made a **VIBR-O-LITE SPINNER** blade in sizes from 3/4" long to 2-1/8" long that could be used as a forward attractor for live bait of the fisherman's choice. The inventor of all of this company's spoons and the owner was John H. Arff, who filed for a patent on April 1, 1946, and received Patent No. 2,503,607 on April 11, 1950.

The company trademark was "VIBR-O-LITE", with the O being a burst of sunlight.

There are two 1948 catalog pages shown (courtesy of the Dan Basore collection).

Most VIBR-O-LITE lures trade in the $15 range, but the VIBR-O-LITE Troll is a little higher, at $20.

At the time I took these pictures from my vast collection (that I sold for health reasons back in the 1990's), I had no plans for this book. Many of these lures are rare, and trying to locate examples for current photography would be near impossible, so you will have to bear with me on these. In the group picture of lures, the two VIBR-O-LITE lures are first and second from the right in the second row. Next is the fish-shaped **VANDES SPOON**, a rare 1946 Vandes Lure Company production from Tacoma, Washington, trading at $50. Next is a 1934 **SILVER DART** by Les Davis of Tacoma, Washington, trading at $10. Above and to the left of that is a **COPPER MINNOW** that is better known by local Wisconsin fishermen as the **WINNEBAGO SNAGGER**, made by Frank Denslo of Stockbridge, Wisconsin, in the 1920's and 1930's, trading at $50 and up. At the very top is a carded **CHICAGO MINNOW RIG**, trading at $10 on the silver fish card. Last, on the far lower right, is a rare **WIG-WAG WIGGLER** made in Missouri, trading at $25.

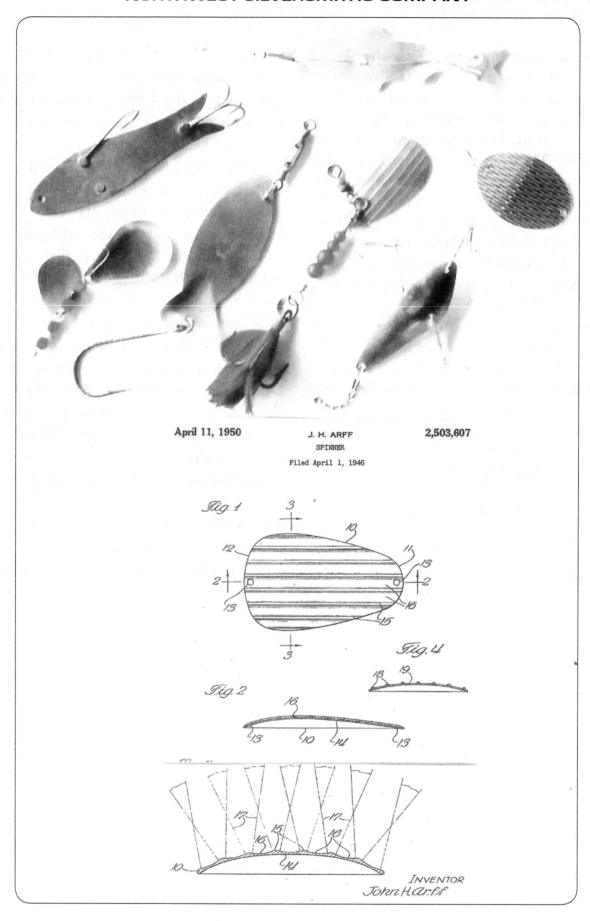

April 11, 1950

J. H. ARFF

2,503,607

SPINNER

Filed April 1, 1946

Fig. 1

Fig. 2

Fig. 4

INVENTOR
John H. Arff

VIBR-O-LITE WOBBLERS
Patents Pending
These products protected by Fair Trade Act
RETAIL PRICES

Cat. No.	No. 4 Wobblers	
W 41	Brass	$ .65 ea.
W 42	Nickel	.70 ea.
W 43	Bronze	.70 ea.
W 44	50/50 Brass and Nickel	.75 ea.
W 45	Silver Plate	.85 ea.

Cat. No.	No. 4 DeLuxe Comb. Wobblers	
C 41	All Brass	$ .95 ea.
C 42	All Nickel	1.00 ea.
C 43	All Bronze	1.00 ea.
C 44	All 50/50 Brass and Nickel	1.10 ea.
C 45	All Silver Plate	1.25 ea.
C 46	Brass Spinner and Nickel Wobbler	1.00 ea.
C 47	Nickel Spinner and Brass Wobbler	.95 ea.
C 48	Bronze Spinner and Nickel Wobbler	1.00 ea.

Cat. No.	No. 5 Wobblers	
W 51	Brass	$1.00 ea.
W 52	Nickel	1.05 ea.
W 53	Bronze	1.15 ea.
W 54	50/50 Brass and Nickel	1.15 ea.
W 55	Silver Plate	1.20 ea.

Cat. No.	No. 5 DeLuxe Comb. Wobblers	
C 51	All Brass	$1.50 ea.
C 52	All Nickel	1.55 ea.
C 53	All Bronze	1.70 ea.
C 54	All 50/50 Brass and Nickel	1.75 ea.
C 55	All Silver Plate	1.95 ea.
C 56	Brass Spinner and Nickel Wobbler	1.55 ea.
C 57	Nickel Spinner and Brass Wobbler	1.50 ea.
C 58	Bronze Spinner and Nickel Wobbler	1.60 ea.

Cat. No.	No. 6½ Wobblers	
W 66	Brass	$1.05 ea.
W 67	Nickel	1.10 ea.
W 68	50/50 Brass and Nickel	1.20 ea.

ALL WOBBLERS AND WOBBLER COMBINATIONS
SHOWN IN ACTUAL SIZES

No. 4
Wobbler

No. 4
Deluxe Comb.

No. 5
Wobbler

No. 5
Deluxe Comb.

No. 6½
Wobbler

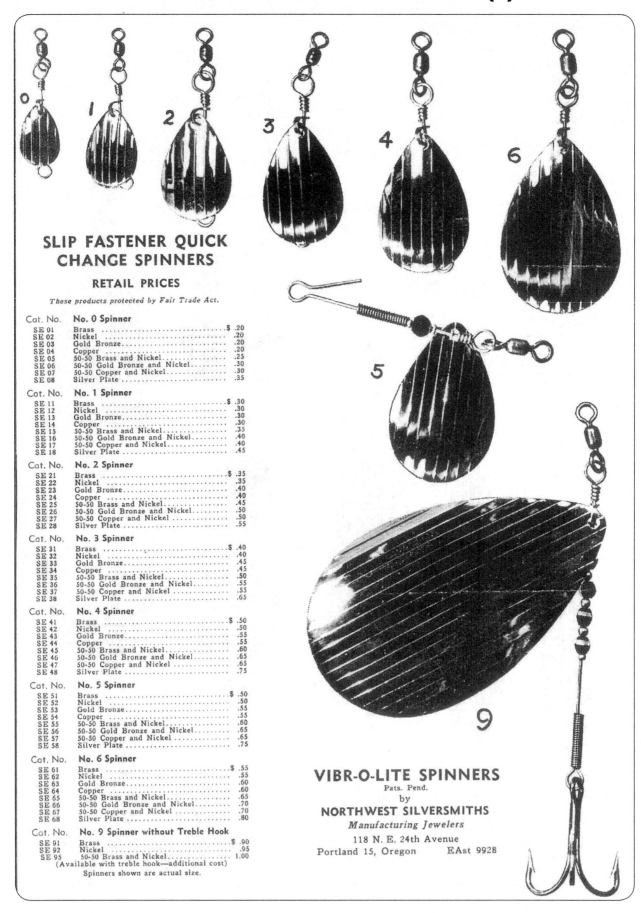

SLIP FASTENER QUICK CHANGE SPINNERS

RETAIL PRICES

These products protected by Fair Trade Act.

Cat. No.	**No. 0 Spinner**	
SE 01	Brass	$ .20
SE 02	Nickel	.20
SE 03	Gold Bronze	.20
SE 04	Copper	.20
SE 05	50-50 Brass and Nickel	.25
SE 06	50-50 Gold Bronze and Nickel	.30
SE 07	50-50 Copper and Nickel	.30
SE 08	Silver Plate	.35

Cat. No.	**No. 1 Spinner**	
SE 11	Brass	$ .30
SE 12	Nickel	.30
SE 13	Gold Bronze	.30
SE 14	Copper	.30
SE 15	50-50 Brass and Nickel	.35
SE 16	50-50 Gold Bronze and Nickel	.40
SE 17	50-50 Copper and Nickel	.40
SE 18	Silver Plate	.45

Cat. No.	**No. 2 Spinner**	
SE 21	Brass	$ .35
SE 22	Nickel	.35
SE 23	Gold Bronze	.40
SE 24	Copper	.40
SE 25	50-50 Brass and Nickel	.45
SE 26	50-50 Gold Bronze and Nickel	.50
SE 27	50-50 Copper and Nickel	.50
SE 28	Silver Plate	.55

Cat. No.	**No. 3 Spinner**	
SE 31	Brass	$ .40
SE 32	Nickel	.40
SE 33	Gold Bronze	.45
SE 34	Copper	.45
SE 35	50-50 Brass and Nickel	.50
SE 36	50-50 Gold Bronze and Nickel	.55
SE 37	50-50 Copper and Nickel	.55
SE 38	Silver Plate	.65

Cat. No.	**No. 4 Spinner**	
SE 41	Brass	$ .50
SE 42	Nickel	.50
SE 43	Gold Bronze	.55
SE 44	Copper	.55
SE 45	50-50 Brass and Nickel	.60
SE 46	50-50 Gold Bronze and Nickel	.65
SE 47	50-50 Copper and Nickel	.65
SE 48	Silver Plate	.75

Cat. No.	**No. 5 Spinner**	
SE 51	Brass	$ .50
SE 52	Nickel	.50
SE 53	Gold Bronze	.55
SE 54	Copper	.55
SE 55	50-50 Brass and Nickel	.60
SE 56	50-50 Gold Bronze and Nickel	.65
SE 57	50-50 Copper and Nickel	.65
SE 58	Silver Plate	.75

Cat. No.	**No. 6 Spinner**	
SE 61	Brass	$ .55
SE 62	Nickel	.55
SE 63	Gold Bronze	.60
SE 64	Copper	.60
SE 65	50-50 Brass and Nickel	.65
SE 66	50-50 Gold Bronze and Nickel	.70
SE 67	50-50 Copper and Nickel	.70
SE 68	Silver Plate	.80

Cat. No.	**No. 9 Spinner without Treble Hook**	
SE 91	Brass	$ .90
SE 92	Nickel	.95
SE 95	50-50 Brass and Nickel	1.00

(Available with treble hook—additional cost)
Spinners shown are actual size.

VIBR-O-LITE SPINNERS

Pats. Pend.

by

NORTHWEST SILVERSMITHS

Manufacturing Jewelers

118 N. E. 24th Avenue

Portland 15, Oregon   EAst 9928

NORTHWEST SPECIALTY MANUFACTURING COMPANY
DODGE CENTER, IOWA

The 1950's Northwest Specialty Manufacturing Company that was located in Dodge Center, Iowa, sold a fisherman's lure-making kit in a neat graphics, colorful, two-piece cardboard box. The kit contained six wooden body blanks, five bottles of paint (clear, black, white, red, and yellow), a paint brush, sandpaper, and all of the necessary hardware and hooks. The examples on the pictured box were Pikie Minnow, Swimming Mouse, Plunker, Bass-Oreno, and Injured Minnow types.

Picture is courtesy of the Larry Sundall collection.

A complete lure-making kit with box trades in the $30 to $35 range.

NORTHWEST TACKLE MANUFACTURING, LTD.
KAMLOOPS, BRITISH COLUMBIA, CANADA

I'll just make brief mention of the 1960's Northwest Tackle Manufacturing Company that was located in Kamloops, British Columbia. The company made small metal spoons and spinners primarily for trout fishing, and most were of very common shapes made by hundreds of companies in both the USA and Canada. They sold their oval-shaped, regular spoon-shaped and spinner-type lures on cards that each pictured a trout fisherman in waders about to land a trout in a hand net. I will say one thing about the company: they favored the color pink. Many of their lures, or the blades on spinner baits, were pink. I won't picture their lures because there is nothing unique about them, but I will show their lure card for one of their best sellers, the **WONDER SPOON**.

Carded Northwest Tackle lures trade at less than $5 at this time.

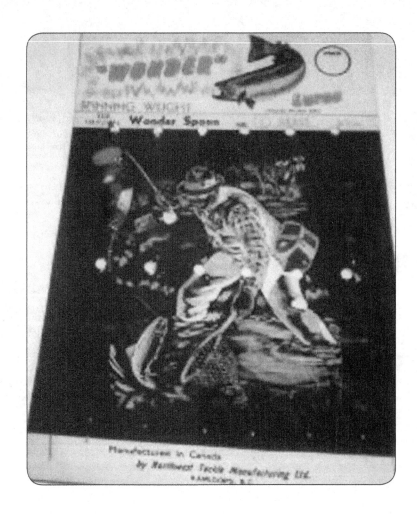

NORTHWOOD TACKLE COMPANY
ROYAL OAK, MICHIGAN

The **CURV-A-LURE** was introduced to the fishing world in 1950 by Robert A. LaFluer. LaFluer received Patent No. 2,536,553 on January 2, 1951, for his shark-tooth-shaped plastic lure. He actually invented it in 1946 and filed for a patent on February 21, 1946. However, he did not enter into production until 1950, and that was short lived, for less than a year. The lure was made in a 3-1/2" casting size and in a 2" spinning size. The Curv-A-Lure was designed with both horizontal and vertical curves, which gave the lure a wiggle and a dive-and-climb action. In fact, LaFluer advertised, "Curve-A-Lure-Exclusive Duo - Plane Curves Give The World's Most Realistic Live Action." The most common color was (YS) yellow with red and black spots. Other colors were (GR) gray with red and black spots, (OR) orange with black back

stripe and red spots, (RB) rainbow, (FR) frog, and a few others. One of the rare colors was dark blue back blending into a white belly with a red-tipped nose. The lure was packaged in a colorful yellow and red one-piece cardboard box with black print and a plastic cover. For a relatively young lure, it is very rare, as it was only produced for one year. Due to the thin nature of the bodies, there was not enough depth to set a solid hook screw eye, resulting in the hooks pulling away on a decent-sized fish. The result was that fishermen stopped buying the lures, and production ceased by the end of 1951.

Don't be fooled by the number of lures pictured that I'm fortunate to have in my collection; the lure is rare. Curv-A-Lure in box trades $25 to $35 and alone $15 to $20.

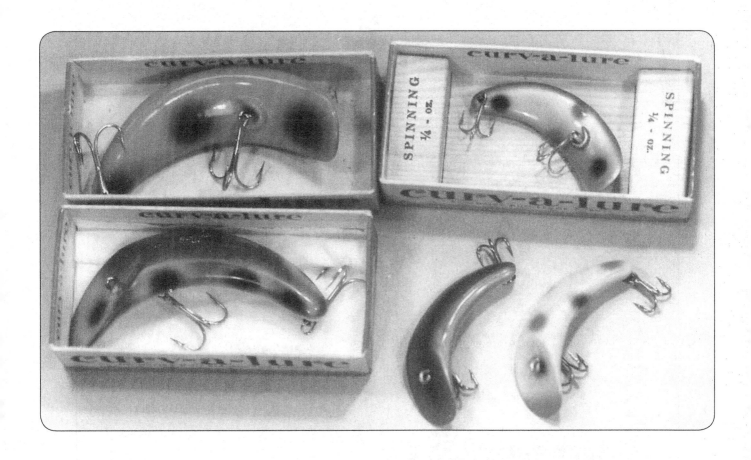

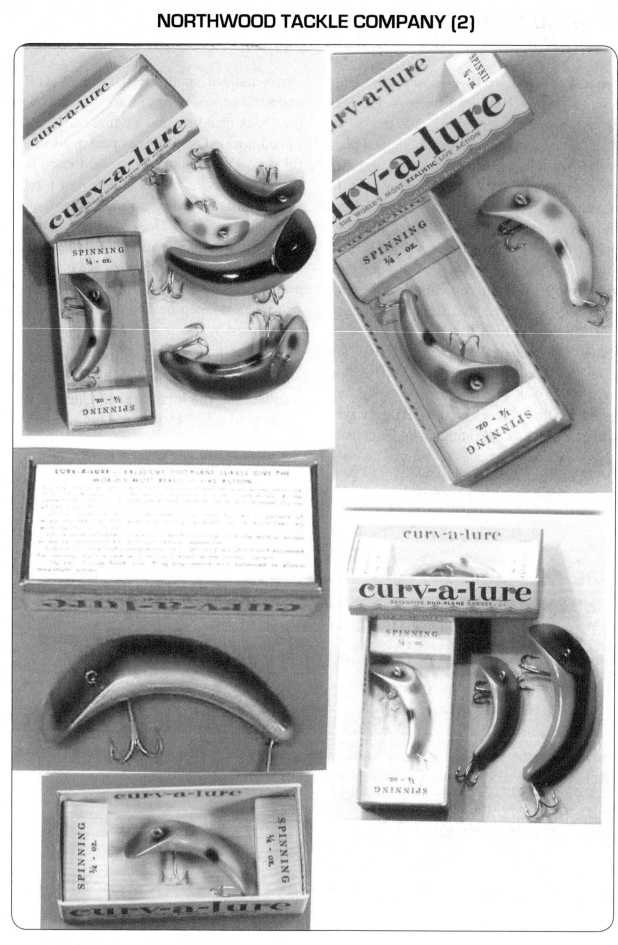

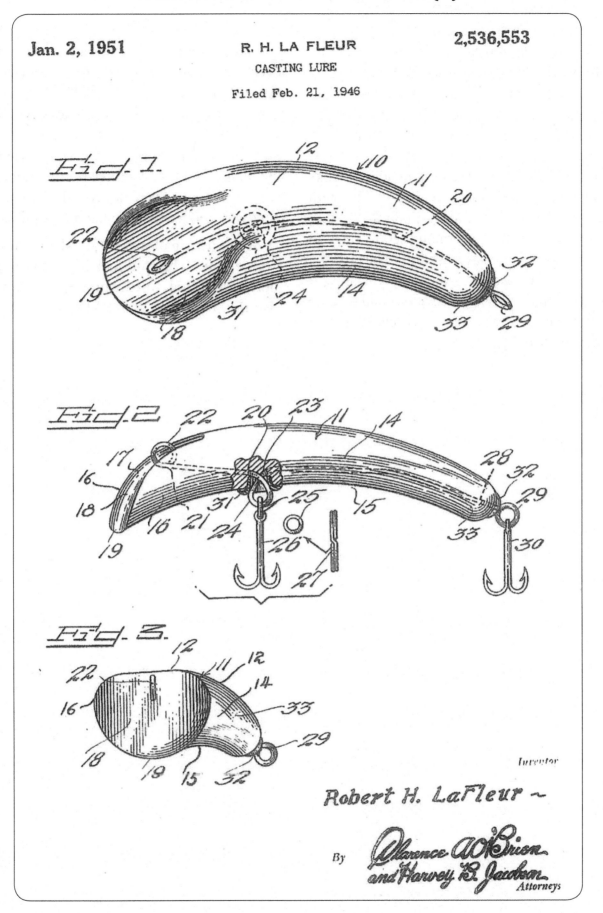

Inventor

Robert H. LaFleur ~

By Clarence A. O'Brien

and Harvey B. Jackson

Attorneys

NORVIEL, TIM
BUCKEYE LAKE, OHIO

The wooden muskie lures made by Tim Norviel would be classified as "folk art" if they were not so popular with Ohio area muskie fishermen. It appears that, when Norviel made the early-1970's lures, he was upset with no luck catching muskies at the end of one day and just took his muskie dispatch club and added hooks to it, making it into a lure. Really, the lure with a long, pointy nose had a big knob at the tail, just like most muskie fishermen used to carry to dispatch big fish. (I say "used to" because it's all catch and release these days. Right, guys?) The surface lure was weighted at one end so as to stand vertical in the water and was designed to be retrieved with jerks, which straightened the lure out in the water, and was then allowed to return to a vertical position to be repeated. Norviel called them **GO FASTER LURES**. They were usually painted with darker colored backs and lighter colored bellies. I'm am sorry that I do not have pictures for this story, so my word description will have to suffice. Pictures for this story, along with some others, were destroyed when my basement was flooded prior to the books publication.

I'm not aware of any established trade value, due to limited numbers only found locally in Ohio, but I would guess they would be in the $20 to $30 range.

NORWICH FLORIDA CORPORATION
ST. AUGUSTINE, FLORIDA

I guess if a lure maker worked out of Florida, Louisiana, or Texas, it would only be natural to develop a shrimp-shaped lure for both fresh and saltwater fishing. The Norwich Florida Corporation out of St. Augustine, Florida, was one of a dozen different companies making a transparent or semi-transparent plastic shrimp lure. This company's lure was named the **NORWICH SHRIMP LURE NO. 600**. It was 3-1/4" long and weighed 5/8 oz. Like some of the others, this shrimp had a lead weight inserted in the belly, but, unlike the others, this one had the line tie on the tip of the nose. The principle colors were either red or natural. Each was packaged in a clear plastic box with ID card insert. In August of 1949, the company advertised in a major fishing magazine, "The NORWICH SHRIMP…It's a Natural….Here is a replica of the natural and quickly napped food of your favorite fish - tantalizing in action, sure in results."

The boxed Norwich Shrimp trades in the $50 to $75 range.

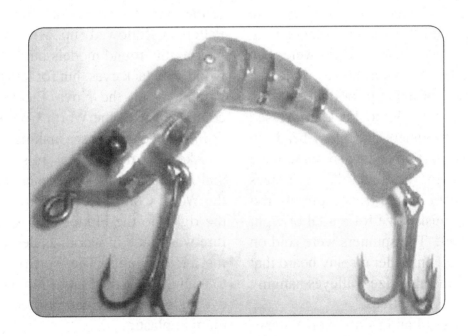

NOVA TACKLE COMPANY
WILD ROSE, WISCONSIN

The Nova Tackle Company was started in 1939 by Delbert F. Patterson and Charles F. Larzelere in Wild Rose, Wisconsin. In the early years of the company, Patterson was still employed as a Wisconsin Game Warden and only worked part time in the production of the company's line of spinner baits. The two men shared in Patent No. 2,212,294 granted on August 20, 1940, for their **AVON SPINNER**.

The blades for their Avon Spinner lures were made in three different styles. One was oval shaped and flat with nine tiny holes drilled in it to give the blades a sonic attracting sound and create a bubble trail. The other two styles were one-bend rectangular blades and the other a two-bend rectangular blade. These blades were then rigged single blade, of tandem blades, followed by a safety-pin type of tail clip for quick change from plain live bait hooks to bucktail-dressed hooks. The early spinners had glass beads in line, later models plastic beads, and some were rigged with no in-line beads at all. The sizes of the Avon Spinners ranged from a tiny fly rod size up to a large musky size for a total of eight different sizes in all. The spinners were sold on an attractive two-dozen dealer display board that had a picture of three nice size walleyes hanging on a stringer between two trees.

The company used an in-line Avon Spinner blade attached to a flat metal type of stand-up jig with a hair tail and named it the **NOVA SPINNER BAIT**. The metal body was just 1" long, but, with the inline wire rigged nose spinner and hair dressed hook, the lure measured 3-1/4" long overall.

In 1964, Delbert F. Patterson made some modifications in the Avon Spinner and was awarded a new patent, No. 3,264,774, on August 9, 1966, for the newer version.

The most famous production by the Nova Tackle Company was the **FLUTTER FIN**. The Flutter Fin was invented by Delbert F. Patterson

after he had fully retired as a Wisconsin State Game Warden. Patterson filed for a patent on the lure on February 26, 1959, and Patent No. 3,003,276 was granted on October 10, 1961. The early models were not round, like the later productions, but rather were egg shaped with squared-off tails. The wooden lure had external glass eyes and unmarked nose metal-whiskers, and the treble tail hook was dressed in feathers. These lures were painted in solid colors and are ultra-rare. (Bob Worth, of the Worth Tackle Company in Stevens Point, told me in an interview in the 1990's that he believed only a dozen of the oval-shaped wooden models were made.) Patterson followed up with that design by making the round models but still made them in wood with tack eyes, but for less that six months. Patterson and the Nova Tackle Company had contracted with the Worth Company of Stevens Point, Wisconsin for the making of the metal nose whiskers for these lures. In short order, Joseph and Edythe Worth, the owners and founders of the Worth Company, made arrangements to buy the rights to the Flutter Fin. Consequently, the lure was made in wood, as described above, for just a few months. The Worth Company went on to manufacture the Flutter Fin with two different eye styles for a number of years, but they made them in plastic.

I'm picturing the very first glass-eyed, wooden, oval, square-tail, no-name-whisker-props **PATTERSON FLUTTER FIN**.

Also pictured are the first **WORTH FLUTTER FIN** production and the second model Worth Flutter fin. Notice the difference in the eyes. The first Worth model had stem bead eyes (red and black), and the second version had built-up tack eyes (brown and yellow). Both of these lures were sold in the earliest style Worth square lure boxes. These pictures are courtesy of the Robin Wickham collection of Louisville, Kentucky.

In the group picture of seven Flutter Fins, the second version round wooden lure made by the Nova Tackle Company is in the center. See "Worth Tackle Company" for more pictures.

Full dealer cards of Avon Spinners trade $75 and up, individual spinners under $5. Early wooden, oval, square-tail Flutter Fins have traded between $400 and $600.

The next Patterson wooden, round, tack-eyed models trade from $200 to $225. The earliest Worth square-box Flutter Fins trade in the $75 range. The second Worth version square-box Flutter Fins trade in the $65 range. The rectangular orange-black and green boxed Worth Flutter fins trade $35 and higher.

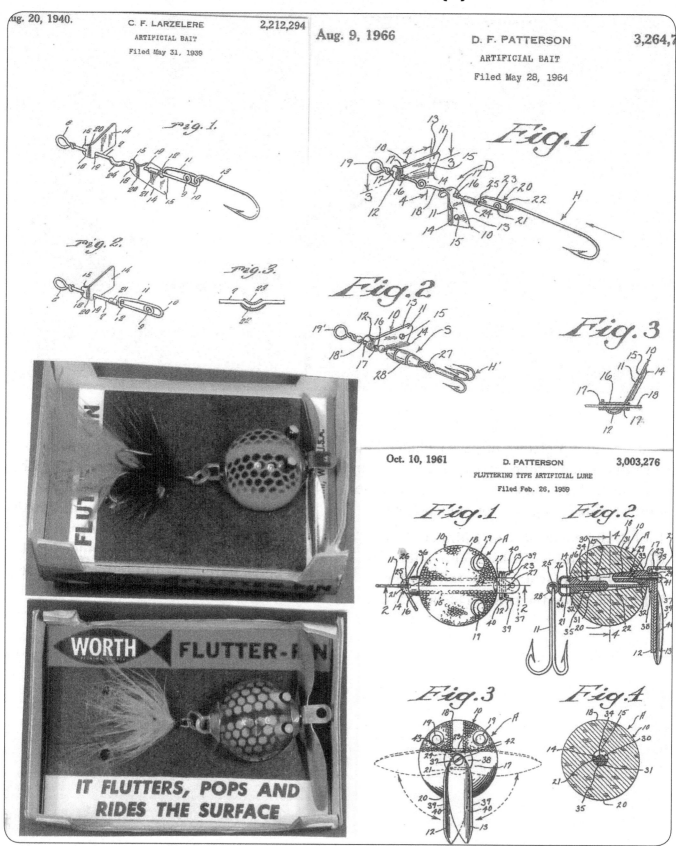

IT FLUTTERS, POPS AND RIDES THE SURFACE

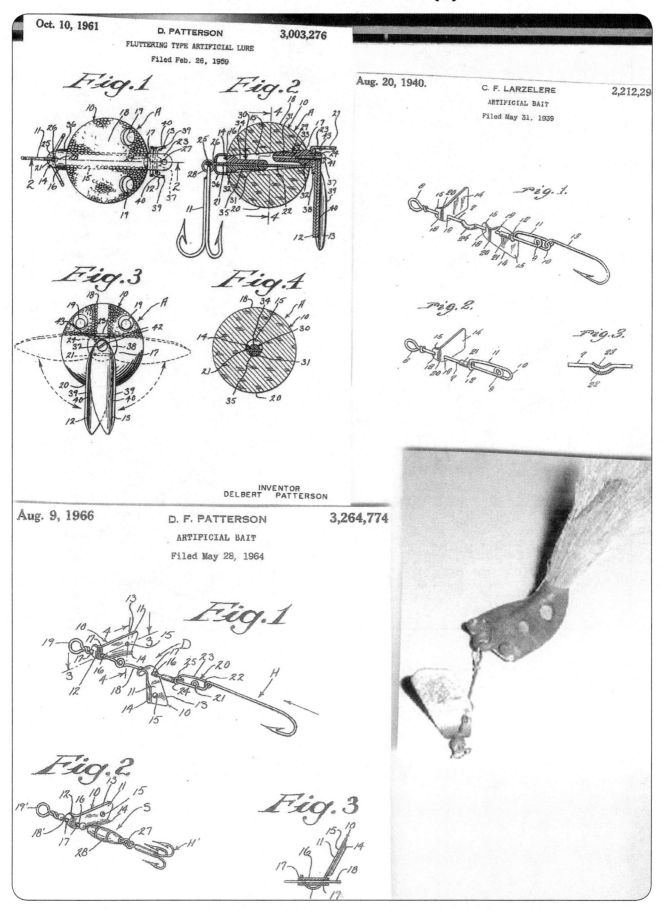

Oct. 10, 1961
D. PATTERSON
3,003,276
FLUTTERING TYPE ARTIFICIAL LURE
Filed Feb. 26, 1959

Fig.1
Fig.2
Fig.3
Fig.4

INVENTOR
DELBERT PATTERSON

Aug. 20, 1940.
C. F. LARZELERE
2,212,29
ARTIFICIAL BAIT
Filed May 31, 1939

Fig.1
Fig.2
Fig.3

Aug. 9, 1966
D. F. PATTERSON
3,264,774
ARTIFICIAL BAIT
Filed May 28, 1964

Fig.1
Fig.2
Fig.3

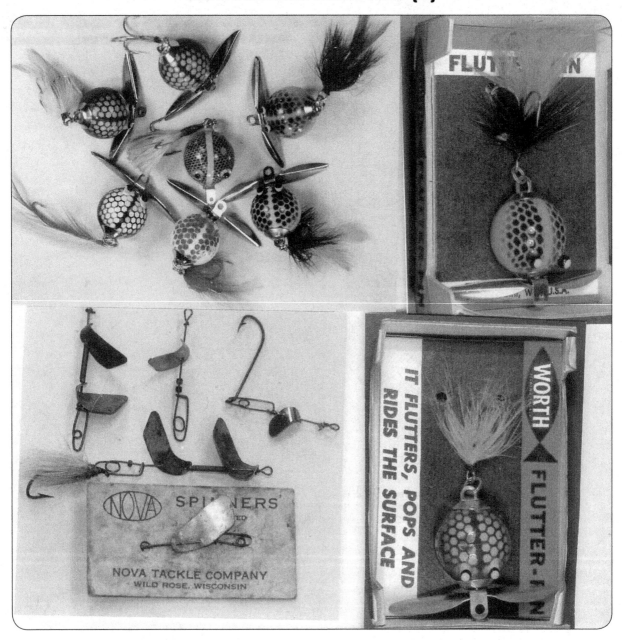

NOVELTY LURE COMPANY
LINCOLN & GRAND ISLAND, NEBRASKA

W-V MANUFACTURING COMPANY
LINCOLN, NEBRASKA

The W-V Manufacturing Company of Lincoln, Nebraska, was started in the later 1940's by Jim Hill. Their first production was the **FINDER FLOAT**, a plastic float with a cord and lead weight that would unwind and stay in place so a fisherman could return to find his marked fishing hole. In 1951, the company introduced "Sam-Bo", and, by the mid-1950's, Hill changed the company name to the Novelty Lure Company, still in Lincoln, and produced his plastic nude black man in a barrel lure that, fifteen to twenty years ago, traded for over $100 in mint condition. That may seem like a lot for a 50's plastic lure, but the 3"-plastic-body, 3-3/4"-overall **SAM-BO** was a cross-collectible. What I mean is that, first of all, Sam-Bo was a fishing lure of sorts, or at least until the first fish struck the lure, at which time its value would have been destroyed. Second, it was a novelty lure, and third it was a black memorabilia collectible. Therefore, there were three different groups of people interested in Sam-Bo, which drove the values up. (Another example is the Connecticut-based Winchester Repeating Arms Company. Their lures are also cross-collectibles because both fishing and gun collectors have interest in them.)

The original Sam-Bo was packaged in a two-tone-green box with a window for the wide-eyed one-toothed man to look out of. Over time, the printing on the box changed, after the company became the Novelty Manufacturing Company, but the uniform consistency was the lure picture on one side and the statement, "The Gloom Killer." At different times the different sides of the boxes read the following ways: "Not a Lure…Just a Cure for Dull Fishing, Hunting.", "A Lure For Fun and Fishing.", "Start The Season Right with SAM-Bo, Pass a Bass and Pickle the Walleyes.". Most boxes each had a circle with a picture of a fisherman in a boat with a fish on the line; others illustrated a silhouette of a hunter with his dog on point.

At a much later date, new owners reintroduced the lure in various color boxes, and, still later, a white "HOMO" version came along, which cheapened the whole concept of the lure. For example, one of the new versions was sold in a white box with purple print and trim and called the **JOCK-E-JO**. Consequently, these later versions trade only in the $15 to $20 range and have also pulled down the trade values of the original boxed lure to an average of a $45 to $50.

Believe it or not, some firm or individual has gone to the trouble of producing a female version of SAM-BO, named **MINNIE THE MINK**. She was sold in a yellow end-flap cardboard box with the print, "Minnie the Mink," on the end flap and on one side of the box. Each side of the box had a big printed "?" with the words "WHEN", "WHAT", "WHERE" printed on each side. Her rubber-band-operated barrel had the print, "MINNIE THE MINK…FIND THE FUR." This lure, by an unknown maker, trades in the $25 range.

The last set of pictures shows the boxed Jock-E-Jo and also a Finish version called the **FINN OR HATTIE**, both were made in Nebraska.

Another novelty production along these lines was made in India and imported to this country. That was the **JUMBO SAM-BO** that was carved in teak wood at a full 12" long in more than one respect, but I'm only picturing this lure in the closed barrel position. The Jumbo Sam-Bo had a propeller-spinner at the top of his head and a treble hook at his feet.

This version of Sam-Bo trades in the $20 to $25 range at this time.

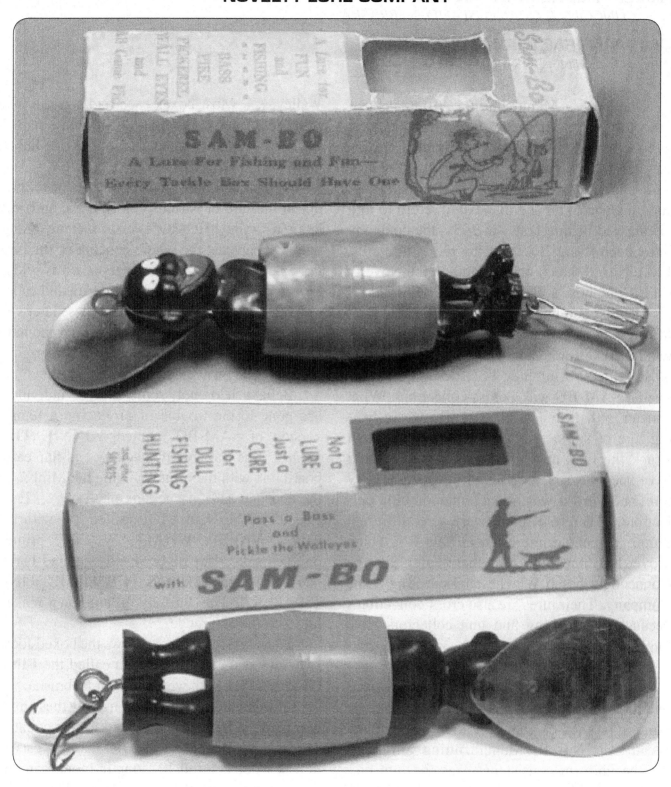

NOVELTY LURE COMPANY (2)

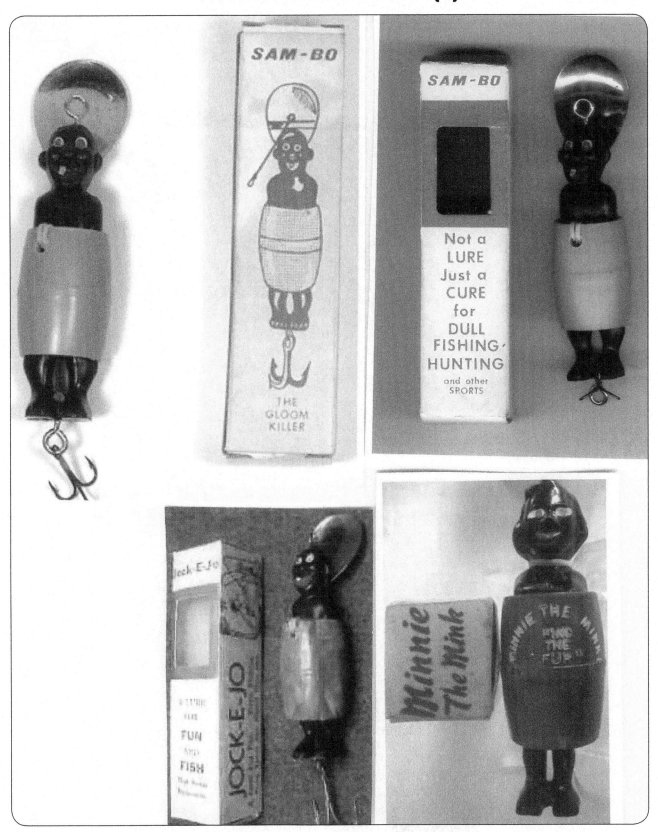

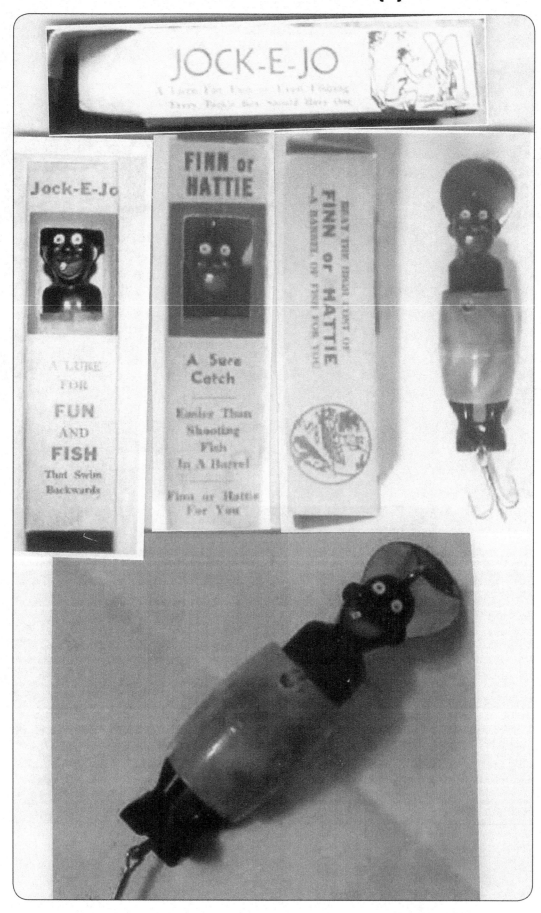

W-V MFG. CO.

BOX 164   LINCOLN, NEBR.

Originators of the "first finder float"

Novelty Lure Co. — "Designers of Lures for fun and fishing"

April 2, 1952

Read - April 7, '52

Mr. R. Walton
2301 Franklin St. North
Wilmington, Delaware

Dear Mr. Walton:

Thank you for your letter of the 30th. We
are enclosing a descriptive ad of "Sam-Bo" which
we hope will be self-explanatory. He is about
3 inches long, complete with hook and bib -- and
when he becomes aroused things really happen.

It is significant, since you are a collector,
that you would be about the 12th such a person to
request information on "Sam-Bo". All of the others
have felt he is certainly unusual from a fishing
standpoint. They felt he certainly ads color to
a collection. We hope you would feel the same way.

He sells for $1.25 -- postpaid -- anywhere in
the United States.

Thanks again for the inquiry -- and please
advise if you wish to add "Sam-Bo" to your collection.

Very truly yours,

W-V MFG. CO.

Jim Hill

JWH/ms

Purchased - October 9, 1952
Murta Appleton
Phila, Pa.

NOVELTY PLUG SHOP
FORT SMITH, ARKANSAS

I'm covering a story here about a fishing plug that absolutely everybody makes. This particular plug, however, was made in the early 1950's and was called **EVERYBODY'S PLUG**, a 4-3/4"-long plastic representation of human excrement. The two-piece pale orange cardboard box read, "Streamlined To Precision… Untouched By Human Hands…Endorsed By Millions Of Men and Women." I have heard sto-ries by seasoned fishermen that on some days the fish will just about hit anything, but I think this might be stretching it a bit. The Novelty Plug Shop was located at 1122 North 15th Street in Fort Smith, Arkansas.

The boxed Everybody's Plug trades in the $20 to $30 range.

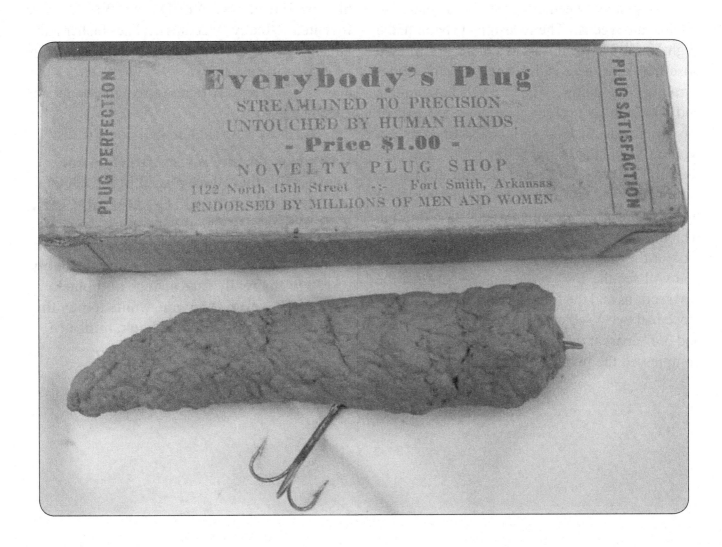

NOWEED BAIT COMPANY
DETROIT, MICHIGAN

The Noweed Bait Company, of P. O. Box 3767, 2170 Coplin, Detroit 15, Michigan, was formed in late 1945. The 3-5/8" brass spoon weighed 3/8 oz. and was a completely weedless "Dardevle" type called the **NOWEED**. The lure was developed by Ewalt Seiter, who sold his **SEITER SPOON** for about six months before he redesigned and renamed it the Noweed spoon. The problem with the first spoon was that it was not completely weedless and did manage to catch some weeds. The redesigned spoon had a slight up-turn at the nose and a more streamlined nose that kept the weeds away from the center pyramid cut window. The lure was both unique and clever in its design. The brass top half of the spoon was made of spring steel and that cut window was folded straight down 1/4", and then the point was folded again to the rear. Just opposite of this fold, the nickel-plated lower half of the spoon had a rectangular cut slot through which the folded-over tab was passed. If you look at the side, tail, and bottom view pictures, you will see the 1/4" vertical piece between the two sections and the folded-over tab. This center piece had two V'ed cuts at 1/4" apart at the base and 3/4" apart at the top. Therefore, when a fish compressed the two sides together on the strike, the lure's two rivet-held pivotal long shank hooks (within the V'ed slots) were extended out from between the two sides for the catch.

The Noweed was advertised in 1946 in finishes of all nickel, all copper, red and white wave with nickel belly, and red and white wave with copper belly. (I have one in red and white and also one in an unlisted color of orange and black.) A fishing magazine with a 1946 coupon mail-in ad read, "NOWEED is NOWEED…Just Invented…Really Weedless…The Fisherman's Dream Come True at Last!" This Field & Stream ad was not repeated in 1947, and, I feel that due to this lure's extreme rarity, all production ended in 1946.

The lures were sold on individual cards.

Although the lure is very rare, I do not agree with the values placed in the 2006 published book, SPRING-LOADED FISH, TRAPS & LURES, of $400, plus. In my opinion, the carded Noweed Spoons have a trade value in the $125 range and probably $150 in the really rare orange and black color. However, if anyone wants to pay the prices listed in that other book, mine are available in a heart beat!

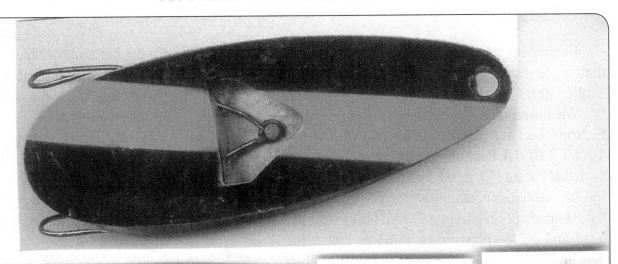

"NOWEED" is "NOWEED"!

Pat. Pending

JUST INVENTED!
REALLY WEEDLESS!

BEFORE — AND — AFTER

THE FISHERMAN'S DREAM COME TRUE AT LAST! INTRODUCING A NEW PRINCIPLE TO HOOK A FISH. SO SIMPLE IT WILL AMAZE YOU!

Supreme in casting or trolling for bass—pike—walleyes and muskies. And one bait the muskie won't shake out—because it hooks fish in the sides of the mouth. No snags—as hooks are not exposed—till fish strikes. Size 3½ in wght. ⅝ oz. Price $1.50. No C.O.D.—Please send money order. Money back if not satisfied.

So get the jump on your fishing pals and order yours TODAY!

Noweed Bait Co.
P. O. Box 3767, Detroit, Mich.

Please send me ☐ Noweeds @ $1.50   ☐—Red & White—Copper underside
     ☐—Red & White—Nickel underside   ☐—All Nickel   ☐—All Copper

Name ....

Street ....

City ....State ....

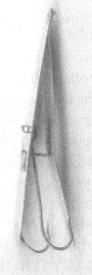

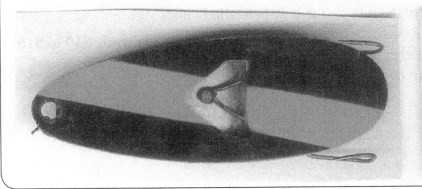

NUNGESSER, R. E. -TROLLER BAIT COMPANY
WASHINGTON D.C.

I can think of only a half dozen companies that made lures in Washington D.C., and the Troller Bait Company, of 3705 Brandywine, N. W., Washington D. C., was one of them. Robert E. Nungesser started making his **NUNGESSER 4 IN 1 TROLLER** lure in early 1942. He was awarded Patent No. 2,313,572 on March 9, 1943, for his adjustable stainless steel spoon. The fish-shaped spoon had two drilled holes near the head and a 3/4" rectangular window cut in the base lure. A second curved-tail spoon was then bolted to the first by two rustproof brass bolts. That piece had a tail slot through which the single hook shank passed. By removing the nuts and bolts, the fisherman could change the shape of the lure in several positions and, thus, completely change the action of the spoon in the water. The spoons were made for both fresh and saltwater fishing, and the colorful box papers listed several species: Rock Fish, Bonito, Blue Fish, Mackerel, Tarpon, Sea Trout, Tuna, Muskies, and many others. The spoons were made in four sizes: non-adjustable 1-3/4" **MIDGET TROLLER** and 3" **BABY TROLLER**; 4-in-1 adjustable troller 4-1/4" size and 5-1/2" size, the largest. Each lure was sold in a white end-flap cardboard box with green border and print. One side of the box had the trademark, a spoon silhouette, with "4 in 1 **TROLLER**" printed inside. Another side had a lure picture and another showing how the spoon was adjustable.

Pictured are the big and the small boxed No. 7731, 1-3/4" MIDGET TROLLER and NO. 3, 5-1/2" 4 In 1 TROLLER. All spoons were stamped, "R. E. NUNGESSER...4 IN 1 TROLLER...PAT 2,313,572," but only "Pat. 3-9-43" was on the smaller spoons.

The 4 In 1 Troller consisted of two separate spoons and hooks that, by removing two bolts, the fisherman could reconfigure the lure into four different size and action lures.

Nungesser also made some smaller 1-1/2" freshwater spoons called the **NUNGESSER SHAD KILLER SPOONS**. The little gold-plated spoons were sold on two-dozen dealer display boards that were white with green border and red print. Nungesser also sold his spoons on one-dozen dealer display boards. This board had a picture of a fisherman with his catch on the left and in red print, "NUNGESSER TROLLER BAIT COMPANY...Gold Medal Award Winner Lure...Rock-Blues-Trout-Bass-Many Others...Remembered by Sportsman Club of America." Pictured is a No. 0, 2 3/8", gold-plated **NUNGESSER SHAD KILLER** from one of those boards. The lure was covered with gold flitter, and a gold artificial hair tail dressed the bolt-held single hook.

Boxed Nungesser spoons trade $10 to $15 and boards to $50.

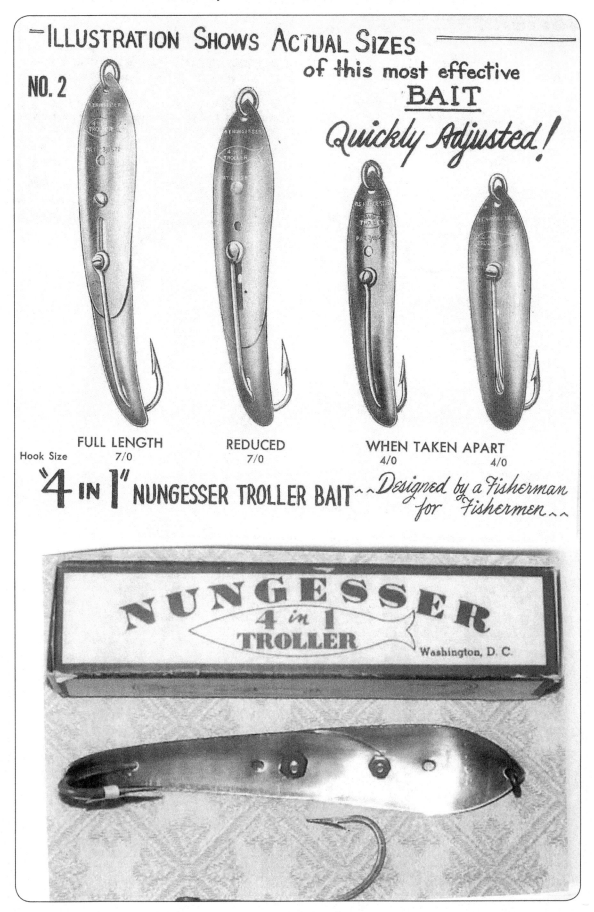

ILLUSTRATION SHOWS ACTUAL SIZES
of this most effective
BAIT
Quickly Adjusted!

NO. 2

| FULL LENGTH | REDUCED | WHEN TAKEN APART | |
| 7/0 | 7/0 | 4/0 | 4/0 |

Hook Size

"4 IN 1" NUNGESSER TROLLER BAIT ~~Designed by a Fisherman for Fishermen~~

NUNGESSER
4 in 1
TROLLER
Washington, D.C.

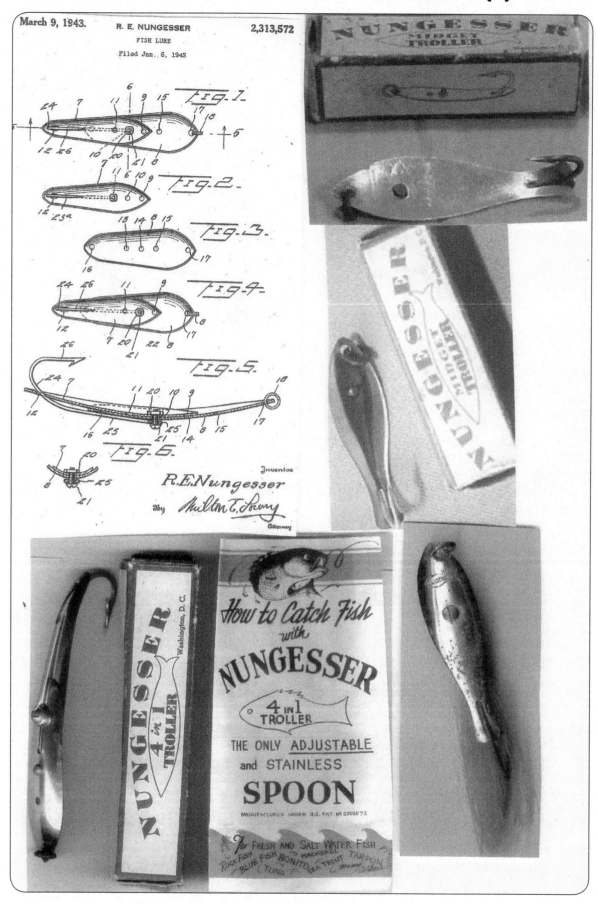

March 9, 1943.

R. E. NUNGESSER

2,313,572

FISH LURE

Filed Jan. 6, 1942

Inventor

R.E.Nungesser

By Milton T. Lowry

Attorney

NUVALU MINNOW USA COMPANY
CHICAGO, ILLINOIS

The Nuvalu Minnow USA Company, located at 2222 Diversey Parkway, Chicago, Illinois, produced a wooden lure in the early 1940's named the **NUVALU**. By the time World War II started, the company disappeared, so the production time was maybe only a year and a half. The NUVALU was a 3-3/4"-long, pointy-nose lure with large cup-rigged hardware for the two screw-eye belly hooks. It had a painted red arrow head with a white body.

The two-piece cardboard box was dark blue with red border trim. The lure name, Nuvalu, was in red angled print on the left side of the cover with an arrow through the name. The box cover stated, "NUVALU...THE BEST BAITS." The boxed lures are very rare; in all of my 47 years of collecting, I have only seen two or three.

The company did produce at least one metal bait that is slightly more common. The **VIM SPINNER** was a forward attractor spinner to be attached in front of a bait hook or trolling fly. It was sold on an ID card that read, "An Eccentric Spinner for Combinations....It spins, Wabbles, Wiggles the Lure."

The official distributor of the Nuvalu lure line was the Vim Chain Stores, with stores in Illinois, Michigan, Wisconsin, Minnesota, Colorado, and Washington D.C. Their trade logo was, "BETTER QUALITY and BETTER PRICES."

Boxed Nuvalu Lure trades $75 to $100. Lures alone trade $50 and higher. The carded Vim Spinner trades in the $10 to $15 range.

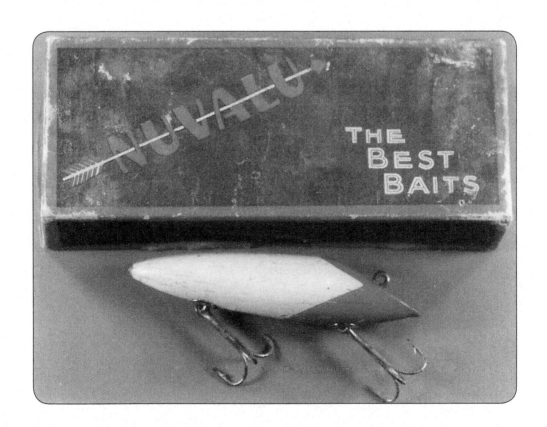

NYGLO PRODUCTS
HOPE, BRITISH COLUMBIA, CANADA

In the 1950's, a company was established in Hope, British Columbia, Canada, that was a manufacturing, importing and distribution company called Nyglo Products. The company developed the trade slogan "With a NYGLO LURE You're Always Sure!" Most of their manufactures were of the smaller spinning lure size. Their lures were sold on a one-dozen dealer display board that had green print and pictured a trout fisherman in waders about to land a trout in a stream. Pictured with this story are the top halves of two dealer boards, one holding 2-3/4"-overall-long **T-DEVONS** and the other holding 3"-overall-

long **PROP-BOBBERS**. The T-Devon consisted of a spinner-propeller with two round, red-fluorescent beads and one oblong one. The Prop-Bobber spinner consisted of a spinner-propeller, two orange fluorescent beads, and an oblong cork body. Although both lures did reflect light in a glowing matter, they were not glow-after-dark lures.

Pictures are courtesy of the Mike Potthier collection.

A full dealer board of twelve of either type of the Nyglo Lures trades in the $20 to $25 range.

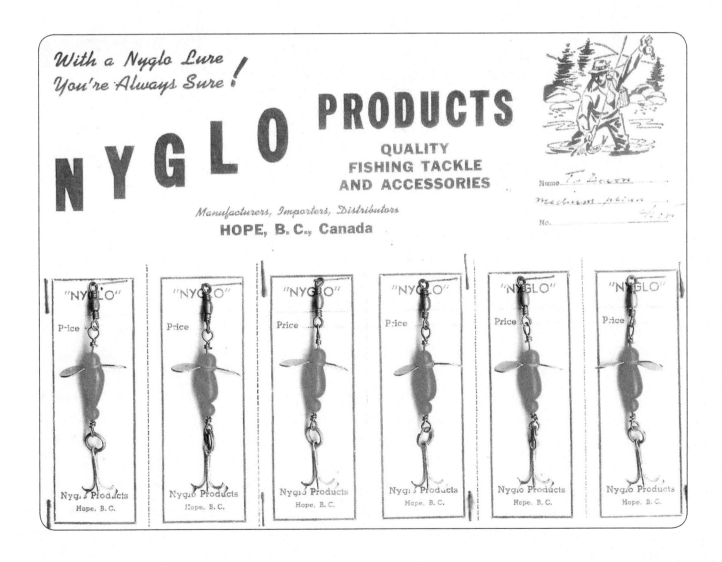

*With a Nyglo Lure
You're Always Sure!*

N Y G L O PRODUCTS

QUALITY
FISHING TACKLE
AND ACCESSORIES

Manufacturers, Importers, Distributors

HOPE, B. C., Canada

Name *Prop. Bobber*

Small

No. *40*

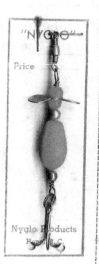     

NYLURE BAIT COMPANY
BRADENTON, FLORIDA

The 1950's Nylure Bait Company that was located in Bradenton, Florida, made a series of artificial bristle tail jigs made with nylon flared tail strands. There were rather neat graphics on their half-dozen dealer display board of a talking fish that says in red print, "Don't forget NYLURE." The pictured example of these patented jigs includes the No. 105 **NYLURES** at 1/4 oz. with yellow lead heads and red painted eyes.

I believe there was some kind of connection between this company and the E. C. Gregg Company of Tampa, Florida, who made the "CRAZY SWIMMER."

Individual Nylures, even on cards, have little trade value, but a six-pack dealer board will trade in the $5 to $10 range.

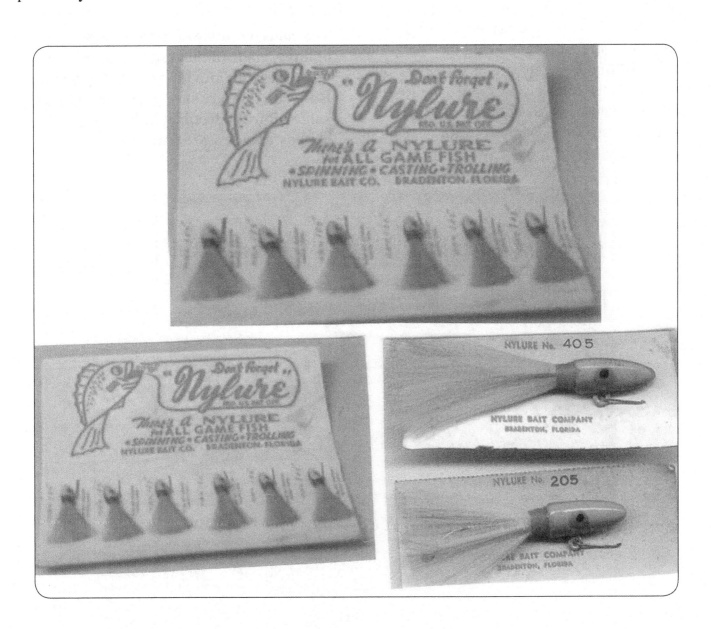

O-RIDGE LURES
OAK RIDGE, TENNESSEE

The mid- to late-1970's O-Ridge Lure Company, of Box 3042 Oak Ridge, Tennessee, made balsa wood crank bait types. There was just an explosion of lure makers in the 1970's in this part of Tennessee making the "pregnant guppy" or Boots Anderson type of balsa crank baits, and this company was just another one of them. The lures, made in the 3" to 3-1/2" range, were sold in plastic sacks with stapled-on blue or tan ID cards. The cards read, "Custom Made Balsa Wood Lures by Skilled Craftsman... Balance Guaranteed."

The collector value of most of these types of lures, made in that era in that part of Tennessee, fall into the $5 to $15 range. However, they are sure to become a higher-value future collectible; in fact, some already exceed a $75 trade value.

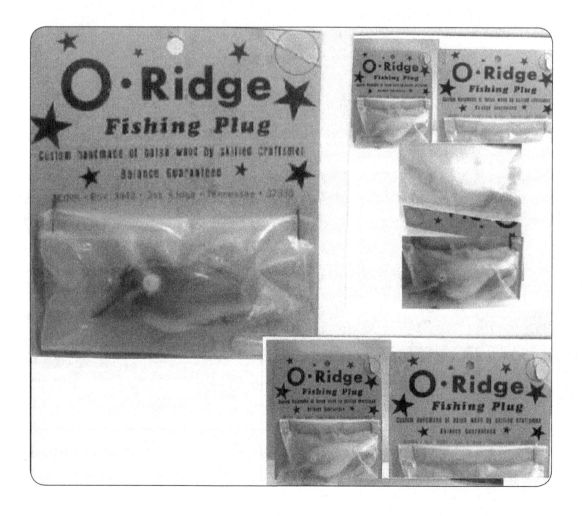

O. K. BAIT CO., NOT INC.
CHICAGO, ILLINOIS

I don't know exactly why, but I have found a number of companies from the 1930's and early 1940's that made mention of the fact in their company name that they were not incorporated. George T. Buddle invented the **BLACKJACK SHAMYHOOK** in 1931, and production started in that year at 3720 Dickens Ave., Chicago, Illinois. He later received Patent No. 1,928,367 for the lure on September 26, 1933. He did assign 25% of the patent rights each to Julius J. Sturm and Minnie N. Sturm.

The BLACKJACK SHAMYHOOK was a pork rind boat-shaped spoon made in two sizes: No. 3, bass, at 3-1/2" long and No. 5, musky, at 5-5/8" long (these were the overall measurements including the leather forked tails). The tail of the red and white painted lure had three holes. The center hole held the single up-turned hook, and the other two held the leather tail piece. Box papers suggested that Al Foss pork rind strips would be ideal to add to the tail hook and further said, "The Bait That Removes Alibis From Your Fishing Jaunt." The one-piece end-flap colorful lure box had a multi-color picture of two men fishing in a boat on a lake surrounded by trees and cattails.

Buddle also developed a 2-3/8" metal lure called the **BLACKJACK PORK RIND LURE** that was also red and white and had two wire weedguards. Later the name was shortened to **BLACKJACK SPOONHOOK.** The two-piece red cardboard box for this lure had the patent number on the cover and the lure name on one end and the company name and address on the other end. George T. Buddle also patented this lure. He received Patent No. 1,939,291 on December 12, 1933, for this 1931 invention. This lure, which was also made in an all-nickel finish, was created with a unique idea for the two wire weedguards. Some fishermen of that era felt that weedguards interfered with setting the hook on a striking fish. With this lure, there was a sliding soldered-together metal ring on the hook shank onto which the fisherman could lock the wire weedguards. The lure is pictured with the weedguards down and also in the up-and-out-of-the-way position.

A third lure made by this company was the jointed **BLACKJACK BUG HEAD SPOON** that measured 3-1/2" long and was split-ring joint-hinged just behind the head. The head was in the shape of a reverse "kite" painted red with holes in the flat metal piece for eyes. There were two dangling spinners at the tips of the ears of the head, and the trailing second section was more or less "Dardevle" shaped.

Boxed Blackjack Shamyhooks with box papers are rare and trade in the $35 to $50 range. The Spoonhooks and Bug Head Spoons are very scarce and trade in the $35-plus range on cards or in their two-piece red cardboard boxes.

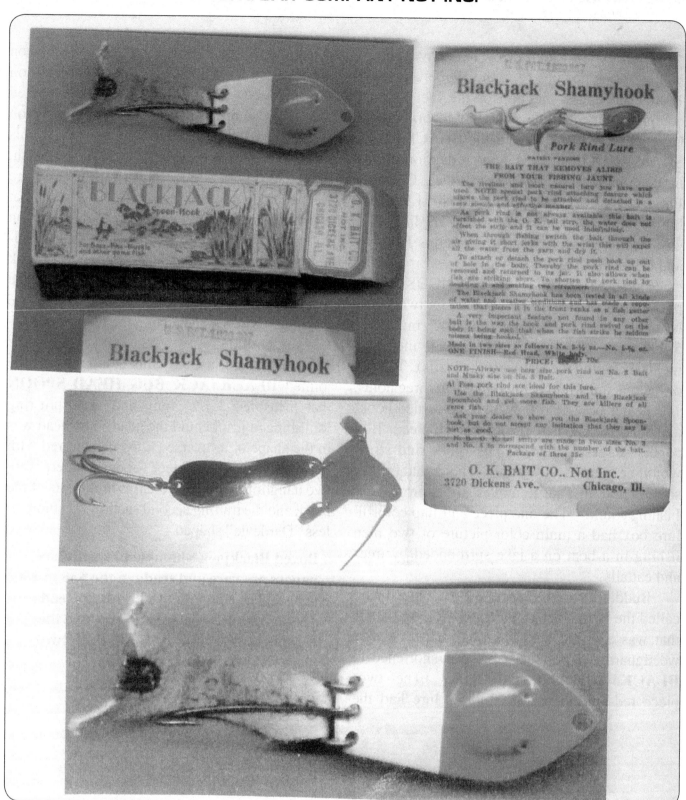

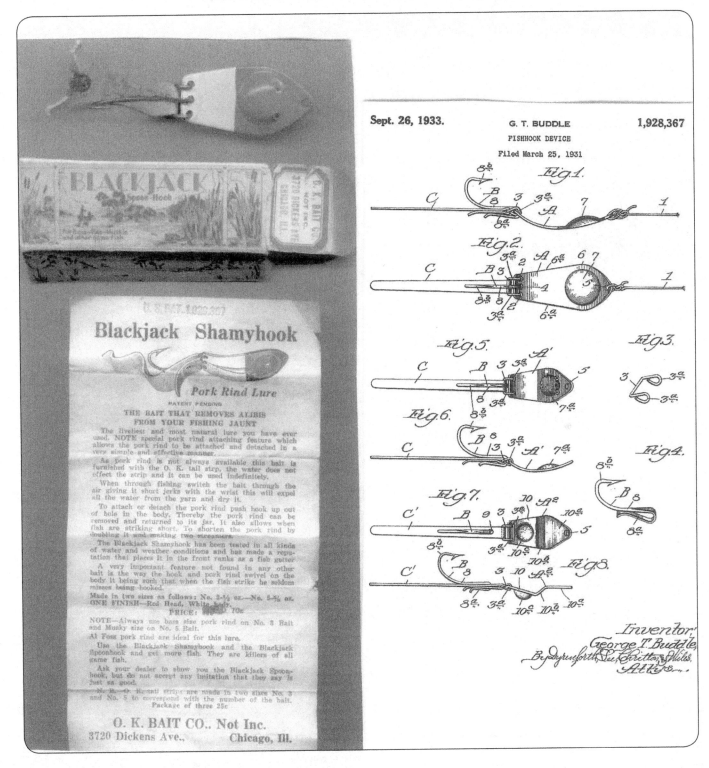

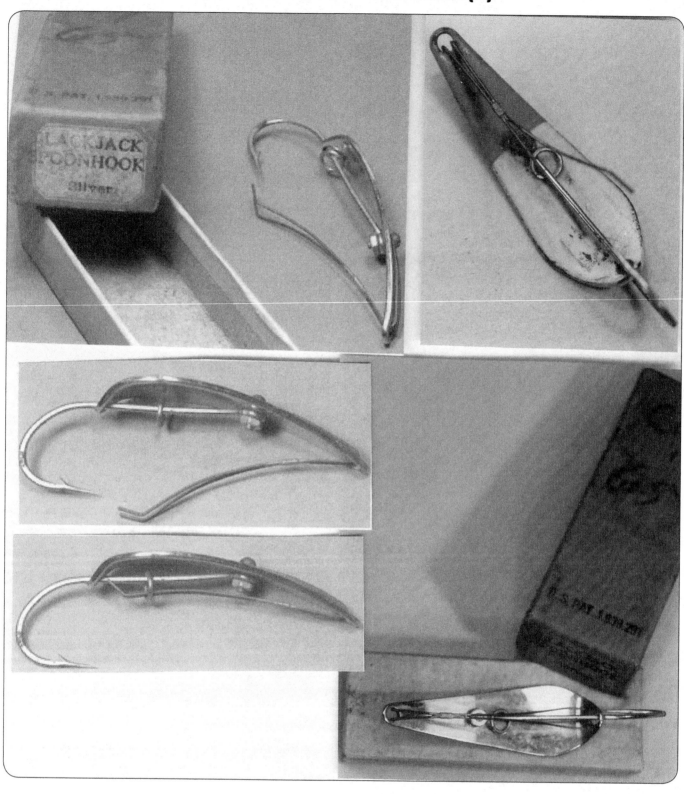

O. K. MACHINE COMPANY
FORT WAYNE, INDIANA

An early reel- and lure-making company from the 1910's era of Indiana was the O.K. Machine Company located in Fort Wayne. The company produced a 5-1/2"-diameter Indiana-style casting reel that also served as a line dryer, which they patented on June 27, 1911. The **OK REEL** had the typical U-shaped line holders at the tips of the arm posts, or spokes, and the entire reel was chrome plated. As far as I'm concerned, this company was the first of several to make reels that we call the "Indian Style Reels".

The company also made metal baits that can be found stamped "OK", such as the pictured **OK CRAB**. This 3-1/4"-long, solid-copper lure was crab shaped. With its barrel line tie extended, along with its natural gray deer hair and red feather-dressed tail treble hook, the lure measures 7" long altogether.

The OK Reel trades in the $85 to $100 range, and the OK Metal lure trades in the $15 to $25 range.

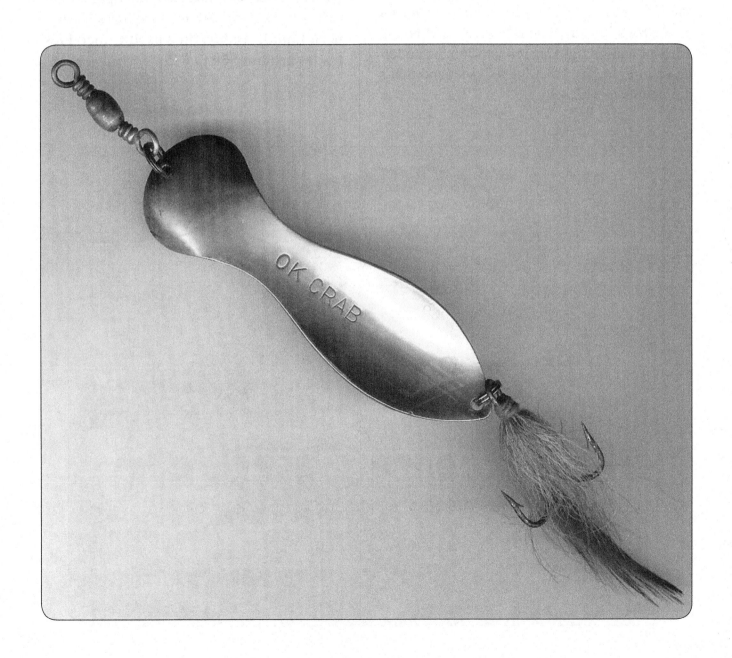

O. M. BAIT COMPANY
HAZEL PARK, MICHIGAN

One of my favorite Michigan-made lures was the O. M. Bait Company's Unner-Flash in frog finish. I used to love fishing for smallmouth bass with this plug in the spring. The late-1940's to early-1950's wooden **UNNER-FLASH LURE** was produced in nine colors numbered 100 through 800: spotted, red head, frog, chub, black, perch, yellow, mullet, and yellow spot. The 2-1/8"-long lure had no eyes and a metal cupped nose piece with a dangling shield type flasher. The 1/2-ounce, slow-sinking lures were relatively shallow runners, diving to three or four feet. Early ads said, "The UNNER-FLASH unit flashes of natural light are reflected on the underside of lure, the part that the fish see, and that's what counts most."

The lure was packaged in a neat two-piece cardboard box. The red and white box cover had the words "UNNER-FLASH" in blue print, surrounded by a red lightning flash, with jumping bass on either side of the box cover with red painted mouths and eyes. At the top of the box cover, along with the company name and address, was the statement, "MORE FISH... BIGGER ONES."

The boxed Unner-Flash lures traded well above $100 ten to fifteen years ago, but prices have dropped as more lures have been found. Today, the boxed Unner-Flash trades around $50 to $75.

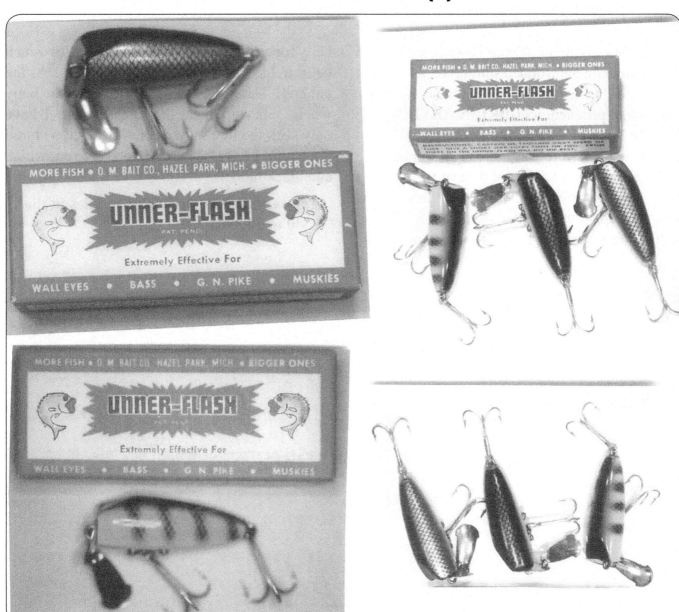

O'BRIEN, RICHARD F.
MINNEAPOLIS, MINNESOTA

On May 21, 1917, Richard F. O'Brien applied for a patent on his wooden spiral lure, and Patent No. 1,256,155 was issued on February 12, 1918. The actual production **O'BRIEN ARTIFICIAL MINNOW** was different from the patent drawing. The 3-5/8" lure was more cigar shaped with a flat nose and tail, but it did have the external wire harness from the lure's wire through that was shaped around under the belly to the tail end of the wire through. There was a loop in the belly for a treble hook (some lures have two such belly trebles) and another was crimped onto the tail end. The lure had cut side flutes so the body would spin within the harness system. I have only seen the lure in one color of white with red flutes, but I have been told there is a red, white, and black model.

The very rare O'Brien Lure trades in the $300 to $400 range.

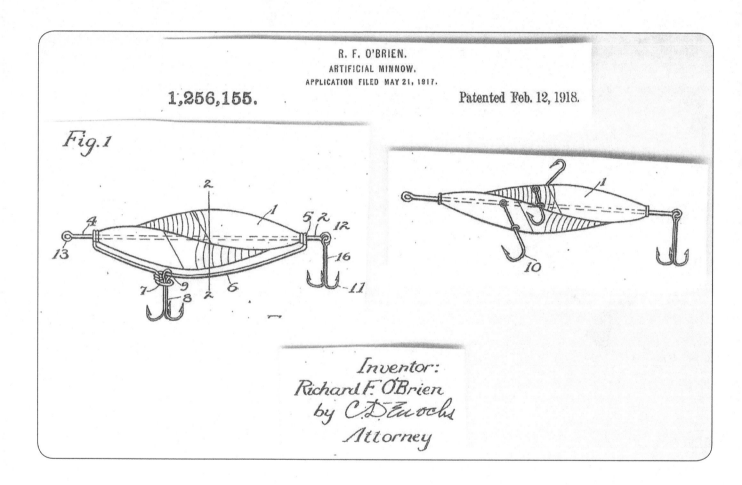

O'KI TACKLE MANUFACTURING, LTD.
SIDNEY, BRITISH COLUMBIA, CANADA

The O'ki Tackle Company, which was located at 7756-A Third Street in Sidney, British Columbia, Canada, was started in the 1970's. The O'Ki Tackle Company produced a line of lures called **PERMA-STRIP** that were made of soft plastic and measured 5-1/4" long. The company advertised, "Salmon and other predator fish will attack a wounded bait fish before they would attack a healthy one. The action of the Perma-Strip is exactly that of a wounded bait fish." Three colors of the Perma-Strip are pictured along with another one of their productions, the **WIGGLE HEAD**.

The soft plastic Perma-Strip and the Wiggle Head lures trade at $5 or less in today's market.

O'NEIL, JOHNNIE, LURES
AKRON, OHIO

In mid 1957, Johnnie O'Neil started making the **WEED WINGS** in the three sizes of 2-1/2", 2-3/4", and 3" lengths at 1805 Preston in Akron, Ohio. They were painted black, gold plate, nickel plate, frog, and possibly other colors. The line tie was on a short metal shaft through the revolving head and fixed to the main body. The head had two extended wings that caused it to spin. There were either single or double weedguards protecting the fixed single hook on the lure body that was shaped very much like the Louis Johnson "Silver Minnow". The lures were all stamped "Johnnie O'Neil" and were sold on individual cards. John "Johnnie" A. O'Neil received Patent No. 3,020,668 for his lure on February 13, 1962.

In the early 1960's, even before this patent was issued, the rights to the lure were sold to Harrison Industries, Inc., and production continued by them for several years in Newark, New Jersey. They sold the lures on large white with black print and red trim cardboard card that read, "The weedless spinner surface lure with fabulous sonic effect…catches bass so big they make headlines," and there was a picture of man holding a largemouth in the eight pound-plus range. Their given address was 250 Passaic Street Newark, New Jersey.

The Ohio carded O'Neil Weed Wings (Pat Pending) are scarcer and trade in the $10 to $15 range, whereas the Harrison versions are in the $5 range and up.

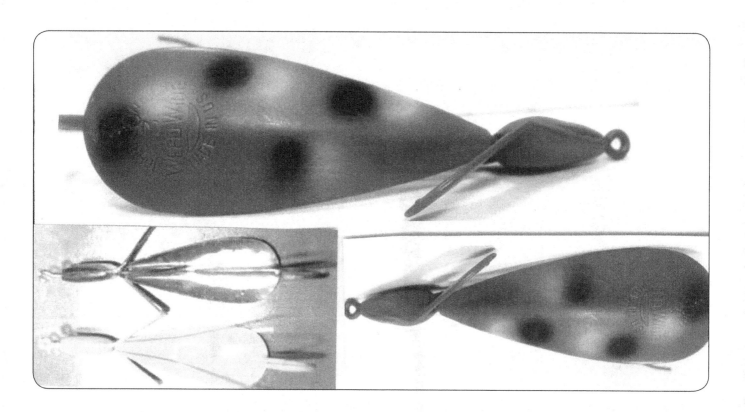

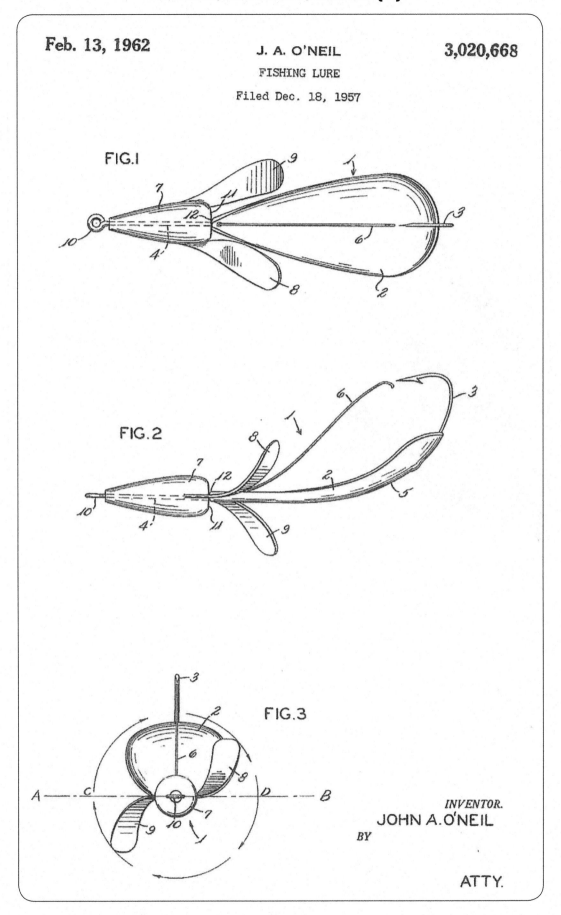

Feb. 13, 1962

J. A. O'NEIL

3,020,668

FISHING LURE

Filed Dec. 18, 1957

FIG.1

FIG.2

FIG.3

INVENTOR.
JOHN A. O'NEIL

BY

ATTY.

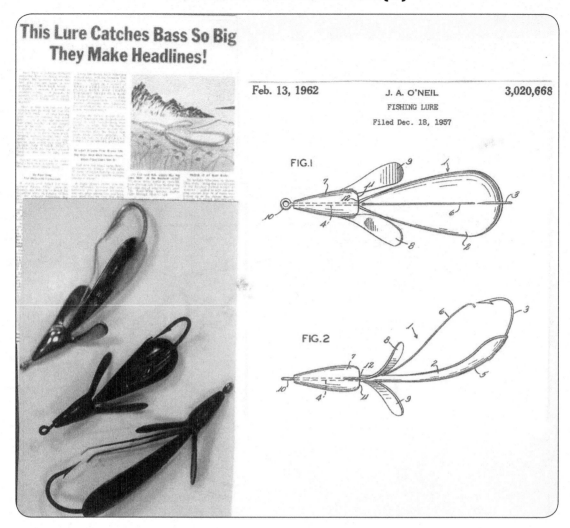

This Lure Catches Bass So Big They Make Headlines!

Feb. 13, 1962   J. A. O'NEIL   3,020,668

FISHING LURE

Filed Dec. 18, 1957

FIG.1

FIG.2

OBERLIN CANTEEN, INC.
OBERLIN, OHIO

As far as I could find in my research, the Oberlin Canteen Company, located at 212 Summer Street in the Ohio town of the same name, only produced one lure: the little 1-1/2" plastic spinning lure called the **DENNY BAIT SPINNER**. The "jellybean" shaped lure had two build-in, curved wings that made it spin on its wire-through axis to its single long shank tail hook. The lure also had a bead spacer and a flat plastic oval attractor spinner at the tail. The lure was primarily designed to be fished with live bait dressed on the long shank hook such as leaches or night crawlers, but minnows could be used as well. The lure received Design Patent No. D231,450 on April 23, 1974, awarded to Thomas A. Denny for his 1973 design.

Also pictured is the **OBERLIN BAIT CANTEEN**, one of the more popular bait canteens ever developed. It was invented by Albert E. Norling, who was awarded Patent No. 2,328,993 on September 7, 1943.

It was Norling who formed the Oberlin Canteen Company in 1942. He was still in business well into the 1990's, and the company is still in operation today with new owner, Keith Delong.

I have not fished for pan fish with crickets for many years, not since the 1950's and 1960's, but, back then, the cricket cage I used was an **OBERLIN BAIT CAGE**. The 6"-tall wire-mesh live bait cage had metal green caps at both ends. The top end had a dial-open access for the insertion or removal of crickets, grasshoppers, roaches, and even small frogs. The bait cage had a 24" elastic cord, so the fisherman could carry it around his neck for quick access. The 2-1/2" diameter cage was sold in a one-piece, rectangular, end-flap cardboard box in a white color with orange border trim and a picture of the live bait cage on the side.

The Denny Spinner trades in the $10 to $15 range. The Oberlin Bait Canteens trade in the $15 to $20 range, and the Oberlin Bait Cage for crickets and other live bait trades in the $35 range and higher.

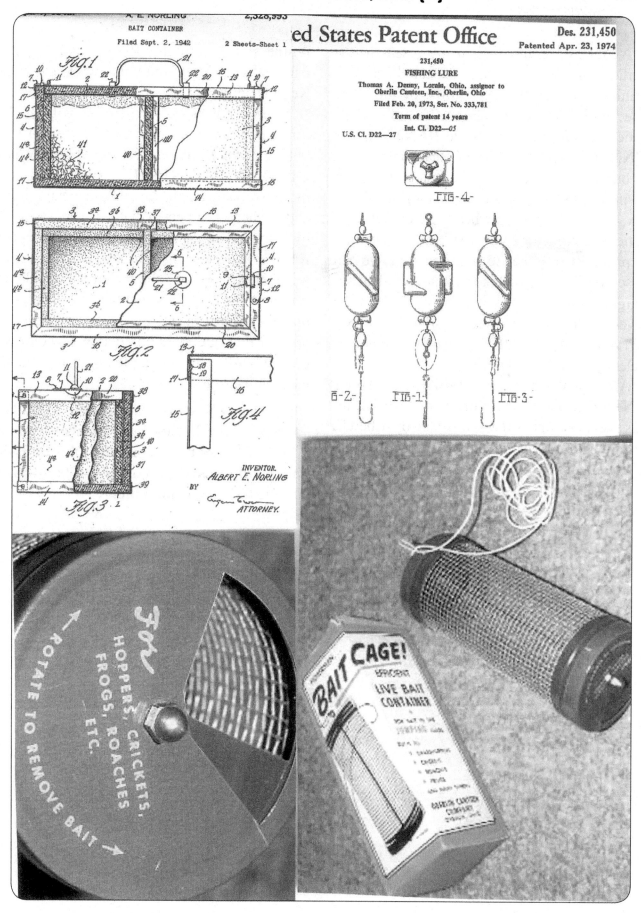

A. E. NORLING
2,328,993
BAIT CONTAINER
Filed Sept. 2, 1942
2 Sheets—Sheet 1

Fig.1

Fig.2

Fig.3

Fig.4

INVENTOR.
ALBERT E. NORLING
BY
ATTORNEY.

ed States Patent Office
Des. 231,450
Patented Apr. 23, 1974

231,450
FISHING LURE
Thomas A. Denny, Lorain, Ohio, assignor to
Oberlin Canteen, Inc., Oberlin, Ohio
Filed Feb. 20, 1973, Ser. No. 333,781
Term of patent 14 years
Int. Cl. D22—05
U.S. Cl. D22—27

FIG-4-

FIG-2-   FIG-1-   FIG-3-

For HOPPERS, CRICKETS, FROGS, ROACHES, ETC.
← ROTATE TO REMOVE BAIT →

BAIT CAGE!
LIVE BAIT CONTAINER

OBIE TACKLE COMPANY
O B'S TACKLE COMPANY
BELLEVILLE, ILLINOIS

Starting in 1973, the Obie Tackle Company, located in Belleville, Illinois, began production and the sale of a 3-1/8" plastic lure they called the **GLITTERING FISH**. The fish-shaped semi-transparent lure had a large, reinforced, built-in dive lip and very distinctive large eyes. The pupils were molded bump-raised and painted black and surrounded by painted bright-yellow irises. The lures were made in two molded halves and then marine glued together. However, before the gluing process, the maker inserted figure-eight clips to hold both the tail and belly treble hooks, and, once sealed, these hooks could never pull out. Also, before the lures were glued, a glitter finish was coated on the inside wall of one of the sides. Then the lure was filled three-quarter's full of water, leaving a large trapped air bubble inside. This air bubble served two purposes. One, it made the lure a slow sinker, and, two, it gave the lure extra sparkle and glitter as the bubble shifted about during the retrieve. The lures were finished in glitter coatings of red, yellow, gold, silver, or green (the latter two colors are pictured). The lure was pat-ented by Donald C. Volenec of 4533 S. 39th Street in Omaha, Nebraska. He was awarded Patent No. 3,885,340 on May 27, 1975, for his invention. The Glittering Fish was sold in a hinged plastic box with card ID insert.

The company later developed a 4-1/2" topwater jerk bait in a torpedo shape with a tail prop. The **SPARK PLUG** was a clear, transparent, hollow plastic lure with activated glitter inside that gave a reflective effect on retrieve. It was sold in a bubble-topped blue and white card with red and blue print. Although Don Volenec gave production rights to the Obie Tackle Company, they were not exclusive production rights. He also gave production right to the Metro Specialties Company, located in Kansas City, Missouri, owned by James T. Sullivan. He manufactured this same lure there, naming it the "Glitter Gitter".

The boxed Glittering Fish and carded Spark Plug lures trade in the $15 to $20 range.

United States Patent [19]

Volenec

[11] **3,885,340**

[45] **May 27, 1975**

[54] **FISHING LURE**

[76] Inventor: **Donald C. Volenec,** 4533 S. 39th St., Omaha, Nebr. 68107

[22] Filed: **Nov. 5, 1973**

[21] Appl. No.: **413,033**

[52] U.S. Cl. 43/42.16; 43/42.21; 43/42.33
[51] Int. Cl. A01k 85/00
[58] Field of Search............ 43/42.33, 42.16, 42.21; 161/18

[56] **References Cited**
UNITED STATES PATENTS

1,451,436	4/1923	Barnia	43/42.21
2,435,612	2/1948	Snyder	161/18
2,909,863	10/1959	Rector et al.	43/42.33 X

| 3,505,754 | 4/1970 | Lawlor | 43/42.33 X |

FOREIGN PATENTS OR APPLICATIONS

| 722,798 | 1/1932 | France | 43/42.16 |

Primary Examiner—Louis G. Mancene
Assistant Examiner—Daniel J. Leach
Attorney, Agent, or Firm—Hiram A. Sturges

[57] **ABSTRACT**

A fishing lure comprising a hollow body portion containing a fluid in which shiny particles move about, the fluid being agitated by motions of the body portion resultant from water interaction with its exterior and from motion of a weight inside the lure, the body being closed.

10 Claims, 10 Drawing Figures

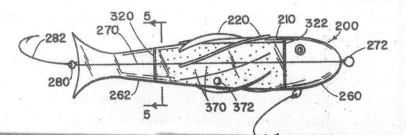

OCEAN CITY MANUFACTURING COMPANY
PHILADELPHIA, PENNSYLVANIA

Most collectors are familiar with the reel production by the Ocean City Manufacturing Company started in 1920 that was located at the corner of A and Somerset Streets in Philadelphia, Pennsylvania. Their early reels included fly rod, bait casting, and larger deep-sea-ocean fishing reels. However, in the 1950's, they also introduced some early spinning reels, such as their **OCEAN CITY 350 SPIN CAST REEL** that was shaped pretty much like the top half of an old kitchen egg beater.

Shortly after World War II, around 1946, the company got involved in the production of a number of different small spinning and casting lures. They advertised and specialized in offering lures of different colors for all conditions, different weights for fishing from one-half foot to twenty feet, and different and unusual actions. The company recognized that fish are attracted to nickel on bright, sunny, clear days and gold on cloudy days even in clear waters. On the other hand copper colors worked best on dismal, rainy days or when the water is dark, riled, and muddy. Consequently, all of the Ocean City's nine different production metal lures were offered in these three color finishes. For actions, they made lures with whirling blades, wobblers with both fast and slow or jerky actions, and lures with slow-floating-fluttering, slow-sinking action. The Ocean City spinning lures with whirling spinner blades included the **ZANI**, **SPIN TWIN**, and **MR. SPIN**.

In the spoon type of lure, the company made the **DESTROYER** that was designed to flutter down slowly and made in six sizes. The three sizes of the **KINGPIN** spoons were made to handle swift water locations. **THE BOSS** was a slow-wobble spoon made in six different sizes or colors. The three sizes of the slow-retrieve **EELIE** were made for freshwater fishing, but the same lure was made for a fast-retrieve saltwater application in three sizes as well. The **DOUBLE TROUBLE** was very similar to the earlier Walton Special made in Fulton, New York. This was a double-V-shaped lure, with the two sides held together with split rings. This stop-and-go-retrieve lure would reverse its spinning direction with each of these intermittent retrieve actions. Another spoon type was the **TINI**, a sink and jerk bait.

The Ocean City lures were sold in clear plastic tubes with a catalog of all company lures and "use" directions.

Pictured are the 1-7/8" size Mr. Spin with its three-surface spinner blade in a copper and red tip blade and the 1" size of the KINGPIN in gold finish. Also pictured is a company catalog that came rolled up in each plastic tube and lure sold.

Scarce Ocean City lures in their plastic tubes trade in the $5 to $10 range.

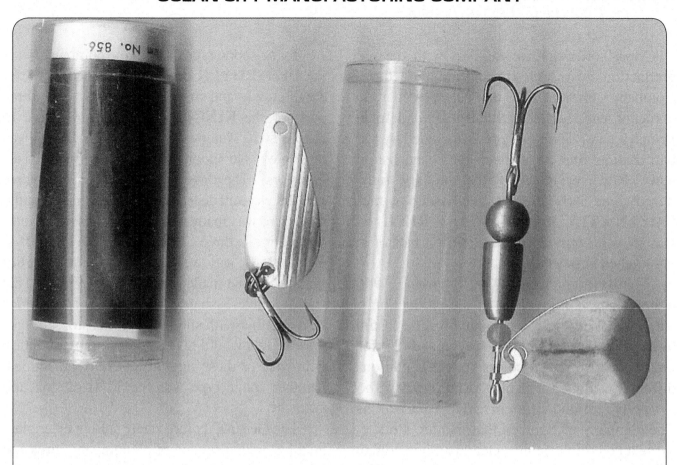

Printed in U.S.A.

Form No. 856-1

FOR BETTER RESULTS

Learn to Fish Your New Lure Properly!

See Over for Other Tips

OTHER OCEAN CITY LURES THAT FISH REALLY GO FOR! (Lures available in various weights and finishes.)

"DESTROYER"
Nos. 829, 830, 831, 832, 833 and 834

This is an all purpose lure which should be fished slowly, should be permitted on the cast to flutter down. The retrieve should be stop and go, and slow.
$.75 and $.85

"SPIN TWIN"
Nos. 863, 864 and 865

The tiny double blades make for fast, whirling action with even a slow retrieve. When used in moving water, the action of the stream itself will usually provide sufficient motion without much help from the fisherman.
$1.00

"KINGPIN"
Nos. 826, 827 and 828

Especially good in swift deep water. Make short casts and retrieve as slowly as possible so that this lure will flutter above the bottom where the big ones lie.
$.65

"EELIE"
Nos. 849, 851, 852, 853, 854 and 855

This lure for fresh water fishing should be fished at a slow rate of retrieve, stop and go action. However, contrary to its fresh water use, for salt water this lure should be retrieved at a high rate of speed.
$.65, $.85 and $1.50

"THE BOSS"
Nos. 835, 836, 837, 838, 839 and 840

This spoon is best fished at a slow rate of retrieve. No special working of the spoon is necessary.
$.65, $.75 and $.85

"MR. SPIN"
Nos. 841, 842, 843 and 844

This spinner should be retrieved at medium speed to get best results. May also be fished as a wobbler by slowing the retrieve to a point where the blade doesn't quite "spin" but only wobbles.
$.85 and $1.00

"ZANI"
Nos. 845, 846, 847 and 848

A fine type of spinner. Upon a cast it should be permitted to sink so it can start working properly. Retrieve should be slow.
$.75 and $.85

"DOUBLE TROUBLE"
Nos. 859, 860, 861 and 862

This is an unusual type of lure. Upon a cast it should be permitted to sink so it starts vibrating and works properly. A retrieve method of stop and go, slow and fast, should be employed since this lure reverses when speed of retrieve changes.
$.75 and $.85

OCEANIC TACKLE SHOP
MIAMI, FLORIDA

I believe that Ralph Miller started making the four sizes of his wooden **LEAPING LENA** in the late 1930's, but I don't know whether of not he was active during World War II. His Oceanic Tackle Shop was located at 240 S. W. 17th Court in Miami, Florida. I do know that he was still making lures at least in the 1946 to 1948 era. The lures were made in a 2" size, the more common 3-5/8" size, and in 3-1/2" and 2-5/8" sizes. The no-eyed lure was torpedo shaped with a slight curved chin undercut. This undercut gave the lure a slight leaping or jumping action on the surface on retrieve, thus, the name for the lure. Lure colors were red head with white, red head with white with silver flitter, red arrow head with white, red head with green, dark blue with black spots and silver flecks, and other colors.

The real collector value is in the Leaping Lena's rather plain, colorful, two-piece card-board lure box. Actually, there were four box styles, three of which were a pale yellow, an all white, and a brighter yellow color. Each had a cover picture of a green leaping tarpon in the foreground on a water scene with two men in a boat in the distance. The fourth box style was a tan color box that had blue trim and purple print that read, "LEAPING LENA...A proven Salt Water lure." Some boxes were white with a green jumping tarpon and dark blue print.

Another Ralph Miller lure, a fat-cigar-shaped wooden production with a single, one-piece, surface-rigged treble hook and no eyes, was called the **RIP-JACK**. It represented a frightened bait fish on the surface.

The boxed Miller lures trade in the $35 to $45 range.

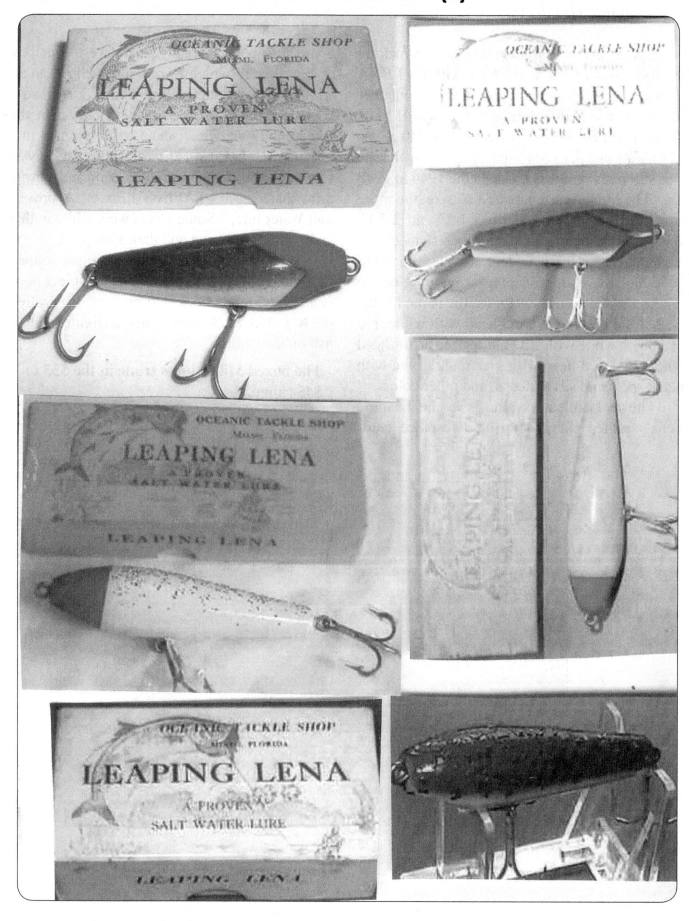

ODON BAIT COMPANY
BRADENTON, FLORIDA

The Odon Bait Company was located at 5536 25th Street West, Bradenton, Florida. "Odon" is a play on the word "odonata", which is the name for an insect more commonly know by most of us as the dragonfly. The company's only lure production was the 3-1/4" wooden **DRAGONFLY**. The lure had a rounded head and annular grooves in the tapered body, simulating the body of a dragonfly. All fishermen know that the dragonfly comprises one of the main foods that bass feed upon. This lure was very realistic with flexible plastic wings attached by screw-bolts to the top of the lure above the thorax portion of the body. The three screw-eye treble hooks were so positioned as to balance the lure to land flat on the surface of the water when the lure was cast. Dennis Y. Jacobs, the lures' inventor and manufacturer, was awarded Patent No.3,871,122 for his 1973-developed lure on March 18, 1975. Two colors are pictured courtesy of the late Art Hansen collection in all yellow with black trim and in brown and red trim.

The Jacobs Dragonfly trades in the $15 to $20 range.

United States Patent [19]

Jacobs

[11] 3,871,122
[45] Mar. 18, 1975

[54] FISH LURE

[76] Inventor: Dennis Y. Jacobs, 5536 25th St. W., Bradenton, Fla. 33507

[22] Filed: Jan. 15, 1973

[21] Appl. No.: 323,694

[52] U.S. Cl. 43/42.27
[51] Int. Cl. A01k 83/06
[58] Field of Search 43/42.27, 42.26

[56] References Cited
UNITED STATES PATENTS

1,540,586	6/1925	Adam	43/42.26
1,738,617	12/1929	Scharrer	43/42.27 X
2,242,708	5/1941	Lancaster	43/42.27
2,448,523	9/1948	Fibiger	43/42.27
2,719,377	10/1955	Bennett	43/42.27
2,760,294	8/1956	Morrill, Jr.	43/42.27

Primary Examiner—Louis G. Mancene
Assistant Examiner—J. Q. Lever

[57] ABSTRACT

The present fish lure or plug is a simulation of an Odonata, more familarly known as a dragonfly, which is well known to be one of the most natural surface foods that bass feed upon and comprises a body simulating the body of the dragonfly which is made of wood and has annular grooves in it to form a simulation of the head of the dragonfly, a pair of flexible wings attached to the top of the body above the thorax and a plurality of annular grooves cut in the wooden body rearwardly of the wings spaced in such manner as to simulate the body of the dragonfly. A line attaching eye is threaded into the outer end and centrally of the head portion of the body and a series of treble gang hooks are attached to the body, for instance, two at spaced distances to the abdomen of the body and extending downwardly therefrom and a third attached to the tail end of the body, all of which hooks are so located that they will cause the body to fall approximately flat on the water when the lure is cast.

1 Claim, 3 Drawing Figures

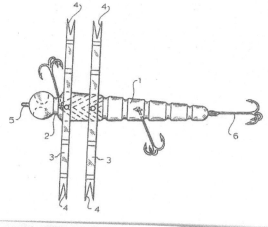

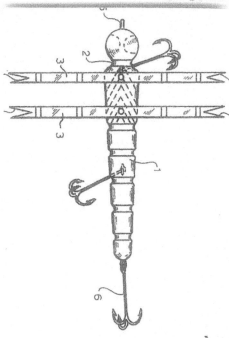

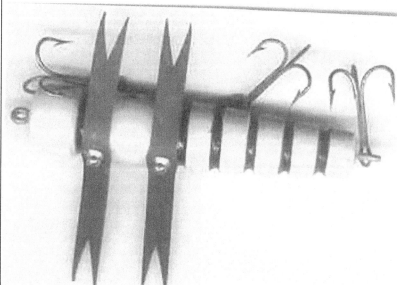

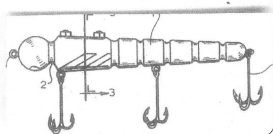

OGENE COMPANY
ABILENE, TEXAS

GAMBILL BROTHERS
ABILENE, TEXAS

The Ogene Company is much older than most collectors realize, dating back to 1939 when they were first located at 309 Alexander Bldg., Abilene, Texas. In that same year, the founder of the Ogene Company, William Milton Gambill, also founded the Gambill Brothers Company at that same address. He left his brother, Carroll Gambill in charge of that operation while he busied himself with the Ogene Company.

The first Gambill Brothers production was the **GAMBILL WEEDLESS SPINNER BAIT**. The lure measured 3-1/2" long overall and was a very well designed and pretty jig-spinner combination. The lure consisted of a 1" oval contoured metal head (not the traditional lead head) that simulated a bug's head. This metal head had molded-in, protruding bump eyes with painted pale yellow irises with center black pupils with red stripes across the pupils. The single-hook lure had a plush dressing of natural color deer hair bucktail with a simulated red blood streak in the hair. You can't see it in the picture, but the piano wire weedguard continued through the metal lure body to the tail hook and formed a lock-over clip to hold a pork rind trailer if the fisherman chose to use one. The off-balance vibrating "All Foss" type prop had just one blade. William Milton Gambill was awarded Patent No. 2,219,225 for that lure on October 22, 1940, following a July 18, 1939, application date.

He also received Patent No. 2,523,949 for a **GAMBILL DIVING JIG** on September 26, 1950, that also had a metal body with a reverse dive lip. The unusual dive lip was secured to the top of the head, which forced the lure up, as opposed to being pulled down with the traditional type of dive lip.

The first lure that "Bill" Gambill produced through the Ogene Company out of the Alexander Building was named the **GLITTERBUG**. This lure was a metal bait with an "Al Foss" type forward spinner blade. This vibrating spinner blade was first made thin and the following lure body was round with a single hook and a shredded rubber skirt. This lure was made this way up to the time that World War II started.

I don't believe there was any lure production by either company during the war years of 1941 through 1945. After the war, Gambill decided that more weight was needed to make the lure work properly, so a thicker through-blade was developed and was followed in-line with a tiny metal bead, a bent metal deflector, and the lure body. This main lure body had also changed to an arrow shape, or lop-sided heart shape, that was hollow inside, although these later lures were still name stamped "GLITTERBUG". (These pre- and post-war Glitterbug pictures are courtesy of the Mike Potthier collection.)

After the war in 1946, William Milton Gambill had relocated his Ogene Company to 1826 Grape Street, Abilene, Texas. There, he developed a 3-1/4"-overall-long lure he named the **ACRO-JET** and a wooden 2-1/4" lure he again named the **GLITTER BUG BAIT**. His first 1947 Acro-Jet production was made of wood at 2 1/4" long with a 1" pyramid-shaped nose dive lip that made the lure 3" long overall. The lure formed a hump in the middle and tapered down at both ends, with the nose end slightly fatter than the tail end. The nose end had a "Luxon" line tie-connector and a dive lip that swiveled from one side to the other. The one-color painted eye was located just back of center in the tail section. The lure had external convex-cup rigged trebles at the belly under the head and at the tail. The early two-piece cardboard box for the wooden model was rather plain and read,

"THE ACRO-JET…Triple Action Lure…(Patent Applied For)." I imagine there were other colors, but I have only seen the lure in yellow-silver scale with black trim and eye blush.

A year earlier in 1946, Gambill had introduced his wooden version 2-1/4" GLITTER BUG BAIT. This short-lived lure was torpedo shaped with a wire through shaft. The lure had a metal two-blade nose floppy prop with a metal bearing, a "Foss" one-blade vibrating spinner at the tail, followed by a treble hook. The Glitter Bug had a reinforcing wire emanating from its tail end and then reaching across the lure's back and down through a tiny drilled hole near the head. This provided the lure with a sturdy hook-up to the belly treble hook. The Glitter Bug Bait, made for only two years (1946 - 1948), was sold in a plain, two-piece, orange-red cardboard box with "GLITTER BUG BAIT" in big print across the cover.

Both lures had unique painted eyes: all yellow or white with black eye shadow blush around the outsides.

Gambel applied for a patent on the Acro-Jet on May 2, 1950, and Patent No. 2,570,338 was granted to him on October 8, 1951. Shortly after the patent was granted, Gamble switched to making the Acro-Jet exactly the same way but in plastic. The new plastic version was simply called the **TRIPLE ACTION LURE**, and the name was so stated on the new red two-piece cardboard box

in which the lure was sold. However, when first introduced in plastic, the box had a pinkish paste-over label that read, "TRIPPLE ACTION LURE (Patent Applied For)…Three Distinct Actions Plus Action…Two More Distinct Actions Than Any Other Lure Of This Type Plus Action." The boxed lure came with an external hanging lead weight on a wire that could be attached to the bottom ring of the "Luxon" line tie connector if the fisherman desired more depth.

The first set of pictures is of the first and second metal versions of the Glitter Bug.

The next set is of the three William Gambill patents.

The third set is of the three metal lures invented and produced by Bill Gambill in order of their introductions.

The fourth and fifth sets of pictures are of the later wooden and plastic lures.

Carded metal Glitter Bug lures made prior to World War II are rather scarce and trade in the $25 to $35 range on cards. The post-war carded metal Glitter Bugs trade in the $15 to $20 range. Boxed early wooden Glitter Bug Baits trade in the $25 to $35 range, and so do the wooden Acro-Jet lures. The later plastic Triple Action Lures can be acquired for around $20 to $25 in their boxes.

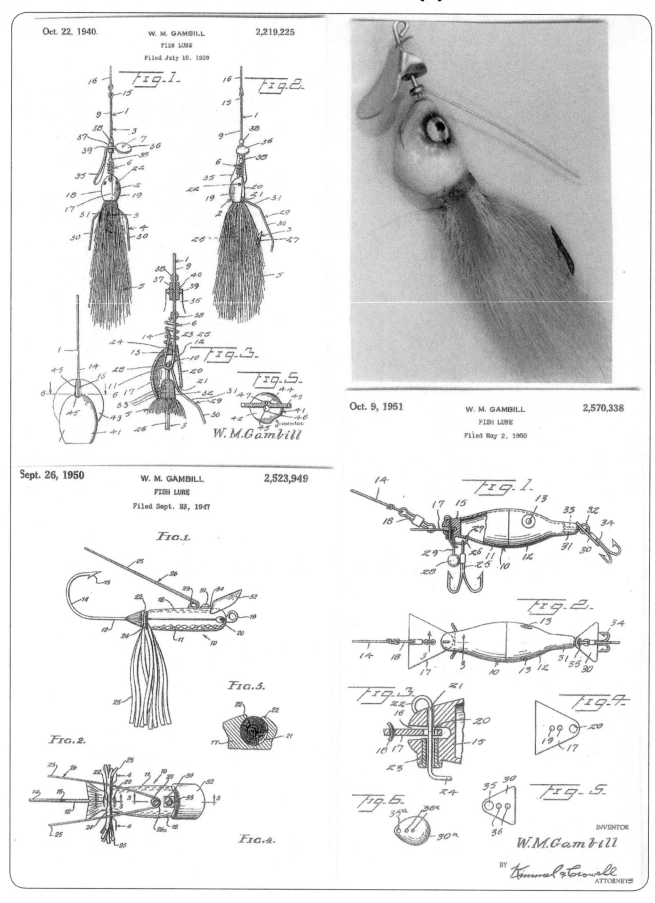

Oct. 22, 1940.   W. M. GAMBILL   2,219,225
FISH LURE
Filed July 18, 1939

Oct. 9, 1951   W. M. GAMBILL   2,570,338
FISH LURE
Filed May 2, 1950

Sept. 26, 1950   W. M. GAMBILL   2,523,949
FISH LURE
Filed Sept. 23, 1947

INVENTOR
W.M.Gambill
BY
Kimmel & Crowell
ATTORNEYS

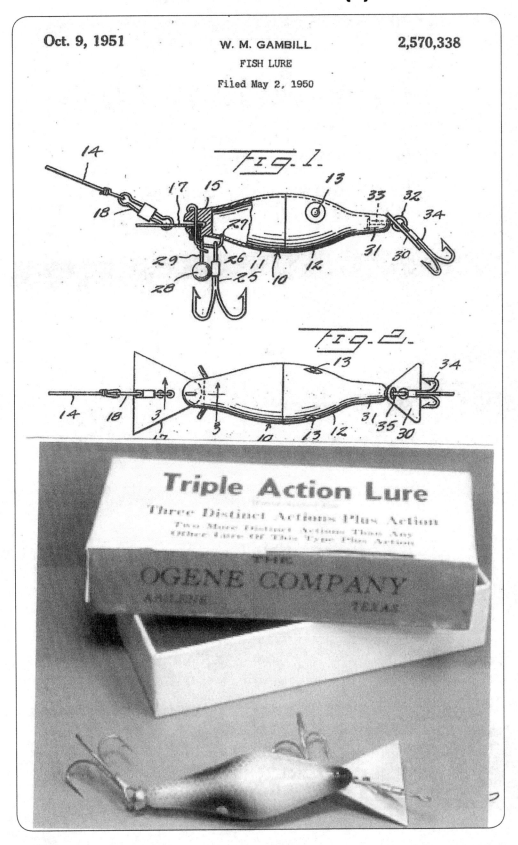

Oct. 9, 1951

W. M. GAMBILL

FISH LURE

Filed May 2, 1950

2,570,338

Triple Action Lure

Three Distinct Actions Plus Action

Two More Distinct Actions Than Any
Other Lure Of This Type Plus Action

THE
OGENE COMPANY

ABILENE   TEXAS

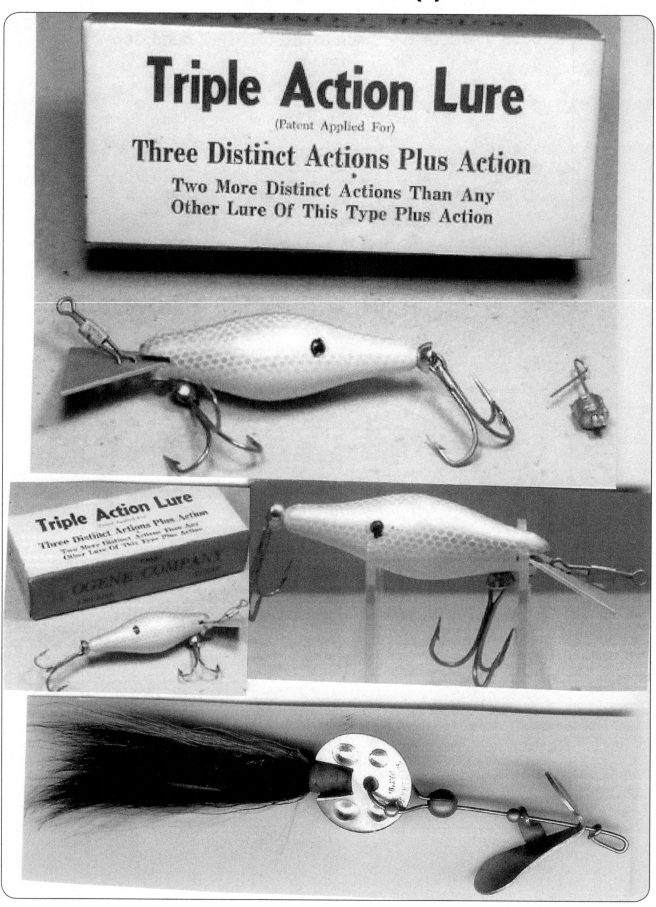

OGILVY, ROBERT, COMPANY
HAWK-OGILVY
NEW YORK, NEW YORK

The Robert Ogilvy Company, of 79 Chambers Street in New York City, was an early distributor of fishing tackle. They carried a long line of both salt and freshwater reels in names like Pflueger, Redifor and Acme. Their main line of braided fishing line was a pure Irish lynen (spelled linen today) under the trade name Crest Brand **CUTTYHUNK**. They also distributed fly rod and regular size fishing lures such as Pflueger and even the Hasting's Frog. Some of their generic reels and metal baits were stamped with the trademark "**OGILVY**". After Ogilvy teamed up with a partner named Hawk, they developed a trademark "Iron Cross", which appeared on many of their metal spinning lures.

Robert Ogilvy Company catalogs of that era trade in the $25 range and higher. Hawk-Ogilvy metal spinner baits trade in the $50 to $75 range.

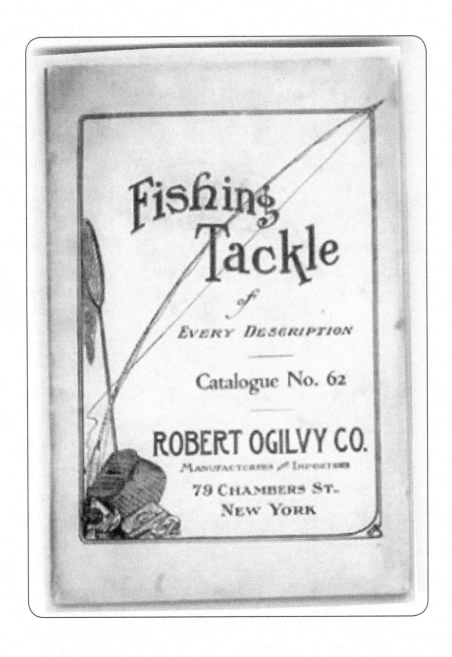

OHIO OUTDOOR PRODUCTS
CLEVELAND, OHIO

The 1950's Ohio Outdoor Products Company primarily made terminal fishing tackle accessories. Their spinner baits were designed to be used in conjunction with any lure of fishermen's choosing or with live bait as forward attractors. The carded lure examples are the double **RAINBOW PEARL SPINNER** and the plated nickel **WILLOWLEAF SPINNER**. The lure had one of two types of quick connectors at the tail end of the spinner's shaft. One was a simple spring wire lay-over clip and the other the pull-forward tight-wound spring wire sleeve. The lure card gave the full company address as 4926 Eichorn Avenue, Cleveland, Ohio.

Carded lures trade up to $5, but, without cards, they have no collector value.

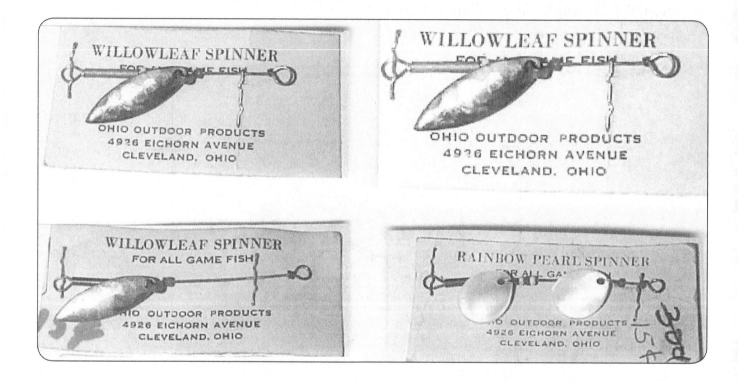

OIL CAPITOL ELECTRONICS CORPORATION
TULSA, OKLAHOMA

I'll just make a brief mention of this company located at 923 East 4th in Tulsa, Oklahoma. This Oil Capitol Electronics Corporation gave out complimentary promotional lures in the late 1950's that were made for them by Heddon. They used the larger size of the **HEDDON HEP** **SPINNERS** and placed them in clear plastic hinged boxes with a green card inserts.

These boxed complimentary lures trade in the $10 to $15 range.

OJIE BAIT & TACKLE COMPANY, THE
CRYSTAL FALLS, MICHIGAN

The "OJIE" spoon was shaped like a fat bullet with a fish tail. It was manufactured at 16 S. Third Street, Crystal Falls, Michigan, a little town north of Iron Mountain in the Upper Peninsula. The company started production shortly after World War II and was in business until around 1955. The brass, nickel-plated, and polished copper spoons were made from a little fly rod size up to a big musky size. The exact five sizes were 1-1/8", 2-1/4", 3-1/4", and 5-1/4" long.

There was also a special 2-1/2" two-tone brass and copper spoon called the **ICER** that was especially made for jigging through the ice in winter. The yellow two-piece cardboard box had green print. Around 1953, the company moved to the Lower Peninsula, at 9650 Commerce Street, Walled Lake, Michigan, and continued business there for two more years.

Lure pictures are courtesy of the Larry Sundall collection.

For a company that was in business for eight years, the boxed lures are quite scarce and trade in the $15 to $25 range with Michigan collectors and less elsewhere.

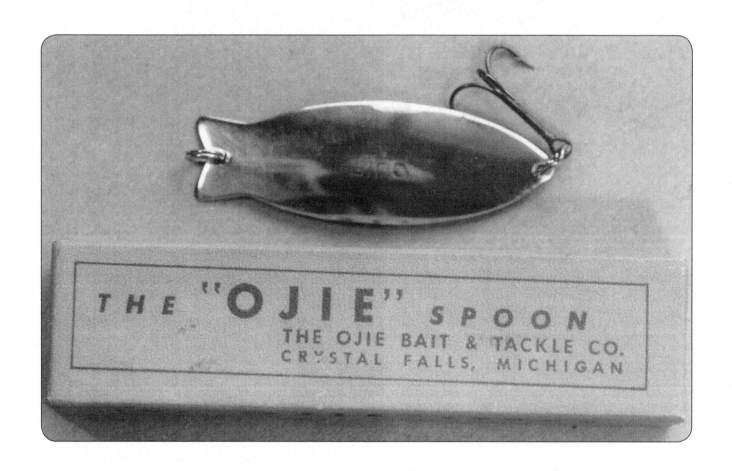

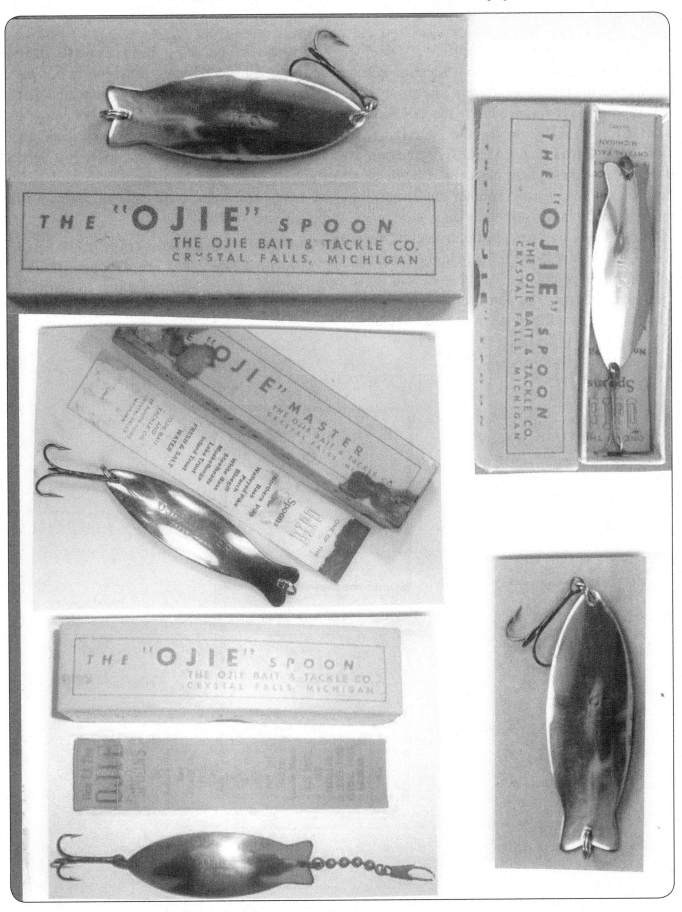

OKIELITE LURES
TULAS, OKLAHOMA

The mid-1970's to late-1980's Okielite Lures Company, of 8712 E.46th Street in Tulsa, Oklahoma, made a little different power set buzz bait type of bass spinner bait: the **OKELITE SINGLE BLADE** and the **OKIELITE DOUBLE BLADE CLACKER**. The major difference in these buzz baits was that the traditional V-spread for the spinner blades and the lead-headed, plastic-skirted bodies were made of unbreakable buoyant plastic instead of metal wire. This allowed the arms holding the buzz-spinner blades to collapse easily when fish strike the lures, reducing the number of short strikes. Also, instead of tying to the front yoke, like most other bass spinner baits, the fishermen tied direct to the lead-headed hooks. These lures had faster rise than standard bass spinner baits and stayed in the strike zone longer. The company also made **SLOW FALL JIGS**, which sank about four times slower than most other jigs, giving the bass more time to make the decision to bite or not. The lures were sold on cards within plastic sacks.

The Okielite Buzz Baits trade in the $5 to $10 range, since they are no longer made, whether as a collectible or just to fish.

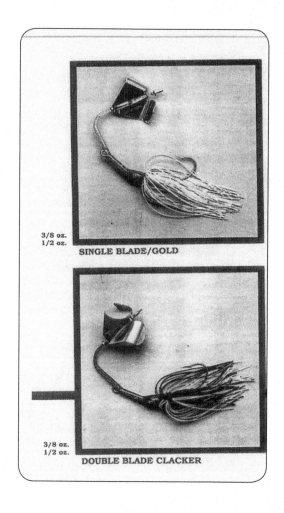

3/8 oz.
1/2 oz.

SINGLE BLADE/GOLD

3/8 oz.
1/2 oz.

DOUBLE BLADE CLACKER

3/8 oz.
1/2 oz.

SINGLE BLADE/SILVER

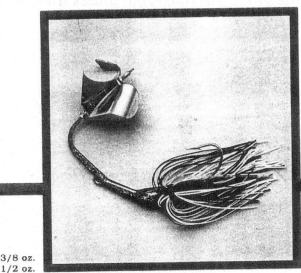

3/8 oz.
1/2 oz.

SINGLE BLADE/GOLD

3/8 oz.
1/2 oz.

DOUBLE BLADE CLACKER

Power Set BUZZ BAITS

Power Set BUZZ BAITS are also made from the same unbreakable plastic and come in the same color combinations as the Original Slow Fall JIGS. It also has a faster rise than standard buzz baits and a much slower retrieve to stay in the STRIKE ZONE longer. The unique design of Power Set BUZZ BAITS transmits stronger vibrations from the lure, because the vibrations travel through the plastic and out of the hook instead of passing through the lead head.

"Keep your lure in the Strike Zone." You have heard this advice dozens of time from many different sources. Good advice, but difficult to do with traditional lead head jigs and spinner baits because they quickly sink through the strike zone to the bottom. Okielite Slow Fall Lures answer the problem of keeping a jig or spinner bait in the Strike Zone. A new unbreakable, buoyant plastic moulded to the traditional leadhead of jigs, spinner baits and buzz baits allows for a slower fall rate keeping your lure in the Strike Zone longer. Although, Okielite lures look similar to traditional jigs, spinner baits and buzz baits the similarity stops there.

Okielite Slow Fall Skirted and Barehead Jigs come in five models, each with a specific rate of fall, from a super slow 3-1/2 seconds per foot to one second per foot. Head colors are moulded into the unbreakable buoyant plastic, meaning that the lure color will never chip, or fade like painted lures. A snake-tongue weed guard, and the two barbs on the shank, will hold a Getzit, skirt or other plastic trailers in place.

Okielite Power Set SPINNER & BUZZ BAITS are also made of the same unbreakable buoyant plastic. This plastic allows the lure arms to collapes easily when a fish bites, reducing the number of short strikes. Also, if the lure arm becomes bent, it can be straightened again by just bending it back with your fingers: it will not kink like wire. Incorporated into the Power Set SPINNER and BUZZ BAIT design is a special power-set hook. Your line is tied directly to the hook, so when you set the hook all of the setting force transfers directly through the hook for a stronger set. Okielite spinner baits fall at about half the speed of traditional spinner baits and the buzz baits rise much faster than the buzz baits on the market.

Fishing a Slow Fall lure takes a little getting used to. There is no need to learn any new techniques, because Slow Fall lures can be fished similiarly to traditional leadhead lures. The difference comes down to adjusting your thinking a bit by slowing down your retreive. Think about it. They slow-fall to give you time to work them through the strike zone. You get the maximum benefit from these lures by working them slowly, giving them time to fall, and bass time to make the decision to bite. If you want to fish fast, standard lures may work best.

With Slow Fall lures a bass does not need to be in a hurry to strike. It can wait and watch, and still have time to bite. Good fishing from **Okielite Slow Fall Lures.**

**MADE WITH GENUINE SAMPO
BALL BEARING SWIVELS**

5 YEAR WARRENTY

OkieLite *Lures*

8712 E. 46th Street
Tulsa, OK. 74145
(918) 663-2219

MADE IN THE U.S.A.
COPYRIGHT 1988 — All Rights Reserved — Patent Pending

OL' BILL'S ORIGINAL LURES
ROYAL PALM BEACH, FLORIDA

William "Bill" Howington started his small company, Ol' Bill's Original Lures, at 142 Saratoga Blvd., E., in Royal Palm Beach, Florida, where he makes his original design wooden lures. His intention was to recycle discarded wood scraps and make quality fishing lures that would actually catch fish, but collectors also hang his lures in their collection rooms as folk art creations. Bill takes great well deserved pride in the lures that he makes from recycled wood. The fourth set of pictures with this story shows the various scrap woods used and the lures made from them.

Bill Howington actually developed three trade names and lure box styles for different categories of lures he makes. There are the original design **OL' BILL'S ORIGINAL LURES**, the lures made from natural and recycled wood, **OL' BILL'S HANDCRAFTED WOODEN LURES**, and repaints of some old classic lures, **FISH A CLASSIC OL' BILL'S REPAINTS**.

One of my favorite Howington original lure designs is the jointed 3" **OL' BILL'S BANJO**, which is actually shaped somewhat like the stringed musical instrument. The pictured red head with white lure has raised tack eyes, a one-piece surface rigged belly treble, and a convex washer- and screw-eye-held tail treble hook. The 4"-overall-long **OL' BILL'S CRAB** has a 2" heart-shaped stainless steel dive lip inserted in the tail, and the lure is designed to retrieve backwards with the painted tack eyes and head facing the rear. Next is Bill's 5-1/2"-overall-long **FROG-PROP BAIT**, painted in a green bullfrog pattern, with a green and white shredded plastic tail skirt, black-iris, yellow-pupil tack eyes, and a 1-3/8"-wide nose prop. One of Bill's smaller lures is his 1-7/8"-long **OL' BILL'S MOUSE** that has a 3/4" leather tail, a one-piece surface-rigged small belly treble hook, and tack eyes. These lures all fall in the original design category, as seen in the first set of pictures.

The next two sets of pictures show his other two categories, handcrafted from natural and recycled wood, and classic repaints. There are several sizes and shapes of frog lures, including some folk art examples of the old James Heddon frog. There is a snake bait and some surface and near-surface stick baits, along with classic repaints of a Bass-Oreno, and a Creek Chub Pikie.

All lures made by Bill Howington have his trademark on the bellies, a signed letter "H" within a circle.

Some of Ol' Bill's Original Lures average in the $10 to $15 range, but others trade much higher.

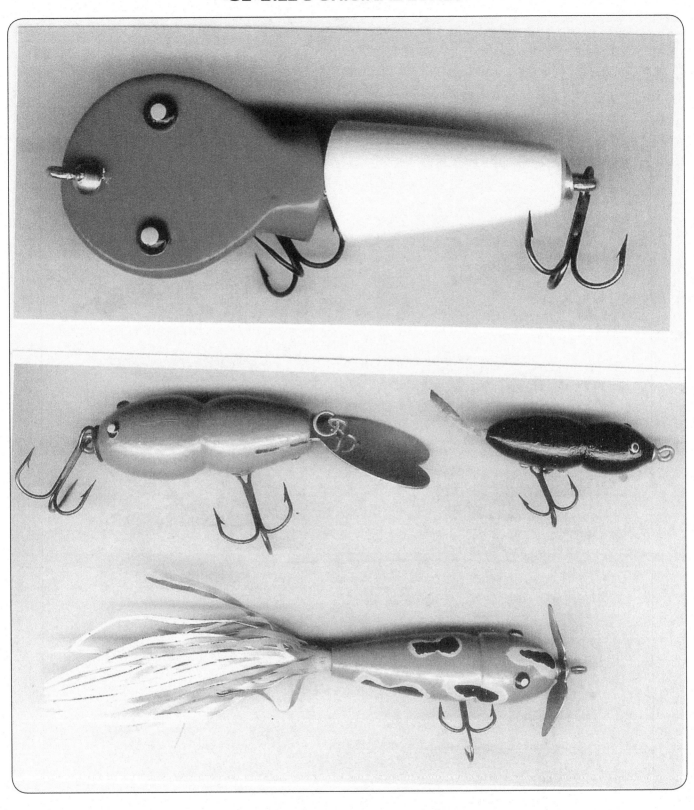

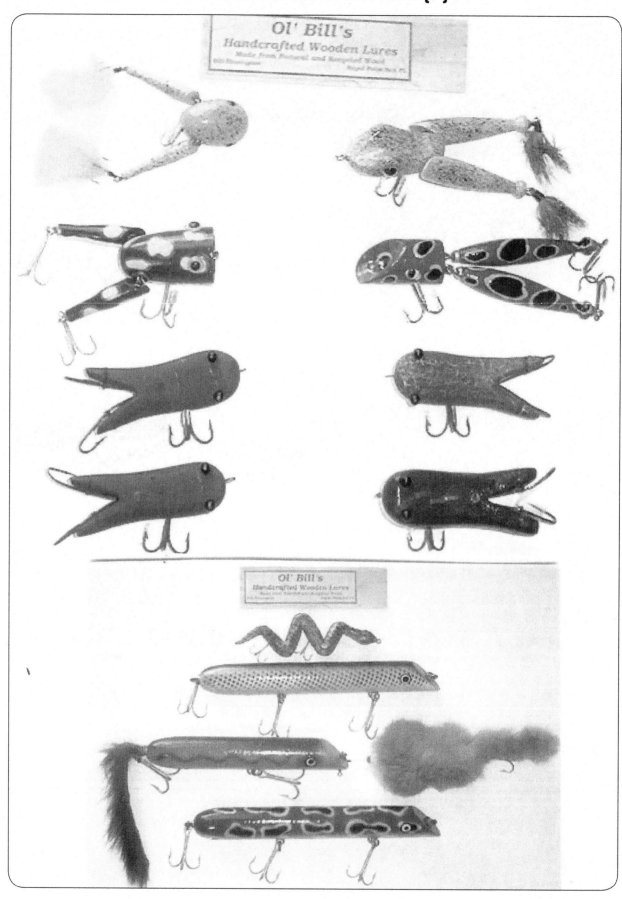

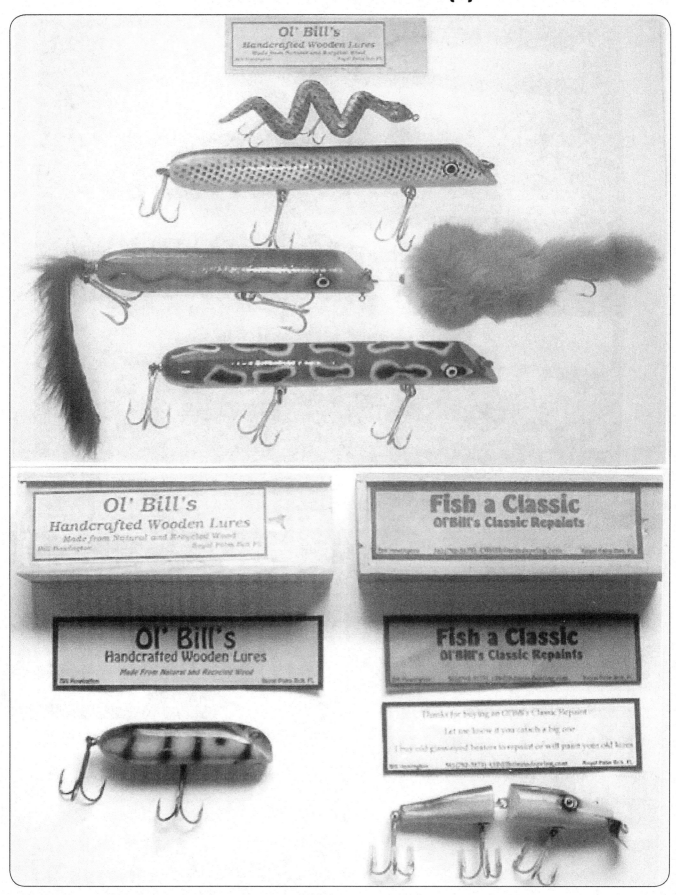

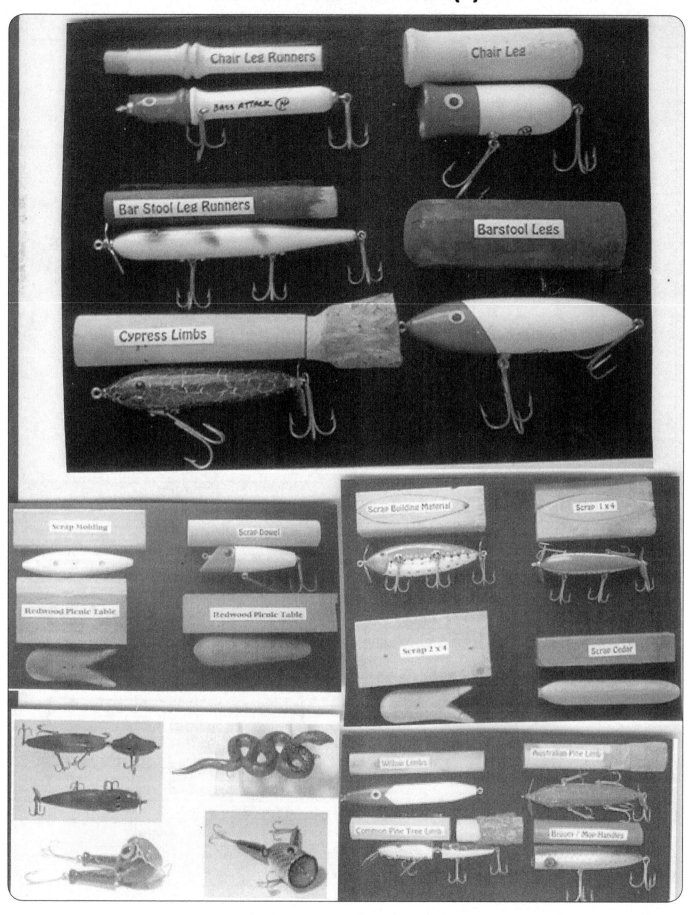

OL' RALPHIES LURES
TRAFFORD, ALABAMA

Ol' Ralphies Lures is a trade name logo for contemporary folk art lures made by Greg and Debbie Hays of 2368 McClellan Road in Trafford, Alabama. I wanted to put Ralph Greg Hay's lures in these books for two reasons. First, the state of Alabama needs more representation in these books, as there just were not that many lure makers from that state in its history. Secondly, not only are Ol' Ralphies' bass wood carved lures beautiful folk art representations, they also catch fish.

Each hand-crafted and -painted lure is signed and placed in a slide-cover wooden box with the name "Ol' Raphies Lures" carved in the cover, along with a jumping bass.

Greg Hays (He prefers to be addressed by his middle name instead of his first name, Ralph.) has also written and published a book, entitled Basic Fishing Lure Carving, to help new wood lure carvers get started.

One of the Hays couples' more interesting and original designs is the 1-1/2" pan-fish-shaped **BLADE RUNNER LURE**. This round-shaped lure has a special tail notched area with an eye screw holding a swivel equipped Colorado spinner blade that spins like a propeller on retrieve. The lure has red-bleeder hooks, typical of all of the Hays' lures, to simulate bleeding to trigger fish strikes. Another original design is the 3-3/4" jointed **PRO-FLEX PRO RUNNER LURE**. This lure (pictured in orange with black spots) has a notched area in the rear of the front section and a jointed tail section that is considerably smaller than the front section. Another pair of similar jointed lures is the **PRO FLEX MINO** and the **PRO FLEX STRIPER LURE**. The latter has a raised dorsal fin and is painted in a white with black tiger stripe pattern with red painted eyes. I believe the largest lure made by Greg Hays is the 5-1/4" **RAGIN MADMINNOW** that is a jointed top-water or near-surface swimmer.

Pictured is the Ol' Ralphie wood lure box, two colors of the Blade Runner lure, the Pro-Flex Pro Runner, the Pro Flex Striper Lure, the Raging Madminnow, and the Pro Flex Minnow, in that order.

In more recent times, Greg has developed some new lures. One he calls the **GOOBER BAIT** that is made out of peanut hulls. In past years, at least three lure makers made lures out of walnut shells, but, to my knowledge, this is the first lure maker to use peanut shells. The last set of pictures shows several examples painted in frog, worm, bee, and other fish foods.

Also pictured are his wooden slide box styles, a **HULA POPPER TYPE**, and his **SPITTIN SPIDER**.

The lures made by Greg Hays trade up to $20 alone, higher in wooden boxes.

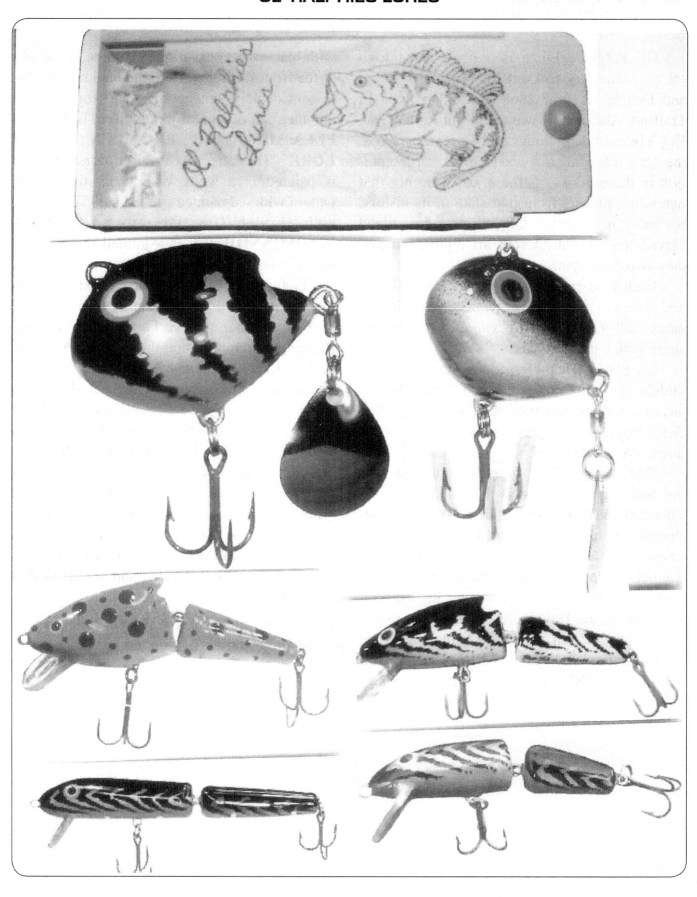

OLD DOMINION LURE COMPANY
KENTUCKY & CREWE, VIRGINIA

The Old Dominion Lure Company is really not an old company. They made lures from the mid to late 1970's. Undoubtedly, their best known lure was the 4-7/8" **SNEAKY BIRD # 2**. The lure had three screw-eye-held treble hooks and hollow plastic inserted eyes with white irises and rolling black metal ball pupils. The lure pictured was in all black with white belly with its one-piece, plastic-covered cardboard box and also in all black with red head blush trim.

This wooden lure had a distinctive 7/8"-long protruding nipple nose. The purpose of the long snout was so the fisherman could grab it to help land and unhook his catch without the use of a landing net. This lure's inventor, William M. Finch also designed the finger hole in the bait "FINCHEROO" for that same purpose.

The lure was originally made the same way in Phoenix, Arizona, by the Robfin Company. The lure was invented by William M. Finch, who was awarded patent No. 3,653,142 on April 4, 1972, for the lure that he called the "FINCH".

Although the Old Dominion lures were marketed out of Kentucky, they were made at 212 Virginia Ave in Crewe, Virginia, and marketed out of Lynchburg, Virginia, as well as in Kentucky by "Doc" Shelton.

Doc Shelton was, in fact, David R. Shelton, and, with the exception of the Sneaky Bird, he designed all other Old Dominion lures. In addition to the Sneaky Birds #1 and #2, Shelton also made lures named **BIG MAMA, LITTLE MAMA**, and **MR. WHISKERS # 1** and **#2**. The Mamas were surface plunker types, and the Mr. Whiskers was made with a round, collar type head and a bushy bucktail. There were several lure body colors and hair colors of natural, gray, black, or white. The two sizes of the Big and Little Mamas were very close in size as to the wooden bodies, but the major difference was the length of the bucktails. Doc Shelton was awarded Design Patent No. D252,583 for his Big and Little Mama lures on August 7, 1979.

By the way, the **SNEAKY BIRD #1** was a whistle lure (made a whistling sound on retrieve). The lure had a carved tail of natural birch wood and was left in varnished natural two-tone birch colors with burned-into-the-wood face details. All of the Old Dominion lures had the hollow plastic eyes with white irises and roll-about metal black ball pupils, except for the Sneaky Bird #1, which had large black glass inserted eyes.

The Old Dominion one-piece, plastic-covered, light-green cardboard lure box had dark green print and trim that said on the side of the box, "OLD DOMININON LURES," in white print on a dark green banner. Below that was a picture of a three-treble-hook lure and the statement, "Old Fashion Wooden Plugs with a New Design."

A 3" (5"overall with the double bucktail) all-black Big Mama and a 2-7/8" (4" overall with double bucktail) with dark green back and white belly Little Mama are pictured with their boxes. In the first set of photos are pictures of a rare color blue splatter Sneaky Bird #2, a common black splatter color, and two pictures of the rarer Sneaky Bird # 1.

In the second group picture, along with David "Doc" Shelton's August 7, 1979 patent, are pictures of the No. 1 3" and No. 2 2-1/2" Mr. Whiskers and the Big Mama and Little Mama lures.

In the third set are pictures of three different colors of Sneaky Bird # 2 and the rarer Sneaky Bird #1.

Boxed Old Dominion lures traded higher several years ago, probably because collectors thought they were older than what they were, but now trading is moderate, at $10 to $20, when in their original boxes.

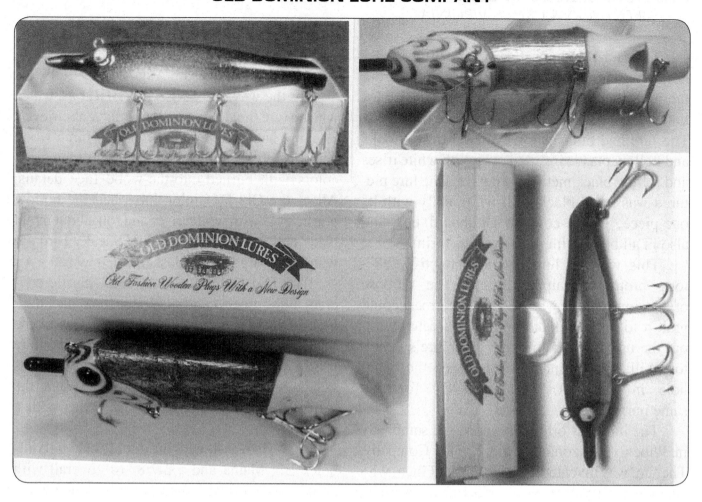

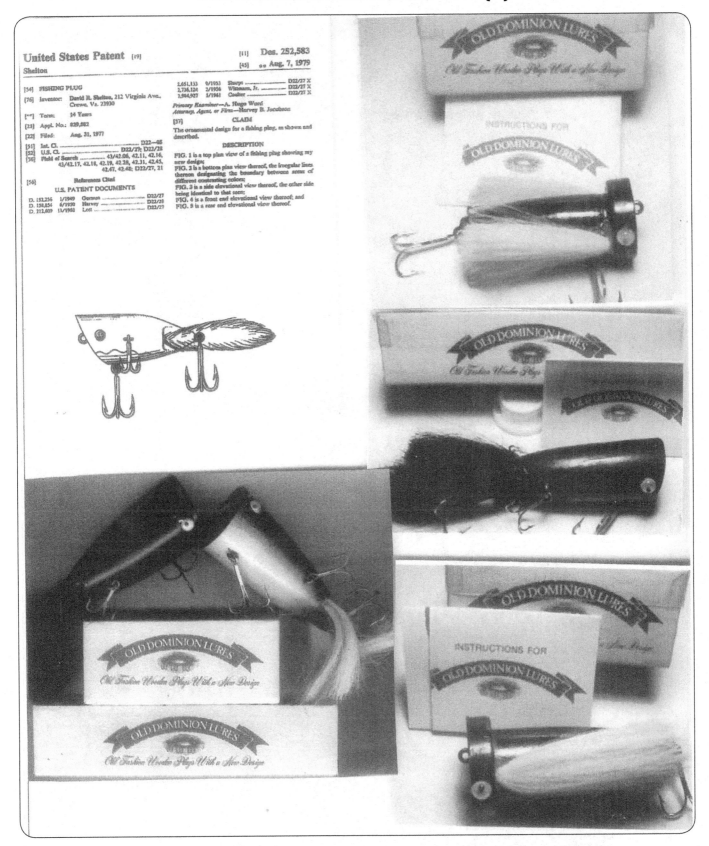

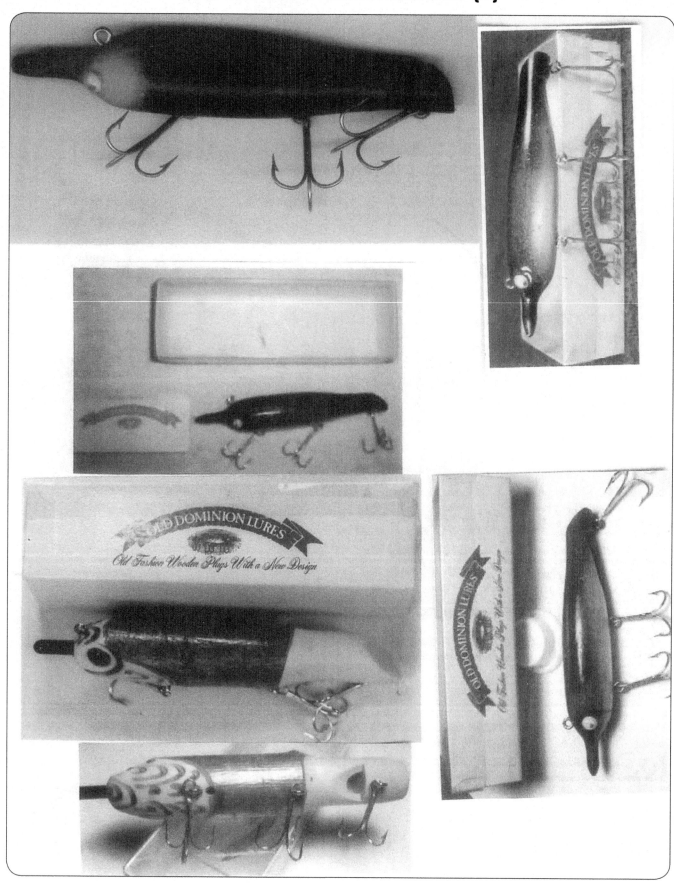

OLD HUTCH, INC.
NILES, MICHIGAN

The collector should not be confused with the "Arrowhead Minnow" made by H & M Mfg. in Eau Claire and this **ARROWHEAD MINNOW** made in Niles, Michigan. The lures were exactly the same, sold in exactly the same boxes, except for the different company names. Old Hutch, Inc., made their pointed Arrowhead Minnow in a brass 2-3/4" length spoon in chrome plate or copper finish. Although scarce, they also painted the spoons red with white center stripes or red with yellow center stripes. The one-piece brown color cardboard box had white print and a clear plastic cover that said, "WEEDLESS WITHOUT GUARD". The lure was weedless because of the body design. At the tail, the sides were curled down, forming a center tail hump, and the rivet-held single hook was bent in the opposite direction of these side curls. This design made the lure ride nose down on retrieve, and the entire lure itself became a weedguard, blocking weeds from catching the hook. I guess the two men who developed this lure in early 1957 wanted both of their home towns represented in the sale of the Arrowhead Minnow. John H. Hutchins of Niles, Michigan, and Paul M. Michalke of Eau Claire, Michigan, were awarded Patent No. 2,908,104 for this lure on October 13, 1959.

Boxed Arrowhead Minnows are scare and trade in the $20 to $25 range.

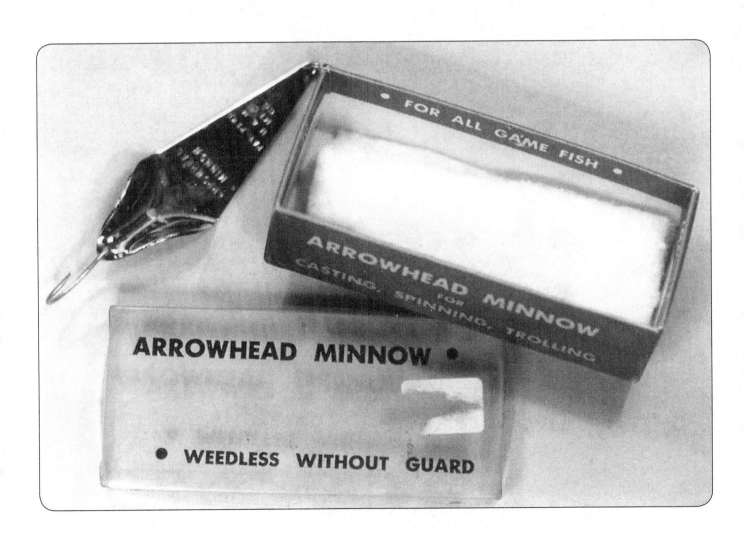

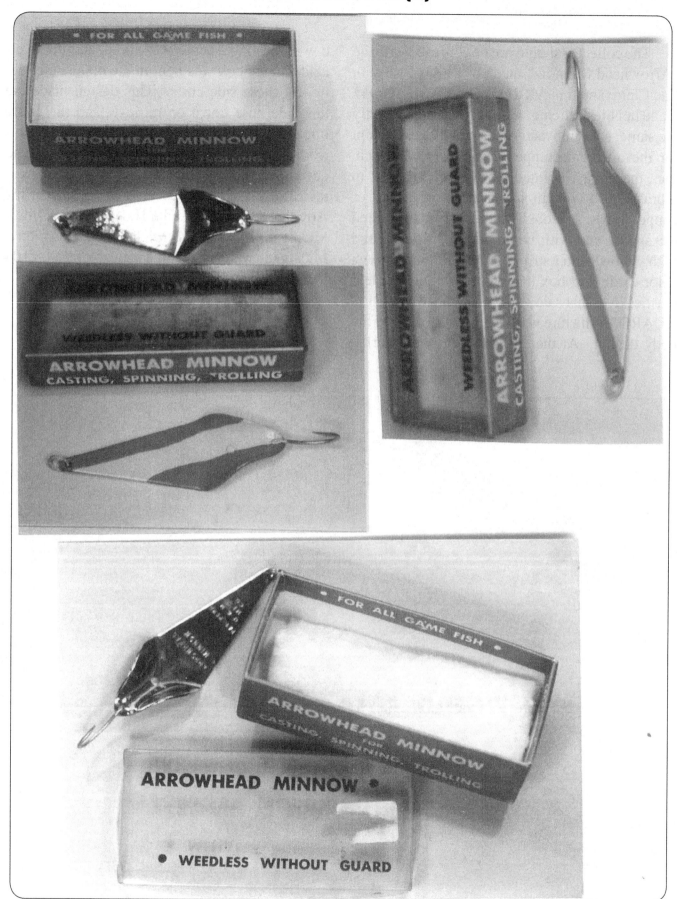

Oct. 13, 1959   J. H. HUTCHINS ET AL   2,908,104

FISHING LURE

Filed April 2, 1957

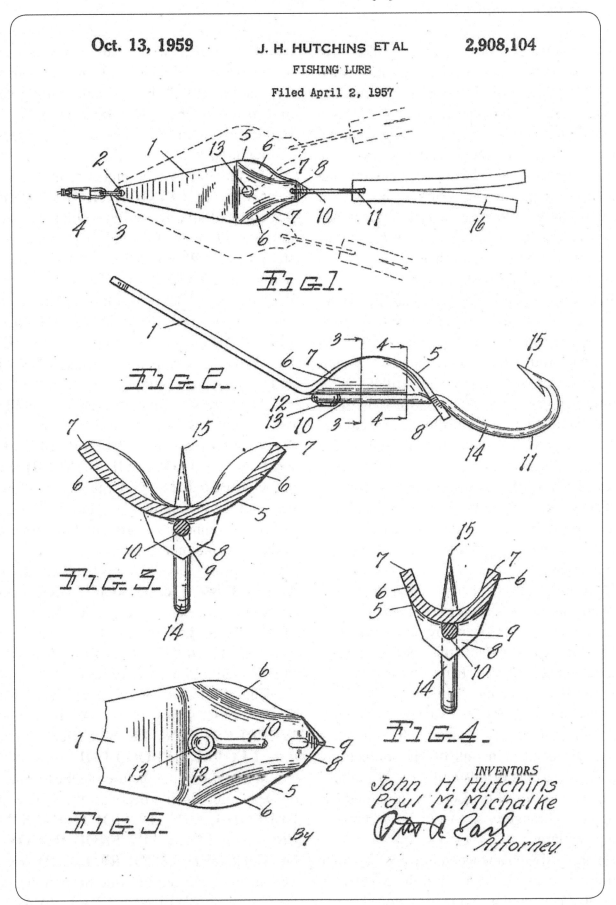

Fig.1.

Fig.2.

Fig.3.

Fig.4.

Fig.5.

INVENTORS
John H. Hutchins
Paul M. Michalke

By

Attorney

OLD OREGON LURES
GRESHAM, OREGON

Dean Crouser has been carving wooden lures for over 30 years, and, some time ago, he formed his Old Oregon Classic Fishing Lures Company at P. O. Box 2242 in Gresham, Oregon. Dean's early carvings or whittlings included animal figurines, chess set pieces, and even a Santa Claus figurine, of which he has been carving one for each of the past twenty years for his wife at Christmas time. However, Dean Crouser has always been an avid fishing and hunting enthusiast, so it was only natural that he also carved fishing lures and ice fishing decoys.

In addition to the recognition that I'm giving him in these books for his excellent folk art type carvings, he has many accolades from others as well. Dean Crouser has been featured on Oregon Public Broadcasting shows and written up in Sporting Classics Magazine, Gray's Sporting Journal, and Hunting & Fishing Collectibles. Dean even made a mark for himself while attending college at the University of Oregon on a track scholarship. He competed in shot put and discus meets in college and won four Pack Ten and three NCAA Championships and was eventually inducted into the College Hall of Fame in 2003.

Dean makes most of his lures using select bass wood and installs glass eyes in his lures and ice fishing decoys. He starts by drawing a template for his ideas and traces this pattern on basswood and makes a basic band saw cut. From there, he uses a Foredom or a carving knife to bring his lure or decoy into shape. He uses a detail knife for fin ray, eye, mouth, and other details. He hand paints all of his productions using acrylic paints or oils and then coats them with up to ten coats of lacquer. His lures and ice fishing decoys range in size from 2-1/4" long to 4" long and larger.

He has designed a wooden lure box in which he burns his company name into the cover, and he has also designed a two-piece colorful cardboard lure box as well. This two-piece box has a neat cover that depicts a fisherman wearing a red plaid shirt with his Labrador sitting next to him in his green wooden boat while he fishes. In the background there are evergreen trees and rolling hills.

In the first set of pictures, at the top, is Dean's beautiful **BROOK TROUT LURE** that has cup and screw-eye side hooks and a bucktail-dressed treble at the tail. Below that are his sleek **COPPER SALMON LURE** and a very real-looking **TARPON LURE**.

The second set of pictures features an absolutely gorgeous **STEELHEAD TROUT LURE**, a **FOLK ART CATFISH LURE**, and a **MUSKY LURE** that is equipped with a single belly hook and a bucktail-dressed treble hook at the tail.

The third set of pictures includes, at the top, one of Dean's wooden boxes for his productions, which, in this case, is the **SPIN BELLY LURE**. Next are his **BUCKTAIL SUNFISH LURE** and **COPPER MINNOW** that is a combination lure and ice fishing decoy with a hanging belly weight, a spinner nose prop, and line tie options at the nose and on the back.

The fourth set of pictures features a **LARGE MOUTH BASS & PERCH LURE** with the bass about to engulf the perch. Next are two of Dean's **SALMON PLUG LURES** and a **BROWN TROUT LURE** with a top view showing the unique side hook system.

The fifth set of pictures has two of Dean Crouser's frog lures. At the top is the **WEEDLESS POND FROG LURE**, and below it the **LEOPARD FROG LURE**.

In the sixth set of pictures, at the top, are four of Dean's ice fishing decoys: the **FOLK ART BLUEGILL**, a **SMALL MOUTH BASS WITH FROG**, his **FOLK ART FROG DECOY**, and his **McCLOUD RIVER REDBAND DECOY** that all have the pig tail line tie options. Next are Crouser's **WALLEYE LURE, PEACOCK**

BASS LURE, **WEEDHOPPER LURE**, and **BUG LURE**.

The seventh set of pictures features one of Dean's unique two-piece cardboard lure boxes for another of his **LEOPARD FROG LURES** that is only 2-1/4" long and has a through body double hook system. Next is a **RAINBOW TROUT LURE**, a **BLUEGILL LURE** that is equipped with a bucktail-dressed tail treble hook, and a **PIKE LURE**.

The eighth set of pictures shows a 5-3/4" Rainbow Trout, a 5-1/2" Brown Trout, and a 6-3/4" Catfish. The three-section snake has five-line tie options.

The ninth set of pictures includes a close up of Dean's burned-wood, copper-hinged cover on his dark stained 5" by 2-1/2" by 2-1/4" lure box. The wooden **LARGE MOUTH BASS MOUSE** lure is 2-1/2" long, but, with the combination deer hair and leather tail dressed treble hook,

the lure is a full 6" long. The lure has Colorado spinner blades as hind feet, bent-up smaller spinner blades for the ears, black bead mouse eyes, and deer hair mouse feeler-hairs on the nose.

I consider the lure in the tenth picture to be a masterpiece by Dean: the 7"-long basswood **TARPON WITH BAITFISH** with its special western cedar wood box. The Tarpon has textured scales, glass eyes, and a hand-tied bucktail tail treble hook. The dorsal and pectoral fins are copper and hand painted.

This is one example of Dean Crouser's beautiful work of art Old Oregon lures that trades above the $100 level. Dean Crouser's Old Oregon lures and decoys trade from $30 up to several times that amount; in fact, I have seen several top the $100 level.

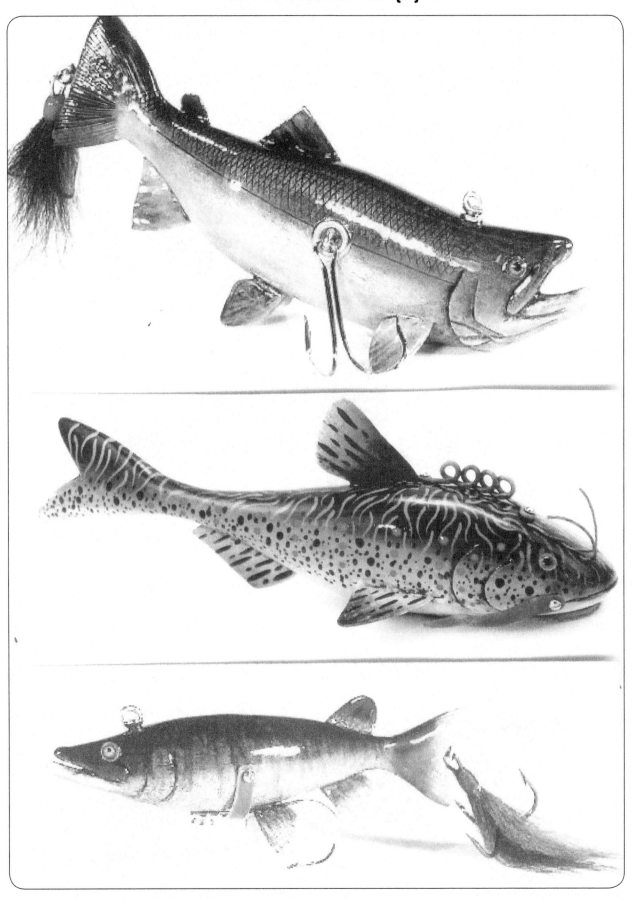

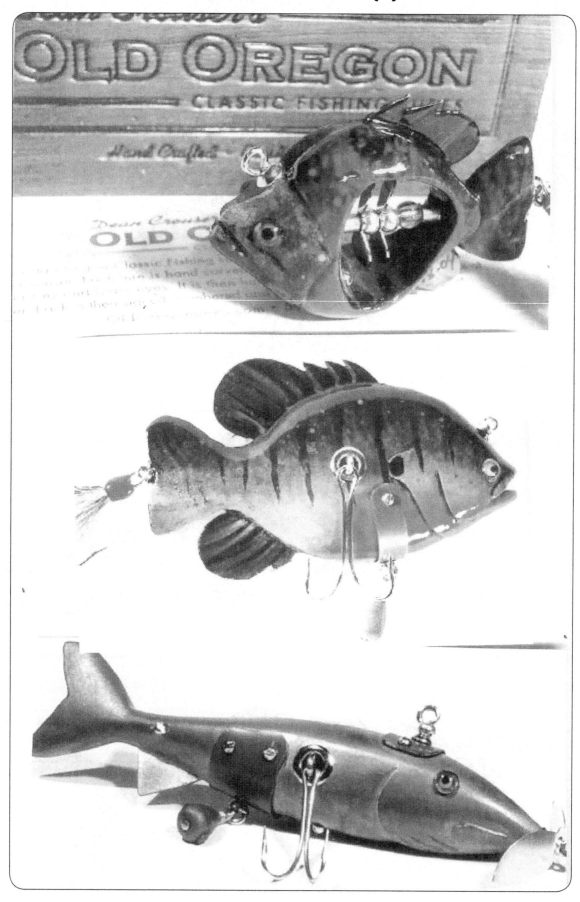

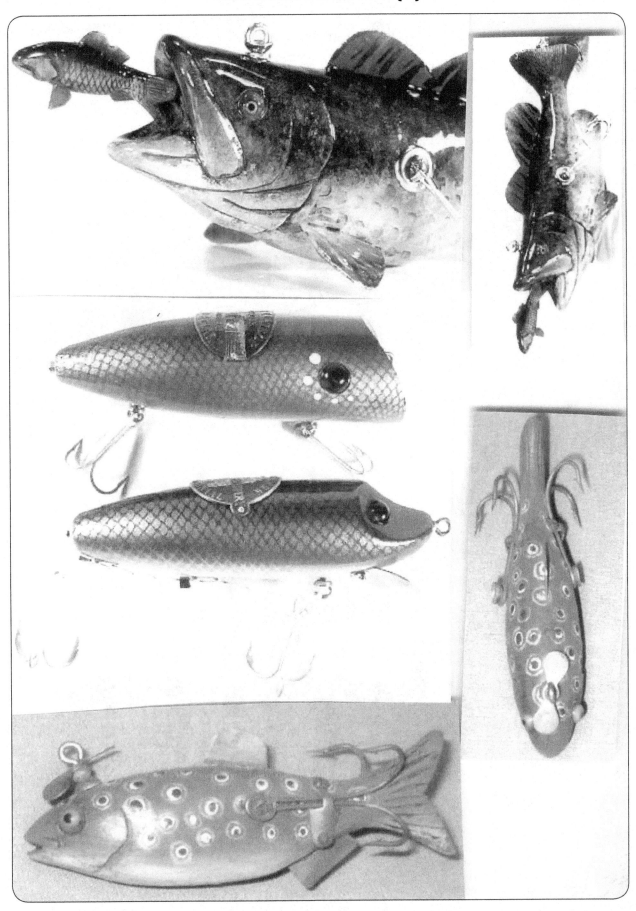

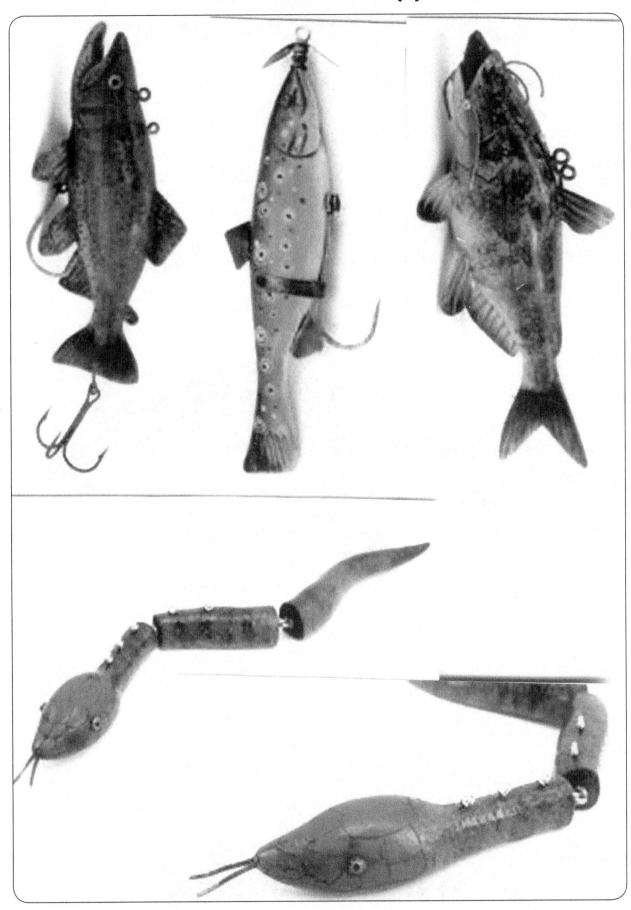

Dean Crouser's
OLD OREGON
CLASSIC FISHING LURES

Every Old Oregon Classic Fishing Lure is hand made by native Orego
Dean Crouser. Each lure is hand carved from select basswood and fitted
copper fins and glass eyes. It is then hand painted, given up to six coa
lacquer. Each is then signed, numbered and presented in a cedar wood box

OldOregonLures.com • 503.669.8747

OLD RELIABLE BAIT COMPANY
BOSTON, MASSACHUSETTS

I'm afraid there is not much known about this early-1900's company located in Boston, Massachusetts. The stamped **OLD RELIABLE** 1-5/8" fluted blade was also stamped, "BOSTON...JANUARY 1902 NO.4." With the older style box swivel and white and red feather tail hook, the lure measured 4-1/2" long overall.

The Old Reliable spinners trade in the $10 to $15 range.

OLD ROW BOAT TROLLING MINNOW FLOATS

Back in the days when few fishermen had the newly developed outboard motors and most were still rowing wooden boats to fish out of, various people and manufacturers developed pointed-nose, torpedo-shaped trolling minnow buckets. These metal minnow buckets were designed this way so as to have live minnows at hand beside their boats while not creating a lot of drag weight.

SHINNERS HARTFORD MINNOW FLOAT
HARTFORD, WISCONSIN

There isn't any question in my mind that the earliest of the trolling minnow floats was made by William Shinners of Hartford, Wisconsin. As I said before, in the early 1900's, a fisherman had to row his boat about, as outboard motors were not in the picture yet or were just being developed, and, even when they did show up, the average fisherman could not afford one, so he still rowed his boat. The SHINNERS HARTFORD MINNOW FLOAT was designed with a torpedo shape and had a pointed cone nose and tail so it would glide through the water with little drag resistance in either direction. It was made of galvanized iron to help prevent rust. The bucket had a 12"-long middle section that was 7" in diameter. Each of the cone end sections was 8-1/2" long, bringing the total length of the float to 28" long overall, and it weighed 3-1/2 pounds. The important thing about this minnow float was that the inside walls were smooth so as not to injure the minnows like many other wire mesh minnow buckets of that day. The float was weighted on the bottom so the minnow bucket would always float with the access door upright. The flotation was the end cones, which were hollow air chambers. The sliding access door on the top of the float was secured in a locked position by a push-down leaf-spring. The middle section of the float had holes in half of the sides to allow for an exchange of fresh water as the bucket was pulled through the water. The carrying handle was on the same end of the float as the water exchange holes; thus, the fisherman could carry it and still keep minnows alive for a while in the bottom half of the bucket. There was a neat brass plate on the top of one of the cones that gave the patent date and maker's name and Hartford, Wisconsin address. Shinners received a patent for his float on Dec. 19, 1905. Most of the Hartford Floats were in natural galvanized metal color, but some are found painted red and white.

The SHINNERS HARTFORD MINNOW FLOAT is quite rare, but there is a very rare super-sized HARTFORD STORAGE FLOAT that is 7'6" long and 1-1/2' in diameter. This float is of the same torpedo shape and was primarily designed for resort owners and boat rental bait shops situated on lake shores. They stored their live bait in the floats for customers, but they were also used by musky fishermen for very large 12" and larger size live suckers. A 1907 ad read, "THE HARTFORD MINNOW FLOAT...The Great Minnow Life Saver. The Most Noiseless, Lightest Running Float Ever Hitched to a Boat. Most Perfect and Practical Bait Receptacle Ever invented."

The smaller Hartford Minnow Float trades in the $850 to $1,200 range, and the giant one trades over $1,500.

CARLSON MANUFACTURING COMPANY
READING, PENNSYLVANIA

In the pre-World War II era, the Carlson Manufacturing Company, located in Reading, Pennsylvania, made a metal minnow float called the **CARLSON BAIT & FISH CONTAINER**.

The shape of this float reminds one of old Dreadnaught Battle Ships of that time. It had a pointed ship type of nose to cause less water drag or resistance as the fisherman rowed his wooden boat about. The metal float had a raised round entry port in the center and two air-pocket round raised areas either side of that door. The float was 24" long stern to stern and 6" high and had a beam of 8-1/2" wide. The galvanized metal minnow float had fish-shaped ID paste-on labels in three locations on the side of the bucket.

Picture is courtesy of the Alan Bakke collection.

The Carlson Bait Float is rare, and trading is infrequent with no established values at this time, but trading would, for sure, be well over $200 to start a trade discussion.

J. FOX MINNOW FLOAT COMPANY
NEW YORK, NEW YORK

Sometime in the post-World War II years, J. Fox of New York produced the smallest of the trolling minnow floats. The **J. FOX MINNOW FLOAT** was only 15" long and 4-1/2" in diameter. The bucket appeared to be larger, as it had a half-moon-shaped keel in the belly to keep the bucket in line while being rowed about. The Quonset-hut-shaped sliding cover had runner-tracks on both sides of the bucket to keep the lid in place. There were two posts on the top with round ball tops for a catch to slide over to keep the sliding cover closed. There is no trouble in identifying this float, as there is a brass fox head symbol on the nose with the print, "J. FOX N. Y."

The J. Fox Minnow Float trades in the $150 to $175 range.

MINNOW FLOAT
UNKNOWN MAKER AND LOCATION

The next float has similarities of both the Hartford and Carlson Minnow Floats made in approximately the same sizes.

It trades in the $200 range.

Pictures of all minnow floats are shown in order of their stories.

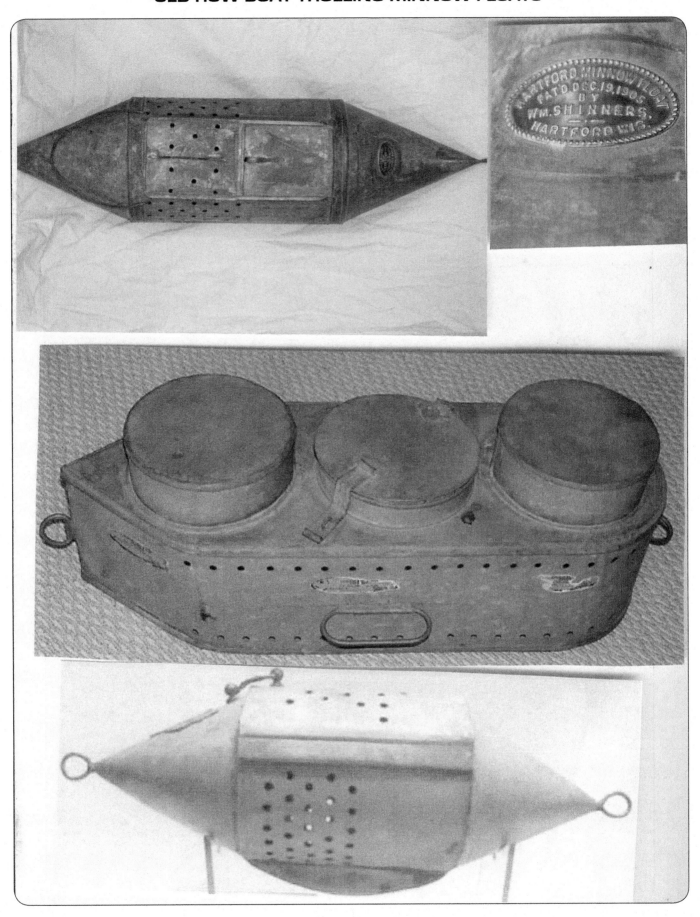

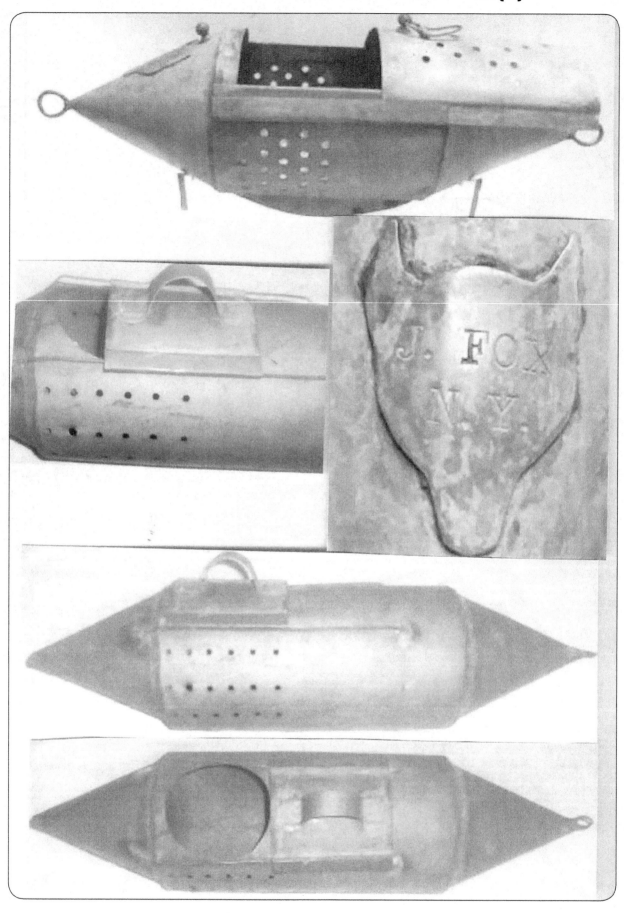

OLD SETTLER LURE COMPANY
GAYLORD, MICHIGAN

The Old Settler Lure Company had a neat name but was really not old, as they introduced their plastic **OLD SETTLER LURE** in the late 1960's. The lure was shaped like a bowling pin, except there was a large, deep-cut nose slant in the forehead of the lure. There were two screw-eye held treble hooks, and the line tie was set back a bit in the nose slant from the tip of the lure. This caused the lure to dig deep and wobble at a 65-degree angle, nose down. The lure was sold in a clear-plastic-top hinged box with a pink address label with ID card insert. The address label read, "SURFACE BAIT," and, "OLD SETTLER BASS LURE...Old Settler Lure Co., P. O. Box 429, Gaylord, Mi." Some of the colors for this 3" plastic lure included the following: 001, black with red throat, 002 white with red throat, and 003 blue with red throat. Pictured with a box are surface bait models 001 and 003.

The boxed Old Settler trades in the $10 range or less.

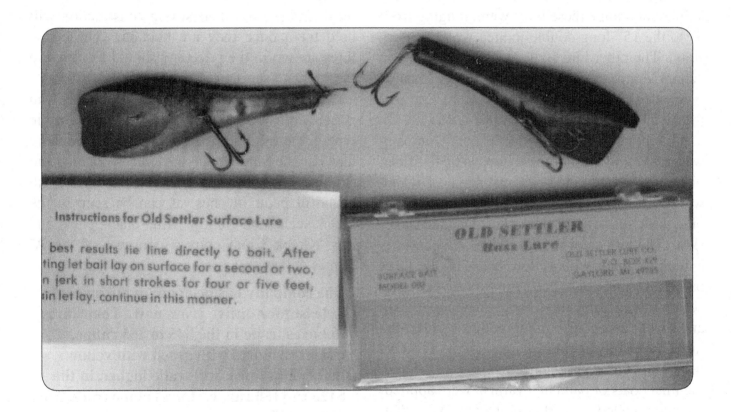

OLD WOODEN BAIT COMPANY
COBOURG, ONTARIO, CANADA

Rick Shepherd was carving wooden duck decoys and giant Creek Chub "Pikie Minnows" for his own use for some time throughout the 1970's. By 1979, he realized how scarce the old wooden baits had become to everyone, so he started producing them commercially. He formed the Old Wooden Bait Company at 499B Walton Street in Cobourg, Ontario, Canada. His company primarily concentrated on four lure types, one of which was the Creek Chub "Giant Pikies", which he named **LEVIATHANS**. Leviathan is the Biblical name for a huge sea animal, and huge these lures were, ranging from 8" to the 15"-long double-jointed wooden monsters. The other lure styles were of the Heddon "Giant Vamp" type, Creek Chub "Husky Musky" type, and the Pfleuger "Mustang" type. Some of the metal-lipped lures are stamped OWL.

Eventually, the Old Wooden Lure Company was producing most of these lures in up to fifteen different painted color patterns, some of which were red and white, perch, pike, spotted frog, blue flash, black tuxedo, lake herring, and snakeskin. The rare color for the Old Wooden lures is evidently green with yellow belly, as the lures painted in this color trade for triple what other colors trade. Early lures had a tendency to chip and crack, especially on the bellies. Later, the lures were dipped in a sealer and let dry for days before applying an enamel white base. Later, the final coats of paint and varnish were applied, which corrected the earlier problems. After that, other lure colors were perch firebelly, strawberry, yellow flash, green firebelly, green yellowbelly, silver flash, and walleye. The lures were sold in a natural wood color one-piece cardboard box with a plastic cover with a silhouette of a jumping musky on the cover corner, as well as on the box-end label, identifying the enclosed lure and color code.

Famous muskie fishing guide and lure maker, Peter Haupt of Hayward, Wisconsin, had this to say about these lures: "The Leviathans are a return to the quality found in lures built prior to World War II. Their action is correct to attract muskellunge, and their strong construction will hold them once they are hooked. These fine lures are worth the price and should be found in the serious fisherman's tackle box."

One of the pictures (courtesy of the Dan Basore collection) is of a No. 960 Husky Muskie type in the tuft color SNAKE SKIN. One thing that can be said about the Old Wooden Lure Company is that they made some lures with beautiful paint finishes, as can be seen in the green scale and yellow with black back and ribs "Creek Chub" types (courtesy of the Al Tumas collection).

The company has been out of business for at least four or five years now. Their lures in boxes trade in the $45 to $65 range, except the lures with green with yellow belly paint finish will trade higher, in the $125 to $150 range. Lures alone trade from $30 to $45.

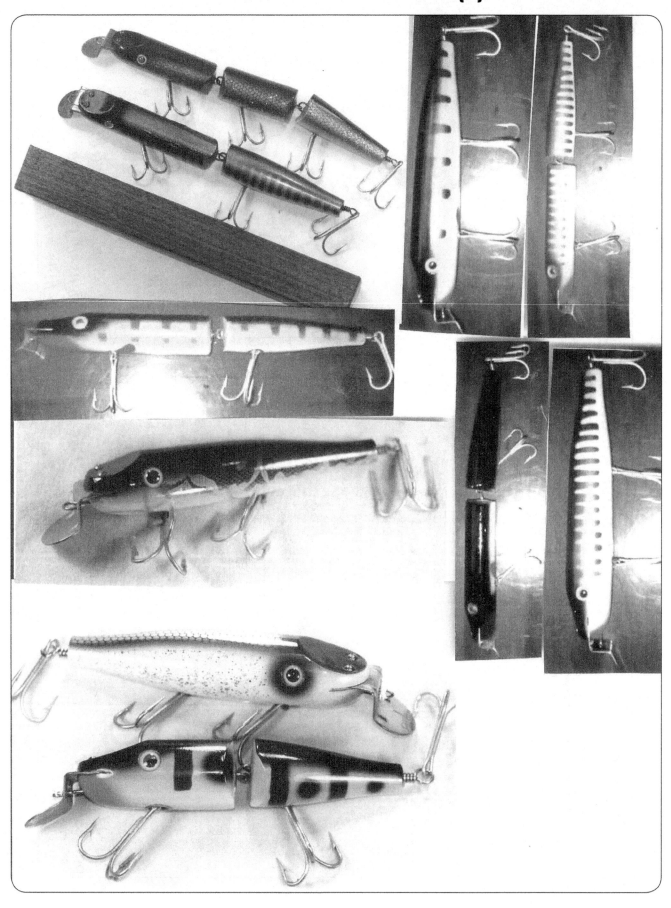

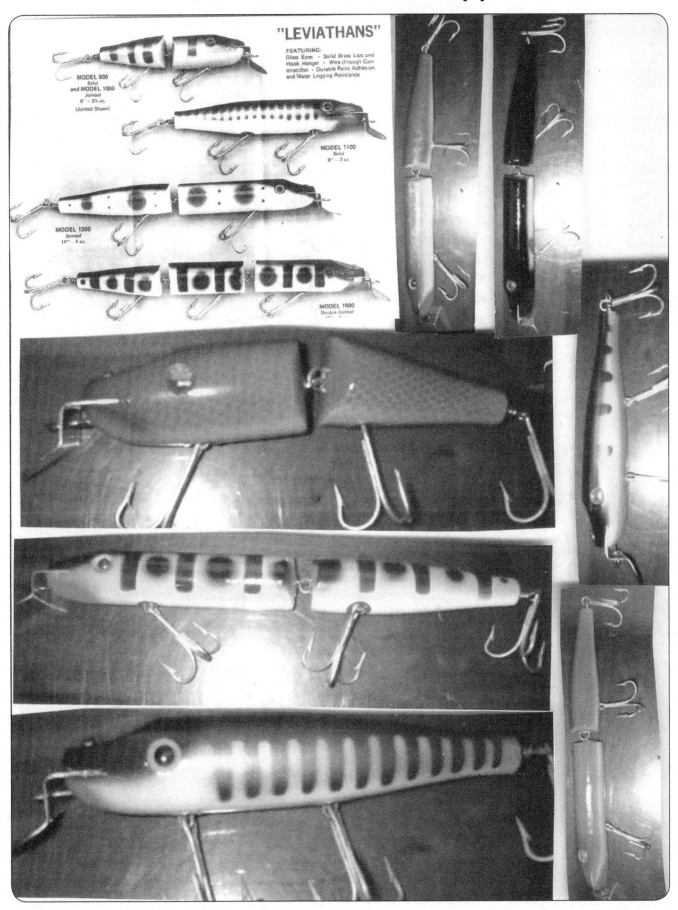

"LEVIATHANS"

FEATURING:
Glass Eyes • Solid Brass Lips and Hook Hanger • Wire through Construction • Durable Paint Adhesion and Water Logging Resistance

MODEL 900
Solid
and MODEL 1000
Jointed
8" – 2¼ oz.
(Jointed Shown)

MODEL 1100
Solid
8" – 3 oz.

MODEL 1200
Jointed
14" – 4 oz.

MODEL 1500
Double Jointed

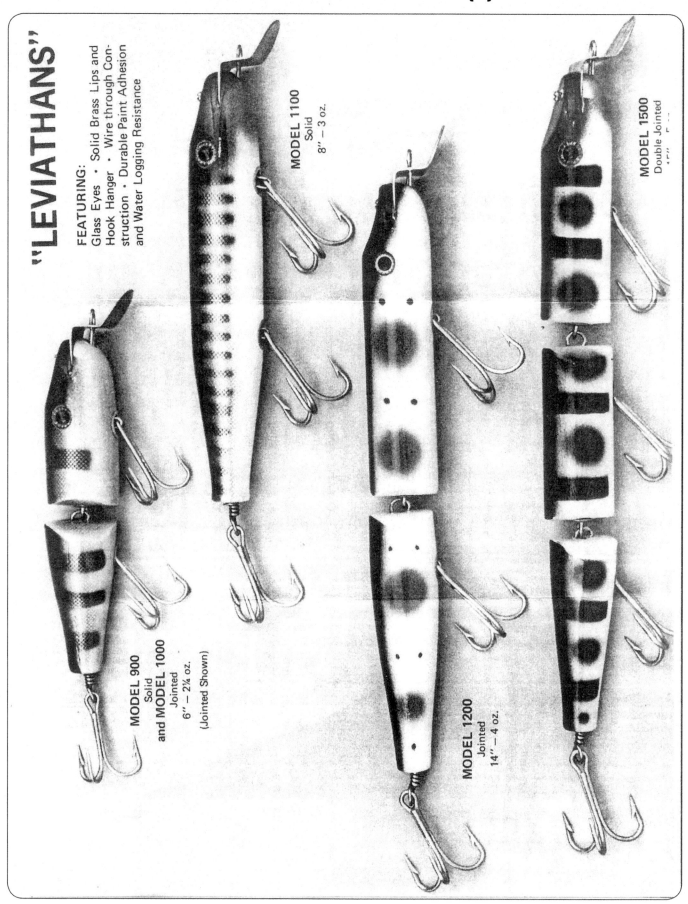

"LEVIATHANS"

FEATURING:
Glass Eyes • Solid Brass Lips and Hook Hanger • Wire through Construction • Durable Paint Adhesion and Water Logging Resistance

MODEL 1100
Solid
8" — 3 oz.

MODEL 900
Solid
and MODEL 1000
Jointed
6" — 2¼ oz.
(Jointed Shown)

MODEL 1200
Jointed
14" — 4 oz.

MODEL 1500
Double Jointed

OLDEST FISHING LURE IN THESE BOOKS: 800 A. D.

Without question, the oldest fishing lure that you will find in these books is this 3-1/4" carved **INUIT IVORY**. Museums have dated this piece to 800 A. D. The lure was made by Alaskan Inuit Indians. Historians think that it was made from ivory of a frozen Mammoth or Mastodon tusk dating back 7,000 to 8,000 years ago. This rare piece, courtesy of the Al Tumas collection, was photographed by me.

This rare Indian artifact does not have an established trade value.

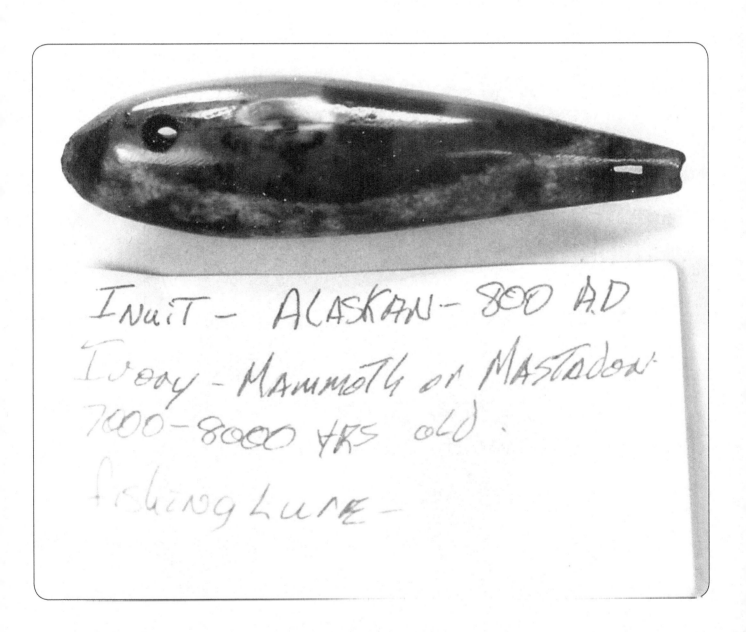

OLDFISHERMAN'S BASS LURES
DURANT, OKLAHOMA

The late 1950's, Fisherman's Bass Lures Company made a **BASS SPINNER BAIT** of a different nature, a near one-of-a-kind. The lure had a stainless steel wire yoke holding two raindrop-finish copper Colorado spinner blades on the one arm and a typical lead head on the hook arm. However, the difference was that this lead head had a red, orange, and black chenille-wrapped insect type body with black and red tied bristly hair. The spinner baits were sold on gray cards with red ID print.

The Oldfisherman's bass spinners trade in the $5 to $10 range today.

OLE OLSON LURES
100% WEEDLESS BAIT COMPANY
MILWAUKEE, WISCONSIN

Ole Olson started making lures in 1936 in Milwaukee, Wisconsin. His first known lure is also the rarest: the 3" **OLSON SPINNING MINNOW**. The lure was made in two metal parts with a 3"-long mushroom-shaped copper base. The head looked like on open umbrella and had a long body, slightly fatter at center, with a spread-out tail with each tip turned slightly in the opposite direction. To this copper base, Olson soldered an arrow-shaped, nickel, hollow body. The hollow body had a direct wire from the tail treble hook to the box swivel line tie up front. The lure was stamped on the belly, "O. Olson". The lure is pictured (courtesy of the Dale and Sally Dalluhan collection of St. Croix, Minnesota) in top and bottom views.

The 3"-long (6" overall) **ARROWHEAD** was made in two parts with a nickel base with curled, swept-back wings and the hollow copper body soldered in place.

A distinctive trademark on both of these Olson lures, other than that both were stamped "O. OLSON", was the hammer and chisel marks he made in the hollow bodies. This feature is easily seen in both lure pictures (courtesy of the Steve O'Hern collection).

Many collectors confuse O. Olson lures with the ice fishing decoys made by a different spelled Oscar Olsen (1884 - 1958) from Anoka, Minnesota. He made hollow copper ice fishing decoys, like the 10-1/2" one pictured. The decoy had glass inserted eyes and painted red mouth and gill trim. The fisherman could fill the decoy with water to arrive at the desired buoyancy.

Two years later, the Milwaukee Ole Olson developed his 2-1/2" and 3" 100% **OLE OLSON WEEDLESS SPOONS**. The nickel-finished spoon had a leaf type spring that was channeled to accept a single hook shank soldered to it. The spring and hook were then ring-riveted to the nose, with the ring forming the lie tie. Olsen formed a cut and pressed recessed area in the tail in which the hook point rested, making the lure 100% weedless. When a fish struck the lure, it compressed the hook into a catching position.

In 1938, Ole Olson formed his 100% Weedless Bait Company in Milwaukee, but it only survived one year. By the end of 1939, Ole Olson had sold the rights to this spoon to Karl "Ruddy" Larson of Minnesota. Earlier in that same year, on June 6, 1939, Larson had formed the Paul Bunyan Company as a corporation. Paul Bunyan continued to make this spoon, actually, name stamping it "OLE OLSON WEEDLESS SPOON", which Olson had not done in Milwaukee. However, Paul Bunyan made a slight change: They cut a slot at the end of the leaf spring, slid in the hook shank, and then riveted the hook eye to the spring and then again with a ring-rivet at the line tie.

In the second set of pictures, the original 100% Weedless Spoon appears in a drawing and two of them are on the right in the picture of five spoons at the bottom. On the lower left is the second Wisconsin version, and the top two are the Paul Bunyan versions. The Ole Olsen Spinning Minnow is the featured lure on the cover of this book.

The very rare Ole Olson Spinning Minnow and Arrowhead trade in the $75 to $100 range. The Oscar Olsen decoy trades in the $150 range and higher. The collector should easily be able to identify the original Milwaukee Olson Weedless Spoon from the Paul Bunyan one based on the descriptions above. The Original trades in the $25 to $35 range and the Paul Bunyan in the $10 to $15 range. Note in the picture of the five Olson Weedless Spoons that the two at the top are by Paul Bunyan and the three at the bottom are Olson originals. Make note that there were two different styles even with Ole Olson; the oldest two are on the right and the one on the left was made just before the sale to Paul Bunyan.

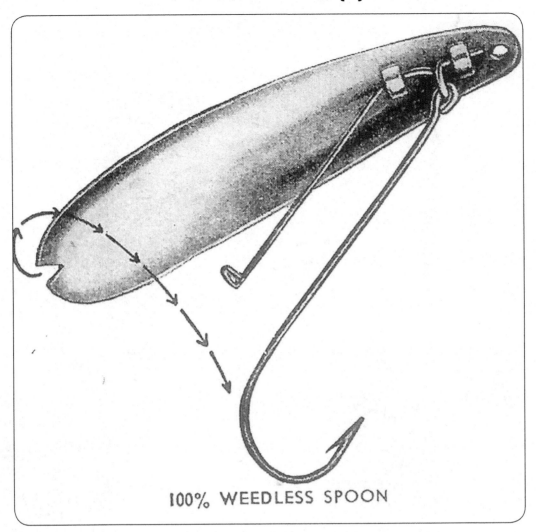

100% WEEDLESS SPOON

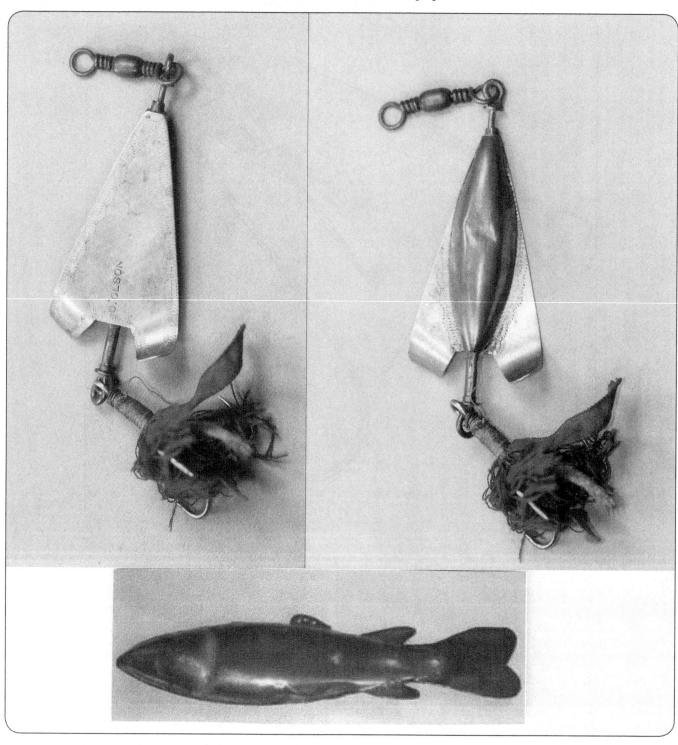

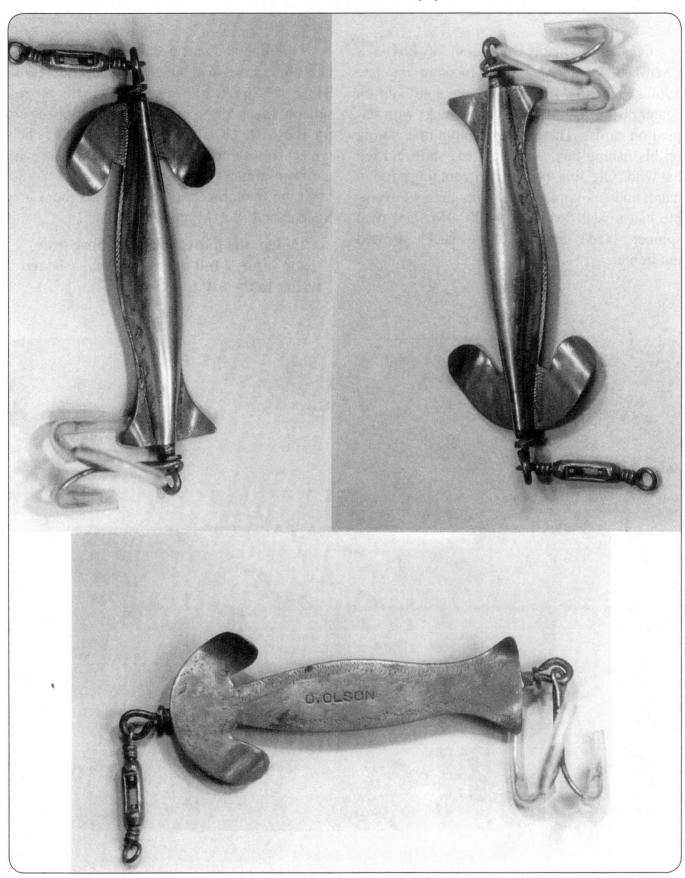

OLE' JIMS QUALITY LURES
CHEROKEE, OKLAHOMA

Ole' Jims Quality lures, out of Box 378 Cherokee, Oklahoma, made lures in the late 1960's and early 1970's that were sold both on dealer display cards and in plastic sacks with stapled-on cards. The card depicted a man sitting on his fishing box, wearing a red shirt and red hat with "Ole'Jim" printed on it, holding a rod in hand, and smoking a pipe. The pictured example had a pearl lead body with a forward oval spinner blade and a black hackle-dressed tail treble.

Ole' Jim later changed the company name to Ole' Jim's Lure Co., Inc., with a new address of 313 E. 5th Street, still in Cherokee. His biggest seller at that address was the bubble-topped card for the **MR. LUCKY BASS KILLER**. This typical bass spinner had a double wire-yoke with a rubber minnow attractor.

Lure pictures are courtesy of the Larry Sundall and Rick Minter collections.

Although the individual lures have little trade value, a full one-dozen dealer board trades in the $10 to $15 range.

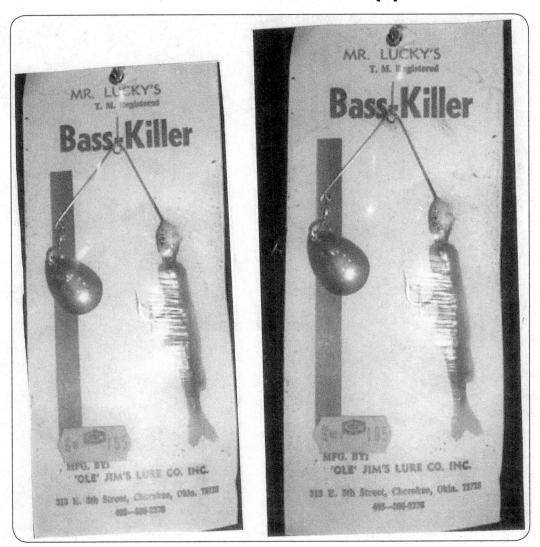

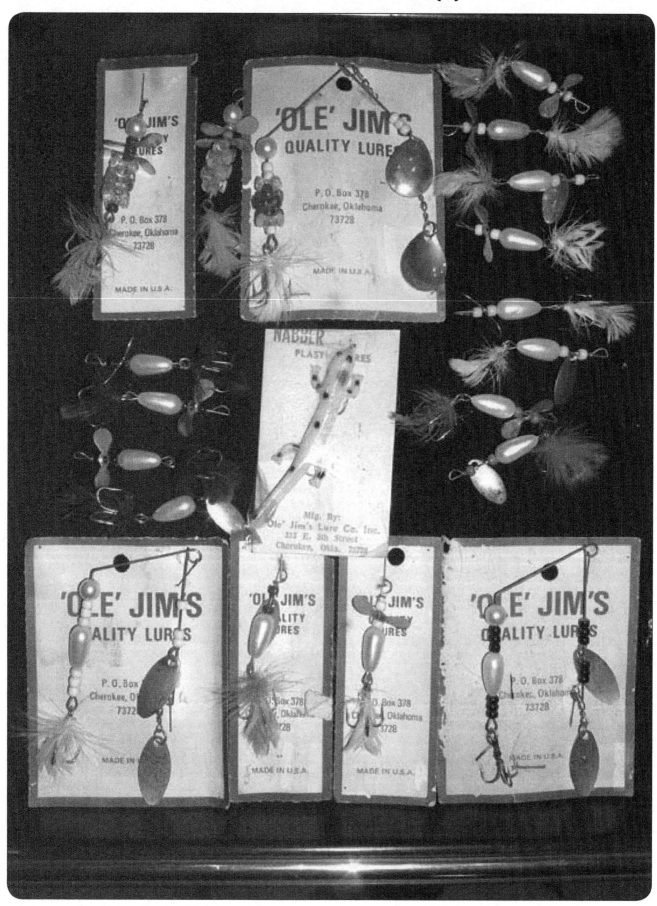

OLETIME WOODSMAN'S LINE COMPANY
PAXTON, MASSACHUSETTS

In the pre-war 1930's and early 1940's, the husband and wife team of Osborn and Josephine Sherer owned a small company that primarily made wet and dry fly rod flies. The Oletime Woodsman's Line Company, of Paxton, Massachusetts, did make some trout and bass lures as well, called the **OSBORN SPINNERS** and **OSBORN SPOONS**. The spinner had a teardrop-shaped spinner blade followed by a chenille-wrapped single hook with hair- and feather-dressed combinations representing vari- ous insects. The spoon had the same metal blade as a belly platform onto which insect bodies of the same nature were mounted. Osborn Sherer received at least one patent for his lures, applied for in 1938 and granted on July 23, 1940, under Patent No. 2,209,096.

Carded flies and lures by the Oletime Woodman's Line trade in the $10 to $15 range.

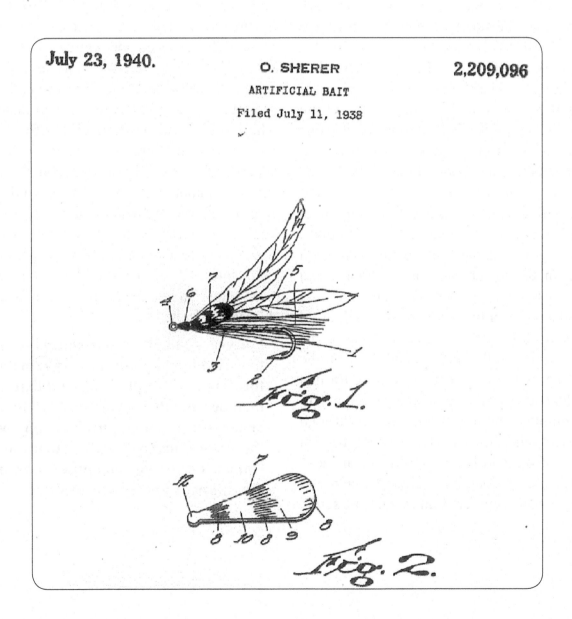

OLIVER & GRUBER
MEDICAL LAKE, WASHINGTON

The 1920-patented 4-1/4", double-jointed wooden **GLOWURM** was produced by Doctors Alfred S. Oliver and James S. Gruber and a cast of mental hospital patients. Oliver and Gruber were employed by a Medical Lake home and hospital for the mentally retarded in their mid-teens. Starting in 1916, the doctors enlisted the help of patients as part of their therapy in forming the wooden bodies and painting the lures. They also cut and made the lures' two-piece wooden lure boxes.

The unpainted wood-grain box had dark purple print on the side that read, "THIS LURE WORKS BEST WITH A SMALL SNAP SWIVEL OR LOOSE LOOP OF LINE THROUGH SCREW EYE." The top of the box read, "The GLOWURM Fish Lure, Patd. Nov. 1920...A Lure for Bass, Pickerel, Pike, Muscallonge (that is one of the many ways muskellunge was spelled in those days) and Lake Trout...Price $1.00." The lures wooden box was cut into two halves held together with only a tape hinge. These two cut wooden halves had a longitudinal rounded internal cut to accommodate the round body with slots cut in the lower half for the hooks, and the box ends were left open. The lure, cut on a lathe, had a series of indented grooves and raised collars on its three sections (three grooves on the tail section, five in the middle, and three on the head). The two joints for the lure were formed by interlocked eye screws, which gave it a life-like swimming motion when drawn through the water. The no-eyed, slanted face had an unmarked Colorado-blade-shaped metal nose piece that extended slightly below the chin and was held by both a top screw and the line tie screw

eye. The lures were made in just three colors: red and white stripes, yellow and green stripes, and a very rare luminous, which is the only lure that had eyes – painted eyes. Oliver and Gruber were awarded Patent No. 1,359,618 for their Glowurm on November 23, 1920, having applied on May 16, 1918.

The lures, made for eight years (1916 - 1924), were relatively rare fifteen years ago and more, reaching a peak trade value of $600 for a pair in 1995, one of each color at a Lang's auction in Chicago. However, starting in 1980, I believe, at lure shows and then much later on E-Bay, a large cash of the red and white models surfaced. On E-Bay, there were as many as 25 or more a week showing up, and, after several months, the trade values plummeted to well under $100. The large mother lode (over 1,000) of the red and white color lures was found in Sandpoint, Idaho, in the hands of the grandson of one of the original founders. It should be noted that this is true for the red and white color only; the boxed yellow and green color is still rare and trades upwards of $350 today. The very rare luminous color lure will top the $600 level, but few have been found; in fact, I have never seen one in over 47 years of collecting.

For years, collectors have heard the story that Heddon had purchased the rights to this lure in the mid 1920's and that this then became their "Gamefisher" lure. Whereas this patent purchase may be true, there were three separate patents on the Gamefisher, one by an outside man from the company and two by Heddon.

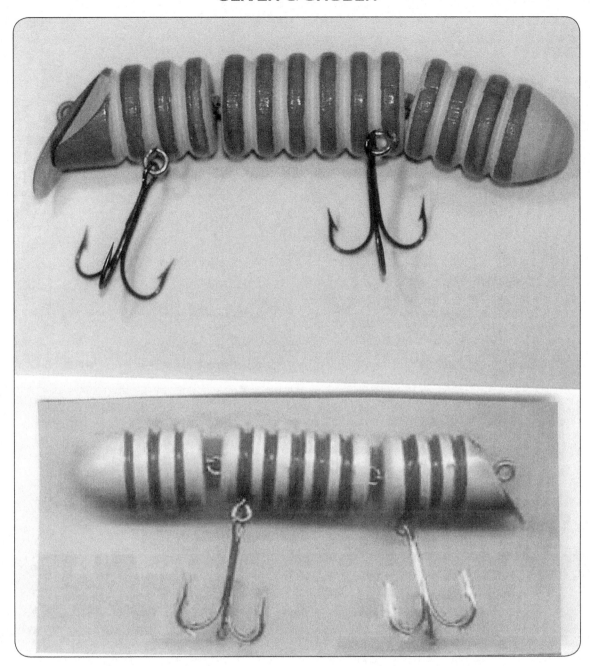

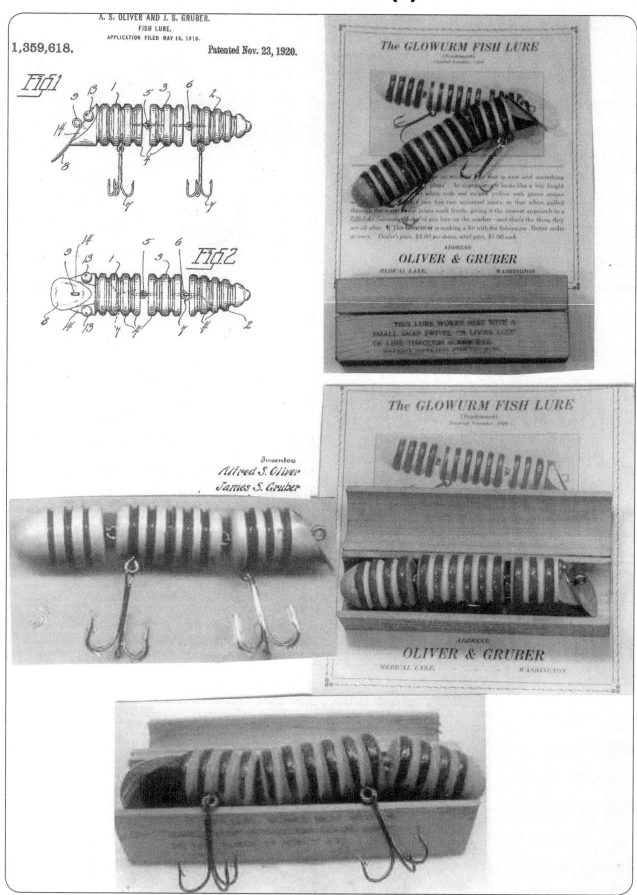

A. S. OLIVER AND J. S. GRUBER.
FISH LURE.
APPLICATION FILED MAY 16, 1918.

1,359,618.

Patented Nov. 23, 1920.

Fig.1

Fig.2

The GLOWURM FISH LURE
(Trademark)

ADDRESS
OLIVER & GRUBER
MEDICAL LAKE. WASHINGTON

Inventors
Alfred S. Oliver
James S. Gruber

The GLOWURM FISH LURE
(Trademark)

ADDRESS:
OLIVER & GRUBER
MEDICAL LAKE. WASHINGTON

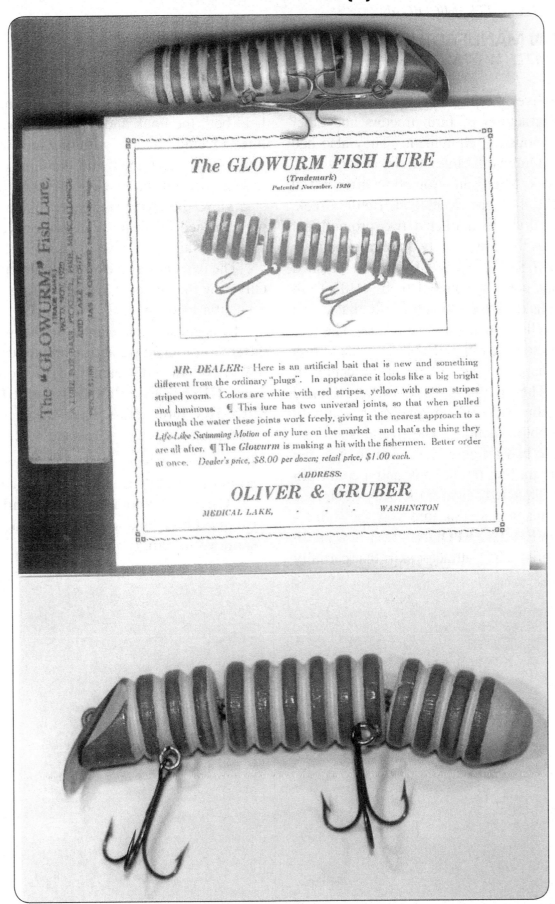

OLIVER OUTBOARD MOTORS
BATTLE CREEK, MICHIGAN

HINKSON MANUFACTURING COMPANY
SEATTLE, WASHINGTON

The Oliver Corporation was a well known early manufacturer of farm tractors and other farm and industrial equipment. They also had an Oliver Outboard Motor Division located in Battle Creek, Michigan. Sometime after World War II, the 440 East Michigan, Battle Creek, Michigan, division marketed two promotional fishing lures that are actually quite rare today.

The 2-7/8" **OLIVER LURE** was finished in the same color as some of their 1940's farm tractors, khaki or olive green on the back side and with yellow spots on the top side. The lure had a dish soldered in place on the nose with a pyramid-shaped raised line tie in the center of the dish. The satellite-shaped dish was cocked slightly to one side, which gave the lure a wild swing wobbling action. The overall-minnow-shaped lure had a figure-eight connector at the tail for the trailing treble hook and a cotter pin type, with flattened head for the belly treble.

A companion to this lure was the 2-3/8"-long **OLIVER JIG SPOON**. This lure had a synthetic bristly hair attractor skirt that partially concealed the single tail hook. A single screw held both the hook and skirt to the belly of the lure. Overall, the lure with this skirt was 3-1/2" long. It was equipped with the same disk at the nose as was on the first lure described. From a side view, this lure was shaped like a horn and was finished in nickel plate with a yellow and silver tail skirt.

The two Oliver lures were contract-made for Oliver by the Hinkson Manufacturing Company of Seattle, Washington.

Hinkson also made and sold the two lures in different colors for western salmon and trout fishing for both inland streams and off-shore fishing. Their **HINKSON SPINNER** and **HINKSON SPIN-JIG** lure colors were all nickel-plated finish, polished brass, or red and white.

Both lures are very rare. The Oliver Lure trades in the $40 and higher range and the Oliver Jig Spoon in the $25 and higher range. The Hinkson versions trade in the same value ranges.

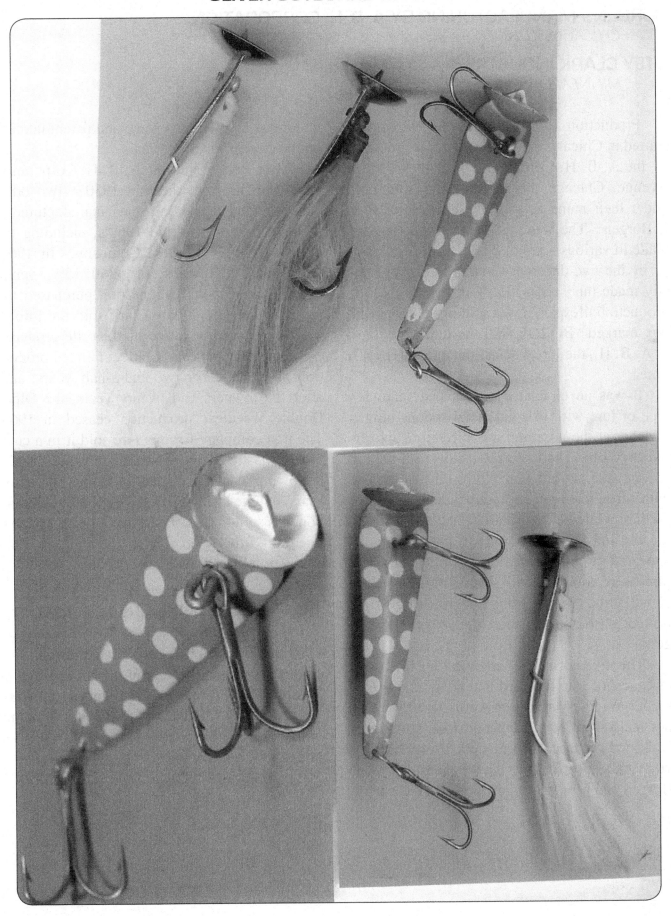

OLLIE'S DOUBLE WEEDLESS COMPANY
BORGENS MANUFACTURING BY A. B. H. CORPORATION
CHICAGO, ILLINOIS

OTEY CLARK INDUSTRIES
MINNEAPOLIS, MINNESOTA

Production for the Double Weedless lure started in Chicago in late 1948. It was produced by the A. B. H. Corporation at 4240 W. North Avenue, Chicago 39, Illinois, and sold both under their name as well as the inventor's, L. I. Borgen. The weedless casting spoons were made in various sizes of 2-1/2", 2-3/4", 3", and 5" by the five different companies that eventually made this spoon. Early in this lure's long production lifespan, it was sold in a clear plastic box marked "BORGENS", the lure's inventor, or A. B. H., the lure's actual manufacturer for a time.

It was an elongated egg-shaped sandwich type of lure with two flat metal spoons hinged together at the nose and was offered in six different colors. There were two slots near the tail on one side and a single slot on the other side with three fixed single hooks hidden inside of the lure while being fished. When a fish struck the lure and compressed the two sides, the hooks appeared through these slots for the catch. The lures were equipped with several different types of tail attractors, including flat pork rind strips, forked plastic strips, and shredded plastic fingers.

The inventor of the lure was Leif I. Borgen of Chicago, who received Patent No. 2,675,639 for his Weedless spoon on April 20, 1954. I'm not really sure why the patent took so long to be issued because Borgen applied for it on July 10, 1948. By the time the patent was issued, Borgen had been selling the lure in a clear plas-

tic hinged box with his name and patent number on the cover for several years.

After Borgen and the A. B. H. Corporation made the lure into the mid 1950's, two other Chicago land area companies manufactured it and carried into the mid 1960's, including the Ollie's Double Weedless Company. In 1965, Otey Clark Industries, of 4340 15th Avenue South, Minneapolis, Minnesota, purchased the rights to the lure. Otey Clark sold the lure in a plastic hinged box, and his favorite produced color was frog pattern. Clark continued production of the lure for two-and-a-half years, and, after five owners and twenty years, the Ollies Double Weedless production ceased in 1968. The first company for this lure sold it in a clear hinged plastic box with a card and papers inside. Following companies did the same for many years, but the last Otey Clark Minnesota production was sold in a plastic sacks or just on a card. There is virtually no way to distinguish a 1948 production from a 1968 production.

Boxed or not, the Ollies Double Weedless, which is quite common, trades in the $10 to $15 range and occasionally will reach $20 in a box or package. The common color is red and white, but others are frog pattern, half nickel and half copper, as well as various painted-blend and splatter-paint finishes, like the pictured Borgen's with box.

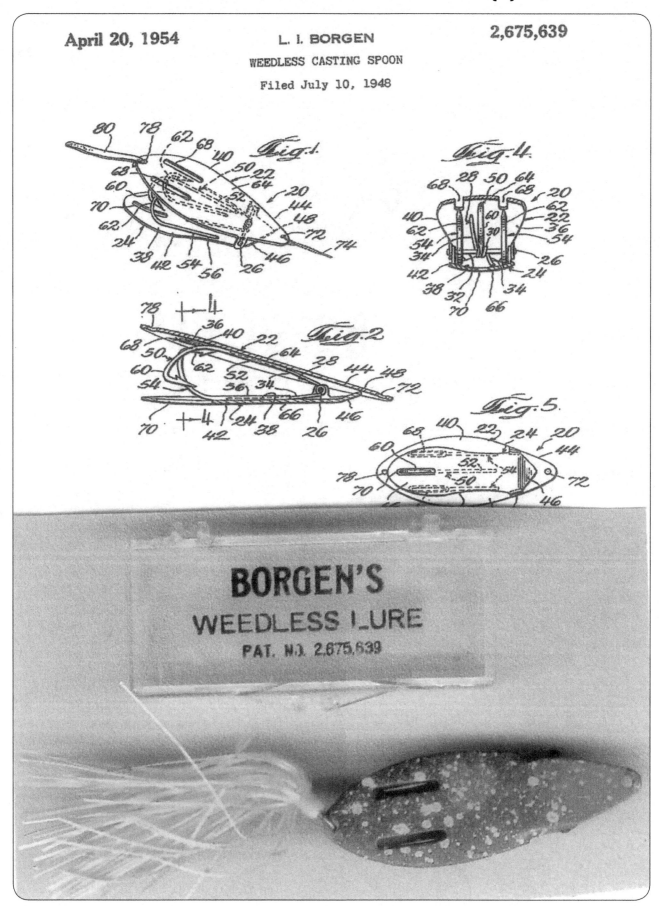

April 20, 1954   L. I. BORGEN   2,675,639

WEEDLESS CASTING SPOON

Filed July 10, 1948

Ollie's Double Weedless
"The Fishermen's Dream"

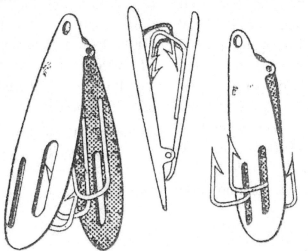

Recd.
July 23, 1949
2

Hooks exposed

In keeping ahead of modern fishing lures. The A. B & H. Corporation proudly introduces "*OLLIE'S DOUBLE WEEDLESS*" for casting and trolling. This lure is the only perfect double weedless lure on the market today. You will be amazed with this perfect fishing lure, how easy it travels through weeds and lily pads.

This lure comes in 6 different colors, it can also be used with pork strips, feathers or bucktails.

In open water you may use it with exposed hooks, only by tying the clams together.

A. B. & H. Corporation has again made a tremendous step forward in building up this line of sport, for the betterment of the fishermen. So ask your dealer for *OLLIE'S DOUBLE WEEDLESS*.

2½" Long Ollie's Double Weedless retails for 98 cents
5"   "   "   "   "   "   " $1.50
       "   Surface   "   " $1.25

Freight allowed on one gross or more

A. B. H. Corporation
MAKERS OF
Ollie's Double Weedless

4240 W. North Ave.   SPaulding 2-0088   Chicago 39, Illinois

OLSEN BAIT COMPANY
CHIPPEWA FALLS, WISCONSIN

In a way, Joseph and Edythe Worth, of Stevens Point, Wisconsin, enabled the Olsen Bait Company to live on beyond their days. They bought the financially troubled company in 1940 at a sheriffs' auction, and it became part of the founding of the Worth Tackle Company. Ryder Olsen had founded his Olsen Bait Company around 1936 and was kept on as a consultant by the Worth Company after the 1940 buyout. The Eppinger "Dardevle" type spoons made by the Worth company in all metal and metal and pearl had been developed by Ryder Olsen, although he did not make the ones with pearl in-lays. He did, however, make the fish-shaped **WATER DEMONS** and the down-turned-tail **DRAGON SPOONS**. His company also made a number of smaller size **CHIPPEWA SPINNERS** sold on cards (pictured).

Carded Olsen Bait Company productions trade in the $5 to $15 range.

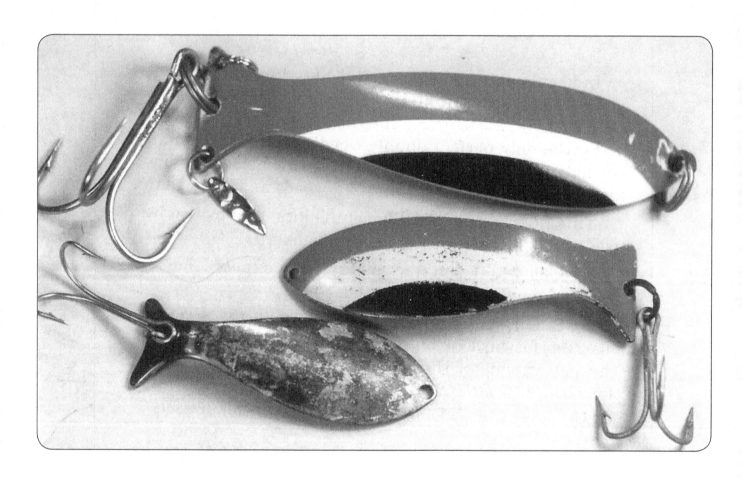

OLSON BAIT COMPANY
RACINE, WISCONSIN

ROLLING PLUG BAITS
CHICAGO, ILLINOIS

The Rolling Plug Bait was first made at 1144 Blaine Street in Racine, Wisconsin, during and after World War II, from 1944 to 1951. The company then moved to 3143 Normandy Ave, Chicago 34, Illinois, as Rolling Plug Baits and was in business there for two more years until 1953. In Wisconsin, the company was the Olson Bait Company owned by Hans P. Olson, who invented the lure in 1944. He filed for a patent on May 29, 1944, and Design Patent No. D140,296 was granted to him on February 6, 1945. I believe Olson retained ownership of the company with the move to Chicago. I say that because on October 13, 1950, he filed for a new patent on what was to become his 2-3/4"-long wooden **OLSON WEEDLESS KNOTHEAD** lure. This very rare lure was awarded Patent No. 2,651,877 on September 15, 1953.

The lure was basically made in the shape of the Bomber Bait Company "Knothead", except this lure had a single large hook held in a tail slot in the weedless position. The lure had an egg-shaped metal nose piece held in place by the line tie screw and two dangling side willow leaf spinners held by a screw similar to the Pflueger "Neverfail" hardware. The hook had a large rounded sway-bend in the hook shaft, and the hook point rested in a long cut slot in the tail. The slightest bump by a fish on the hook shank released it from that tail slot for the catch. The lure was made with nail and washer eyes.

The Wisconsin Rolling Plug lure box is pictured (courtesy of the John Collen collection) with a couple of the Olson manufactured red head with white lures. The two-piece white cardboard box had a blue top label that read, "ROLLING PLUG BAIT...for BASS-PIKE-PICKEREL...It Rolls and Swings...It Gets The Big Ones."

The wooden lures were similar in shape to the late production years Paw Paw "Platypus". The overall egg-shaped lure had a long, down-slanted nose with deep fingerprint, elongated indented dimples on both sides of the head. The lure had the appearance of pinched-in sides, as if though they were made of clay and a person squeezed the sides in with his fingertips. The 3-1/8" **ROLLING PLUG BAITS** had metal tack eyes painted with bright yellow irises and center black pupils. The eyes were placed in the forward part of the side indentations.

The smaller 3" model, called the **BASS SNOOPER**, appeared to be shorter than the 1/8" difference from the big ones, but that size was deceiving because the larger one had a fatter body. The Bass Snooper had built-up tack eyes looking forward in the forward part of the slanted forehead. The lures were painted in several different quality paint patterns, like the blood red head with aluminum, red head with yellow, red head with white, olive green with faint pepper specks, and yellow and green splatter finish (pictured). Some of the two screw-eye-held treble hooks were of the patented "John Walsh" pressed collar types made in Chicago by Land-O Tackle, Inc., just after the war. The top of the Chicago two-piece white cardboard lure box stated in red print, "Gets the big ones...It Rolls - Swings... ROLLING PLUG BAITS 3142 Normandy Ave., Chicago 34, Illinois."

The rarest size and color is the little 3" plug, pictured in dark green black-speckled back and in an off white-yellowish body with green side ribs. Although the example is not in the best condition, it does show the tack eyes without paint, as compared to the like-new-condition red head with white 3" model with built-up eyes with yellow irises and black center pupils.

In the first set of pictures, the 1945 patent is shown with both lure sizes and the four different eye types. With the patent is an early Racine painted-eye lure. On the right, with the paint off the eye, is a solid tack eye and, below it, a tack and washer eye model. All three of these lures are the larger 3-1/8" size. In red head with white is the smaller 3" Bass Snooper that has the forward-located built-up tack eyes.

In the second set of pictures, at the top are the two lure sizes with the early Racine two-piece cardboard box (close ups), and the same two lures are below. The last picture is of two of the Chicago-made lures with their two-piece cardboard box.

In the third set of pictures, at the top is a rare version of the Bass Snooper, in which there is only one dimple in the center of the back, rather than the two dimples on the sides. The tack eyes are also larger in size on this version. Pictured is a rare color yellow head with gray-aluminum from both side and top views and to the right a red head with white rare painted-eye version. The other two lures pictured are the side-dimple versions for comparison. Note that the two top rare versions also have fatter bodies than the more narrow, more common versions.

The fourth picture is of the 1953 patent for the Olson Weedless Knothead lure.

The Racine plugs are the rarer of the two manufacturers and trade in the $150 to $200 range in box, and the Chicago productions are close behind at $125 to $150, except the smaller and scarcer 3" models trade higher. The back-only dimpled versions also trade higher, starting at the $150 level and up. The very rare Weedless Knothead lures start in the $175 range and up.

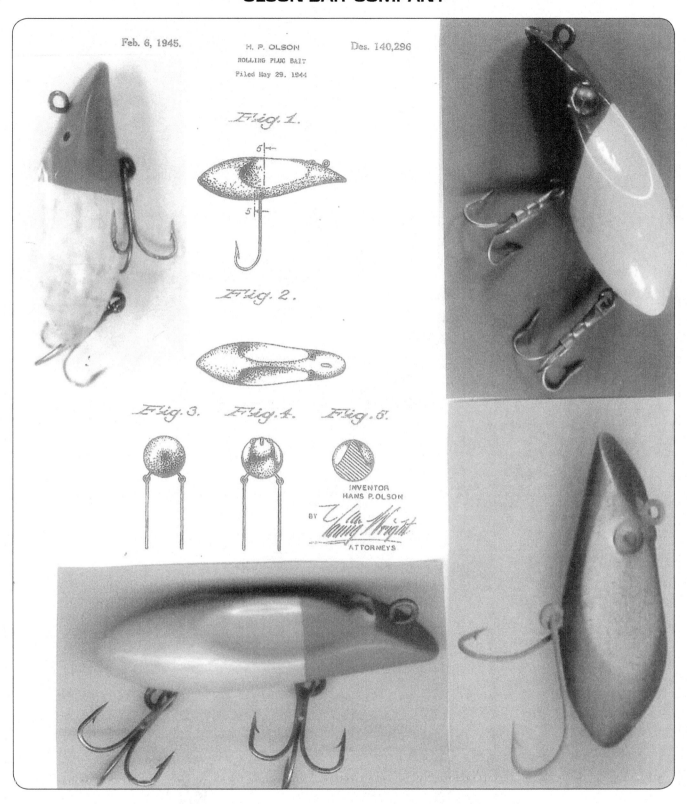

Feb. 6, 1945.

H. P. OLSON
ROLLING PLUG BAIT
Filed May 29, 1944

Des. 140,296

Fig. 1.

Fig. 2.

Fig. 3.   Fig. 4.   Fig. 5.

INVENTOR
HANS P. OLSON

BY

ATTORNEYS

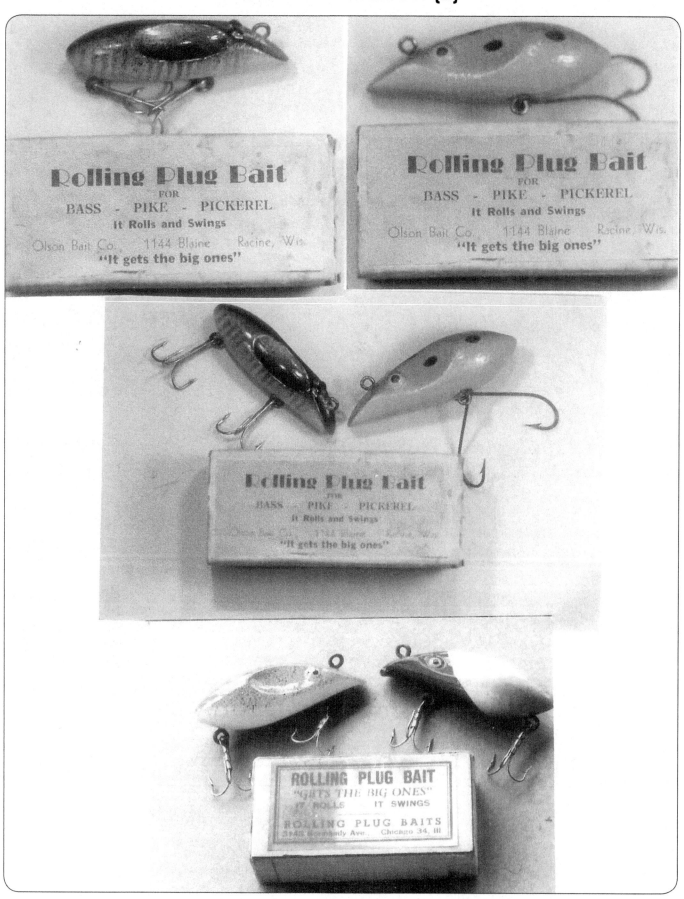

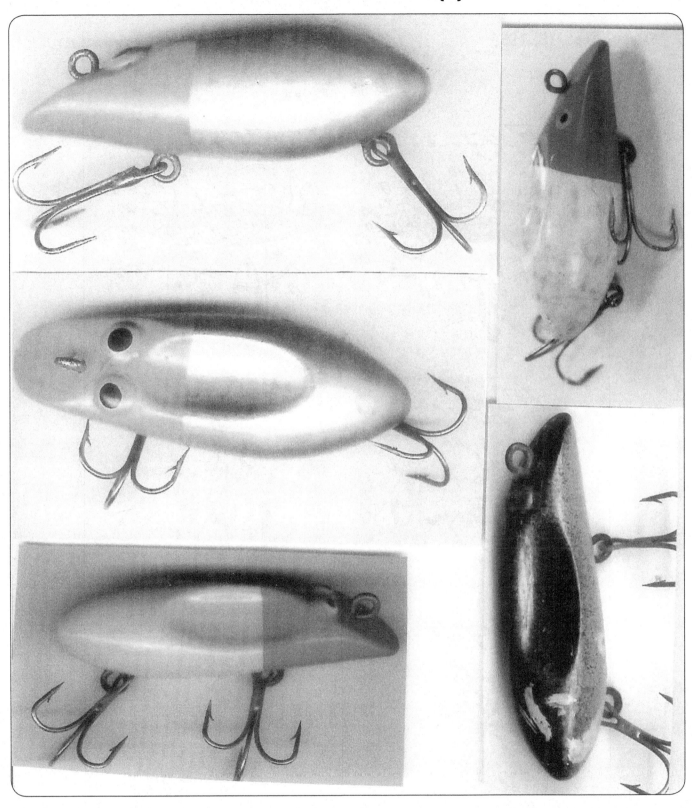

Sept. 15, 1953

H. P. OLSON

2,651,877

WEEDLESS HOOK AND LURE

Filed Oct. 13, 1950

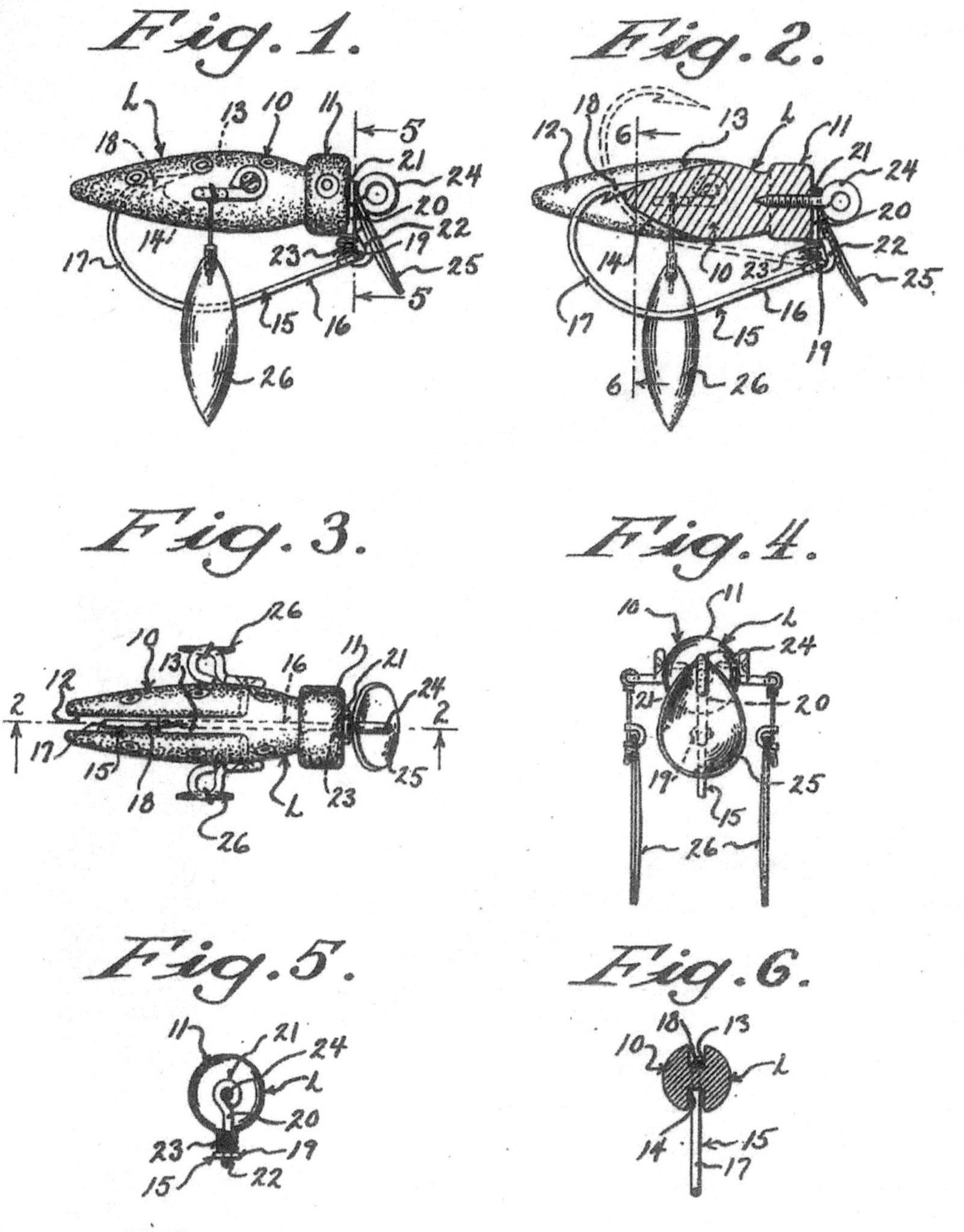

Fig. 1.

Fig. 2.

Fig. 3.

Fig. 4.

Fig. 5.

Fig. 6.

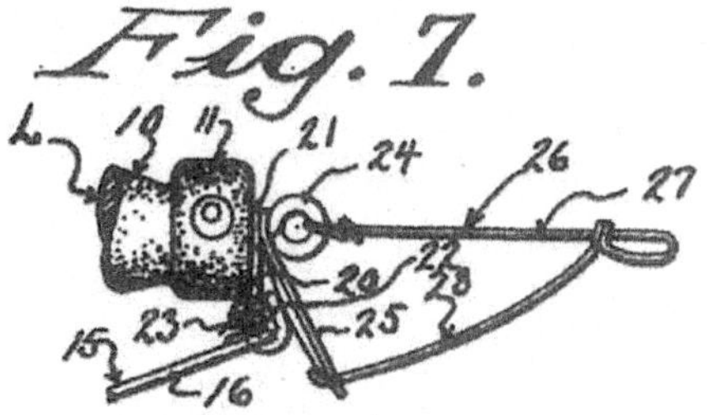

Fig. 7.

INVENTOR
HANS P. OLSON

BY

Young Wright

ATTORNEYS

OLSON FLY & LURE COMPANY
CASHTON & LA CROSSE, WISCONSIN

Other than Ole Olsen of Milwaukee, who dates to the 1930's, the Olson Fly & Lure Company is the next oldest of the four Wisconsin Olson companies. They were started in the early 1930's in La Crosse, Wisconsin, primarily making just fly rod lures and flies at that time. The flies were initially sold in round tins, such as the pictured examples of the **ROYAL COACHMAN** and **DIVIDED WING** flies. Later, the company sold flies on both individual cards and dealer display cards. A pictured example is the carded 3"-overall-long streamer fly, named the **TROUT FIREFLY**.

Sometime prior to 1940, the company moved or had a second location in Cashton, Wisconsin. Far more lure productions are found with that address than with the La Crosse address, but I don't believe this company was in business after World War II started. Pictured is one of their hen pheasant feather **SILVER MINNOW STREAMER** flies sold out of their Cashton location.

One of the company's most popular and successful sellers was the large squirrel tail, rabbit hair, and bucktail **MUSKY DRAGON**

spinning lures. A variety of different spinner blade types were used, but the most common was a fluted blade. These lures were sold in two-piece yellow cardboard boxes, each with a cellophane-covered picture window on the cover and "OLSON" printed in yellow inside of a red shield.

Another Olson production was the **WEEDLESS SPINNING POPPER** that was sold both on individual plastic covered cards and on half-dozen dealer display boards (like the ones pictured courtesy of the Alan Bakke collection).

To be honest, I can't remember how I determined that this company made these 4-1/4"- and 4-3/4"-overall-long "butterfly" type spinner baits covered in my first book. They have 2"-wide, large, swept-back wing propellers. Let's just call them suspect Olson Fly & Lure Company productions.

Olson Fly & Lure Company productions are rare today and trade from $35 to over $50. Early catalogs, like the one pictured, trade in the same range.

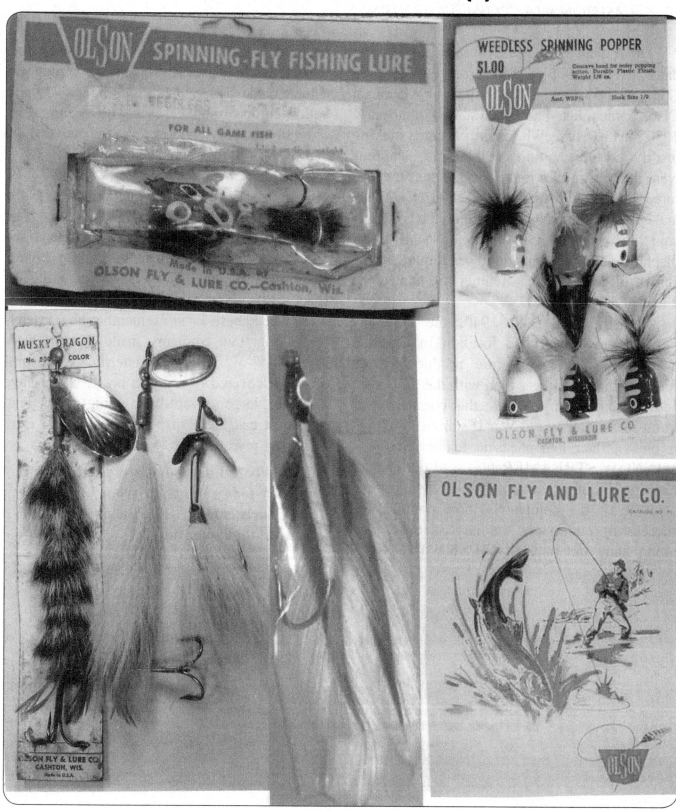

OLSON LURES
PARK FALLS, WISCONSIN

Olsen and Olson were popular names in the 1930's to the 1960's in Wisconsin. Five different unrelated lure makers had those names and made lures during that time frame. One such company was Olson Lures that was located at Shady Knoll Road in Park Falls, Wisconsin. The company was started in the mid 1960's, and they were still in business into the late 1960's.

They made two sizes of a soft-sponge-body lure that varied in length from 4" to 5" long, depending on how many 1"-round sponges were strung on the lure's wire shaft. This wire was attached to the back of the **SOFTY** lure's 1-1/4" hard plastic head that had a down-slanted nose. Actually, the lures were made with different head styles, the one described and a second one shaped like a child's top. The eyes were set in deep drilled sockets with the inside of each hole painted yellow for the iris and with a black pupil

at the base of the hole. The Softy was a weedless and snag-proof lure, as the box papers claimed, because the three or four in-line sponges were followed by a hidden treble hook and a shredded plastic skirt. The last sponge in line protected the hook points until a striking fish squeezed the sponge, exposing the hook for the catch. Not only did this lure present a soft natural feel to the fish, it could also be scented with liquid scent of the fisherman's choice to further attract fish. The lure was colorful with a red painted head and yellow in-line sponges. It was sold in a clear plastic hinged box with blue paper inserts for ID and instructions.

The Olson Softy is quite scarce today and, in box, will trade in the $20 to $25 range and sometimes even higher.

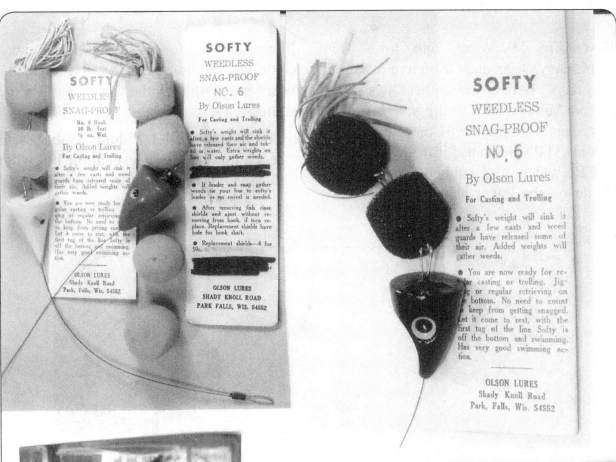

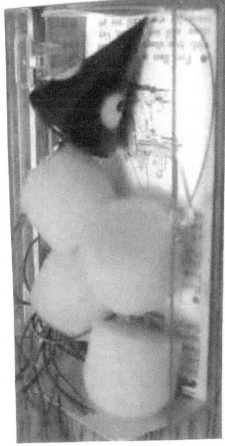

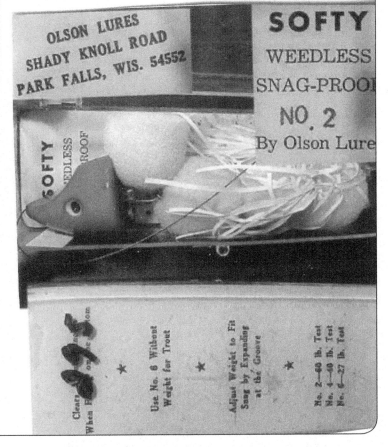

OLSON, NELS
BURLINGTON, IOWA

Wisconsin, Minnesota, and Iowa were homes of many Olsen and Olson lure makers in the early days. Here is yet another Olson: Nels Olson from Valley Street, Burlington, Iowa. He introduced his August 17, 1901-patented wooden bobbers in 1900. He named it the **SNAGLESS BOBBER**, which was painted green on top and white on the lower half most commonly.

It was also made in red and white, but each color was sold in a plain, two-piece green cardboard box with only the lure maker's name and address on it.

The unmarked 4-1/4"-long bobbers seldom reach the $10 trade level alone but will top the $35 level in box with papers.

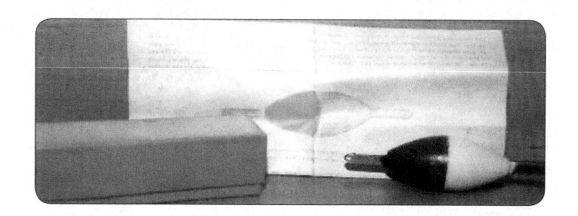

OLSON, O. F., LURE COMPANY
FENTON, IOWA

The 1931 - 1935 O. F. Olson lure company, of Fenton, Iowa, made some interesting metal **OLSON'S LURES**. Each of Oscar F. Olson's lures had a flat metal body with a vertical, soldered-in-place, three-quarter's slant oval head. One style was the 3" **OLSON FROG** that had split frog legs at the rear end with a split-ring-held treble hook in between the legs. These lures were painted in either green frog spot or red head with white.

Another lure was the 2-3/4" **OLSON MINNOW TAIL**, a flat, fish-shaped spoon with the soldered-on vertical head that served as a plane and stabilizer. These lures were finished in either nickel plate or red vertical head with white.

More ommonly were his 2-1/2", 2", and little 1-5/8" **OLSON LURES**. These were just flat, oval bodies with the soldered-on three-quar-ter's oval vertical head. These lures were finished half nickel and half frog, half nickel and half red, or all nickel plate.

All of his lures were stamped "Pat. Pend." Oscar F. Olson Received patent No. 1,875,122 for his lures on August 30, 1932. The white two-piece cardboard lure box read, "OLSON'S LURES...Patent Pending...Price $1.25...Reel with slow to moderate speed."

Lure pictures are courtesy of the Larry Sundall collection.

These Olson lures are rare, and the box is very rare. A boxed lure will trade in the $50 to $65 range, with the boxed frogs reaching the $75 level. The lures alone are $25 to $35, with the frogs pushing $45.

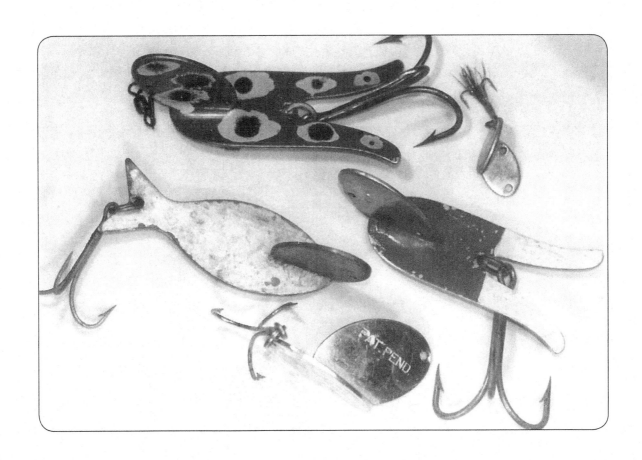

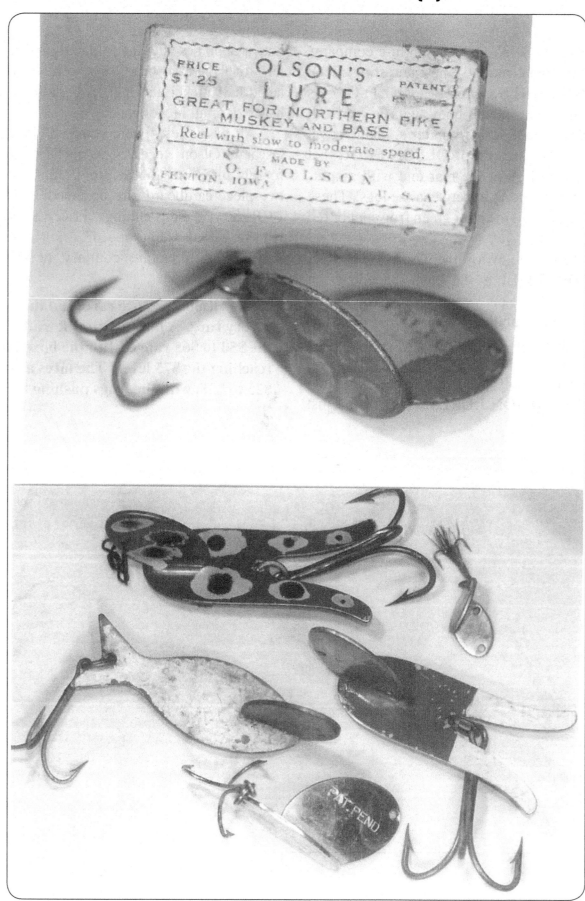

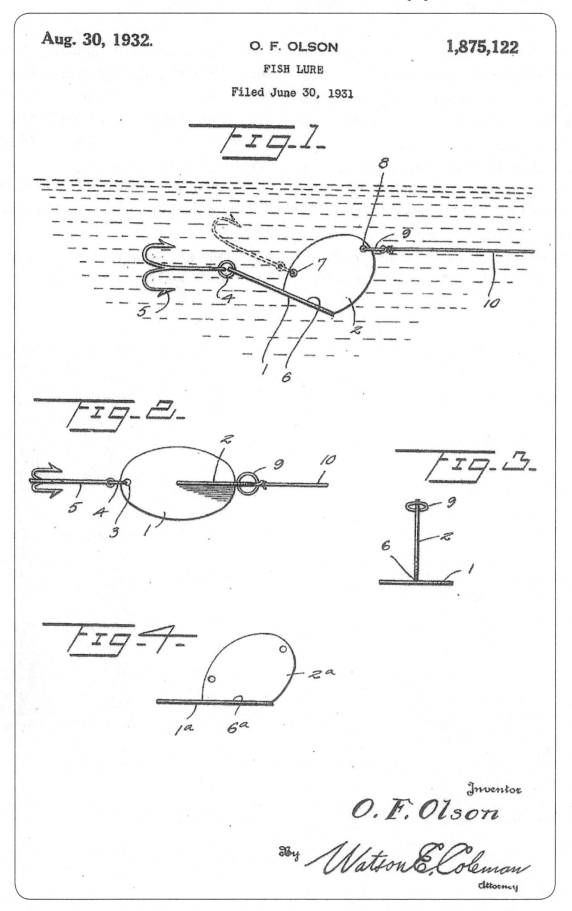

Aug. 30, 1932.

O. F. OLSON

1,875,122

FISH LURE

Filed June 30, 1931

Fig.1.

Fig.2.

Fig.3.

Fig.4.

Inventor

O. F. Olson

By Watson E. Coleman

Attorney

OLT, PHILLIP S.
PEKIN, ILLINOIS

Phillip S. Olt was more famous for his waterfowl calls than he was for his fishing lures. However, his **OLT O. K. SPINNER MINNOW** is quite famous as well. The lure had a series of three descending-size cultivator-blade-shaped arrowhead spinner blades mounted on a wire shaft with guinea hen feathered tail treble hook. It should be pointed out that the O.K. Spinner pictured in Karl White's book was not made by Philip S. Olt. I believe that spinner was actually a Loftie because the Olt Spinner is as described above, made of aluminum and bent at a 90-degree angle to the axis and designed to spin in opposite directions. Phillip S. Olt received Patent No.1,292,865 on January 28, 1919, for his O.K. Spinner.

A picture (courtesy of Don Kramer) of the patent is shown along with two lures. The ad is courtesy of Dick Streater.

P.S. Olt O.K. Spinners are very rare and will trade well in excess of $200.

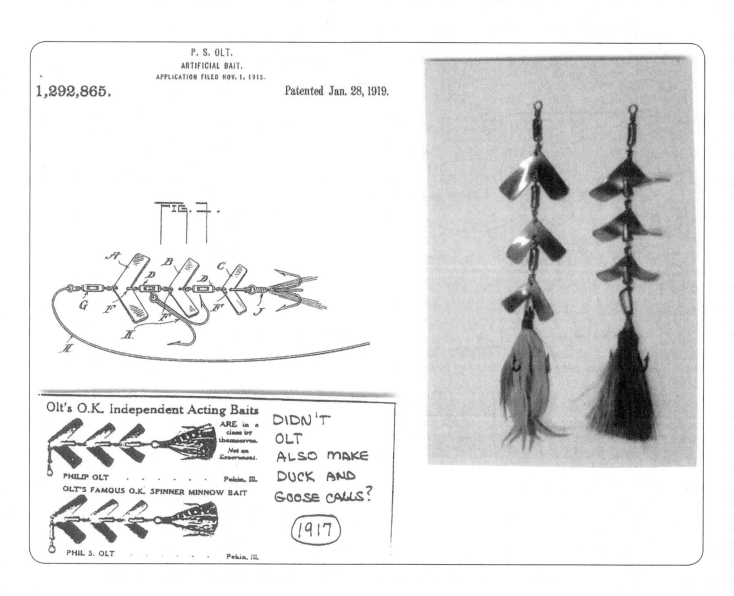

OLYMPIC DISTRIBUTING COMPANY
PLEASANTON, CALIFORNIA

In 1923, Ueno Seiko Company, Ltd., formed a manufacturing company at 3859 7 chome Shiinamach toshima-kn, Tokyo, Japan. They manufactured reels, landing nets, flies, jigs, and lures under the trade name **OLYMPIC**. Their trade symbol was of five interlocked rings, or circles, in a row with a saltwater flying fish etched above these rings. The company made reels for Ocean City, OLM, True Temper, Sears, even some for Heddon, and others. One of their reels, made in their own trade name, was the **OLYMPIC NO. 71** (pictured courtesy of the Merv Bortner collection). Take note of the trademark symbol on the reel's cloth sack. The major distributor of this company's products in this country was Olympic Distributors out of Pleasanton, California, but the Compac Company, also in California, distributed their productions as well, particularly reels.

One of this company's lures was the 2-1/2" **TWINKLE** that had a cigar-shaped body with side swept-back wings that made the lure 3/8" wide. The metal fish-shaped lure had a teardrop-shaped mouth that also served as a line tie, a hole for an eye, and a cut hole in a half circle for a side gill. In the slot between the body and the wings, there were two rivet-held red plastic beads. The lure was stamped, "TWINKLE... PAT." The only patented lure like this one that I know of was manufactured in the late 1940's by the Alexander Bait Company out of Clifton, New Jersey. Their 1-5/8"-long "ALEXANDER SPIN FISH" lure was awarded patent No. 2,493,693 on January 3, 1950, to Alexander Maista and Lawrence Tony Pareti. I'm picturing their lures alongside the Twinkle for comparison.

Another lure made by the Olympic company was the 2-1/8" **PEARL ROCKET** that had built-up tack eyes with bright yellow irises on either red head with white or red head with yellow painted bodies. The lure had an under-the-chin, three-screw-held metal lip that was pretty much straight up and down, more of a wobbler-plane than a dive-plane. One type of lip was smooth and slightly shovel-nosed, but the older model's lip was made from a fluted spinner blade. On both metal nose pieces, the name "PEARL ROCKET" was stamped on the blades, along with the five-interlocked-rings Olympic trade symbol. The lure had a flat washer that was shaped to the belly's contour and a screw eye for the belly treble hook and a simple screw eye for the tail treble. Olympic also made other lure designs that they also stamped as "Pearl Rocket" with their trade symbols. The pictured "Pikie Minnow" type that measured 4" long and was finished in green head with silver scale with red ribs had the dive lip stamped in the same print.

Along with at least three USA companies making the "Lur-All" type of tin Beetle Bug lures, there were also two in Japan, including this company. The **OLYMPIC BRAND WATER BEETLES** were sold on tan cards with green print and were made in pan fish and trout sizes as well as in a bass size.

Much of this company's history and the pictured Olympic Reel is courtesy of the Merv "The Reelman" Bortner collection.

The Olympic Twinkle trades in the $5 to $10 range and the Pearl Rocket in the $15 to $20 range. Carded Water Beetles trade in the $20 to $25 range. I have not seen enough trading in the reels to know into what trade ranges the boxed reels fall.

OMAN, JOHN
MINNEAPOLIS, MINNESOTA

John Oman has been a recognized carver of lures but, primarily, of ice fishing decoys in the Minneapolis area since the early 1970's. Pictured (courtesy of the Steve O'Hern collection) is the 4-1/2" **OMAN FROG**. This realistic-looking wooden frog has large, glass frog eyes, a humped frog head, and a two-ridge back. The lure body is 3-1/4" long, and the hinged hind legs are 1-3/4" long. The lure is painted in a green-spotted leopard frog pattern.

I'm also picturing another wooden frog in the same size range. This frog was NOT made by John Oman but, rather, by some unknown lure maker. I felt this contemporary folk art frog should get its place in history because it is very well made, just like the Oman Frog. It had a Heddon bar type hook hardware piece for the belly hook and two embedded long shank hooks spreading out along the legs. There were cut slots in the ends of the legs that have two nail-held leather feet. The lure had red iris glass eyes.

In the second set of pictures, the John Oman Frog is on the top and the unknown frog is on the bottom of the page. The unknown frog lure pictures are courtesy of the Matt Lollman collection.

Both the Oman Frog and the unknown-maker frog trade in the $50 range and higher. Some of the John Oman ice fishing decoys trade still higher.

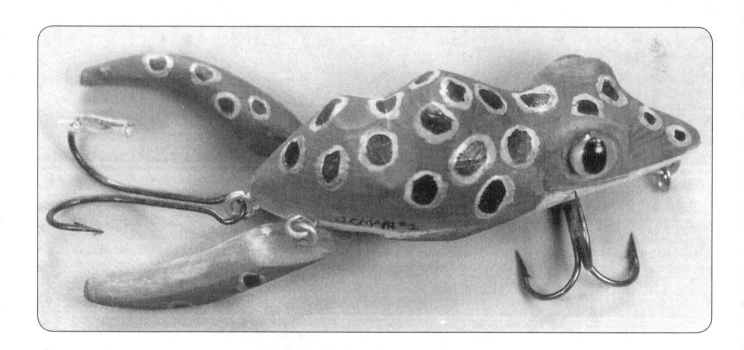

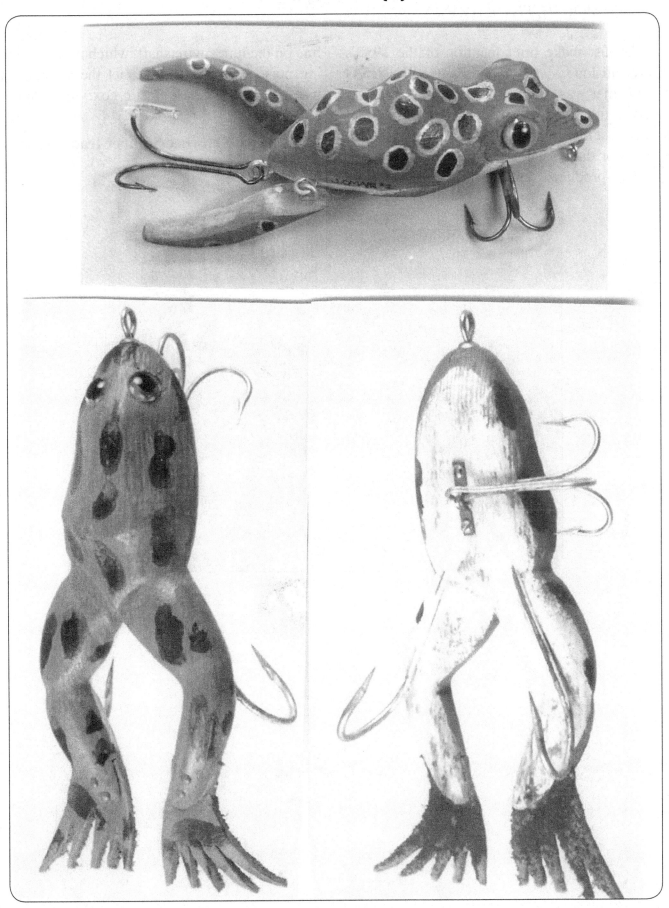

I'll just make brief mention of the 1950's 3"-overall-long **SHAWNEE SPINNING LURE** that was made at 101 Davenport Street in Plymouth, Pennsylvania. The 1/4-oz. spinner looked just like another "Mepps" copy, but it had one major difference: it was noisy. The M. J. Onderko-produced lure had five brass beads in line on the lure's wire shaft, which made a clicking noise on retrieve to attract the attention of fish. It was sold in a plastic box with a tan ID card insert.

The boxed Shawnee Spinner trades in the $5 to $10 range.

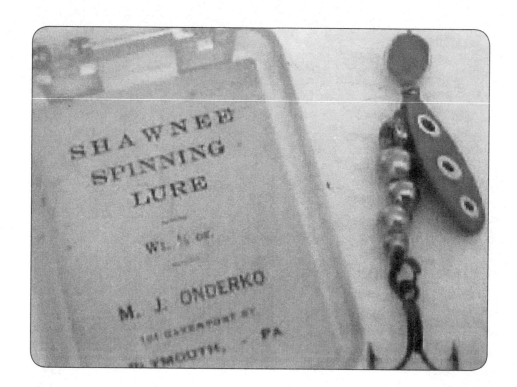

ONE HOOK LURES, INC.
SHREVEPORT, LOUISIANA

The Bacon & Edwards Hardware and Sporting Goods Store of Shreveport was jointly owned by R. R. Bacon and Hartwell M. Edwards, who was known by the nickname Sonny. In 1956, Sonny Edwards founded his One Hook Lure Company at 4233 Chamberian Drive in Shreveport, Louisiana. Edwards designed and produced five different one-hook lures that were basically 98% weedless with their up-turned tail hooks. All five lures were introduced in 1956, with the 1-1/2" 3/8-oz. **BALLYHOO** being the first.

The wooden Ballyhoo was made in nine colors and had a single hook inserted in the tail held by a screw eye that also held a small zip willow leaf spinner blade under the tail. The screw eye line tie had a reverse cup washer and was made with or without a front bow tie spinner blade.

A very similar lure, the **SPIN PLUG**, was made in a 1-7/8" length but had no nose prop and a large Colorado spinner blade under the tail instead of the zip spinner blade. This lure was made the very same way at 2-1/4" long and was called the **TOP WATER SPIN PLUG**.

A departure from the wooden lures was the **SPINFLASH**, which was a typical wire shaft bass spinner bait with a lead head and a rubber skirt covering the single up-turned hook. This lure had the addition of a bow tie spinner blade mounted inline on the wire shaft ahead of the lead head. This lure was made in twelve different color patterns.

The **POT BELLY WATER BUG** was another lead-head bass spinner bait. However, the lead head was a series of three ascending-size dumbbells in series followed by a rubber "Beetle Spin" type rubber body with spider-like rubber side legs. This lure also had the bow tie in-line spinner blade.

Another spinner lure with a lead head, a shredded plastic tail skirt, and a bow tie spinner prop out front was the **ENTICER**. This lure was made with tail skirt colors of white, purple, black, yellow, or green with a blend of white or black mixed in. The lures were sold on card in plastic sacks on large one-dozen dealer display boards that read, "Don't worry about WORMS…MINNOWS…CRICKETS. They Lose Their Popularity When You Use 'SONNY'S' FLASHY ENTICER."

The One Hook Lures were each mounted on a card with a plastic cover that read, "A LIVE ACTION LURE," together with the lure name, company name, and address.

Lure pictures are courtesy of the Adrien A. Delbasty collection. The group picture shows a dealer board of ENTICER lures on the left and two SPINFLASH lures on the right. Below are two TOP WATER SPIN PLUGS that were designed to be used with live bait on the surface, just like an underwater "Floating Jig Head" with a slip sinker. On the right is a 1-7/8" TOP WATER SPIN PLUG. The 1-1/2" UNDER WATER BALLYHOO looks just like this lure, except it is weighted. The first set of pictures includes a green scale Under Water Ballyhoo and a red and a black Top Water Spin Plug.

The packaged wooden lures trade in the $25 to $30 range and the Spinner Lures in the $5 to $10 range, some to $20. Full dealer display boards of spinner baits trade in the $50 and higher range.

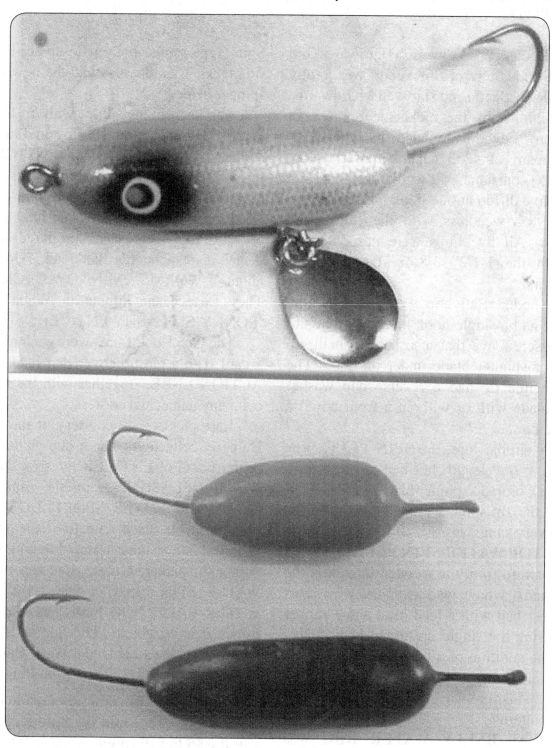

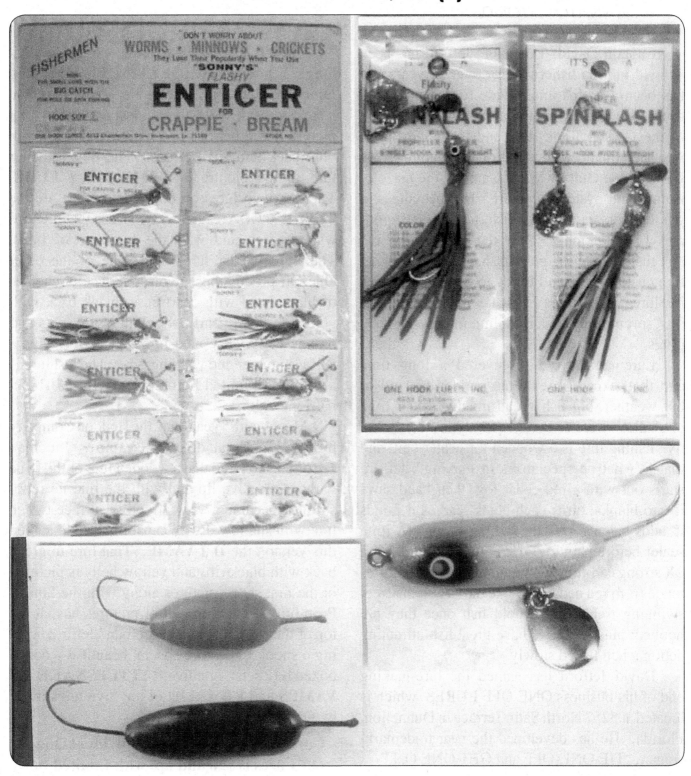

ONE-OFF LURES
DUNNELLON, FLORIDA

Captain David "Lureman" Jefford has been an avid Florida fisherman for over 30 years and has been a professional guide for much of that time. He guides out of a 24-foot skiff based in the Crystal River area and takes customers into the aquatic wilderness of the Nature Coast Keys on the Gulf of Mexico among the maze of islands and oyster bars there. He specializes in guiding for sea trout, redfish, tarpon, and grouper. Lureman makes all of the lures that he and his customers fish, plus he has a following of lure customers from Florida to Canada who fish his lures. The lures he makes include spoons, jigs, soft plastics, and, most importantly, wooden plugs.

Lureman Jefford discovered a long time ago that, except in extreme periods of cold or hot weather, big fish spend much of their time in shallow waters. Consequently, a very effective fishing lure is a wooden top-water bait, and that is what he specializes in making. Jefford starts out with a red cedar log, then band saws it into blanks, turns each blank, carves it, sands it, adds balance weight, and then coats it with a sealer before painting. He equips his lures with 2X strong cad-tinned Mustad treble hooks. Lures made from red cedar cast like darts, and the free-swinging treble hooks hold fish once they are hooked; plus, the lures have great fish-attracting action when fished slowly.

David Jefford has named the lure-making end of his business ONE-OFF LURES, which is located at 5257 North Satin Terrace in Dunnellon, Florida. He has developed the neat trademark/slogan, "TIE ONE-OFF and GET ONE ON."

One of his recent lure productions is a 3"-long, painted-eye, tail-prop, glazed wooden **SQUIRT-PROP**. That lure is pictured in two different colors with its plastic-tub type box and red card ID insert.

One of Jefford's first lures was his 3-5/8"-long, 7/10-ounce **ZARDEEN**, a shallow-running minnow twitch bait. The lure is pictured in blue head and back with silver sides, and below that picture is another one in a red headed color with blue back and silver sides. The other smaller lure in the picture is a **WEEDEEN LURE**. The next two lures on this picture page are the **SUPER-CEDAR** lures in two sizes that are top-water twitch and walk-the-dog type of lures. The Super-Cedar lures and some of the other One-Off productions are offered in color choices of black head with chartreuse, black back with gold sides, and pearl body with black spots and orange belly. The next lure is a **BYTE-ME**, a surface popper and walking type. The last lure is a 12"-long Limited Edition **WAHOO LURE** in patriotic colors.

More than 85 years ago, the Heddon Company produced a metal dive lip "Vamp". Lureman Jefford discovered that a wooden lure of this type without the dive lip and with the line tie repositioned became a very effective surface-twitch lure with shallow diving capabilities. He named this version the **D J VAMP**. That lure in green back with black ribs and yellow belly is pictured in the first set of pictures along with the Squirt-Prop lures. The third set of pictures has, at the top of the page, Captain "Lureman" Jefford holding a snook. Next are special beautiful wooden boxed lure sets: first five **RATTLESNAKE D J VAMPS** and a boxed set of any five lures made by One-Off lures.

Current trade values for individual One-Off Lures is $20 and up, with Limited Editions higher. Boxed sets trade at over $100 and up.

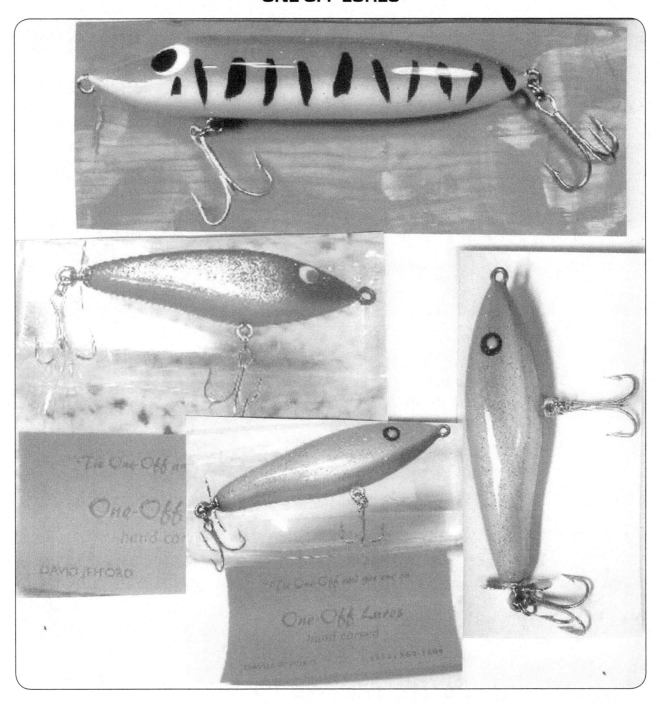

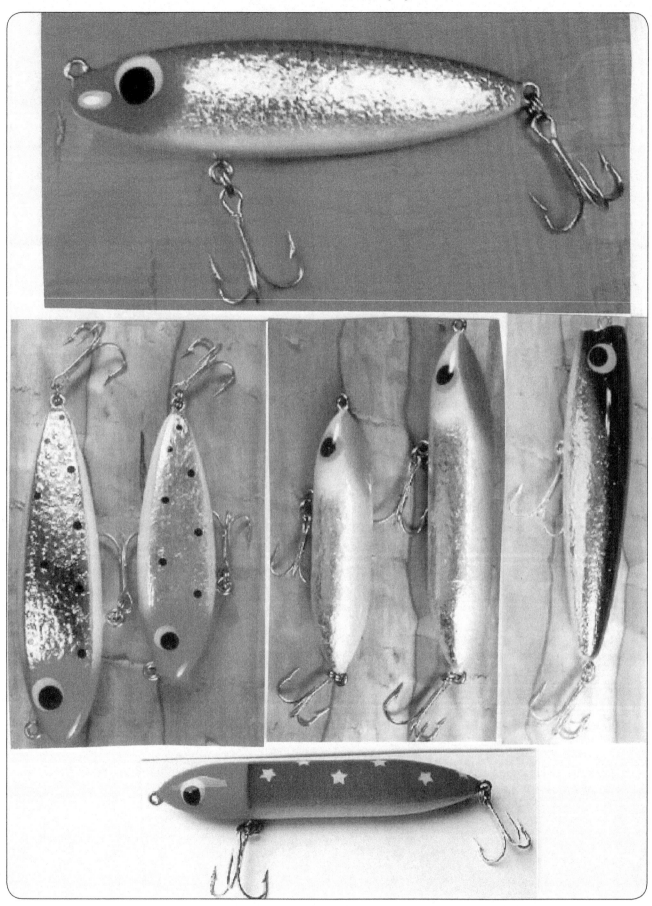

ONLY MANUFACTURING COMPANY
INDIANAPOLIS, INDIANA

For an impressive company name like The Only Manufacturing Company, their production was pretty much of a common deer hair spinner bait. The company was located at 113 to 125 Capitol Ave. S in Indianapolis, Indiana, and they date to 1939 and possibly earlier. They made a kidney-shaped blade spinning lure with a series of two sets of two spread hooks in tandem, followed by a tail treble hook hidden in three distinct clumps of deer hair bucktail. The lure was also made in single and tandem kidney blade spinners. The lure was called **THE ONLY TROLLING WORM** and was made in five sizes: two in fly rod sizes and three in trolling sizes. See the picture of a "jobbers list" mailed to dealers. The lure was developed by an Ohio man by the name of Manly Phillips, who received Patent No. 2,277,350 for his spinner lures on March 24, 1942.

The Only Trolling Worm trades in the $20 to $25 range on card, but, unfortunately, the blades are unmarked except for "Pat Apl'd For".

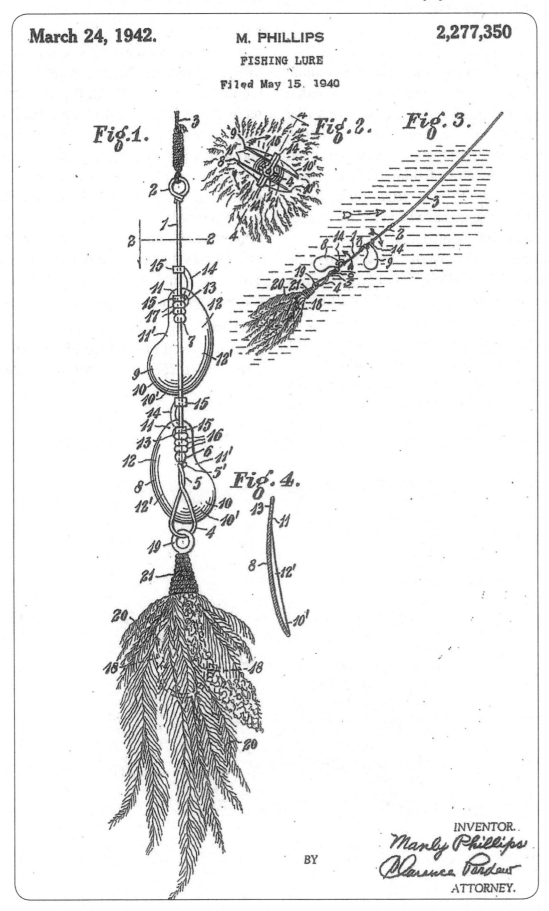

March 24, 1942.

M. PHILLIPS

FISHING LURE

Filed May 15. 1940

2,277,350

Fig. 1.

Fig. 2.

Fig. 3.

Fig. 4.

INVENTOR.
Manly Phillips
BY
Clarence Pardew
ATTORNEY.

ONONDAGA SPECIALITY COMPANY
SYRACUSE, NEW YORK

In the early 1920's and into the late 1930's, the Onondaga Company introduced a unique "Flat Top" type of lure. Most of the wooden no-eyed lures did not have metal dive lips like the one pictured. The lure resembled a "Rush Tango" cut in half horizontally, giving it a flat upper surface. Several of their lures also had paint patterns similar to some Rush Tango lures, and there very well may have been some connection between the two companies.

The hand-painted wooden lure pictured is the 3-1/2" **IDEAL UNDERWATER FLOAT**. The lure had a red painted metal dive lip starting on the flat head and bent down over the nose. The lure was equipped with over-sized screw eyes for the line tie and two belly trebles. Another version of the Onondaga Minnow did not have the metal nose dive lip and had a single belly eye screw. The idea was for the fisherman to place a spinner of his choice on this screw eye, and, when trolled or reeled, the lure would dive and give the spinner action. When the fisherman stopped reeling, the lure would wobble back to the surface. A hook could be substituted for a spinner and fished just that way as well, if desired.

The two-piece cardboard lure box was off white with black print and gave the full address of Mercantile Press, 345 W. Fayette Street (Onondaga County), Syracuse, New York.

Thanks to Joe Stagnitti of Manlius, New York, for making his boxed lure available for photography.

All lures by this company are very scarce to rare. Boxed Onondaga Minnows trade in the $45 to $55 range and lures alone $25 to $35

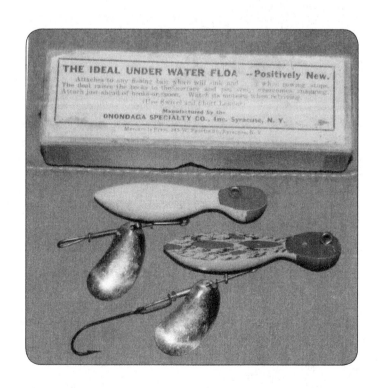

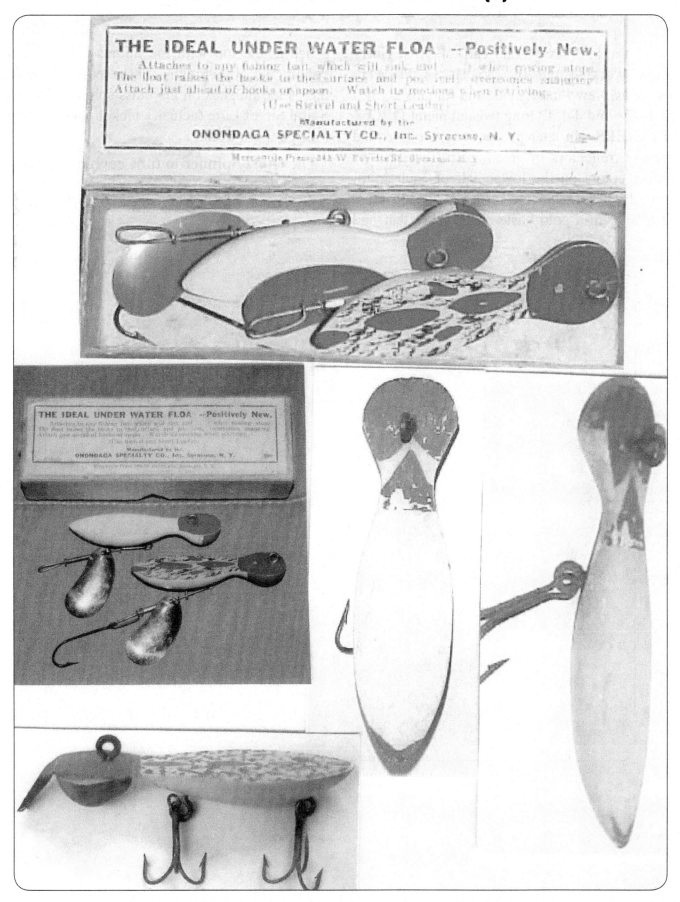

OPITZ, HARRY
SECAUCUS, NEW JERSEY

In the late 1960's and early 1970's, Harry Opitz, working out of 285 Hagan Place in Secaucus, New Jersey, made and sold his 2-1/4"-, 3-1/4"-, and 4-1/4"-long twisted metal **OPITZ SPINNERS**. In later productions, Opitz added paste-on reflectors in green, gold, red, blue or yellow colors on the lower half of each spiral lure. He sold each lure in a 4-1/2"-long plastic tube with a gold paste-on ID label that had a fish at the top with the initials SSL or SGL coming out of its mouth. These letters stood for the plated finishes on his brass spirals: SSL for Spiral Silver Lure (actually nickel plate) or SGL for Spiral Gold Lure.

The Opitz Spinner in tube currently trades at $5 or less.

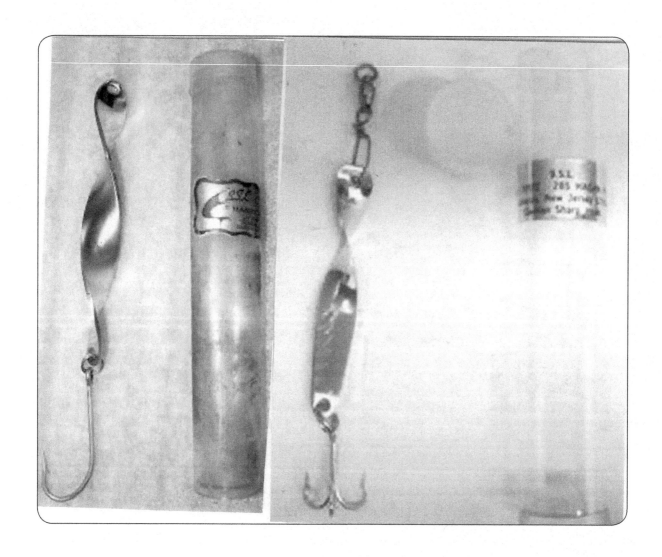

ORAVEC, STEVE, BAIT & REEL MANUFACTURING COMPANY
DETROIT, MICHIGAN

I'm not normally covering Pencil Plug or McGinty type lures in this book. However, Steve Oravec deserves mention because of the variety of lures he made and the fact that he was in the lure making business in Michigan for close to twenty years (1922 to 1942, approximately).

The 4"-longen no-eyed wooden **ORAVEC MINNOW** was a cigar-shaped lure with a long metal dive plane inserted in a slot in its face. The lure had concave-washer and screw-eye hook hardware and a luxon nose clip line tie.

His **PENCIL PLUGS** were long, narrow, no-eyed wooden plugs, not unlike the many other "Pencil Plug' types made throughout Michigan.

The **ORAVEC Mc GINTY** was usually engraved "Oravec" on the metal wings, so they are easy to identify. His first ones, made in the 1920's and 1930's, had cloth bodies and were made in 1 3/8" lengths. In the early 1940s, Oravec started making the **LAST WORD Mc GINTYS** with plastic bodies.

The lures made by Steve Oravec were normally sold on one-dozen dealer display boards; however, he did sell his Mc Ginty lures in two-piece cardboard boxes with lure pictures on the covers.

One of the pictures shows three of Oravec's Pencil Plugs and paint sticks for the cut nose slot 4" Oravec Minnow.

Over any other state, Michigan probably had the greatest numbers of Mc Ginty type lure makers over the years. An early such lure maker was John Popplecheck, from Roseville, Michigan, who made a wide brass blade head with a tight tapered body Mc Ginty in the 2" range. A very similar lure was made by Chuck Hayes of Detroit, Michigan. The lures made by Garmet De Cou, of Marine City, Michigan, had the fabric-composition bodies of the phantom minnow types with smaller metal wings as part of the metal heads.

A full dealer board of any of the Oravec lures trades in the $100 to $125 range. Individual lures trade in the $10 to $20 range. Boxed Mc Ginty lures either with cloth or plastic bodies trade $15 to $20. Most other Michigan Mc Ginty lures trade widely, depending on age and recognition; however, in general, they trade in the $5 to $15 range, some higher.

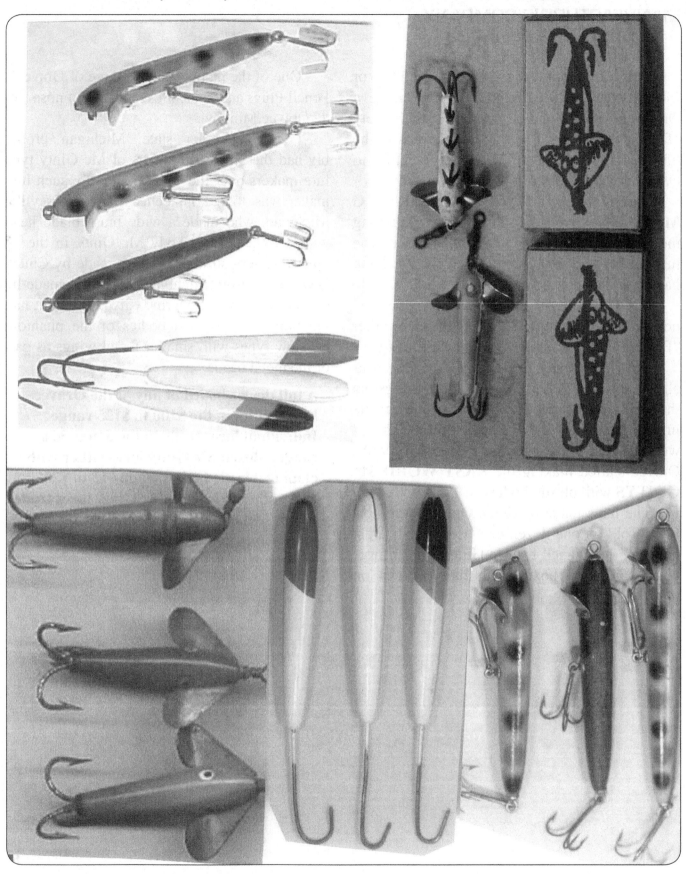

ORBIT AERO COMPANY
WEBBERVILLE, MICHIGAN

This 1972 Webberville, Michigan, company was one of the early pioneers in molded eye and gill detail in soft plastic body fish-shaped minnow lures with the relatively new "paddle tail" concept. The paddle tail for plastic imitation minnow baits gave the lures fast, short, vibrating swimming action. The company's **SUPERMINNOW** was made in 2-1/2", 3-1/4", and 4" sizes and in colors of all yellow, all white, blue back with white, and black back with white. The lures came complete with various weighted round-head or stand-up lead jig heads and were packaged in plastic sacks with stapled-on white cards with blue print.

The half-dozen packaged sack of Superminnows trades in the $5 range, if not for collecting yet, for fishing. It is an excellent bait for bottom-feeding bass, pike, and walleye where a finesse delivery system is required.

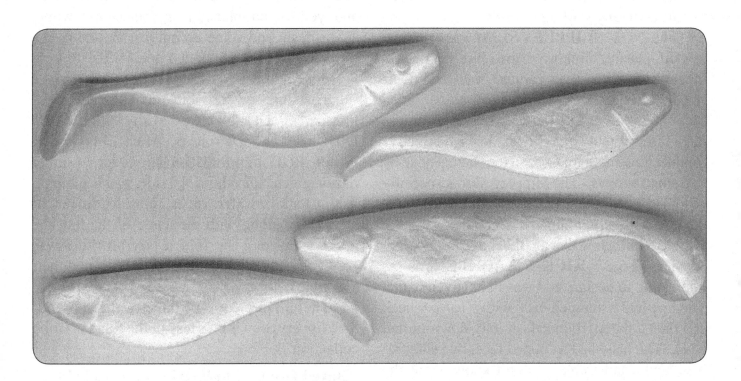

ORCHARD INDUSTRIES, INC.
DETROIT, MICHIGAN

Orchard Industries was founded in 1946 by Lewis D. "Pop" Adam and A. E. Johnson at 18404 Morang Drive, Detroit 5, Michigan. The company's first product was the famous glass **ACTION ROD**, which was very similar in appearance to the Chicago-made "Gep Rod" of the 1920's (Gephart Mfg. Co.). Both companies followed the rod design patented by Joseph Carlson that he developed in 1929 and patented in 1933. In late 1947, Pop Adam teamed up with Nelia G. Poplin, of Ponca City, Oklahoma, and, together, they developed the three lures produced by this company starting in 1948.

The 2-1/2" **SLIPPERY SLIM** was a unique, jointed, plastic, minnow-shaped lure with large, indent eyes with silver painted irises and oversized black pupils. The lure had a slanted-joined section instead of the traditional vertical joint in most lures of that era. The lure had a distinctive rounded nose dive lip fixed to the slanted nose by two small screws. The Slippery Slim's specially designed head plate and knife-edge body gave the lure a slithering minnow action that was irresistible to all game fish at all depths.

The 2-5/8" **KICK-N-KACKLE** was as interesting in design as it was in its given name. The lure had a humped back with a narrow neck and then a flared, rounded, slightly down-turned head. The head had a cupped face, two side trebles, and a tail treble. I don't know about the "Kick", but the lure sure could "Kackle"! The lure made gurgling, popping, blurping, and blooping noises from the end of a cast all the way back to the rod tip. The 2-1/2" **BOTTOM SCRATCHER** had teardrop-shaped silver iris eyes with small black pupils, as opposed to the eyes found on the other two lures. The Bottom Scratcher's nose and chin were both slanted to a point, and the lure had the same dive lip as the Slippery Slim. As the name implied, this was a deep-running lure, up to 8 feet on a normal cast and to 30 feet on a troll. Pop Adam and Nelia Poplin shared Patent No. 2,542,447 granted to them on February 20, 1951, for this lure.

Colors for the three lures included red head with white, red head with yellow, black and yellow, all black, frog, black and white, silver flash, and some colors just as odd as the lure names, such as spotted ape for the Bottom Scratcher and Kick-N-Kackle.

The lures were sold in tall, two-piece transparent plastic boxes with "ORCHARD INDUSTRIES, Detroit 5, Mich...Makers of Action Rod" imprinted on the cover in either red or green. On the right side was a jumping fish just above water waves imprinted in matching colors, along with the name of the lure the box contained. The folded box brochure was very colorful and listed the three lures and their available colors.

The group picture of three of the colors of the Slippery Slim is courtesy of the Randall Cobb collection.

Boxed Orchard Industries lures trade in the $35 to $50 range, with the much scarcer Slippery Slim on the higher end.

ORCHARD INDUSTRIES, INC.

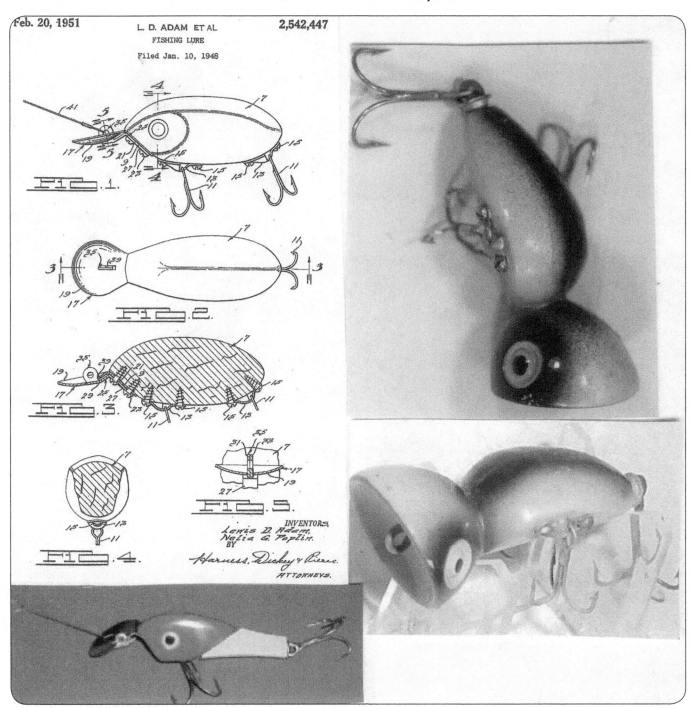

FIG.1.

FIG.2.

FIG.3.

FIG.4.

FIG.5.

INVENTORS.
Lewis D. Adam.
Nelia G. Poplin.
BY

Harness, Dickey & Pierce.
ATTORNEYS.

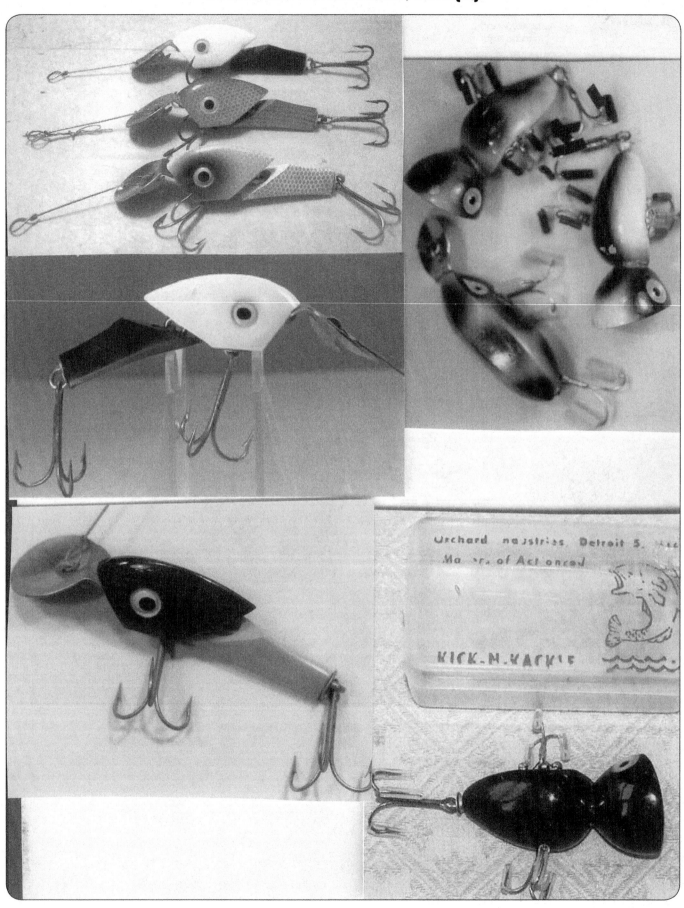

NOW, ORCHARD ANNOUNCES

Slippery Slim

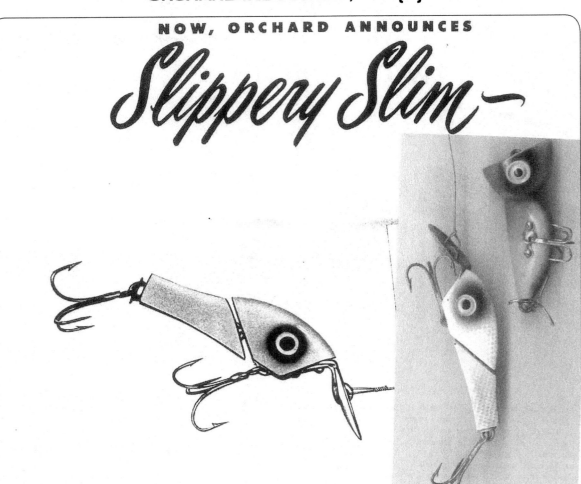

● Here's the weirdest-working bait you've ever seen—Actionrod's new "Slippery Slim."

Specially-designed head plate and knife-edge body lines give "Slim" a slithering minnow action that is irresistible to game fish at any and all depths. Jointed body adds a vicious wiggle on the retrieve—

and without any vibration to your rod tip.

Anchored with two treble hooks. 3⅜" long. Actual weight 9/16 oz. Choice of these six colors:

300-RW (Red and White)
301-SF (Silver Flash)
302-RY (Red Head, Yellow Body)
303-WB (White Head, Black Body)
304-BY (Black Head, Yellow Body)
305-YP (Yellow Perch, Green,
    Black, Gold Scale)

} LIST

Actionrod's famous KICK-N-KACKLE and BOTTOM-SCRATCHER are also available in similar color patterns at the same price.

Every Actionrod bait is packaged in strong, transparent plastic box for attractive display, easy sales.

(Detailed specifications subject to change without notice. Actionrod products are quality protected under Fair Trade laws.)

ORCHARD INDUSTRIES, INC.
18404 Morang Road • Detroit 5, Michigan

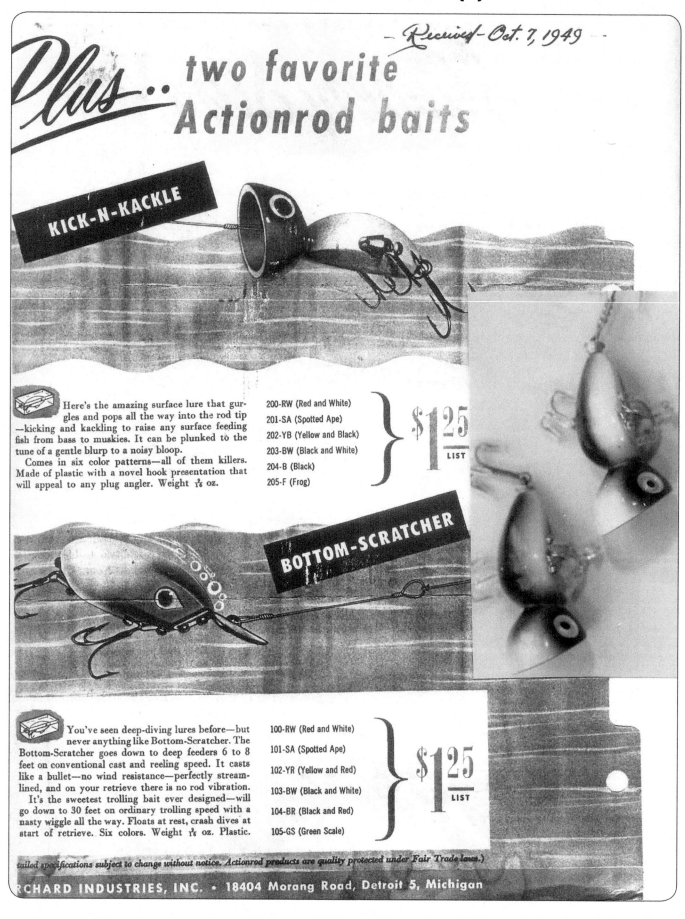

Plus... two favorite Actionrod baits

Received Oct. 7, 1949

KICK-N-KACKLE

Here's the amazing surface lure that gurgles and pops all the way into the rod tip —kicking and kackling to raise any surface feeding fish from bass to muskies. It can be plunked to the tune of a gentle blurp to a noisy bloop.

Comes in six color patterns—all of them killers. Made of plastic with a novel hook presentation that will appeal to any plug angler. Weight ⅝ oz.

200-RW (Red and White)	
201-SA (Spotted Ape)	
202-YB (Yellow and Black)	$1 25
203-BW (Black and White)	LIST
204-B (Black)	
205-F (Frog)	

BOTTOM-SCRATCHER

You've seen deep-diving lures before—but never anything like Bottom-Scratcher. The Bottom-Scratcher goes down to deep feeders 6 to 8 feet on conventional cast and reeling speed. It casts like a bullet—no wind resistance—perfectly streamlined, and on your retrieve there is no rod vibration.

It's the sweetest trolling bait ever designed—will go down to 30 feet on ordinary trolling speed with a nasty wiggle all the way. Floats at rest, crash dives at start of retrieve. Six colors. Weight ⅝ oz. Plastic.

100-RW (Red and White)	
101-SA (Spotted Ape)	
102-YR (Yellow and Red)	$1 25
103-BW (Black and White)	LIST
104-BR (Black and Red)	
105-GS (Green Scale)	

...tailed specifications subject to change without notice. Actionrod products are quality protected under Fair Trade laws.)

RCHARD INDUSTRIES, INC. • 18404 Morang Road, Detroit 5, Michigan

ORIGINAL DOO DAD BAITS
KERRVILLE, TEXAS

Some time in the later 1940's, M. Gray formed his little Original Doo Dad Baits Company in Kerrville, a small Texas town north of San Antonio. He made a 2-1/2" wooden bug-shaped lure he named the **DOO DAD** (pictured in red head with white and in green-gray back with white belly and red side stripes). The lure had washer and screw-eye belly and tail held treble hooks and a metal dive lip that was inserted in a slot cut in the lure's round head at an up-slanted angle. The two-piece cardboard lure box was orange with a heart on the left side of the cover with a fisherman inside landing a fish stream-side.

Another Texas company that dates back well before World War II, that was started in the teens and carried through to the war years and after to the a 1950's, was the Southwestern Fish Tackle Company out of San Antonio. Their "Bingo Mouse" was made almost identically to the Doo Dad, except it had glass eyes.

Lure pictures are courtesy of the Colby R. Sorrells collection.

Boxed Texas Doo Dad lures trade in the $35 to $50 range, sometimes higher.

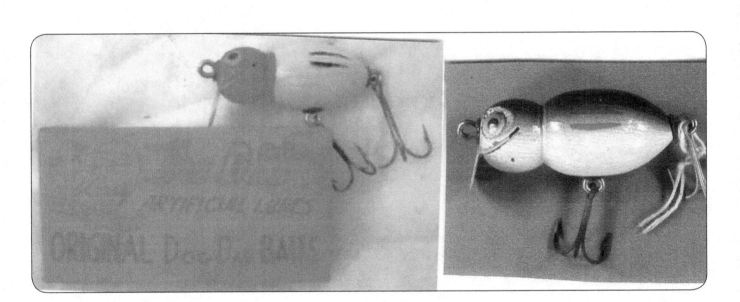

ORLUCK BAIT COMPANY
MINNEAPOLIS, MINNESOTA

Just after World War II, the Orluck Bait Company, of 1421 Park Ave., Minneapolis, Minnesota, introduced the **CRAZY GEORGE** lure. The 5-1/4" plastic lure had a full 1-1/16" diameter. It was advertised as a "two-in-one" fishing lure because it was a casting or trolling plug and a spinner all in one. The spinner was a 1-3/4" flat metal insert with up-turned flaps at the end that caused it to spin inside the body of the main lure. There was a plastic wall at either end to hold the axis for the spinner. The red-headed lure had a clear plastic body that was hollow all the way through. Because of this water-flow system, the lure did not create much drag. The lure had two single free-swinging belly hooks. The lure was sold in a rather plain, one-piece end-flap white box with black print.

Lure made available for photography by the Alan Bakke collection.

Boxed Crazy George trades $45 to $50, and lures alone trade at $25 to $35.

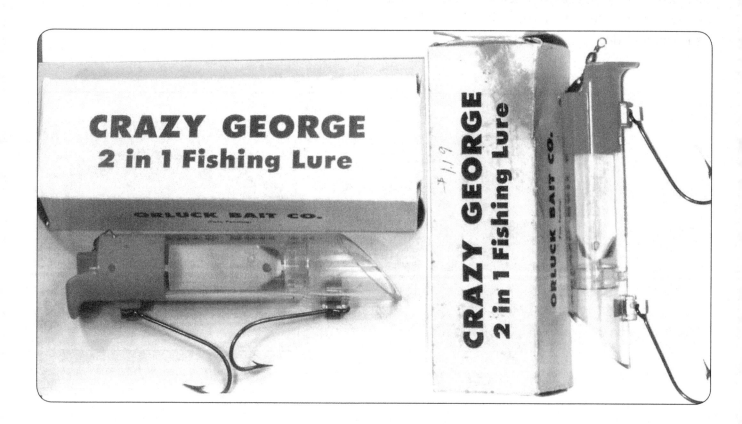

ORMAN'S REELY READY LURES
HARVEY, NORTH DAKOTA

I probably would not normally cover such a simple spinning lure as the 1950's **ORMAN'S TREBLE HOOK SPIN JIG**, but there were so few lure companies ever in this state that I have to cover what I find. The 8-1/2"-overall-long jig-lure consisted of a red, pulsating, plastic finger skirt with several in-line weights and colored plastic beads and a Colorado clevis-

held in-line spinner. The lure was sold on a tan card with blue fish picture graphics and the print "Harvey, North Dakota".

Picture is courtesy of the Steve O'Hern collection.

The carded Orman's spinning and jig combination lures trade in the $5 range.

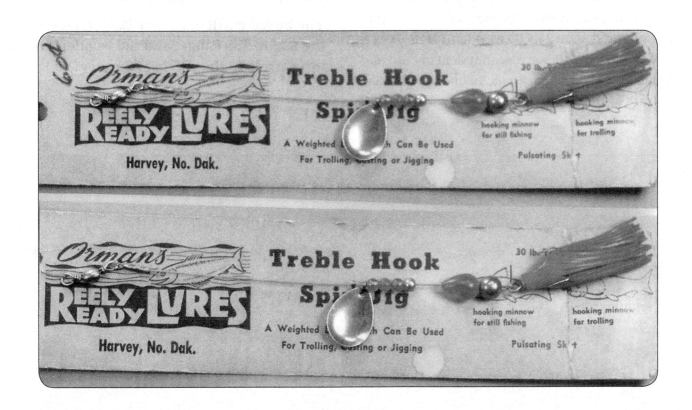

ORR BAIT

TULSA, OKLAHOMA

Kerry Orr started making contemporary folk art type lures in the mid 1980's out of Tulsa, Oklahoma. The little 1-1/8"- and 2-1/16"-long **ORR BASS BUGS** were wooden-body bomb-shaped lures with pointed noses. They had black-bead glass eyes, plastic side flipper feet, and four-wave-shaped-tipped plastic tails. The pictured examples are in a marbled white and red finish and were sold in two-piece white cardboard boxes with yellow borders and blue print. Also pictured is a 2-1/2" wooden **ORR BAIT MINNOW** with glass eyes, an indent carved and painted gill, and a fingertip metal dive lip. Next is the 4-5/8" **ORR FROG** with free-swinging hind

legs secured by a swiveling system and screw-held retaining loops. The 5" **ORR SHRIMP** and jointed **SWIMMIN' BIRD** lures were sold in dove-tail wooden Orr-made boxes. These wood-boxed Orr baits are somewhat scarce, as only between 100 and 150 of these boxes were ever made.

Lure pictures are courtesy of Walter J. Hickerson and Mike Thompson.

The boxed cardboard Orr Baits trade in the $25 to $35 range, and the wooden boxed lures trade in the $35 to $45 range.

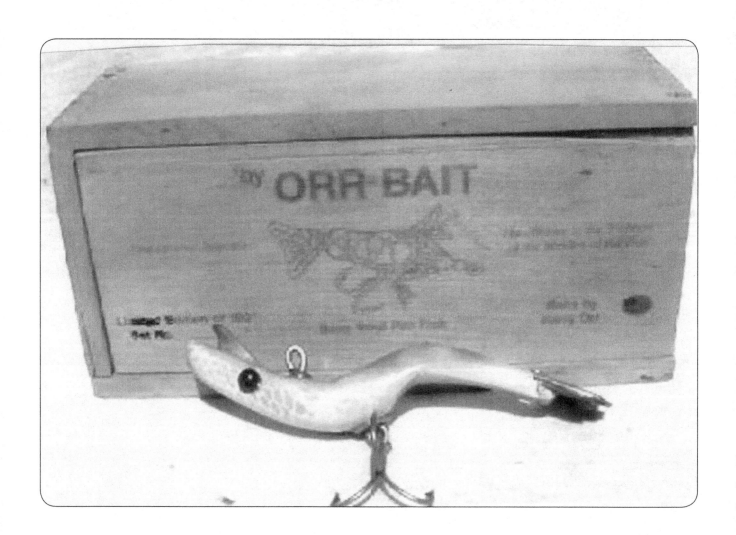

OSPREY LURES
ELIZABETHVILLE, PENNSYLVANIA

The mid- to late-1960's Osprey Lures company, of RD 1, Box 561, Elizabethville, Pennsylvania, was a bit unusual in that, even through they were making their lures out of plastic, they still inserted pretty amber-colored glass eyes in all of their lures. The 2"-long **OSPREY LURE** was similar in shape to the "Layfield" and had a 3/4", flat, rounded-tip metal dive lip inserted and molded in a chin slot. The lures were quality made and were well thought out in their design. The line tie was a through-body wire to the rear belly hook hanger that held a double hook. There was a thin plastic extension tab near the tail, and the fisherman could push the split in the double hook up into that tab, making the lure semi-weedless until a fish pulled the hook down (the lure bag also contained a split ring and a small treble hook as an alternate option).

The lure was sold in a plastic bag that was stapled to a red and yellow card with a pictured osprey in flight, along with lure name, company name, and address.

The Osprey lures were stamped on the div lips "SS" for slow sinking or "FS" for fast sinking. The basic difference in the two models was that the fast-sinking lure had two shallow holes drilled in each side and a small lead weight inserted in a third hole between the other two. Lure colors were marbled red, black, green, yellow, white, or brown.

In the group picture, the two lures on the left have the hooks down in the catch position, and the two on the right are up in the semi-weedless position. The lure at the bottom is a fast sinker, and all of the rest are slow sinkers.

The carded Osprey Lures trade in the $10 range to sometimes $15.

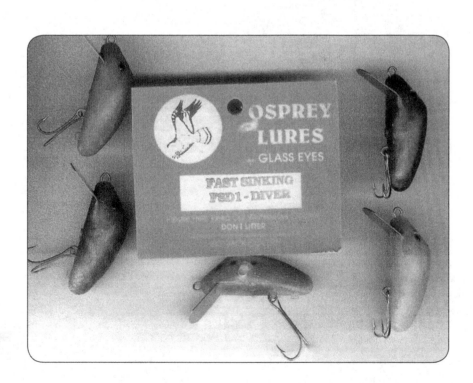

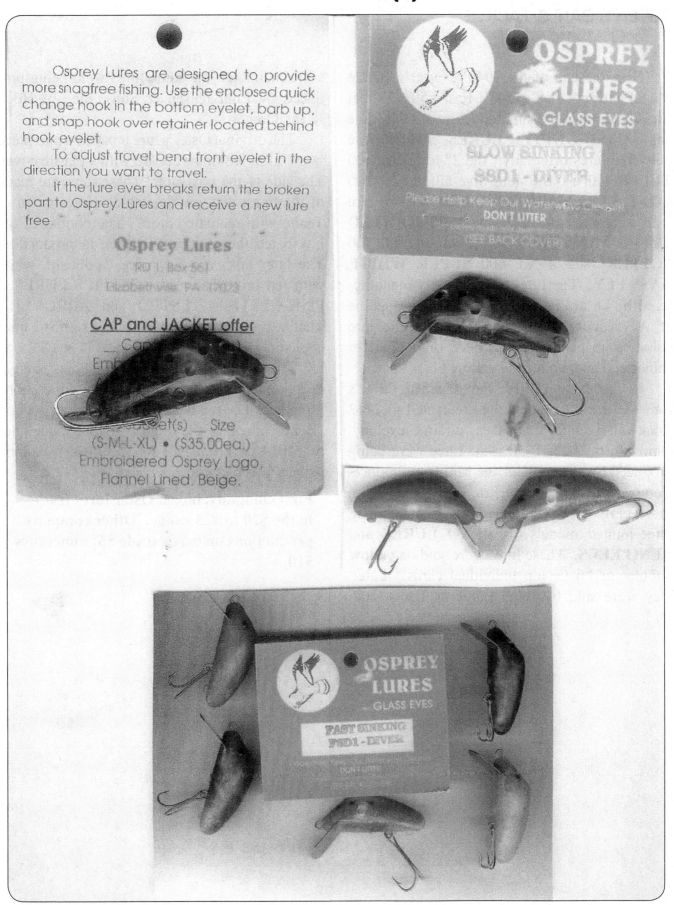

Osprey Lures are designed to provide more snagfree fishing. Use the enclosed quick change hook in the bottom eyelet, barb up, and snap hook over retainer located behind hook eyelet.

To adjust travel bend front eyelet in the direction you want to travel.

If the lure ever breaks return the broken part to Osprey Lures and receive a new lure free.

Osprey Lures
RD 1, Box 561
Elizabethville, PA 17023

CAP and JACKET offer

Cap
Embr
A

Jacket(s) __ Size
(S-M-L-XL) • ($35.00ea.)
Embroidered Osprey Logo,
Flannel Lined, Beige.

OSTER'S TACKLE MANUFACTURING
OSTER'S BAIT & TACKLE
CLEVELAND, OHIO

Near the end of the 1940's, Oster's Tackle Manufacturing, of 1241 East 59th Street Cleveland, Ohio, began production of their trade name "**FISH-GETTER LURES**." There were only five lures originally: the 2"-long No. 400 **TUFFE** with a 1-1/2"-long dive-bill; the No 200 **LONE STREAMER**, a lead-head hair-tail lure with a ponca type blade; No. 300 **JOINTED TUFFE MINNOW**; a short, stumpy No. 500 **POPPER**; and a No. 600 **SUPER WHITE BASS FLY**. The lures were actually manufactured by an affiliate company, Landis Machine of Waynesboro, Pennsylvania. The Tuffe lure colors were perch, green shiner, orange, silver shiner, red and white, and yellow-black spot.

In the early 1950's, the renamed Oster's Bait & Tackle Company had relocated to 2112 Rockwell Avenue, but this was still in Cleveland, Ohio. In the later 1950's, the lures were being produced by new owners, the Mill Run Products Company of 634 Huron Rd., Cleveland, Ohio, in several new styles, including four-segment, three-jointed models, as **BENO LURES** and **BENO EELS**. These lures were sold on yellow bubble- or blister-top individual cards. Later, they were sold by Beno Lures of Texas, and,

still much later, the same lures were being produced by Luhr-Jensen & Sons, Inc., of Hood River, Oregon.

The original Oster's lure box was a one-piece wood-grain-color cardboard with a plastic cover. The side of the box said, "These lures are made of the finest material available. Constructed of Tenite with realistic color." The bottom of the box listed the four models then in production. The later box was one-piece cardboard, white with red print that read, "OSTER'S LURES… FISH-GETTER…TESTED and ARROVED." That box with the overall 3"-long Lone Streamer is pictured.

The second set of pictures includes straight and jointed Tuffe minnows, plus the Lone Streamer. The red head with white, four-section "Beno" is one of the larger versions made later by Mill Run Products. A 1953 Oster's catalog page is also pictured.

First company, boxed Oster lures trade in the $20 to $25 range. Other company productions on cards trade $5, sometimes $10.

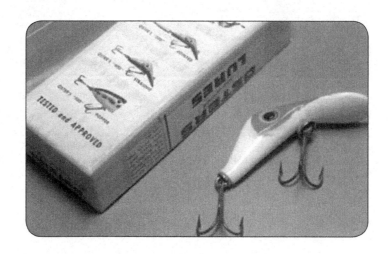

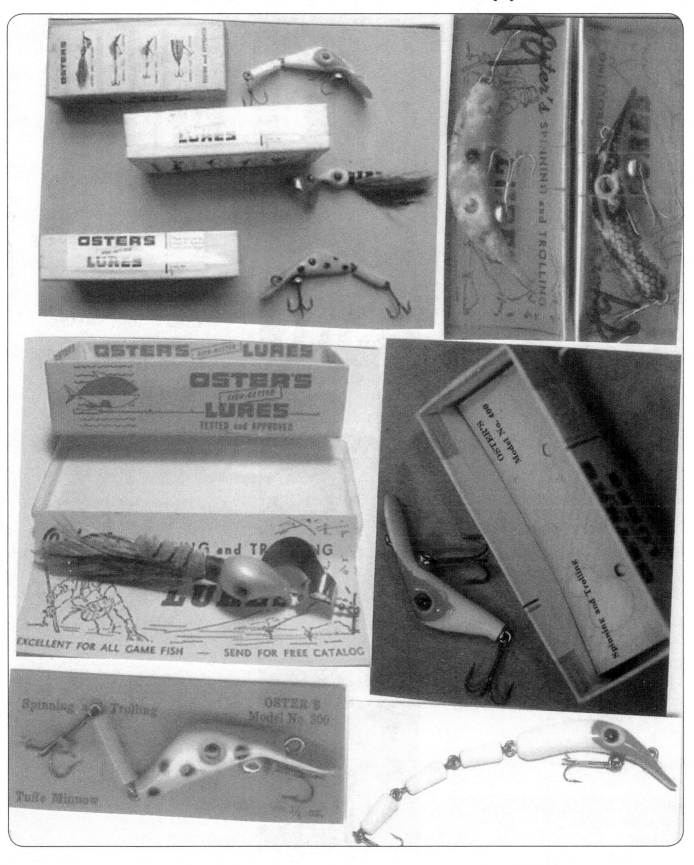

Fish-getting Power with inning Lures

OSTER'S STRAIGHT "TUFFE MINNOW"

Mod. 400

Wt. ¼ oz.
$1.10

400 P		Perch
401	GS	Green shiner
402	OR	Orange
403	SSh	Silver shiner
404	RW	Red and white
405	YBs	Yellow-black spot

Boxed 6 each or asst'd

SUPER WHITE BASS FLY

No. 600 RW
601 RY

2 Doz. on card 20c Each.

THE IDEAL LURES TO MEET THE EVER INCREASING
DEMAND IN SPINNING. A COMPLETE SELECTION
OF SPINNING LURES FOR ALL TYPES OF FISHING.
JUST THE RIGHT WEIGHT AND ACTION. PACKED
IN ATTRACTIVE WINDOW BOXES.

SOLD THROUGH JOBBERS ONLY.

TER'S
ACKLE MFG.
well Avenue
) 14, OHIO

Here is PROOF o

Oster's S

OSTER'S "LONE STREAMER"

Mod. 200

Wt. ¼ oz.
Price $1.00 ea.

		Head	Feather
200	YY	Yellow	Yellow
201	BG	Black	Gray
202	WB	White	Black
203	RW	Red	White
204	YBr	Yellow	Brown
205	RY	Red	Yellow

Boxed 6 each or asst'd

OSTER'S JOINTED "TUFFE MINNOW"

Mod. 300

Wt. ¼ oz.
$1.25

300	P	Perch
301	GS	Green shiner
302	OR	Orange
303	SSh	Silver shiner
304	RW	Red and white
305	YBs	Yellow-black spot

Boxed 6 each or asst'd

Constructed of Tenite in realistic colors.

OSTROWSKY, ZIGGY
MILWAUKEE, WISCONSIN

Ziggy Ostrowsky was an early Milwaukee artisan who deserved more credit than he ever received during the 1930's and 1940's when he made fishing-related carvings. He is best known for his **FISH PLAQUES**, which were carved and painted in great detail, as well as his **ICE FISHING DECOYS**. Ostrowsky sold his carvings by word of mouth and by traveling the local tavern and restaurant circuits, trading his work for food and drinks. He carved numerous fish species and mounted them on thin furniture paneling or just about any scrap of wood he could find.

A few years ago, his 6" **MUSKIE PLAQUE** traded for $650. Pictured are a couple of other ones, a 9" salmon type and a 14-1/2" sail fish type, that were some of his later creations in the early 1950's. He did make a few fishing lures as well. Pictured is a very rare 5-3/4" **ZIGGY JOINTED FISH** that had red-painted screw heads for eyes, a carved forked fish tail, and all-metal hardware that was made by Ostrowsky. The lure had a hand-made etched-in scale pattern and was painted in a brown-silver finish.

I don't know how many fishing lures Ziggy Ostrowsky made, but this one is valued at around $200.

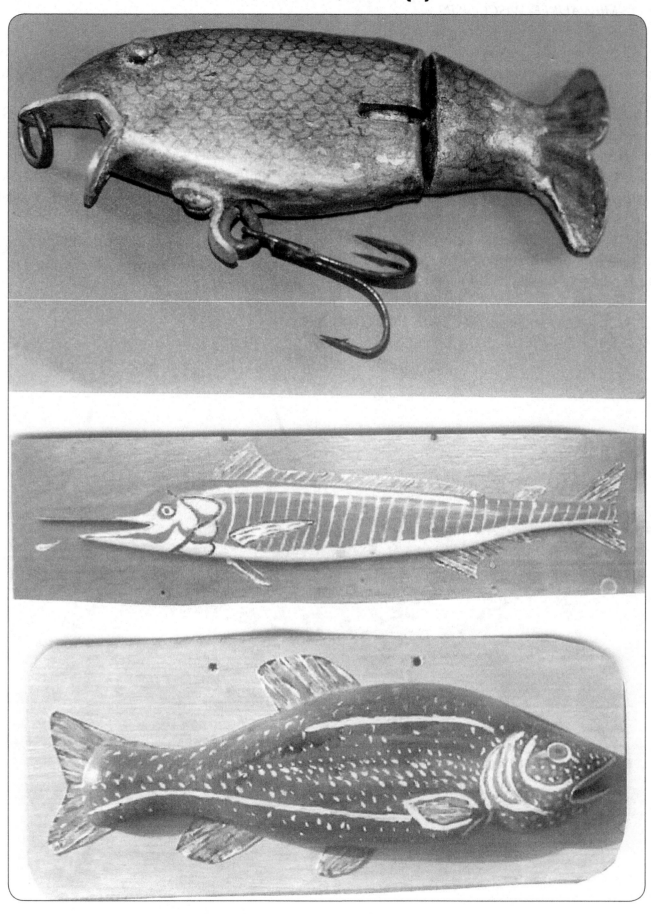

OTT, MIKE
PINE RIVER, MINNESOTA

Mike Ott (born March 27, 1955) grew up in the Minneapolis area and, as a kid, became an avid fisherman. His early fishing years were spent on Medicine, Eagle, and Bass Lakes in New Hope and Plymouth, Minnesota. After a chance meeting with Bruce Dixon of Backus, Minnesota, and other Minnesota ice fishing decoy carvers, he started making carved dolphins, jig sticks, and spearing decoys in 1990. Bruce Dixon, considered to be one of Minnesota's beast decoy carvers, became Ott's mentor, and they spent many hours together field testing on Minnesota waters the lures and decoys that were made by Mike. Most of Mike Ott's lures and spearing decoys are made out of white pine wood. He uses old metal hardware found on beat up lures of the past, and he hand paints all of his creations using acrylic paints, never using an air brush. The final touch for Mike's fish is several coats of polyurethane or classic auto finish.

Mike is somewhat famous for his **CRAPPIE ICE FISHING DECOYS**, made in sizes 2-1/2" to a whopping 13-1/2", that are considered by many to be the most realistic Crappie Decoys ever made. In fact, Mike Ott has been featured in several newspaper, magazine and, book publications, including the Lakes County Journal and North Country Brainerd Daily Dispatch and books Fish Decoy Makers Past & Present by Donald J. Peterson and The Fish Decoy by Art Kimball. Mervin C. Eisel, in an article about Mike Ott for the Lake County Journal magazine, wrote, "Iridescent and pearlescent colors infuse life into Mike Ott's spear-fishing decoys and illustrates the artist's evolution." Mike's carved ice fishing decoys are extremely realistic and painted in very true-to-life color patterns. His decoys include bluegills crappies, perch, catfish, trout, and other species, and the same holds true for his fishing lures. Although I have never in my life been a spear fisherman, the thing that most impresses me about Mike's ice fishing decoys

is that they are not just folk art wall hangers. They are "working decoys", perfectly balanced with lead belly weights, and are designed to swim true.

The first picture is a group photo of some of Mike Ott's ice fishing decoys.

In the second set of pictures, at the top is a 4-1/8"-long wood **OTT CRAPPIE LURE** with a carved raised gill plate, open mouth, and a detailed painted crappie scale pattern. Just behind the gill plate, Mike has installed flush brass cups that hold a cross-body wire with split rings on each side of the lure holding smaller size treble hooks, with another screw eye treble hook at the tail. The fish has painted eyes with yellow irises and black dot center pupils and an under-the-chin finger-type two-screw-held dive lip. There are four small lead belly weights to make the lure swim at the correct attitude in the water. Next is one of his first 4-1/4"-long **SWIMMING FISH ICE DECOYS**. This wooden fish had a carved and curved tail, a carved raised gill plate, and an open mouth. The lure has small glass eyes with yellow irises, a metal back line tie, metal raised dorsal and pectoral fins, and metal side stabilizer fins. The front fins are 2-3/8" wide, and the rear fins are 1-1/4" wide. The decoy is finished in old boat green paint over a basic dark brown color in irregular sized spots. The oval-shaped lead belly weight is marked with Mike's initials, "M. O." These two lure and decoy pictures are courtesy of the Steve O'Hern collection. Below these two pictures are two of Mike's Critter Lures and a Trout Decoy.

The next set of pictures includes ice fishing decoys: a Toothy Northern, a Realistic Bluegill, a Flashy Sunfish, and other fish species. To the right is Mike's version of a Mermaid Lure and two of his famous ice fishing jig poles.

The last set of pictures has a group of decoys, lures, and a curved jig pole. Note Mike's version of the Pflueger "Kent Floating Frog" and

the famous Howard "Pop" Dean 7-1/2" "Dean Bull Frog" that Pop made in 1957. The last picture, taken in 1999, is of Mike Ott hard at work in his workshop.

Mike currently lives just outside of Pine River, Minnesota, with his wife, Diane, and their son, Eric.

Mike Ott's lures trade in the $75 to $100 range, and his ice fishing decoys trade in the $50 to $200 range normally, but there have been trades up to $400.

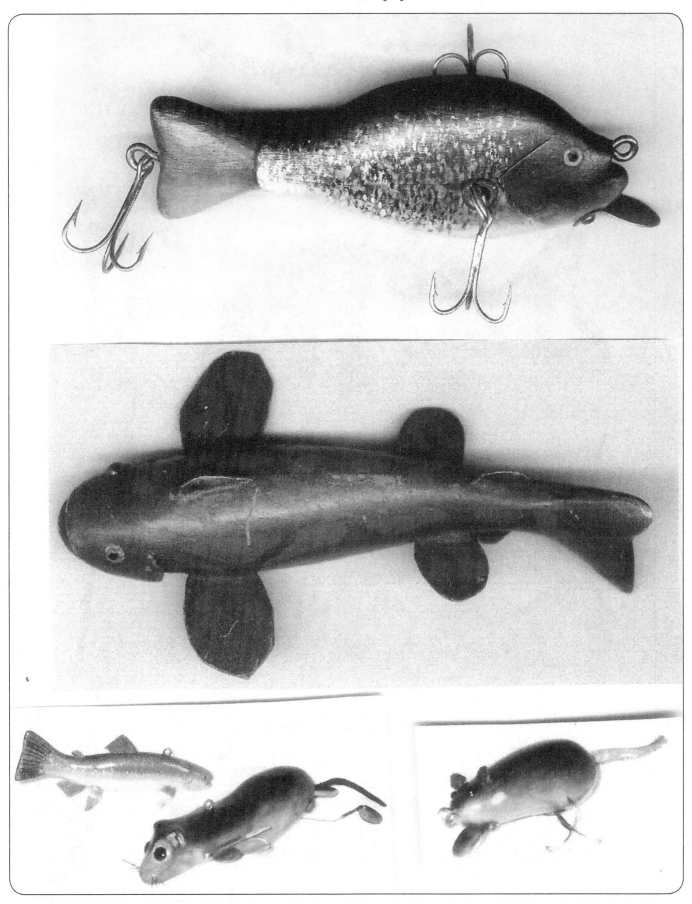

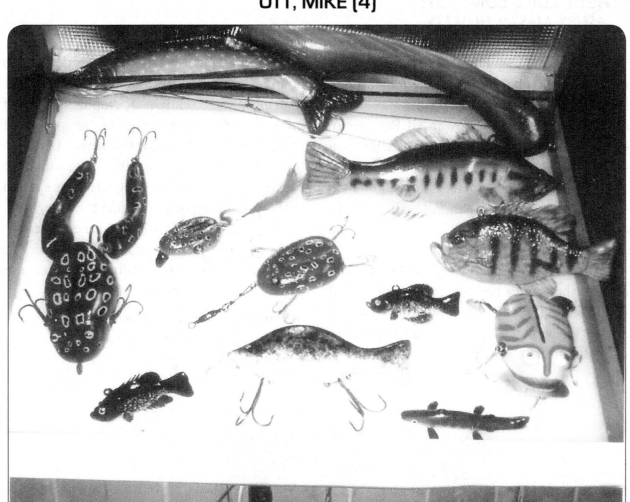

OTTERGET LURE COMPANY
ASHBY, MASSACHUSETTS

In 1959, a man of Finnish descent, known locally as "Aho The Finn", started making a heavy 1/2-ounce lure primarily for land-lock salmon. Eino K. Aho was awarded Patent No. 3,145,497 for his **OTTERGET LURE** on August 25, 1964, in this country and Patent No. 643,499 in Canada. Eino K. Aho established his Otterget Lure Company at P. O. Box 123 in Ashby, Massachusetts, in 1958 and made the lures for approximately four years.

The lure was designed to be a slow rolling action lure that could be cast, trolled, or jigged and was double tapered at both ends with a dimple in the center with each end cupped in opposite directions.

The lures were sold eight to a dealer display board. The board unfolded to an open position to display some really neat graphics. Most of the print was green with evergreen trees on the shore of waters in the background with an otter in the foreground holding a small salmon in its mouth. The lure name, "OTTER LURE" was spelled out with brown twigs cut to shape the lettering.

In the picture with the green background showing eight different color OTTERGET lures, you can see Eino Aho holding a stringer of three small salmon in the background.

A full dealer board with all eight lures trades in the $35 to $50 range.

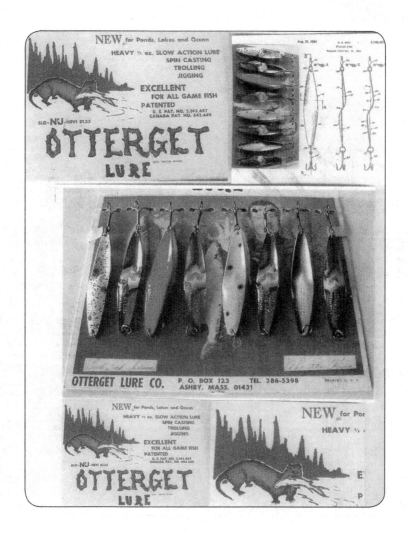

OUSLEY, BOB
HOMESTEAD, FLORIDA

Bob Ousley, who was located at 32800 S.W. 202 Avenue in Homestead, Florida, introduced a neat baby snook minnow in the 1970's. The 3-3/4"-long **SNOOK MINNOW**, made in weights of either 3/8 or 3/4 oz., was actually made in the shape of a yearling snook minnow. The lure had a large round wire loop line tie at the nose that continued on through the lure's wooden body and out of the tail, forming another loop for the tail treble hook. Ousley used one of two different methods for attaching the belly treble hook. One, the most common, was a barrel swivel that was interlocked with the through body wire shaft, and the other method utilized a double eye connector that was 1/2" long and also locked into the through body wire. His lures have indent carved gill plate lines painted red and inserted glass eyes with red-orange irises. There were several lure colors, including silver scale, natural green back with silver scale, and yellow with black and red spots. (The latter two color finishes are pictured.) The lures were equipped with galvanized coated 3X treble hooks to prevent saltwater corrosion. Bob Ousley sold his lures in zip lock plastic bags with ID card inserts and papers that had actual black and white pictures of his lures with "use" instructions.

Plastic sacked Bob Ousley Snook Minnows trade in the $15 to $20 range.

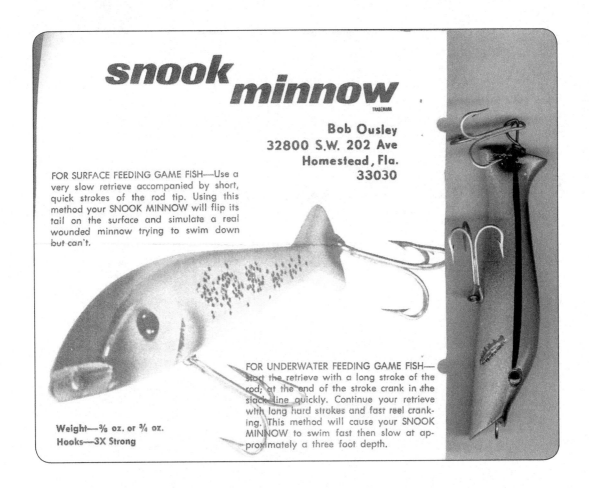

snook minnow TRADEMARK

Bob Ousley
32800 S.W. 202 Ave
Homestead, Fla.
33030

FOR SURFACE FEEDING GAME FISH—Use a very slow retrieve accompanied by short, quick strokes of the rod tip. Using this method your SNOOK MINNOW will flip its tail on the surface and simulate a real wounded minnow trying to swim down but can't.

FOR UNDERWATER FEEDING GAME FISH—Start the retrieve with a long stroke of the rod; at the end of the stroke crank in the slack line quickly. Continue your retrieve with long hard strokes and fast reel cranking. This method will cause your SNOOK MINNOW to swim fast then slow at approximately a three foot depth.

Weight—⅜ oz. or ¾ oz.
Hooks—3X Strong

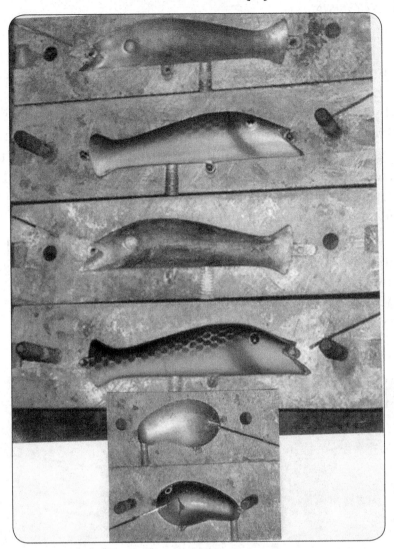

OUTERS LABORATORIES, INC.
ONALASKA, WISCONSIN

Outers produced a neat **REELSLICK CASTER'S KIT** in the 1930's inOnalaska, Wisconsin. The "De Luxe Assortment" kit was packaged in a 4-1/2" by 8" tin, flip-cover hinged red box. The reel and rod-tender kit included the following: Ferrule Cement, Reelslick, Dry Fly Oil, Line Dressing, Reel Oil, Rod Varnish, and a 6" long four-way Outer's Combination Tool.

There were at least a half dozen companies that developed spot-locators for fishermen to aid them in being able to return to a new found "hot-spot" fishing hole. The **OUTER'S LOCATOR** was one of the early ones. It consisted of a black metal wheel with all points of the com-

pass marked. There were three different adjustable spotting arms for the fisherman to line up with distant shore objects and then write down the compass point readings. (I never used any of these devices back in those days, but I doubt they were any more effective than good ole' "dead reckoning".) The Outer's Locator was sold in an aluminum hinged box with a set of waterproof instructions.

The boxed complete kit trades in the $20 to $25 range. The Outer's Locator trades in $10 to $15 range.

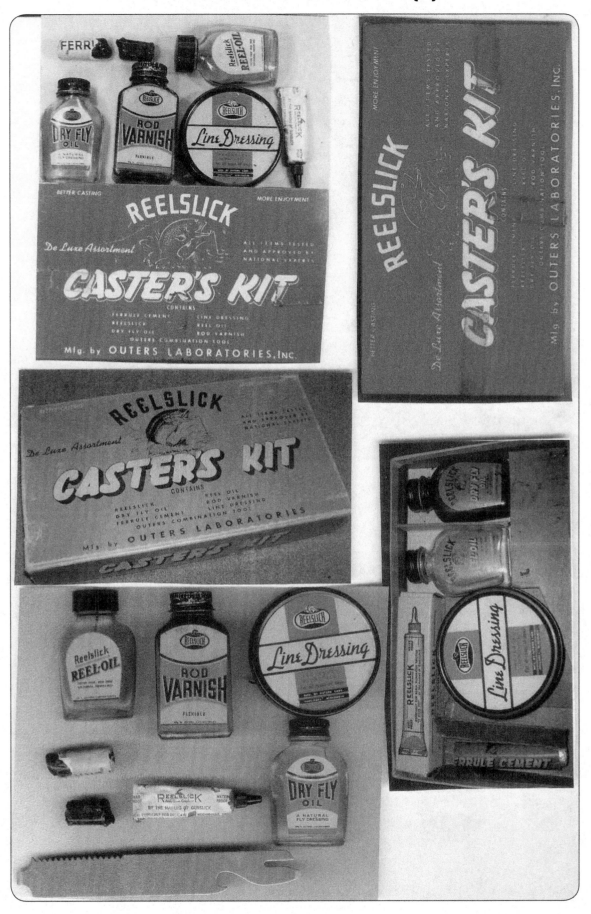

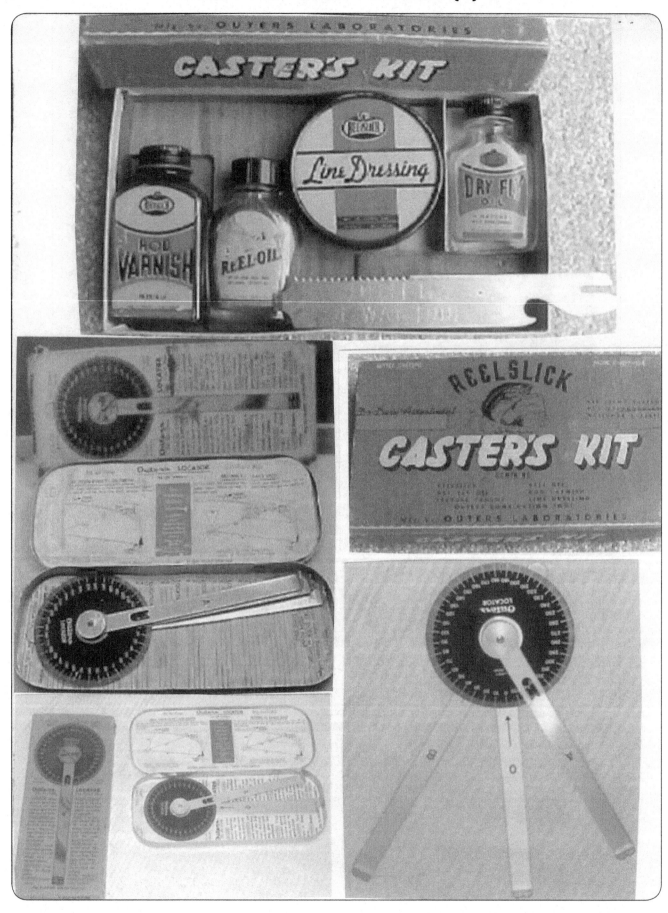

OUTING MANUFACTURING COMPANY
ELKHART, INDIANA

Clarence L. Dewey started the Outing Manufacturing Company sometime in 1923 and designed some, if not all, of their lures. In its short lifetime, from 1923 to 1927, Dewey's company produced six different hollow metal lures as well as several lures designed to be used with pork rind. The company also produced crow, owl, duck, and goose decoys, outdoor folding tables, rods and reels, and the famous metal "OUTING tackle box", which was the reason the Heddon Company acquired Outing in 1927. The company developed a distinctive trademark. At first, it was a triangle with an evergreen tree in the center and said "OUTING" and "MFG. CO." on each side. Later, the trademark was changed to a jumping fish in the center and with "ELKHART, INDIANA" added to the bottom of the triangle.

The Series 700 3 1/8", 3/4-oz. and Series 750 2-3/4", 1/2-oz. **DU-GETUM** lures were almost totally weedless and good hooking surface lures. They were made in six early colors: No.26, Grass Frog (white and green); No. 36, Bull Frog (yellow and green); No. 46, Field Mouse (white and gray); No. 56, Water Bug (gray and brown); No. 66, Doodle Bug (white and red); and No. 76, Nite Bug (black and red). Later on, another color was added: red and aluminum. The lure is pictured in the lures' first, rare picture box that had the above first six colors listed on the side of the box, along with the early trademark described above. Also pictured is the red and aluminum Du-Getum in the more generic Outing box, which was red with mustard color print inside of a blued area.

The Series 1200 3-7/8", 5/8-oz. **BASSY GETUM** was another hollow bronze, celluloid colored lure in the series. It was also offered in six colors, and box papers said, "Just use the dark colors for light days and the light colors for dark days." (This is kind of the opposite philosophy of today's bass fishermen.)

The Series 1000 3-5/8", 1/2-oz. **PIKY GETUM** was finished in nine different celluloid colors. The Piky Getum was made in two halves marine glued together. There was a down-turned nose flange with a ring-rivet through it holding an adjustable nose piece. This metal nose piece could be turned up or down slightly as a different depth planer.

The last in the line of the hollow bronze lures is also the rarest: the Series 400 **FLOATER GETUM** made in a 2-7/8", 1/2-oz. size. The lure is pictured in its rare intro picture box, listing, at that time, its four color choices. Later, five more colors were added. Clarence L. Dewey was awarded Patent No. 1,608,375 on November 23, 1926, for this 1924-developed lure.

The company also produced four pork rind type lures. The Series 500 **PORKY GETUM** was in three sizes and initially four colors. The plastic body lure had external metal washer type eyes, a metal nose lip with weedguards, and a single tail hook with an in-shaft smaller pork rind keeper hook.

The Series 600 **FEATHER GETUM** was also made in three sizes and four basic colors. The lure was basically the same lure as the 500 but had a leather fin and tail feather, designed to be fished without pork rind. The lure is pictured in its intro picture box that, with differences in body, leather fin, and feather tail colors, listed thirteen different colors. The Feather Getum received Patent No. 1.568,325 on January 5, 1926, which Dewey had applied for in May of 1923.

The Series 800 **BUCKY GETUM** was made in three sizes and six colors and had a feather tail and could be fished with or without a pork rind trailer.

The 900 Series **LUCKY GETUM** was made in three sizes and six colors and was a bucktail lure without weedguards.

I have pictured a page from a 1920's catalog showing some of the company's other product lines.

Boxed lure pictures courtesy of the Randy Nelson and Bob "Robbie" Pavey collections.

In collecting the hollow body Outing lures, there is a wide range in trade values because of condition. The paint on these lures had a tendency to chip off of the tail, dorsal, and pectoral fins fairly easily. Also, for a company that was in business for such a short time, they did develop several lure box types, which can also affect trade values.

Outing lures in intro picture boxes are rare and trade in the $600 to $1,000 range. Outing lures in the later generic red and blue boxes are still very scarce and trade in the $350 to $500 range. The Porky and Feather Getum lure types trade lower, in the $50 to $100 range. I will have to admit that these trade values were what I was familiar with fifteen and twenty years ago. I have not seen a lot of trading in these lures in recent times, but, based on how all lure trade values have nose dived, I suspect that today's value are much lower than quoted above.

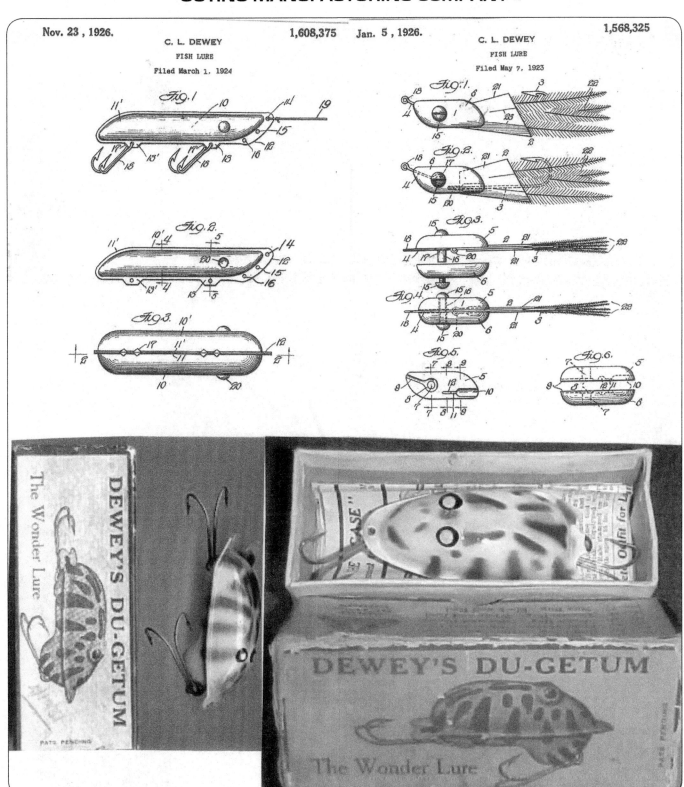

Nov. 23, 1926.

C. L. DEWEY

FISH LURE

Filed March 1, 1924

1,608,375

Jan. 5, 1926.

C. L. DEWEY

FISH LURE

Filed May 7, 1923

1,568,325

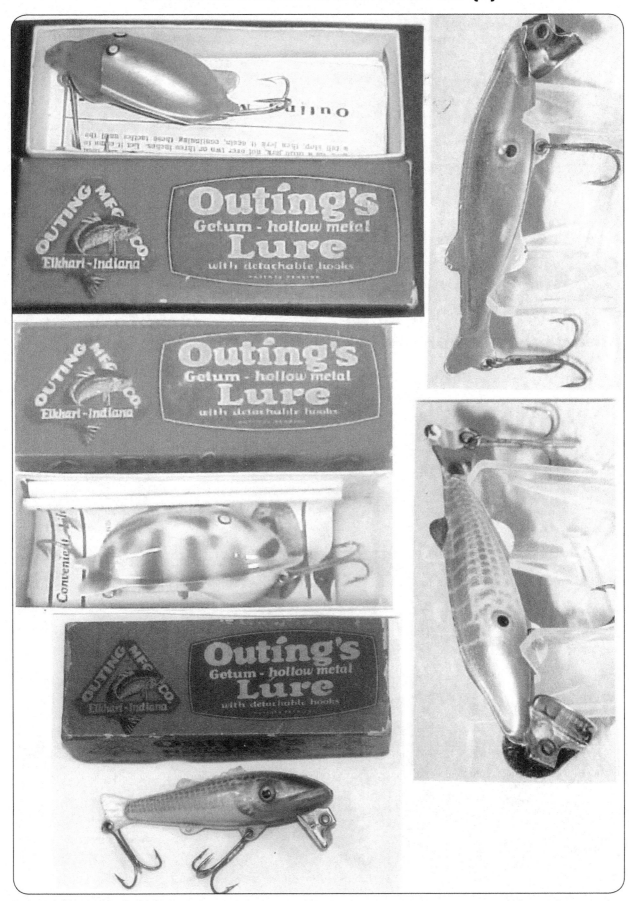

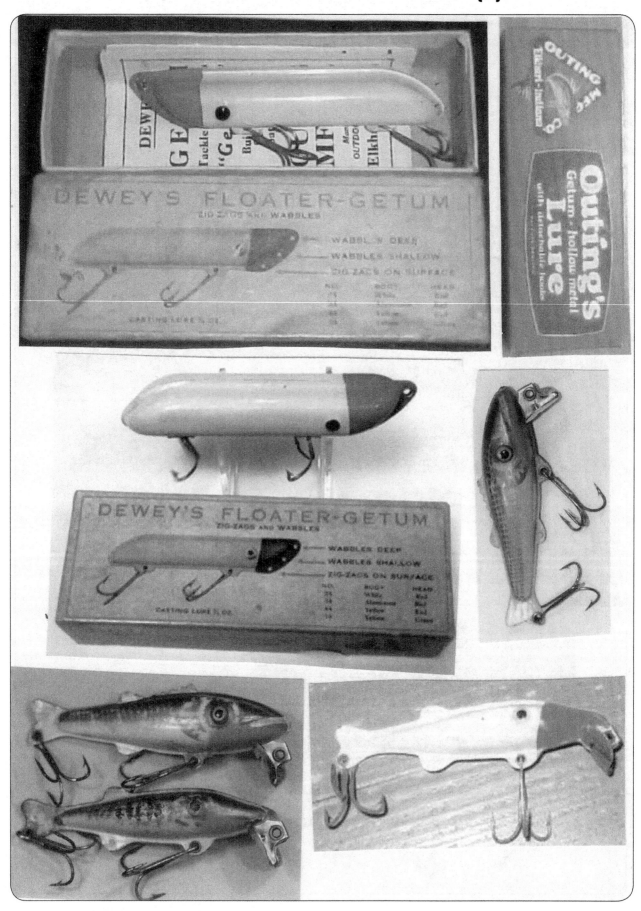

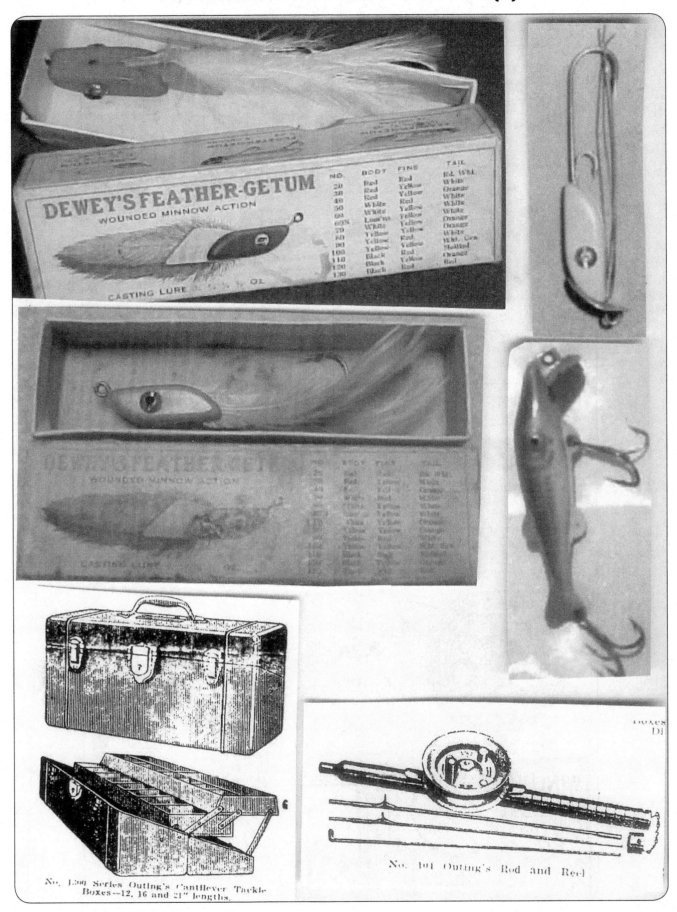

NO.	BODY	FINE	TAIL
20	Red	Red	Rd. Wht.
30	Red	Yellow	White
40	Red	Red	Orange
50	White	Yellow	White
60	White	Yellow	White
60X	Lou'na	Yellow	Orange
70	White	Yellow	Orange
80	Yellow	Red	White
90	Yellow	Red	Wht. Grn.
100	Yellow	Yellow	Nabind
110	Black	Red	Orange
120	Black	Yellow	Red
130	Black	Red	

DEWEY'S FEATHER-GETUM

WOUNDED MINNOW ACTION

CASTING LURE

No. 1300 Series Outing's Cantilever Tackle Boxes—12, 16 and 21" lengths.

No. 101 Outing's Rod and Reel

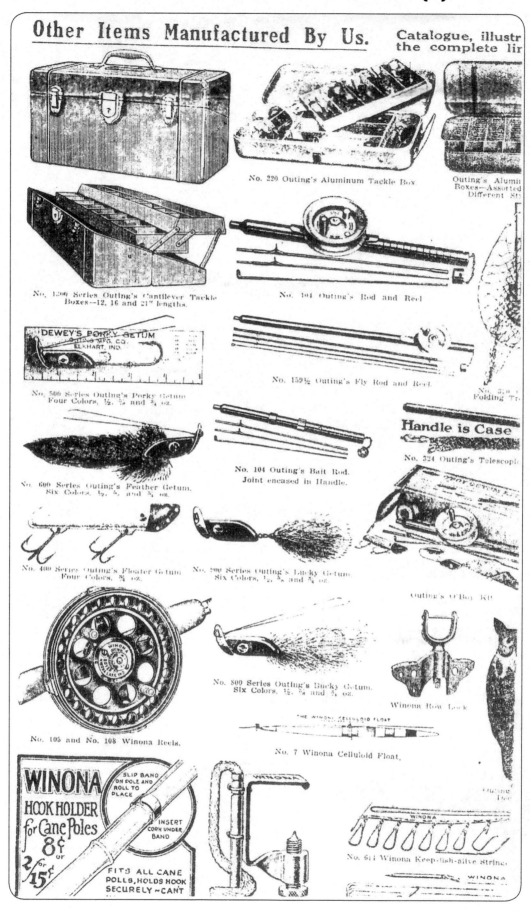

Other Items Manufactured By Us.

Catalogue, illustr the complete lir

No. 220 Outing's Aluminum Tackle Box

Outing's Alumin Boxes—Assorted Different St

No. 1300 Series Outing's Cantilever Tackle Boxes—12, 16 and 21″ lengths.

No. 104 Outing's Rod and Reel

DEWEY'S PORKY GETUM

No. 159½ Outing's Fly Rod and Reel

No. 3,0 Folding Tr

No. 506 Series Outing's Porky Getum Four Colors, ½, ⅝ and ¾ oz.

Handle is Case

No. 324 Outing's Telescopi

No. 104 Outing's Bait Rod. Joint encased in Handle.

No. 600 Series Outing's Feather Getum. Six Colors, ½, ⅝ and ¾ oz.

No. 400 Series Outing's Floater Getum Four Colors, ¾ oz.

No. 900 Series Outing's Lucky Getum Six Colors, ½, ⅝ and ¾ oz.

Outing's O'Boy Kit

No. 800 Series Outing's Bucky Getum. Six Colors, ½, ⅝ and ¾ oz.

Winona Row Lock

No. 105 and No. 108 Winona Reels.

No. 7 Winona Celluloid Float.

WINONA HOOK HOLDER for Cane Poles 8¢ or 2 for 15¢

SLIP BAND ON POLE AND ROLL TO PLACE
INSERT CORK UNDER BAND

FITS ALL CANE POLLS, HOLDS HOOK SECURELY ~CANT

No. 611 Winona Keep-fish-alive String

OVERLANDER SPORTS
YELLOWKNIFE, NORTHWEST TERRITORIES, CANADA

A fishing tackle supplier and complete outdoor travel and fishing trip outfitter by the name of Overland Sports, located at 4909 50th Street in Yellowknife, Northwest Territories, has a colorful advertising spoon that they distribute. The 3-1/2" and 5" spoon sizes have the name "**YELLOWKNIFE**" printed on their backs. The spoons are finished in blends of blue, green, gold, orange, and brown marbled colors. The curved-S-shaped spoons were contract made for this company by the Len Thompson Bait Company out of Lacombe, Alberta, Canada.

The Yellowknife souvenir/advertising spoons currently trade in the $5 range.

OWENS LURES
ALAMOGORDO, NEW MEXICO

The 2-1/2" **OWENS-BUG** was produced at P. O. Box 971, Alamogordo, New Mexico, in the summer of 1960. The body of the lure was a 1-1/4"-diameter round wooden ball with an inserted 1-3/4" metal dive lip in a cut nose slot, which made up the bulk of the lure. The thin metal dive lip itself was 1-3/4" wide at the nose tip with a three-hump wave design on the front leading edge. The lure body had two string side feeler-feet on each side, and the leading edge of the dive lip had large, painted eyes with yellow irises and tiny red dot pupils. The lure was made with a single belly treble hook held by a through body cotter pin with the tips bent and painted over on the back of the ball body. That lure is pictured in black and white and in all red colors. A second lure made by Emmett Owens was his 3-1/2"-overall-long **OWENS-BIG BILL**. This lure consisted of a 1-3/4"-long, carrot-shaped wooden body with a pointed nose with a deep-set, 2-1/2"-long metal nose dive lip. This metal lip extended out in front of the body by another 1-1/4" and was made in the same shape as the Bug Lure dive lip, with the three-hump wave design at the leading edge, and had the same type painted eyes.

The Bug lure had a tiny cotter pin line tie in the metal nose, and the Big Bill had a Luxon line connector. These two lure types were awarded Design Patent No. D190,177 on April 25, 1961, to Emmett B. Owens.

The Owens-Bug and Big Bill trade in the $10 to $15 range.

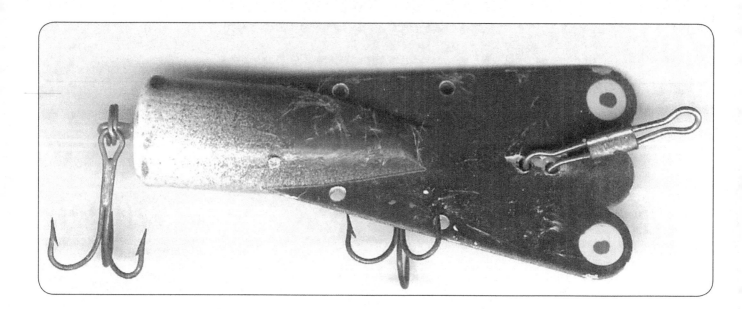

United States Patent Office

Des. 190,177
Patented Apr. 25, 1961

190,177
FISHING LURE
Emmett B. Owens, P.O. Box 971, Alamogordo, N. Mex.
Filed Mar. 9, 1960, Ser. No. 59,681
Term of patent 14 years
(Cl. D31—4)

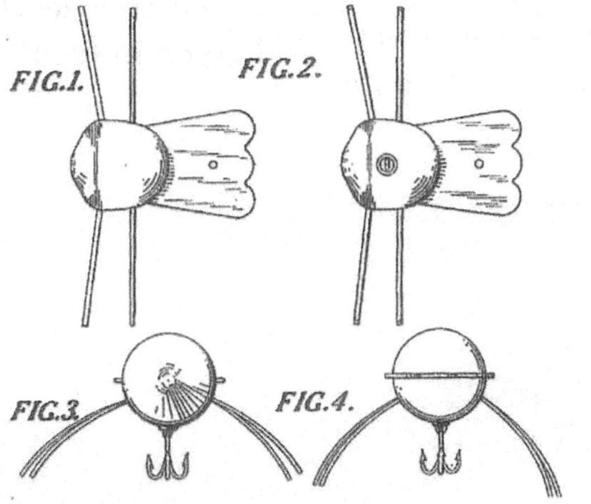

FIG.1. FIG.2.

FIG.3. FIG.4.

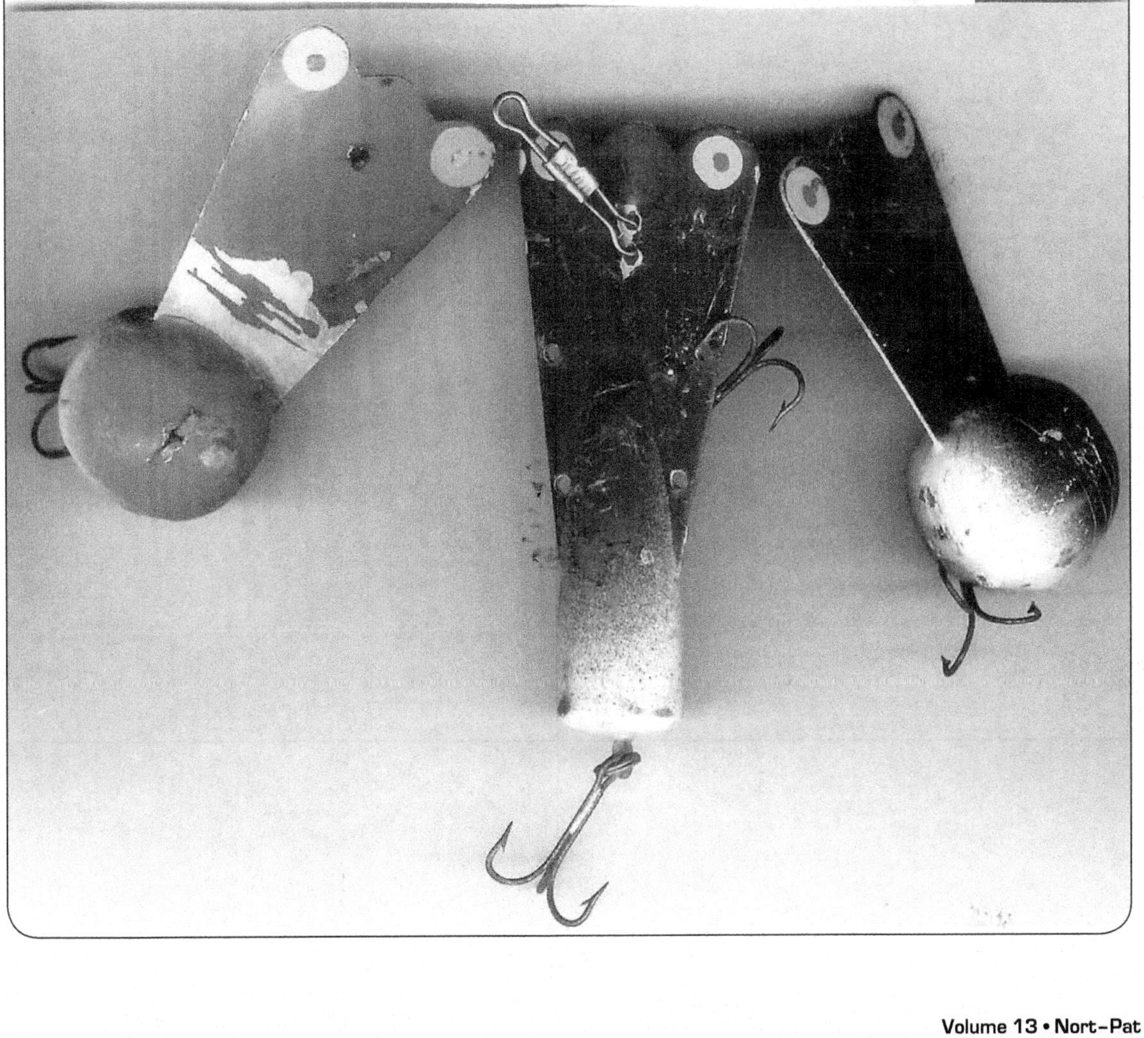

OX-BOW BAIT COMPANY
DETROIT, MICHIGAN

On November 24, 1959, Thomas E. Ware, of Sedalia, Missouri, received Patent No. 2,913,847 for his 2" **FLY-PLUG** lure. His Tom Ware Fishing Tackle Company was located at 913 Crescent Blvd. in Sedalia. At virtually the same time that he was in production until his death in 1960, the Ox-Bow Bait Company, of Detroit, Michigan, was producing the same lure, and both lures are name stamped in the same way. The wooden piggy-back lure body rested on a metal "Russelure" type frame and had a tied fly trailing hook. I suspect that there was also a tie-in with the A & S Stamping Company out of Detroit, who, at nearly the same time, made a similar lure called the "CAMELURE". See the comparison pictures.

Lures by any of the three companies trade in the same level of $20 to $25, and maybe higher, in their boxes.

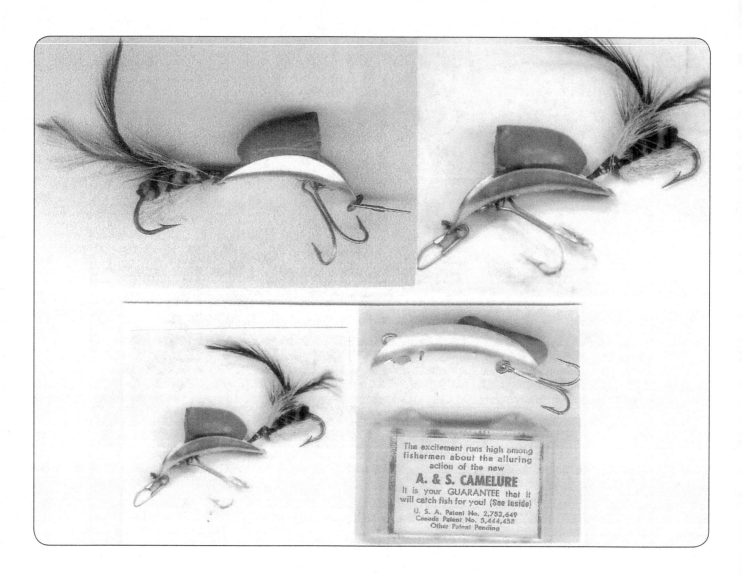

OZARK BAIT COMPANY
SHELBYVILLE, INDIANA

The post-war **OZARK WIG WAG** was made of metal and lead and had a body shaped similar to the "Jake's Bait", except for the "twist-on" plastic streamer tail. The lures were 3" long overall counting the plastic streamer tail. However, the amount of lead filler varied from 1/2 oz. to 1/4 oz. for different fishing purposes. Each lure was sold in a two-piece brownish-color cardboard box with dark blue print. The side of the box read, "The streamers do not deteriorate from heat, grease, gas, or oil. Positively will not stick together." Advertising of the era said, "Genuine OZARK WIG WAG...With the million dollar screw-on plastic streamer....manufacturers of Lifelike lures." There were eight solid colors for the lures and twelve combination colors, such as yellow with black spot, white with red spots, and green with black spots, to name a few. The tail streamer colors were red, white, green, black, orange, or green and yellow mottled. The pictured example is No. 213 all black with the yellow streamer.

Boxed lure picture is courtesy of the Jack Leslie collection.

The rare boxed Genuine Ozark Wig Wag lures trade in the $15 to $25 range.

GENUINE OZARK WIG WAG

"It Wiggles and It Wabbles"

A SURE KILLER FOR ALL GAME
FISH, LAKE OR STREAM

Genuine Ozark Wig Wag

With the million dollar Screw-on Plastic Streamer

Not rubber or Synthetic Rubber — not affected by Grease, Oil or Gasoline
Guaranteed to stand 160 degrees heat

Positively will not stick together. Comes with 1/0 an 3/0 hook — 1/2 ounce. Same size for the extra light
tackle fisherman 1/4 ounce.

"FISH AND STAY YOUNG"

Series 200 — List $1.10

SOLID COLORS		STREAMER COLORS	COLOR COMBINATIONS		
213	Black	Red, White, Yellow, Green, Black,	201—White	Red Spots	
214	White	Orange, Green and Yellow	202— "	Black "	
215	Green	mottled	203—Black	White "	
216	Yellow		204—Yellow	Black "	
217	Red	Any Combination of Colors	205— "	Green "	
218	Orange	On Special Order	206—Red	Black "	
219	Gold		207—Orange	" "	
20	Silver		208— "	Red "	
			209— Green	Black "	
			210— "	Yellow "	
			211—Gold	Black "	
			212—Silver	" "	

Individually boxed 12 to the container
Three black, three yellow, one each of
other numbers unless specified.

Individually boxed
12 to the container.
One Each of above unless specified

OZARK BAIT COMPANY

Manufacturers of Lifelike Lures

SHELBYVILLE, INDIANA

OZARK BAIT COMPANY
SHELBYVILLE, INDIANA

OZARK BAIT COMPANY
WINDSOR, MISSOURI

OZARK BAITS
SEDALIA, MISSOURI

There were a number of 1940's through the 1960's lure companies that incorporated the name "OZARK" in their company names. I have already covered the Shelbyville, Indiana, Ozark Bait Company in another story in these books. That story was for their 3"-long metal-and-lead combination **OZARK WIG WAG** bait. However, because of the cross-over connection with two other companies, I have included that company in this new story. These companies with the name Ozark were spread across the country, located in Indiana, Missouri, Arkansas, Oklahoma, and even California. Here, I will cover three of those companies that not only had similar company names but also made some of their lures that were identical to all three companies.

The Ozark Bait companies, of Shelbyville, Indiana, and also of Windsor, Missouri, are definitely the oldest involved here. One or the other of these companies may have been first and then moved, or they may have existed simultaneously at the two locations. It is my opinion, however, that Shelbyville was first and that they then moved to Windsor and that they were in business there until 1950. In either event, they date to a start up of around 1947 and made identical lures. These 2-1/4"- and 3-1/2"-long lures were made of a latex material with molded-in lure colors that would not crack or chip because the color was not painted on but was rather mixed in the latex mold. This lure, called the **RED FIN MINNOW**, was made of a very poor latex compound that proved to be very unstable and became brittle with age. The Helin "Flatfish"

type shaped lure had a fixed single tail hook, a recessed forehead pocket where the line tie was located, and slightly protruding wing-like flanges on each side of the head. Although I have not been able to confirm it, I believe that the inventor of these lures and company owner was Paul Skeen.

Another latex lure made at two of these locations was the 2-1/4" **PAUL'S PAL**: "The Wonder Bait...A lure for the Sportsman," as it said on the side of the box. The mouse-shaped lure had a slanted and double-dimpled nose with a center ridge. It had external, plastic, white-iris eyes held by tacks, or nails, as the pupils. The lure had an Arbogast type of "Hula Popper" tail skirt placed over a tail nipple.

Around 1951, Ozark Baits was formed in Sedalia, Missouri, by the same or new management. They continued to make the Red Fin Minnow, but in a larger 3-1/2" size. The body shape was the same, however, but the small side projections had grown larger and longer, more in the shape of a seal's front flippers, and the lure was equipped with two underside double hooks. The Sedalia Company also made a lure the others did not, called the **WONDER POPPER**. The 3"-long Wonder Popper was a surface lure that had two protruding plastic side fins.

All three company locations sold their lures in one-piece aluminum-color cardboard boxes with plastic covers.

Boxed Ozark Bait Company lures trade in the $15 to $25 range.

Genuine Ozark Wig Wag

with the Screw-on Plastic Streamers

OZARK BAIT COMPANY
Manufacturers of Lifelike Baits
SHELBYVILLE, INDIANA

PAUL'S PAL
THE WONDER BAIT
A Lure for the Sportsman

OZARK LURES
FOR FRESH AND SALT WATER

Original Red Fin for Spinning Casting or Trowling, Lake or Stream. Hand made lure made by the originator.
OZARK BAITS   SEDALIA, MISSOURI

OZARK BAIT COMPANY

WONDER POPPER — For Spinning and Casting
Handmade Lures For The Sportsman
OZARK BAITS   SEDALIA, MISSOURI

OZARK BAIT COMPANY
CALIFORNIA, MISSOURI

On May 1, 1930, Herman G. Swearingen filed for a patent on a mechanical spring hook lure. On July 7, 1931, Patent No. 1,812,906 was awarded to him. However, Swearingen awarded half of the patent rights to the Popejoy brothers. H. R. and J. R. Popejoy were supposed to be the manufacturers of the aluminum-body lure. The patent called for two hump triggers in the rear back and belly of the lure to release the concealed hooks. However, the actual production model worked on fish pressure against the line tie. This released a tail hook to fall back, catching the fish that then released two more spring-activated hooks from top and bottom slots in the lure to further hook into the fish. The lure had all-black glass inserted bead eyes and a red nose and tail with a white fish-scale pattern in between. The lure had "SWEARINGEN'S" molded into the sides of the aluminum body. The two-piece yellow cardboard lure box had the company name and address on the side and the lure name on the cover, "**THE SHEIK METAL MINNOW**." The box cover also had a picture of the lure patent drawing, which, by the way, was manufactured in a slightly different format.

Pictures are courtesy of the Dean A. Murphy collection. According to Dean Murphy, only a token amount of these lures were ever produced because of a disagreement between Swearingen and the Popejoy brothers, resulting in a lawsuit and no major numbers-production of the lure.

Due to the extreme rarity of these lures, there is no established trade value at this time.

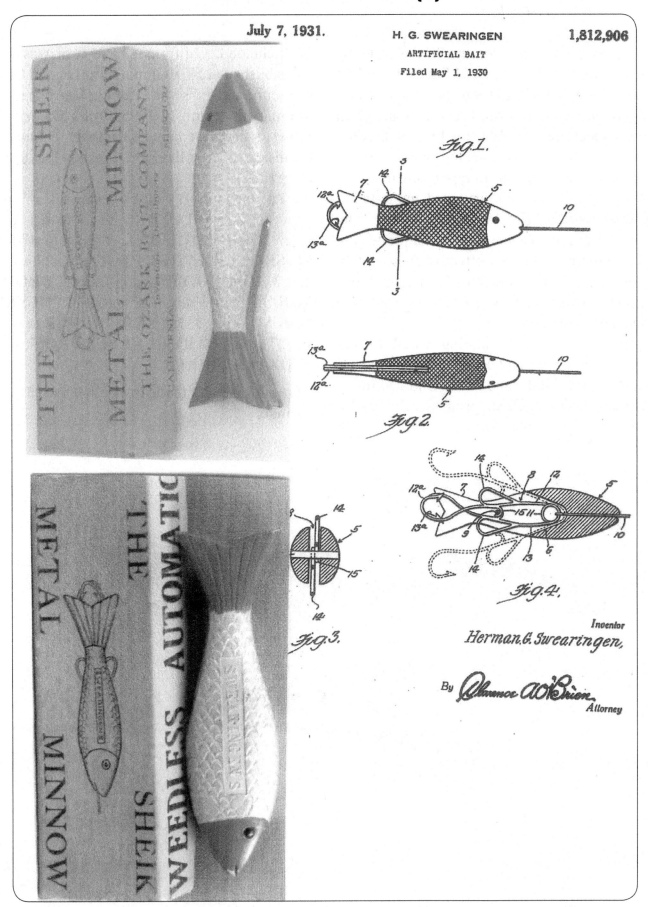

July 7, 1931.

H. G. SWEARINGEN

1,812,906

ARTIFICIAL BAIT

Filed May 1, 1930

Fig.1.

Fig.2.

Fig.3.

Fig.4.

Inventor
Herman. G. Swearingen,

By Clarence A. O'Brien
Attorney

OZARK ED'S LURES
CUBA, MISSOURI

Some might consider the lures made by Patrick Smith and his dad, Ed Smith, under the trade name **OZARK ED'S** to be contemporary folk art. I do not, though, because, although in some respects they probably are folk art, they are also very effective fish-catching working lures. Many contemporary folk art types were made for eye appeal and were not fine tuned and tested to be water worthy. However, the lures made by Ozark Ed's have gone through a lot of pre-testing and fine tuning to be very effective smallmouth, largemouth, walley, and muskie fishing lures. The lures are all hand carved, hand painted, fine tuned, and signed on the bellies.

Ed Smith began whittling wood fishing lures at a young age and using them on Missouri streams in the 1960's and 1970's and had really perfected some very effective lures by the 1980's. At that time, he established Ozark Ed Lures out of Richmond, California. The firm was later reestablished at 57 Hummingbird Lane in Cuba, Missouri, and Ed's son, Patrick, had joined the lure-making team. In 1995, Ozark Ed won the Cabela's best lure contest and was featured on the inside cover of the 1996 <u>Cabela's Tacklecraft</u> magazine.

At the top of the second set of pictures, in its wood OZARK ED'S box, is a 3" green **BUGEYED FROG**. Next is a 4"-long **MUSKIE CRAZY DIGGER**, a shallow-running 3" **HUMINBYRD**, a top-water 2" **BROWN MOUSE**, top-water nose prop 3" **MUSKIE MOUSE**, a big 6" **MUSKIE BEAVER**, a small 1-1/2" brown **BABY BUGEYED FROG**, and a 3" **OZARK SHINER**.

Ozark Ed lures trade in the $10 to $25 range.

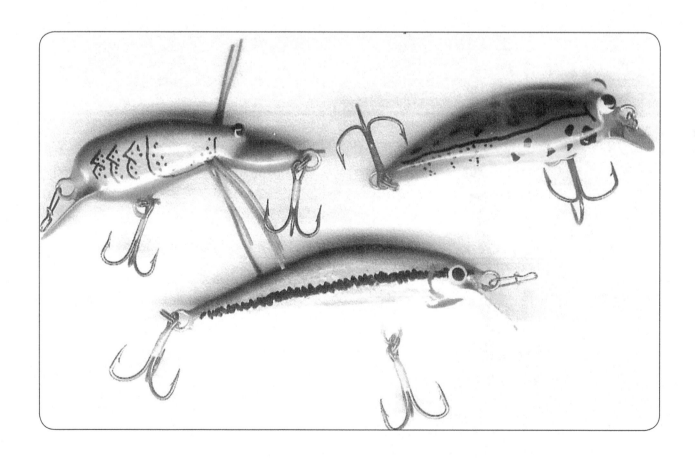

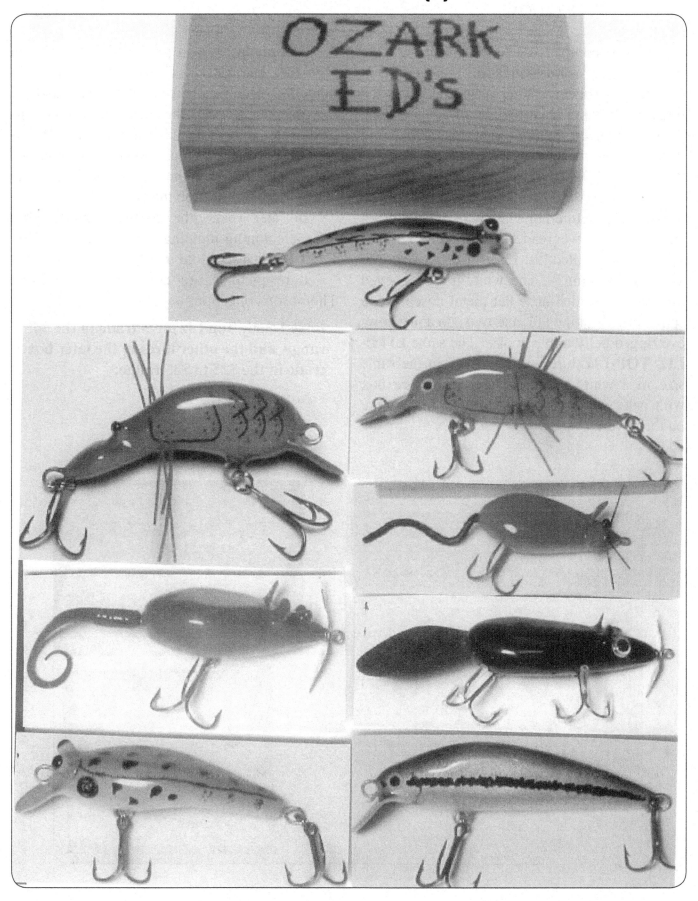

OZARK LURE COMPANY
TULSA, OKLAHOMA

Another company starting in the lure-making business after World War II was the Ozark Bait Company of Tulsa, Oklahoma, who made wooden lures similar to the Martin "Lizard". They made the lure in three different styles and sold them in three different lure boxes. The earliest lure was the 3"-long **TOP-LIZ** that was sold in a colorful lure-picture red cardboard box. The Top-Liz on the box was pictured in white with red and black spots, and the cover read, "Fishing's Top Thrill… Top Liz (also called Litl-Liz Top-Liz)…Casting-Trolling-Spinning." The white-iris glass-eyed lure had a rounded-nose flat metal nosepiece, a spinner blade at the tail, and two cup and screw-eye rigged belly treble hooks. The same **LITL-LIZ TOP-LIZ** lure was later sold in the same size in a white two-piece cardboard lure box with pale green print, but with no lure picture on the cover.

The company also produced a 4" wooden **OZARK LIZARD**. This lure was basically made the same way, except for the size and the fact that the front of the metal nose plate was heart shaped, or notched in the center. It was packaged in a red two-piece cardboard box that had black print that only gave the lure name "OZARK LIZARD" on the cover.

In later years, the company produced a 1/2-oz. spinning-jumping lure called the **TEN-KILLER** that was sold in a plastic hinged box.

Lure pictures are courtesy of the Mike Thompson collection.

Boxed early Top Liz lures trade in the $45 range, and the other lures in the later boxes trade in the $25 to $35 range.

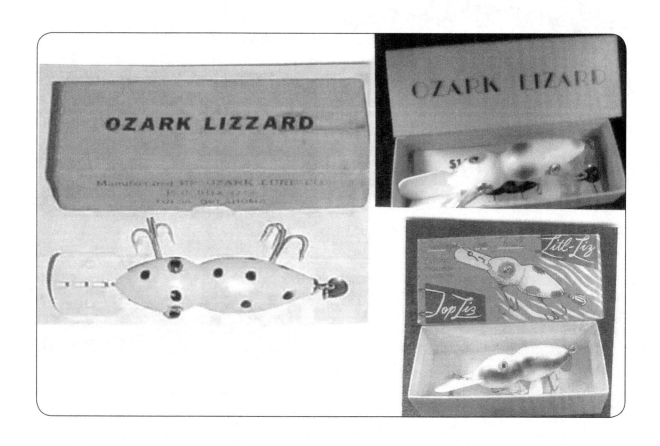

OZBURN, FLOYD A.
HOLLYWOOD & BALDWIN PARK, CALIFORNIA

In 1933, Floyd Allan Ozburn developed his **HOOT SPINNER** and started his little company, briefly located in Los Angles, California. Shortly after that, he moved to Hollywood, California. However, for most of his production years, he was located at that second address and his later address of 13527 E. Corak in Baldwin Park, California. The first lures that he made under Patent No. 1,923,840, issued on August 22, 1933, had some minor problems with the wire arms holding the spinners twisting out of position. The newer version is the one most often found by collectors. It has a more streamlined pollywog-shaped body and a special improved M-shaped wire system to keep the two Colorado type spinner blades in the proper position. This was accomplished by a bend in the wire to form a saddle in which the belly of the lure rested. It was impossible for the water pressure to twist or torque the wires out of position with this new system. Ozburn received a new Patent No.2,125,030 on July 26, 1938, for this improved lure design. The whole purpose of the Hoot Spinner design was to provide the fisherman with a lure that would cause a rippling and bubbling water disturbance at any depth. At the same time, Ozburn designed the lure to be pretty much weed proof without the need of a traditional wire weedguard. As far as appearance was concerned, Ozburn's intent was to make his lure resemble a large insect, probably a hellgrammite. The most common lure color, by far, is a yellow body with black spots in the size of 1-3/4" long. However, there were other colors and one other size. A 1933 ad read, "30,000 Baitcasting Southern Californians can't be wrong!...The proven WEEDLESS, REALISTIC, EASIEST CASTING, DEADLY KILLING HOOT SPINNER." Floyd A. Ozburn, unlike many other lure makers of his era was successful and he was in business into the late 1950's, making his HOOT SPINNER, later named **HOOT TWIN SPINNER**. In fact, in 1956, he introduced a new color: red head with luminous.

In the meantime, over the years, his company moved three times from the 1933 Los Angels, California, address to 4629 Kingswell Avenue in Hollywood, California, in the 1940's to 13527 E. Corak Street in Baldwin, California, in the 1950's.

Hoot Spinners trade widely, mostly because of lack of knowledge of the age of these lures. The Hoot Spinners can trade as low as $25 and as high as $65.

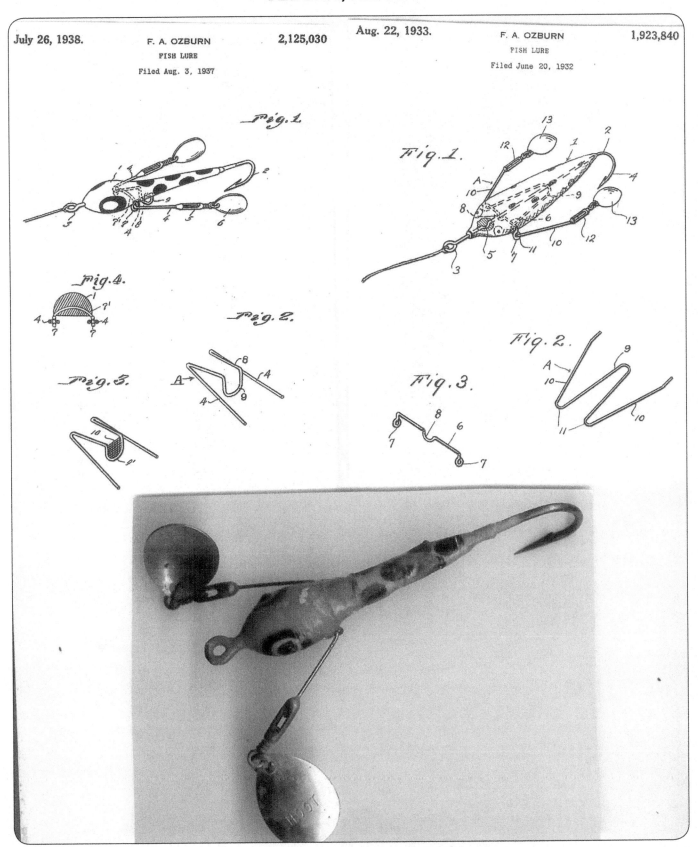

July 26, 1938. F. A. OZBURN 2,125,030
FISH LURE
Filed Aug. 3, 1937

Aug. 22, 1933. F. A. OZBURN 1,923,840
FISH LURE
Filed June 20, 1932

Fig. 1.

Fig. 4.

Fig. 2.

Fig. 5.

Fig. 1.

Fig. 2.

Fig. 3.

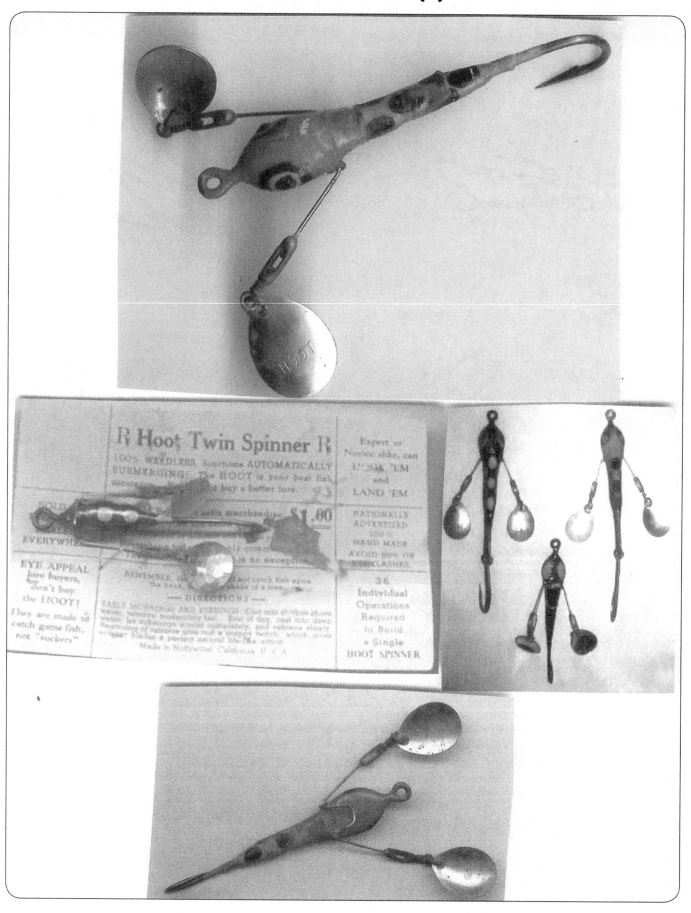

1956 *Address*

Floyd A. Ozburn
13527 E. Corak
Baldwin Park
California

New address
9629 Kingswell Ave
Hollywood Ca.

bait-rod artificial
purchased that
all its claims."
Anderson, M.D.
lk, Virginia

d check for six
which please send
e HOOTS. I
ery much."
Nisley, D.D.S.
yra, Pa.

bait caster selected
alytically, a good
HOOTS would be
kle box. Landed
4 ounce Florida
on INDIAN
15 lb. 10 ounce
EAD HOOT."
ld J. Stephenson
ling Contractor
ta, Illinois.

could get every
think as much
OT as I do, your
ld be few."
S. E. Moncure
Blackstone, Va.

DIAN HOOT
mall mouth Bass
sed."
H. Wofford, Jr.
ox 84
oo, Ga.

how much you
atives, there's no
ncle Sam!

NNER

WEEDLESS. Functions
ORIGINAL INDIAN,
- BLACK BEETLE,
OT ROACH - HOOT
ts.

es his idea of the HOOT:
the yellow and black will
TAKE BASS IF THE
CAN SEE 'EM."
nin - San Francisco, Calif.
J.N PARK
WOOD, CALIFORNIA

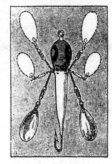

RED HEAD
(LUMINOUS)

New : Different : Weedless

april 5th 1956

Dear Mr Walton:

Received your inquiry regarding Hoot Spinners, I am not actively engaged in the manufacture of Hoots any more, but have a few dozen on hand for old users, but in Two colors only, The "Indian" (see above) and the "Freak" which is a reversal of The Indian Color Combination. They retail @ $1.25 each. Can supply you for your personal needs.

Thanks again. Oh yes, none made for Spining Reels. TOO LIGHT for balance to obtain decent blade action.

Sincerely yours
Floyd Ozburn

P

P & C SPINNERS
ROCHESTER, NEW YORK

The 1950's P & C Spinners Company, located at 140 Woodrow Avenue in Rochester, New York, made a little different version of the common "June Bug Spinner" lure. Their version had a 1-5/8"-long, pointed oval-shaped blade mounted on a wire shaft with a 2"-long shank No. 2 size single hook, making the rig 7" long overall. The **P & C SPINNER** was designed for live bait fishing for walleyes, northern pike, and pickerel. They were sold on one-dozen dealer display boards, like the one pictured.

A full dealer board trades in the $10 range.

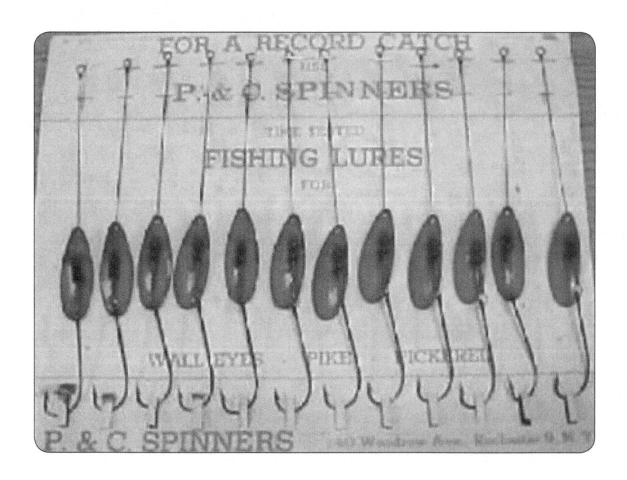

P & H BAIT COMPANY
PALMYRA, MISSOURI

The partnership of Frank C. Pollard and, son-in-law, Paul Hoens (hence, "P & H") formed the P & H Bait Company in 1952 in Palmyra, Missouri. (Palmyra is a small town just a little west of the Mississippi River and Quincy, Illinois. The town name is not all that common, but there was another town of the same name that was home to another lure maker. The 1950's and 1960's Katchmore Bait Company was located in Palmyra, Wisconsin.) Frank C. Pollard was granted Patent No. 2,603,024 on July 15, 1952, for his **RIPPLE TAIL** spinning lure. The lures were made with two different shaped 1" spinner blades, one hammer finished in an oval shape and the other hammer finished in a willow leaf shape. Some of the 2-5/8"-overall-long lures were equipped with an artificial pork rind trailer and others with a second stinger hook. The lures were sold on white cards (pictured with the patent). The one-dozen dealer display board for these lures had red print and pictured a red print bass on the left and a red print trout on the right. A similar metal spinner made by this company was called the **LUTZ SPINNER**.

Picture is courtesy of the Dean A. Murphy collection.

Carded P & H lures trade at $5 or less; however, a full dealer display board will trade in the $30 to $35 range.

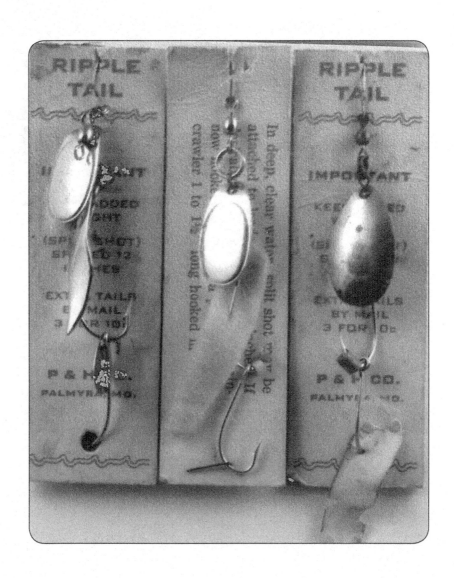

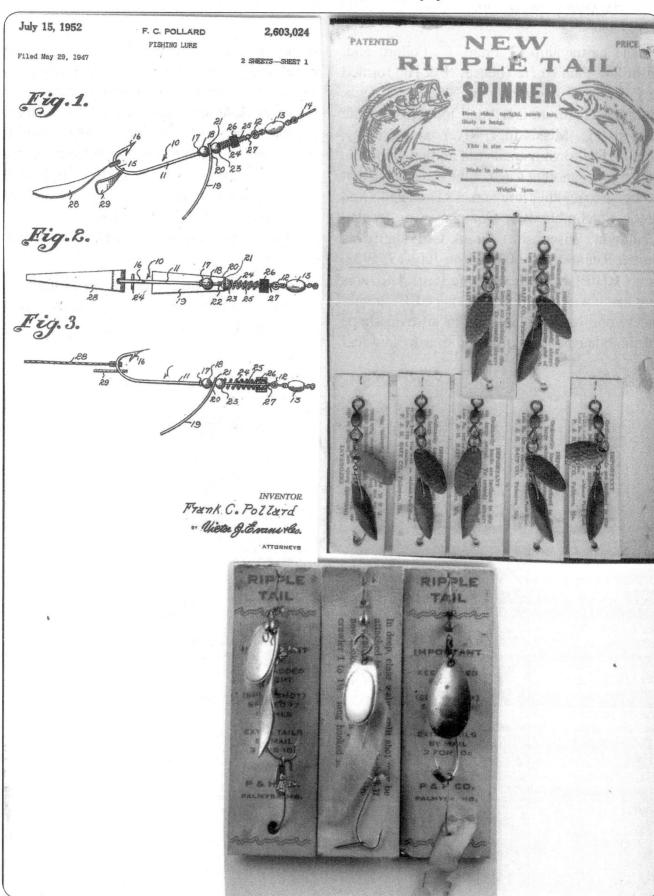

July 15, 1952

F. C. POLLARD

2,603,024

FISHING LURE

Filed May 29, 1947

2 SHEETS—SHEET 1

Fig.1.

Fig.2.

Fig.3.

INVENTOR.
Frank C. Pollard
BY Victor J. Evans & Co.
ATTORNEYS

PATENTED

NEW RIPPLE TAIL SPINNER

Hook rides upright, much less likely to hang.

This is size _____

Made in size _____

Weight ⅝oz.

PRICE

P & M SPORTING GOODS
LAUREL, MISSISSIPPI

The P & M Sporting Goods Company, located at P. O. Box 2506 in Laurel, Mississippi, distributed a copy of the original Missouri "Bass Hawk" Lure. I don't know if this Mississippi company manufactured these 2" plastic reproductions or if they were merely a distributor. In any event, they named their version the **MAYBERRY'S** **SPUTNIK** and sold them on a six-unit dealer display board. The top of the white board with black print depicted a stream fisherman on the left fighting a jumping fish on the right.

A full board of six lures trades in the $35 range.

P & P BAIT COMPANY
BUFFALO, NEW YORK

In the fall of 1932, two brothers formed the P & P Bait Company in Buffalo, New York. The 3-3/8"-long brass lure that they made was unique and is very rare. The lure had a special 3-1/4" wire nose leader line tie that made the lure 6-1/2" long overall from the line tie to the tail hook. In all of my 47 years of lure collecting, I have seen exactly two of these lures that the brothers named **PETER'S SPECIAL**. Otto H. and Albert H. Peters filed for a patent on their invention on December 16, 1932, and Patent No. 1,963,380 was granted to them on June 19, 1934.

The lure was made from a flat, rather thick piece of brass sheet metal and then formed and stamped into the shape of a special kind of minnow. The lure was made to simulate a member from a group of minnows that would dart about and make a series of rapid wiggling motions and then settle down to the bottom of the stream or body of water they inhabited. (This class of minnows was known in that era as skip jacks, mod-docks, mud minnows, Johnny darters, or rainbow darters.) The lure had folded-up sides forming a semi-hollow body channel that flared out to a 1-3/8" width at the eyes and then narrowed again to the nose. From a top view, the lure had the shape of a swimming seal and, from a side view, a bird-like head. The eyes were made by stamping or pressing from the inside, out, forming a convex iris painted yellow and a concave center pupil painted black. A ring-rivet held a circular-shaped dive lip on the nose that was concaved towards the front and then bent straight down. Two tabs were pressed outward from the inside to form the loops for both the belly and tail treble hooks. The Peter's Special was made in finishes of brass, nickel, or gold plating. I have not seen how this lure was packaged for sale. The lure is pictured with the patent, along with two separate pictures of the lure from both belly and side views.

The very rare Peter's Special lure trades in the $40 to $50 range.

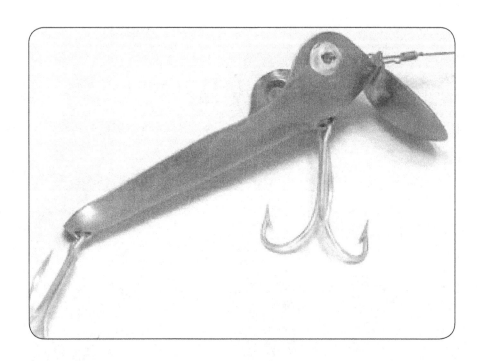

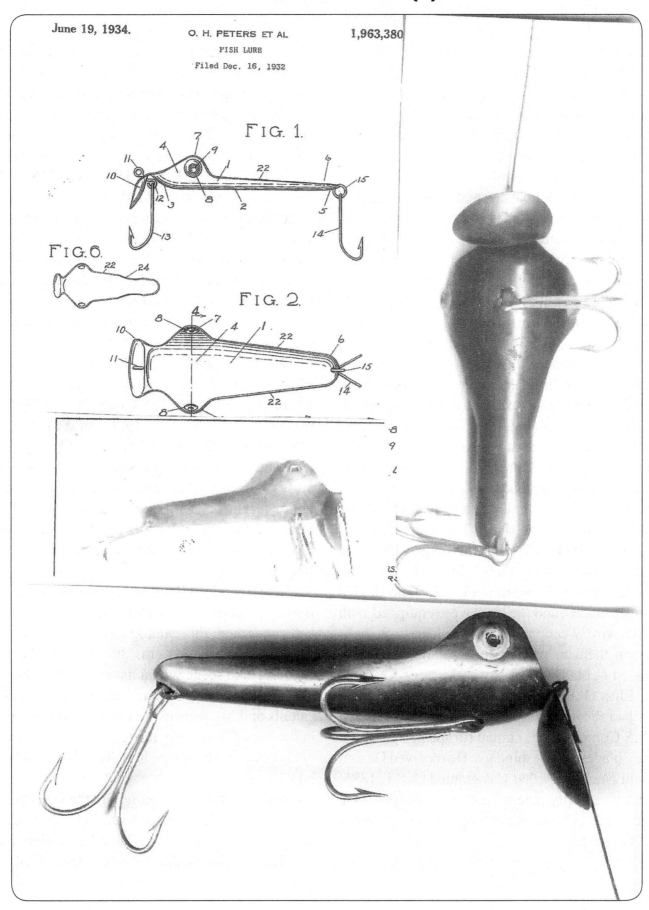

FIG. 1.

FIG. 6.

FIG. 2.

P & S BALL BEARING BAIT COMPANY
SAYRE, PENNSYLVANIA

The Sayre, Pennsylvania, P & S Ball Bearing Bait Company was formed in 1902 by Elias Oliver Pealer and Thruman V. Sloat (hence, "P & S"). Early company advertising claimed, "Once Used Always Used." The metal spinning baits by this company used either wire or metal shaft bases in both single and double spinners. The fancy spinners on the doubles were designed to spin in opposite directions, one of polished brass and the other nickel plated. The men made their lures with hollow point feathered trebles. There were several sizes and styles, such as follows: Style H, a double spinner for bass; Style SH, a double spinner for muskallonge (this was the correct way they spelled it); and Style M, a double spinner on a four-foot piano wire leader, with box-swivel designed for trolling. Most lures had six or more round or diamond-shaped tiny brass bead spacer-bearings. Many of the lures were also stamped with the lure patent date of November 13, 1896. One of the pictured lures with a box-swivel was a pre-P & S era lure made in 1897 by E. O. Pealer alone. The blades on this lure were 3/4" long on a 4-1/2"-overall-long shaft. The later and larger **P & S MUSKY SPINNER** had big 2-3/8"-long blades on a 7"-long shaft. Many P & S Ball Bearing Bait lures were made with one or two spinner blades, and the lures were equipped with piano wire weedguards with soldered-on ball-tips on them to protect either plain or feather-dressed treble hooks.

Elias O. Pealer, was a local jeweler by trade and had received at least two patents before the P & S Company was started for the design of the fancy blades for his spinners. He received Design Patent No. 24,724 that was granted Oct. 1, 1895, and a lure utility patent on Nov. 13, 1896. One of the lures pictured was stamped with both dates and his name.

In 1904, the P & S Ball Bearing Company went bankrupt and was purchased by a man named Robert F. Page, an ex-partner, who continued to run the company for several more years. Shortly after the turn of the century, Robert Page introduced several new lure designs. A good example is the 3-1/8" **P & S SPINNING MINNOW** that had a 1-5/8" torpedo-shaped wooden body mounted on a square barb hook that had a 3-1/8" shaft. The tail of this lure was dressed with short cut white feathers. The nose had a two-blade prop with arms of different lengths that caused the lure to vibrate on retrieve. The tips of the props were bent over forward, and the base of the prop was soldered to a U-clevis.

Many years after Elias Pealer was no longer associated with the P & S Company, he was awarded another patent; Patent No. 1,589,860 was granted on June 22, 1920, for a metal bait. This **PEALER LORELEI** lure was 2-3/4" long and was figure-eight shaped with 1/4" side tabs, or arms. The lures were painted blood red or bright red with a white center wave line. Some of these Lorelei lures were made in just a plain brass finish. I have pictured three lures with this story.

The P & S Ball Bearing Fly-Troll and Casting Baits are featured in a 1903 catalog. As far as I'm concerned, this catalog has one of the nicest cover pictures of that era. It depicted a beautiful quiet lake scene with a fisherman, standing in a rowboat, fighting a fish. The picture included cattails and lily pads in the foreground with trees in the background and, the real kicker, no houses or cabins disturbing the shore line, like in today's lake scenes.

Some pictures are courtesy of the Dan Basore and Steve O'Hern collections. The last set of pictures is courtesy of the Phil Allen collection.

The first spoon blade was stamped "EOP".

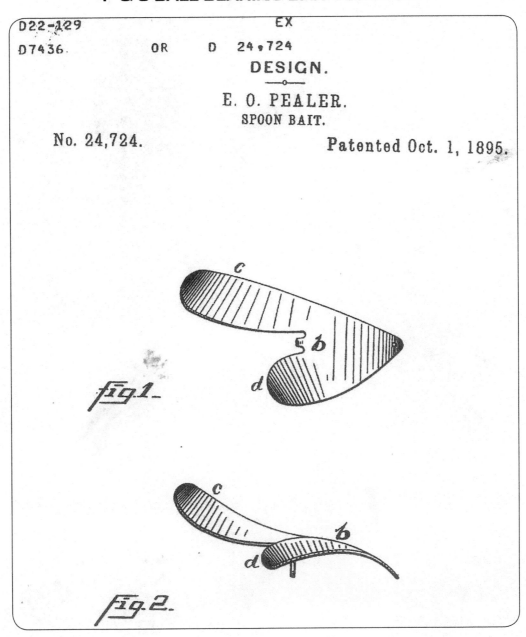

D22-129   EX

D7436.   OR   D 24,724

DESIGN.

E. O. PEALER.
SPOON BAIT.

No. 24,724.   Patented Oct. 1, 1895.

fig.1.

fig.2.

Pre-1902 stamped and carded Pealer lures trade at $100 and up. Un-carded trade at $75. P & S Ball Bearing lures on cards or in boxes trade at $50 to $75 and up.

Un-carded trade $30 to $50. Early P & S catalogs trade in the $50 to $75 range. The very rare Pealer 1920's Lorelei lures trade at $50 and up.

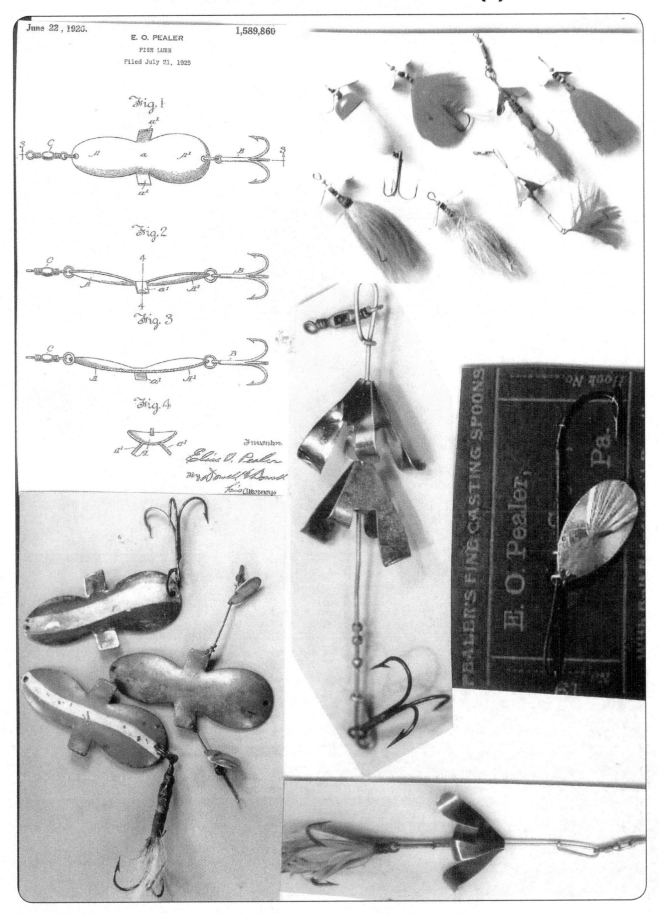

June 22, 1926.

E. O. PEALER

FISH LURE

Filed July 21, 1925

1,589,860

Fig. 1

Fig. 2

Fig. 3

Fig. 4

Inventor

Elias O. Pealer

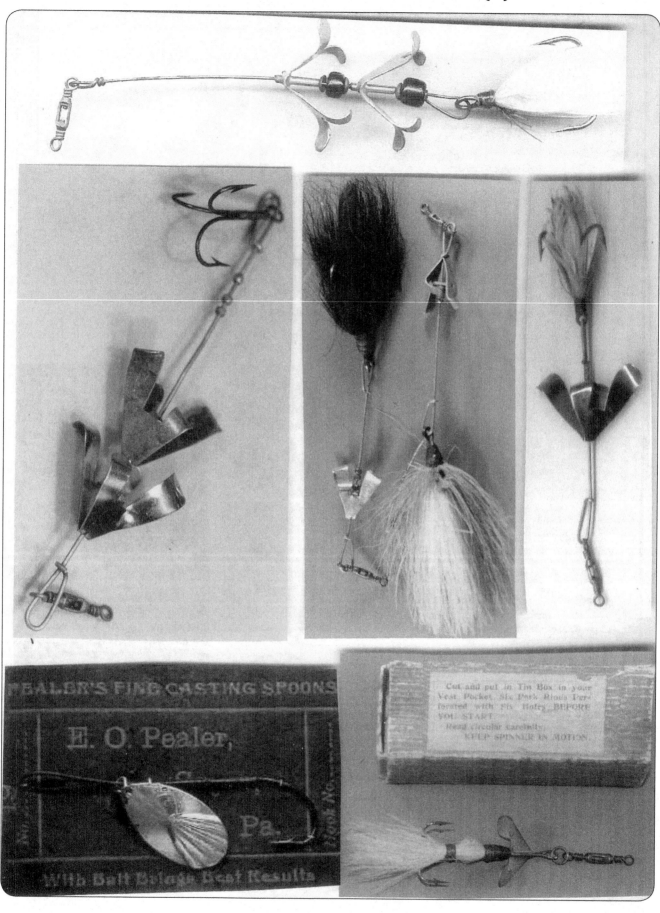

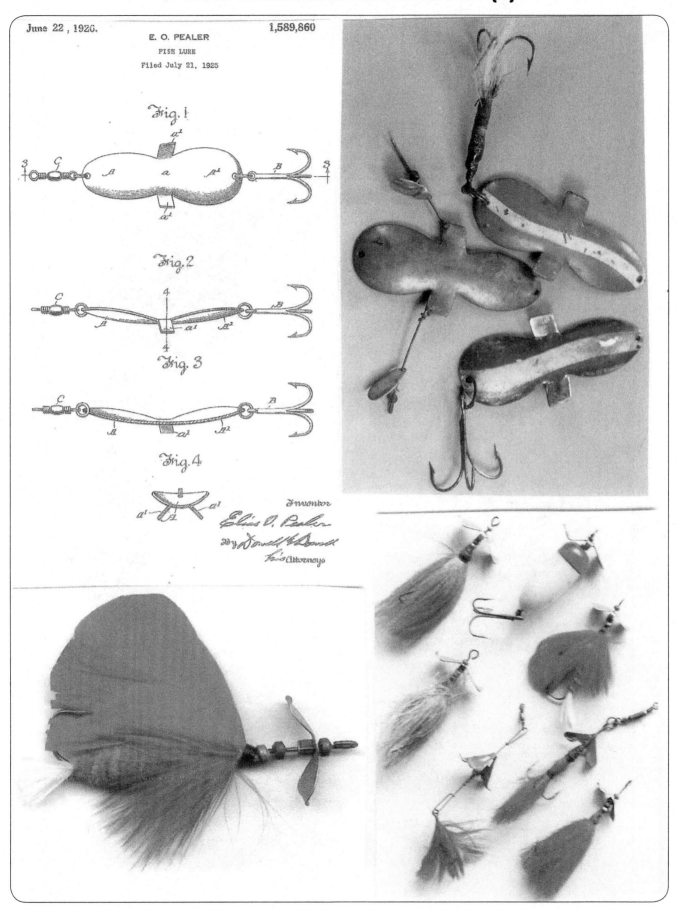

June 22, 1926.

E. O. PEALER

FISH LURE

Filed July 21, 1925

1,589,860

Fig. 1

Fig. 2

Fig. 3

Fig. 4

Inventor

Elmer O. Pealer

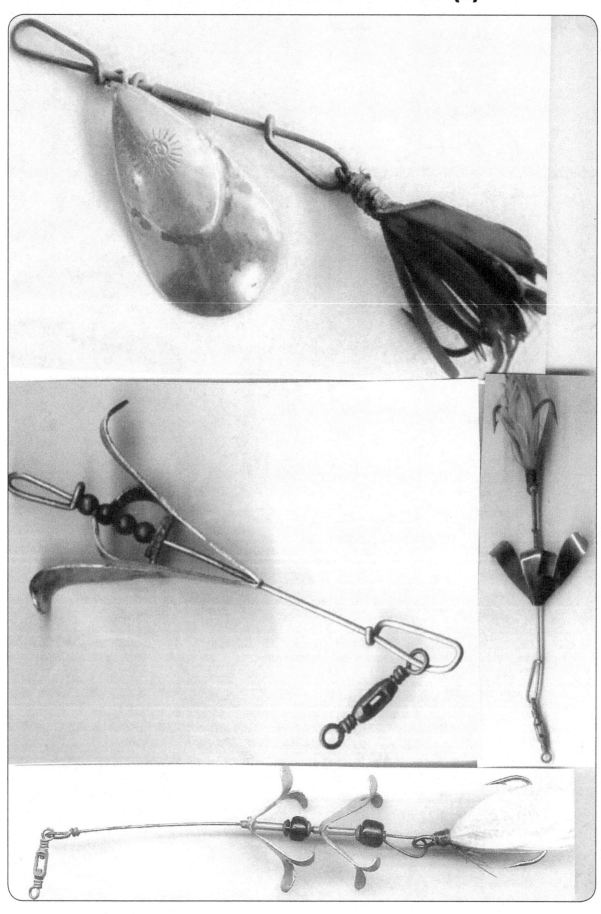

P. & V. BAIT COMPANY
JOLIET, ILLINOIS

The **RED WING BLACKBIRD** lure was the invention of Walter Pius and Frank Vanderheide; thus, the name P. & V. Bait Company, which was located at 1021 Ridgeway Ave., Joliet, Illinois. The lure was made in six colors in both 2-3/4" bass and 4-1/4" musky sizes. The torpedo-shaped bodies were first made of wood, but, if I recall correctly, they were later made of hollow plastic (I could be wrong about the plastic). The lure had two side treble hooks and another at the tail. It had a floppy squared nose prop, side wings made of stranded vinyl, and painted eyes that always faced downward. The six lure colors were black body with either red or yellow wings, yellow body with red or black wings, and red body with yellow or black wings. One of the company's advertising slogans was, "Fish and See with P & V." The late-1940's and into the 1950's two-piece cardboard lure box was a colorful yellow with red and black print and trim with a lure picture on the cover. Box papers said, "To get the best results with the Red Wing Black Bird, let it set on the water about two or three seconds and then retrieve it in jerks of about 12" to 15"."

Boxed Red Wing Black Birds trade in the $65 to $75 range.

P & V BAIT COMPANY

MANUFACTURERS OF THE Famous RED WING BLACK BIRD

FISH AND SEE WITH P&V

P&V BAIT CO. JOLIET, ILL.

P & V BAIT CO.

1021 Ridgewood Ave — Joliet, Illinois

★ ★ ★

Manufacturers of the Famous
RED WING BLACK BIRD

To get the best results with the Red Wing Black Bird, let it set on the water about 2 or 3 seconds after casting and then retrieve it in jerks of about 12" to 15". In the event that you get a follow up, cast again, let it set 2 or 3 more seconds, jerk it 2 or 3 times and then reel in as fast as possible.

PATTERNS and COLORS

3001	Black Body with Red Wings
3002	Black Body with Yellow Wings
3003	Yellow Body with Red Wings
3004	Yellow Body with Black Wings
3005	Red Body with Yellow Wings
3006	Red Body with Black Wings

P. C. FISHING TACKLE, INC.
OWENSBORO, KENTUCKY

Owensboro, Kentucky, is just the other side of the Indiana border and on the south side of the Ohio River. There, in the late 1960's, a 3-1/2"-long wooden **BLUPER** lure was introduced. Because they are very rare, I believe that these early glass-eyed wooden versions were made for less than six months in late 1967. I have pictured one in blue with darker blue spots.

The 2-1/4" plastic Bluper production was started in early 1968, and it was a surface lure with molded, raised bump eyes painted with yellow irises and black pupils. The popper type had fluttering side mounted plastic skirts similar to the tail skirts on the Arbogast "Hula Popper". The nose had a deep, scooped-out cup to give the lure a wobbling action and create noise and bubbles when popped on the surface. Lure colors included frog with green and white skirts, yellow coach dog with yellow and white skirts, red head with white with red and white skirts, and all black with black skirts. The lure had a raised forehead above the eyes and a shallow notch just behind the head and probably most resembled a frog in the water. The 2-1/4"-long, 3/8-oz. Bluper was semi-weedless with a belly and a tail screw-eye-held set of double up-turned hooks. The clear plastic hinged lure box had a white paper insert that said, "Congratulations Sport Fisherman, You have just bought yourself a BLUPER, a lure that was designed to get in the places where the fish are, such as timber, weed-beds and lily pads."

The company was owned by the lure's inventor, Paul C. Lott, who gave the company name his first two initials, P. C. Fishing Tackle, Inc., which was located at 720 West Second Street, Owensboro, Kentucky. At the time that Paul C. Lott filed for his patent on January 10, 1968, he resided at 2974 Cheyenne Drive, Owensboro, and his Design Patent No. D212,609 was granted to him on November 5, 1968.

Lure pictures are courtesy of the Doug Carpenter collection.

The very rare 3-1/2" wooden Bluper lures trade above the $75 level. Boxed plastic Blupers are scarce and normally trade in the $30 to $40 range, except on E-Bay, where I have seen them top $85. (E-Bay is a market place that proves almost every day that a "fool" and his money can easily be parted.)

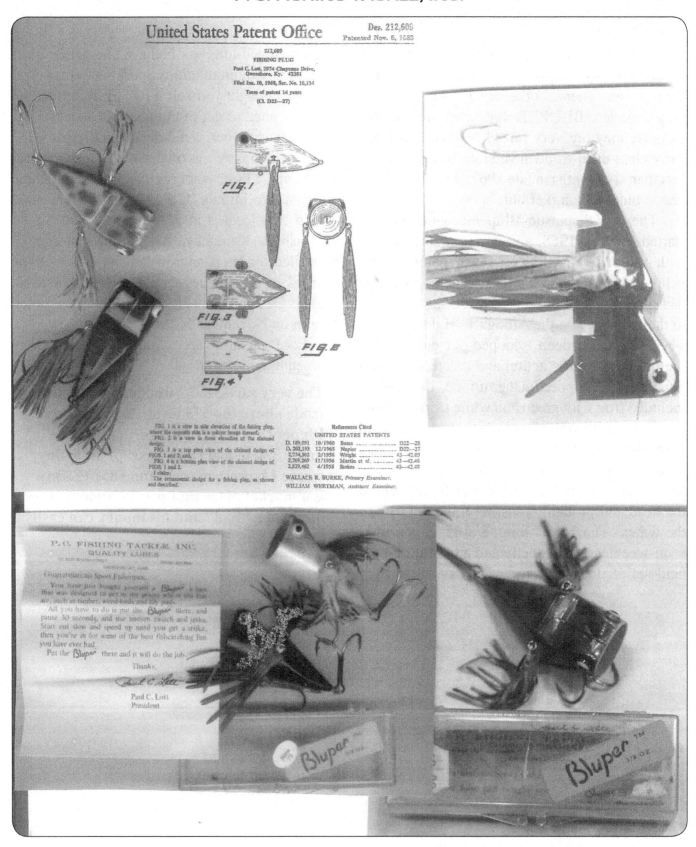

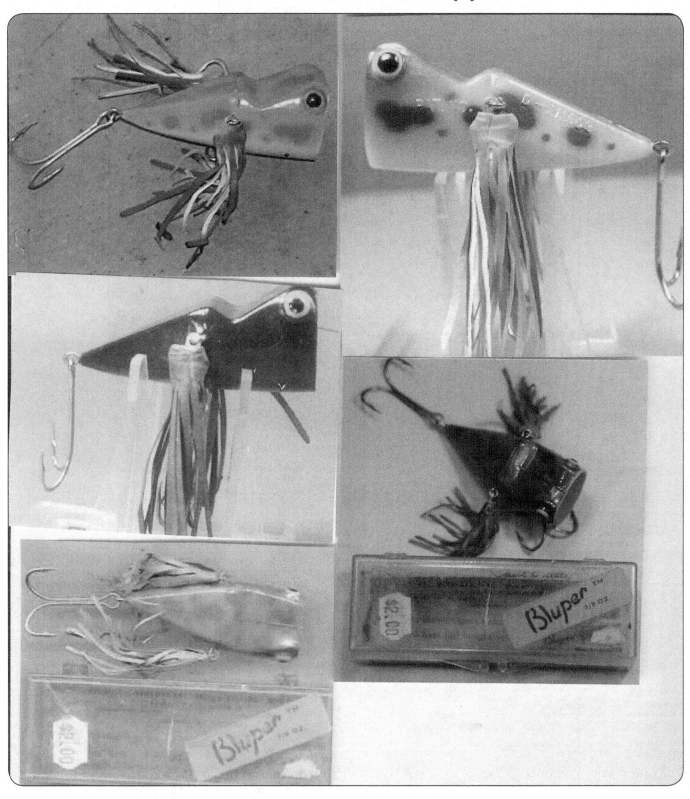

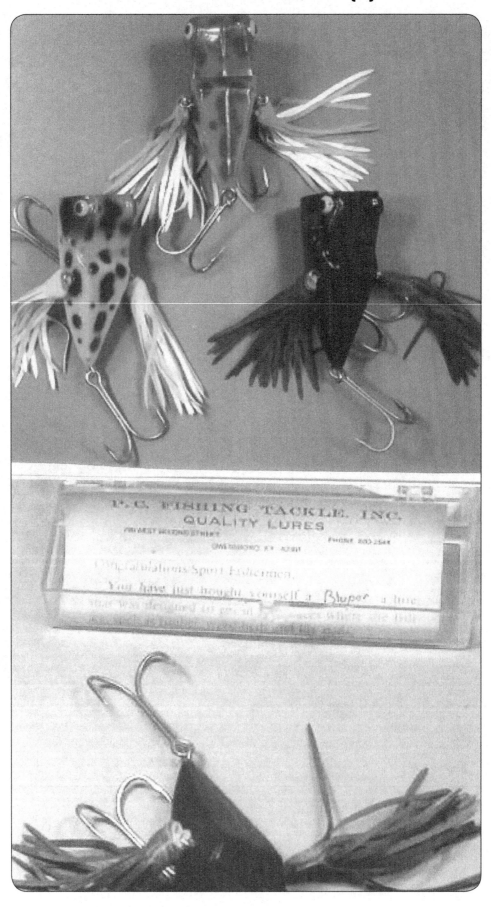

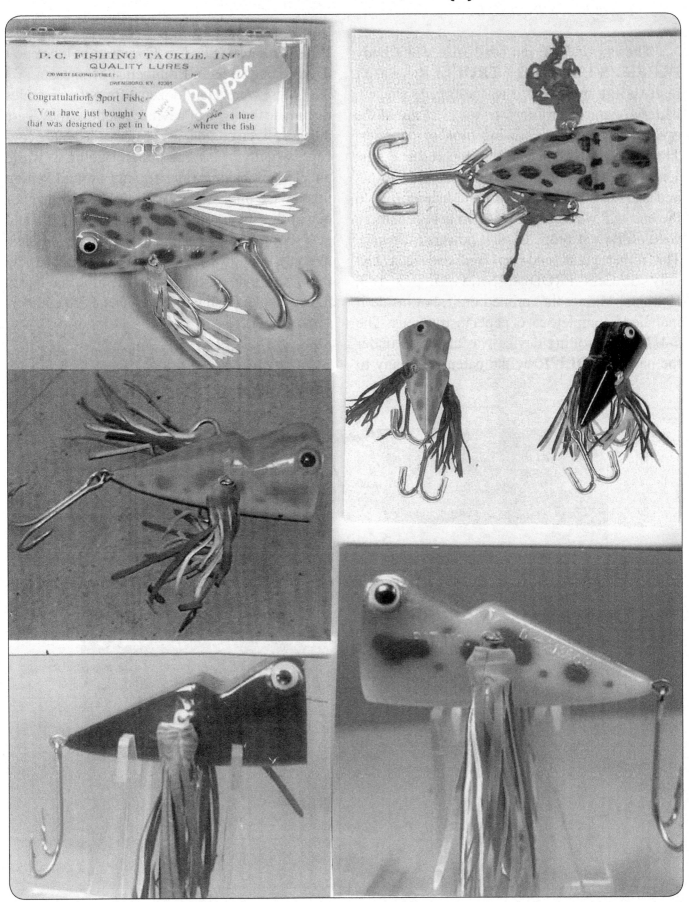

PACER PRODUCTS
HOPKINS, MINNESOTA

The late-1950's, red head with white body **PACER ELECTRIC TROLLER** wasn't really a lure by itself. It was a torpedo-shaped, battery-operated trolling device. It could be opened at the center for insertion of batteries. There were two holes in the double back fins. The top hole was to secure the fisherman's line, and the bottom hole was for the fishing line to the bait that was to be trolled. In between, there was a little red propeller that powered the unit. The rather plain, end-flap cardboard box had only "PACER PRODUCTS....P. O. Box 183, Hopkins, Minnesota" printed on it, but inside it included a complete set of paper instructions. The 5-1/2"-long trolling device was also sold under the name **TROLL'R** by the parent company to Pacer Products, Sta-Tite Corporation located at 277 Steiner Street in Bonifacius, Minnesota.

There were a half dozen different companies that made this type of device. I believe they were all short-lived companies because the whole concept is faulty. Fishermen aren't going to waste all of their fishing time fooling around setting this device up just to get a little further distance out in the stream or lake from what they could get from a normal cast. Then, they would have to contend with wind and wave action changing the troller's direction, not to mention having to fight a hooked fish with all of this extra cumbersome weight.

The scarce boxed Pacer Electric Troller trades in the $15 to $25 range.

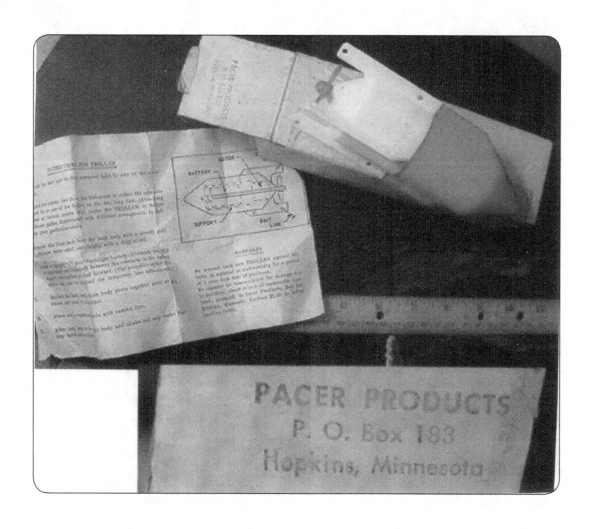

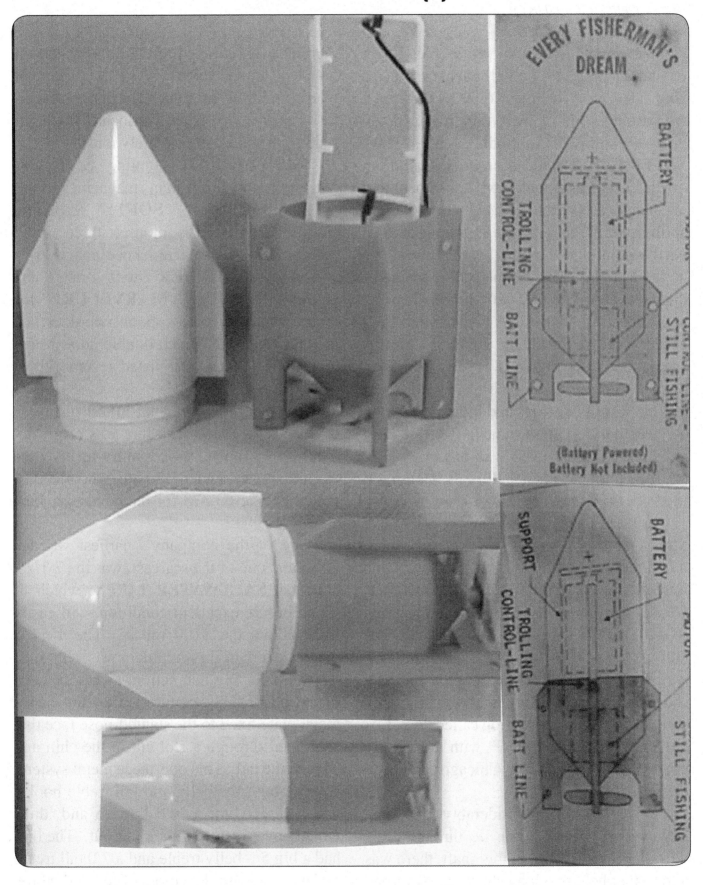

PACHNER AND KOLLER, INC.
CHICAGO, ILLINOIS

The company best known as P & K got its start in 1933 by Leo C. Pachner, who, a year later, took in Fred Koller as a partner. As partners, one of their very first productions was the 1935-introduced **MINNOW SAVER HOOK** made in a no-rust, Cadmium finish. This was actually two hooks bent in a W-shaped fashion and held together by a tight spring wire wrap with one end finished as a needle point and the other as a U-clip. The head of the minnow was placed up inside of this yoke and skewered with the needle point and clipped in place. Leo Pachner and Fred Koller received Patent No. 2,051,651 for this special hook on August 18, 1936. The company also made some take-off variations of this hook for both frogs and minnows.

Another important name in P & K history is Frank Koranda, who was made supervisor of the new Momence, Illinois, plant built in 1945.

In 1939, P & K, located at 2317 West 69th Street, Chicago, was one of the early manufacturers of quality rubber lures with the introduction of **SOFTY THE WONDER CRAB** (invented by a Dr. Deering) and **SOFTY THE WONDER FROG**. The crab was made in four sizes, and the frog was made in two sizes, although a third fly rod size frog was also made of rubber in a different style. A rubber frog called "KICKY, THE SWIMMING FROG" with a similarly shaped body was made in Chicago at close to the same time.

This frog was considerably different, however, as it had a line tie through-body wire shaft. At the end of this shaft, there was a loop that held two long shank down-turned single hooks with molded-on rubber legs. As the lure was retrieved through the water, the hind legs moved about, giving the appearance of a swimming motion. The lure was sold in a square, two-piece cardboard box with reddish print and is extremely rare.

Ads from 1941 Hunting & Fishing and National Sportsman magazines listed the following lures: "SOFTY" crab, four sizes; "LIFELIKE" mouse, three sizes; "SPOTTY" the amazing knee action frog, two sizes; "SHINNER" with orange tail and fins, three sizes; "MARVELURE" the mouse-shaped weedless spoon, two sizes; and the "RIVALURE" fixed double hook weedless spoon. The ad also listed several rubber insect fly rod lures.

The Marvelure was put into distribution by P & K in 1940. The lure was originally made by Advance Devices and was invented in 1938 by Alexander Horvath, who received Patent No. 2,163,378 for the device on June 20, 1939.

One of the company's earliest wooden lures, and one of the scarcest, was the 7-1/2", 3-1/2-oz. **SALTWATER LIPPY**, which, if found in rare excellent condition, will easily trade above the $100 range. The 1-5/8"-diameter lure at the shoulders was very sturdily built for big fish action, as can be seen in the under-belly picture. The lure had a metal plate fixed to the slanted-nose face that continued through a slot cut in the chin and back to the tail. This one-piece metal system, holding both the belly and tail treble hooks, was a direct link to the line tie and, thus, would never result in hook pullout. The lure had a big 5/0 belly treble and a 7/0 tail treble and was made in the colors of red and white, squid, blue scale, and silver.

Another big wooden lure was the 5-1/2" **SALT-WATER WALKIE TALKIE** that had a sturdy metal plate marine glued inside to reinforce the belly and tail treble hooks against pullout. It was made in the same colors as the Lippy.

The company produced a long line of Tenite-plastic lures, including the two sizes of the flat-tail plunker type, **WALKIE TALKIE**, in the lengths of 2-7/8" and the very scarce 1-3/8" long. Pictured is a cute ad from 1946 of a couple of ladies advertising the Bright Eyes and Walkie Talkie lures.

The **AMAZIN MAIZE**, with big eye sockets and fat head, had a small dive lip and a wire line tie. The Amazin Maize was developed by Louis D. Adam in 1946, and he received Patent No. 2,473,324 on June 14, 1949, for the lure. Adam was from Ponca City, Oklahoma, and he developed a number of spinners and lures for Al Foss over the years.

The curved-body lure, **BRIGHT EYES**, with a small nose notch and one-piece surface hardware was made in a 2-3/4" standard model and with a metal deep dive lip, called the **DEEP RUNNING BRIGHT EYES**. This lure was invented by a Ponca City, Oklahoma, person by the name of Nelia G. Poplin in 1945. Design Patent No. D142,305 was granted to her on August 28, 1945. Design Patent D147,102 was granted on July 15, 1947, and shared by Nelia Poplin and Louis Adams for the Deep Running Bright Eyes. Although very rare, the BRIGHT EYES was also made in a fly-rod and a musky size.

Another Tenite lure with a molded, half-moon chin lip to spin the lure and a high raised fish tail was the **WHIRL-A-WAY**. This lure had a long, through-body wire system with a half-moon in-line lead keel weight out front and a trailing long shank double hook.

By far, however, the most popular collectible of the Tenite line was the **SPINNING MINNIE**. This 3-1/4" lure was also made in a 1" fly rod size. The larger one had an external hook hanging harness. The wire harness hung below the lure and was connected to the through-body wire axis at both ends of the torpedo-shaped lure. The lure had a three-quarter round metal spiral orange-peal spinning device that was secured to the lure body by two tiny screws. Unlike the other plastic lures that were offered in ten different colors, this lure was made in just three: frog, aluminum, and copper-gold. The lure entered into production in 1942 or 1943. It was invented in 1941 by Warren H. Flood, of Gurnee, Illinois, who revived patent No. 2,306,692 for the lure on December 29, 1942.

A rather scarce lure by P & K was the 1930's **NIGHT CRAWLER**, which consisted of two folded-over rubber night crawlers, each with a single hook embedded near the tail. The lure had two forward spinner blades with red plastic ball bearings. The Night Crawler was mounted on a pink color selling card. This same spinner-blade system was also incorporated into a **MINNOW HARNESS** and a **JUNE BUG SPINNER**.

The P & K Company also produced the **HAMEL'S HOOK HOLDERS, RAP-A ROUND SINKERS**, fish stringers, glass rods, leaders, fish scalers, folding minnow nets, and small heavy plastic lure boxes.

If you don't know it by now, I never have

been a great believer in or favored any type of spring minnow hooks or lures, or even complicated minnow and frog rigs. They were totally unnecessary in days of old, or any time, in my opinion. Fishing is not so difficult that every bite or strike has to be a catch. I never had any trouble catching all the fish I wanted with a simple single hook in the mouth, with maybe a trailing stinger hook on cold water days, and I can't imagine why old time fishermen would put up with all of those heavy and cumbersome frog and minnow hooks.

The familiar two-piece cardboard red lure box with black trim is well known with the statement, "TESTED AND PROVED LURES AND FISHING ACCESSORIES." A slight variation of this box was the lure picture box, such as for the WHIRL-A-WAY.

A very scarce P & K production was Catalog No. 55, **TRAP BAIT**. This was a rubber spotted frog and a natural color crawfish sold as a set in the traditional two-piece cardboard box. Each lure had a metal clip to attach to a trap pan, primarily for attracting raccoons.

Just as Creek Chub, South Bend, Paw Paw, and other companies had done, P & K introduced a cheaper line of lures-division in their company. CLIPPER LURES was formed at 122 N. Dixie Highway in Momence, Illinois, and they produced at least seven known lures. The **CLIPPER BASS WOBBLER** was a "Bass-Oreno" look-a-like made at 2-1/2" and 3-3/4" long. The 3" **CLIPPER TOP KICK** was a very similar plunker to the "Walkie Talkie", except it did not have a flattened tail. The "River Runt" types of the No. 500 2-3/4" and No. 511 1-3/4" lures were called the **CLIPPER WIGGLERS**. The No.

508 4" and the No. 509 3" **CLIPPER ZIG-ZAG** were notched-mouth darter type lures. A 3-3/4" torpedo-shaped lure with props fore and aft was called the **CLIPPER SURFACE SPINNER**. Another smaller 1-3/4" lure with a fingerprint nose dive lip was the **CLIPPER TINY MITE**. The one-piece blue cardboard with plastic cover Clipper Lures box had a picture of a three-mast "Clipper Ship" on the left side of the bottom box half.

P & K also manufactured a fishing accessory, the **PAPAROUND** universal ribbon sinkers in a white box with red print. There were one dozen of these 1/8"-wide, thin lead sinkers to a box for just 10 cents.

I'm picturing a lure made by an unknown lure maker, I believe in Chicago, who was inspired by the P & K softy, The Wonder Frog. The 4-1/2" hard rubber frog with a soft center was called **KICKY**, The Swimming Frog, with moving hinged hind legs. It was sold in a white cardboard box that gave no maker's name or address. The boxed Kicky Frog trades in the $300 to $400 range.

GROUP PICTURE No. 1: The boxed P & K Whirl-A-Way shows one of the problems this lure had in keeping the red paint on the forward lead weight and stabilizer keel. The frog color lure below it is an exception with all of the paint intact. The rubber **P & K FROG POPPER** is one of the company's scarcer frog lures. The picture of the pipe-smoking man is from the front cover of a 32-page book entitled ADVENTURES IN FISHING written for P & K in 1946 by the famous muskie fisherman, Cal Johnson. Next is an ad for the PAPAROUND Ribbon Sinkers and the P & K **FEATHER SPINNER**.

GROUP PICTURE No. 2:   This set

includes early lures by P & K, including the patent for the Minnow Saver Hook with the hook and box. To the right is the Chicago KICKY, the Swimming Frog by an unknown maker, and a copy of Softy the Wonder Frog. Below that is a **P & K FROG HOOK** that was a take-off of the Minnow Saver hook. Next is a 1930's production of the Night Crawler and the Deering "Softy The Wonder Crab" plus the next boxed version of that crab.

GROUP PICTURE No. 3: First is the very popular collectible Spinning Minnie in all three of its colors, including one of its early boxes and the scarce 1" fly rod size. Next is the patented Marvelure, after P & K became a distributor of it. Also pictured are side views of the P & K Frog Hook and a suspect dive lip frog and minnow hook that may not be a P & K.

GROUP PICTURE No. 4: This set includes some of the rubber baits made by P & K, including two Spotty The Wonder Frogs, along with two plastic Amazin Maize lures. Next is a boxed Softy Crab, made in four sizes, and a boxed P & K Mouse, made in three sizes. Next are two very early **BAIT ROD SHINERS** that were later made with orange forked fish tails. Next is a **FLY ROD RUBBER MINNOW** on its red card. Last is an early closed-leg 3" **RUBBER FROG** with weedless hook.

GROUP PICTURE No. 5: This set includes the scarce 7-1/2" Saltwater Lippy lures, showing both the nose and belly views of the unique hardware. Also pictured are a red head with white lure and a blue scale with blue-tipped tail lure, two colors of the 5-1/2" Saltwater Walkie Talkies.

GROUP PICTURE No. 6: This group includes various colors of the Whirl-A-Way, one with box. Finding a Whirl-A-Way with a coat of full-color, unblemished paint on the forward lead weight is indeed very difficult. Also pictured is copy of a 1946 magazine ad, "P & K HEADLINER!" for the Bright Eyes and Walkie Talkie lures. Next to it is a full page ad from May 1941 that appeared in the National Sportsman magazine.

GROUP PICTURE No. 7: This set includes the cheaper line of baits made by P & K's subsidiary company Clipper Lures that was located ay 122 N. Dixie Highway in Momence, Illinois. First is a 4-1/2" No. 505 **CLIPPER JOINTED PIKIE**. Next is a 4-1/4" No. 506 **CLIPPER MINNOW**, and last is a 3-7/8" No. 501 CLIPPER BASS WOBBLER. To the right are two catalog pages of all of the Clipper lures.

With the exception of the boxed Saltwater Lippy, exceeding $100 to as high as $150, the Saltwater Walkie Talkie, at $50 and up, and the Tenite Spinning Minnie, exceeding $50, most other P & K and Clipper boxed lures trade in the $20 to $40 range.

GROUP PICTURE No. 8: This includes two of the scarcer P & K rubber lures from the 1940's. Pictured is a 1941 ad copy, and No. 8 on this ad poster is for the 2-1/2" **FLY ROD SPOTTY FROG** that is pictured below. No. 14 on the ad poster is for the 4" BAIT ROD SHINER that is pictured to the right. As in this example, finding a P & K Shiner with all of the tail and the top dorsal fin fully intact is difficult.

The Spotty Frog trades in the $20 to $30 range, and a Shiner in excellent condition will trade higher, in the $35 to $45 range.

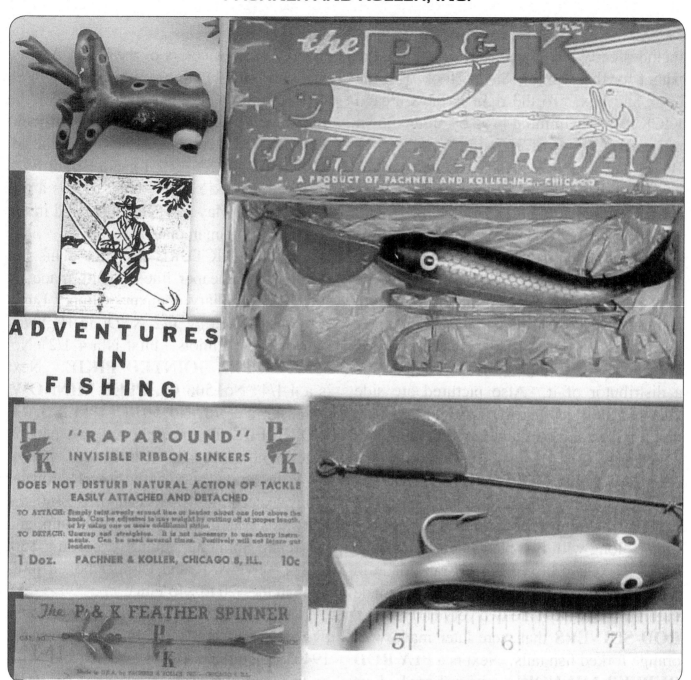

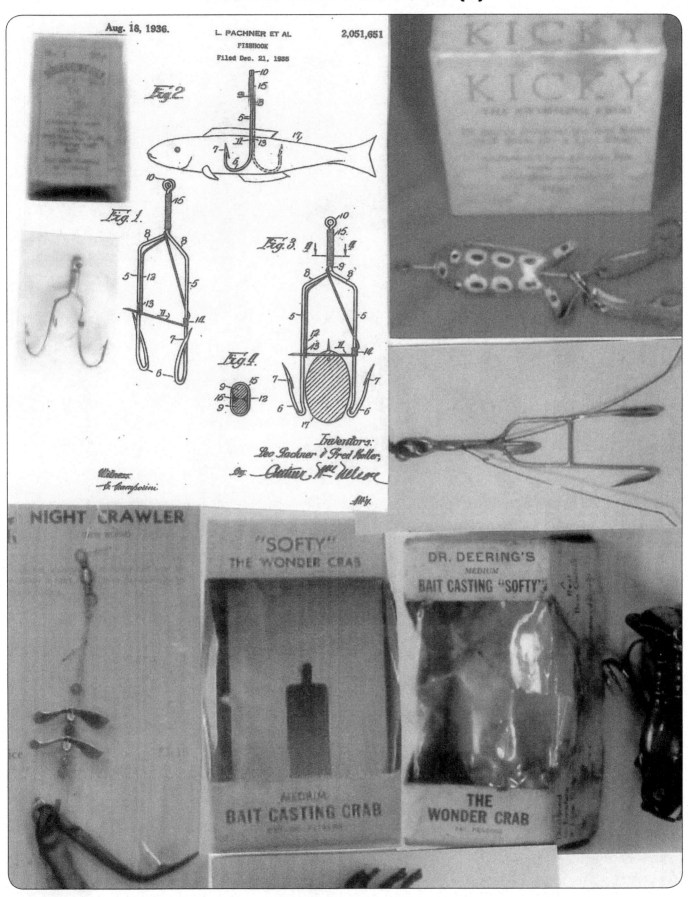

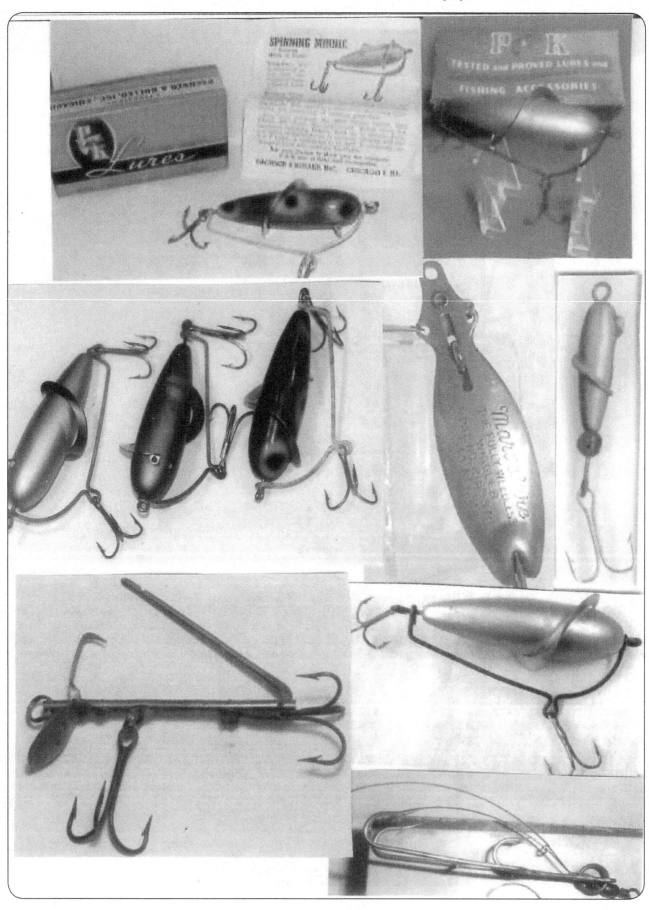

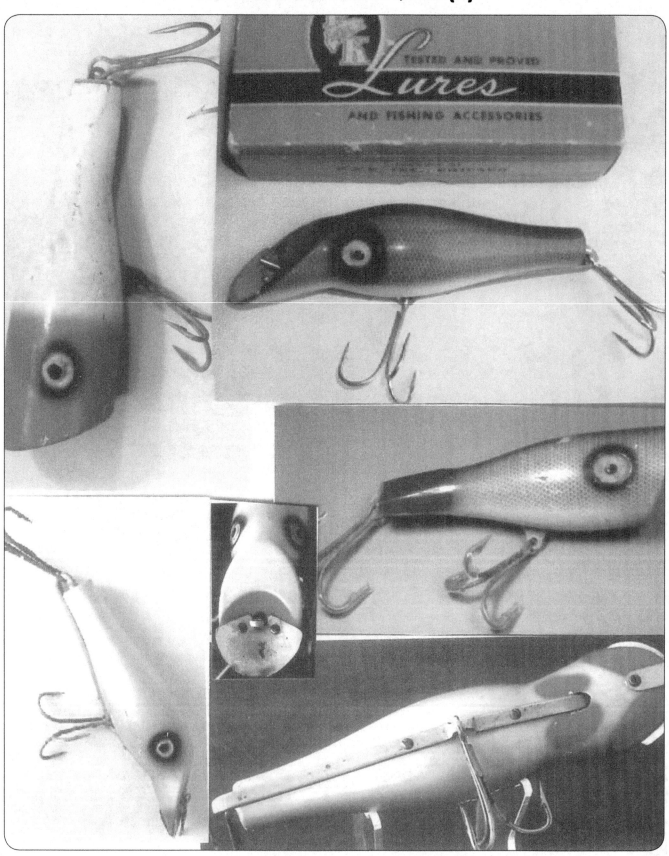

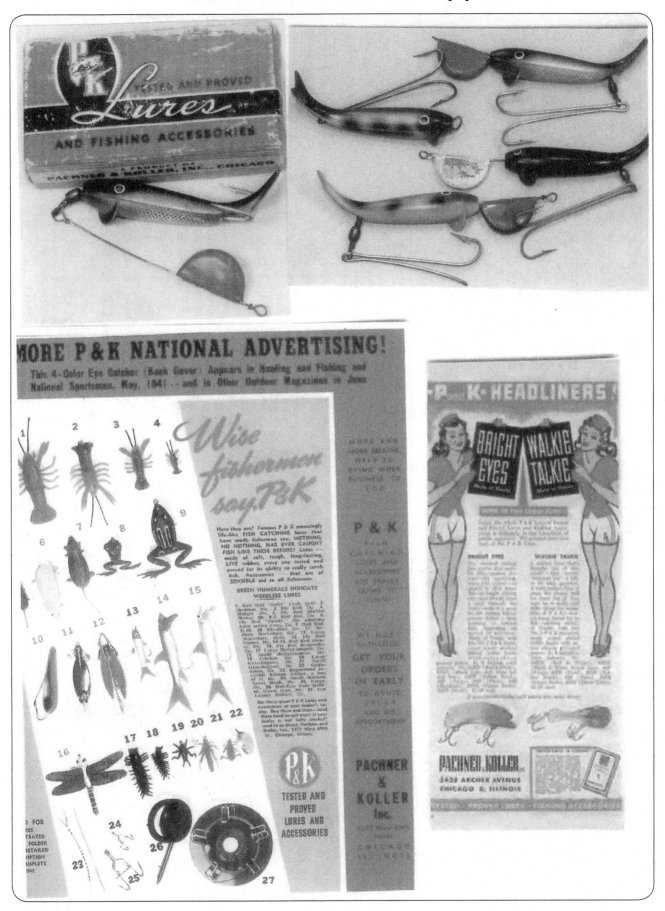

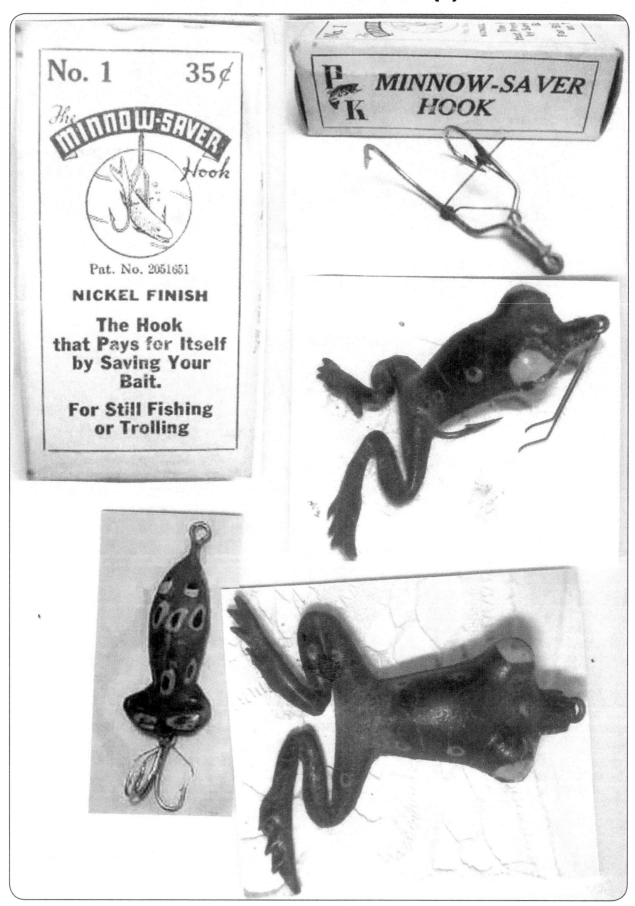

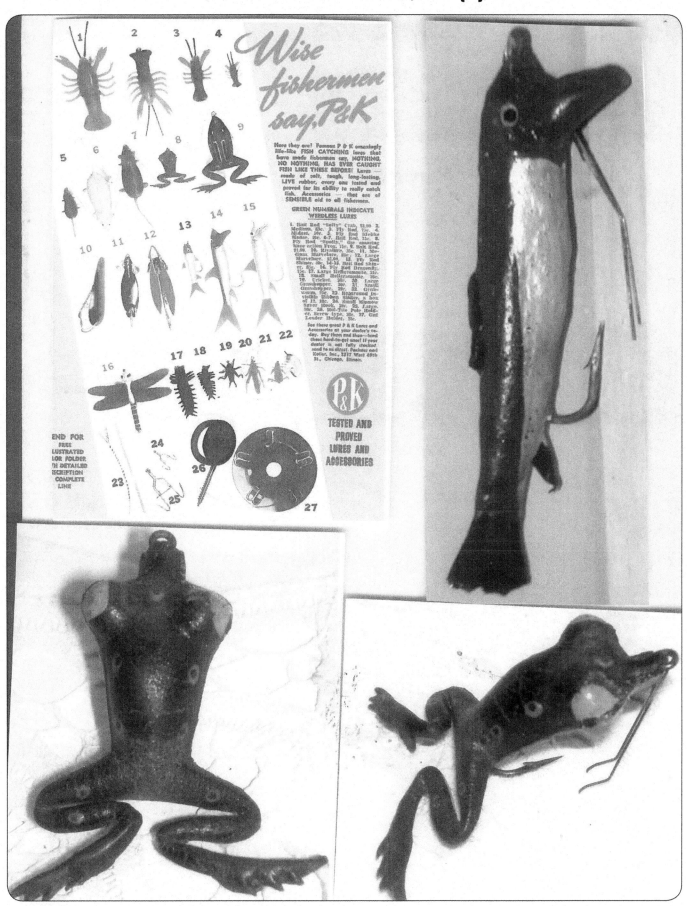

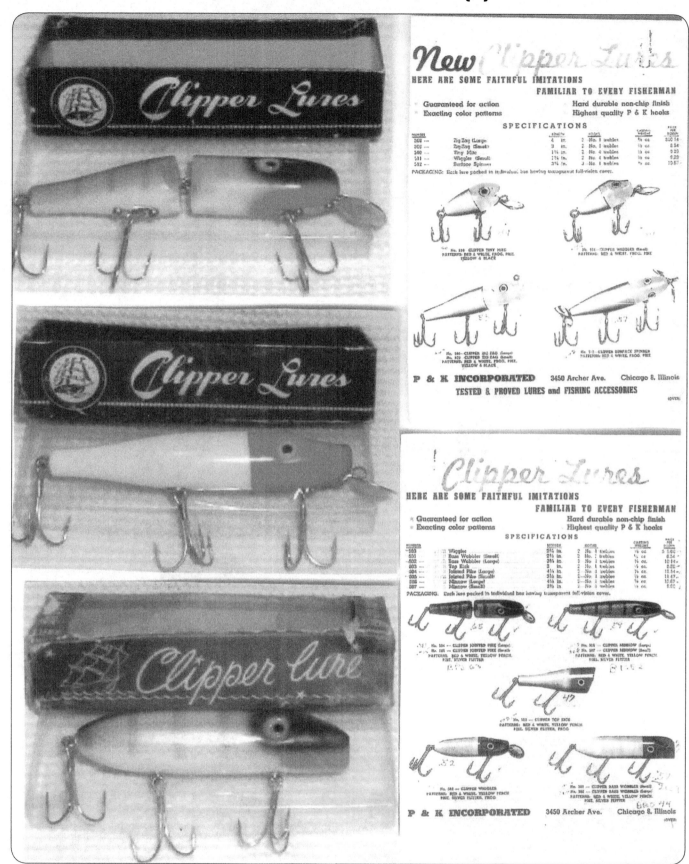

PACIFIC FISHING TACKLE
PORTLAND, OREGON

In the early 1930's, the Pacific Fishing Tackle Company, which was located at 1935 S. E. Hawthorne in Portland, Oregon, developed a new idea for a fishing spoon. The **JONES PROPELLED FISH SPOON** was 4" long overall with a large 2-1/8" brass hammer-finished Bear Valley type spinner blade. What made this spinner different from most was its angle of attack to the water. The blade had a flange soldered to the tail that held it out from the main wire shaft a full 1", causing the propeller to rotate even in slow-moving stream water or on a slow retrieve. The propeller strut was shielded from water currents by the extra-wide spinner blade, making for erratic movements compared to that of a darting minnow. The Propelled Fish Spoon was equipped with a large box swivel and was stapled to a blue ID card.

Lure picture is courtesy of the Arne Soland collection.

The rare carded Jones Propelled Fish Spoon trades in the $15 to $20 range.

PACIFIC NORTHWEST SALMON PLUGS & LURES

From the 1920's to the 1950's, salmon fishing in the Seattle area Elliot Bay-Puget Sound waters was at its best, as well as all up and down the Pacific North American coast line from California to Canada. There was a terrific proliferation of wooded lure makers from 1930 to 1950, the largest of which were Hansen, Hook Brothers, Martin, Minser-Lucky Louie, Rosegard, and others. I may have already covered some of these early Oregon, Washington, and other western salmon lure makers in these books elsewhere; however, between the 1920's and the 1950's there were just too many other Pacific Northwest salmon lure makers for me to dwell on all of them. Besides, unless you are an expert collector specializing in salmon lures, few regular collectors can tell one from the other in most cases, as they were all very similar in appearance and in performance. If there were distinctive features in any of the lure inventors that I'm about to list, I will point out those characteristics. Most of these lure makers used Alaskan yellow cedar to make their lures because it was a hardwood, very tightly grained. This wood was then soaked in a mixture of lacquer and plastic glass in order to waterproof the wood. Most had the traditional slant noses, glass eyes, and quality heavy-duty hooks and swivels. I am also covering metal salmon lure makers, and some of these companies may have also made lures for steelhead, trout, and saltwater fishing for other than salmon. The following list by no means covers all of the 100-plus lure makers making wooden salmon plugs and another 70-plus metal lure makers in that era.

I never had a large collection of Pacific Northwest salmon plugs in my collection, so, for the most part, I'm not going to state any trade values in this book, except on some more obscure lures that are not known to many collectors. It is almost impossible to present realistic trade values on any specific group of lures, such as these, unless you are confronted with them at least once a year or less, which has not been the case with me. My purpose in writing these books was not for them to be a price value guide, anyway; it was to pass on and preserve what history I knew or developed for future generation collectors. At the end of each of these sub-stories, the picture group (PG) number is indicated in parentheses.

ABE & AL TACKLE COMPANY
PORT ANGELES, WASHINGTON

In the later 1930's and into the early 1940's, Gene "Abe" Caulkins and Harry "Al" Coventon formed their Abe & Al Tackle Company at 114 W. 14th in Port Angeles, Washington. They became the exclusive distributors of the Al McKnight-developed **AL MCSPOON**. The spoon (4-3/8" is the size pictured, but there were two other sizes) was shaped like a Herring with a peaked roof high lateral line and a wide forked tail. The lure was made to perform like a crippled herring. It was made in a half nickel and half brass finish with the lateral line dividing the two color finishes. Each lure was named stamped "AL Mc" and was equipped with a large single salmon hook or a smaller double hook.

Al McKnight started making metal salmon lures in the mid 1930's out of Port Angeles, Washington. Most of his spoons were stamped "**AL MAC**" or just "**AL MC**". His most unique spoon was the 4-1/2" **MCKNIGHT SPECIAL** that, at a glance, looked like the Michigan Edson "Fish Fooler". The sleek, long, fish-shaped spoon had raised ridges running the center length of the spoon.

Pictured with this story are two scarce McKnight salmon spoons, the 4-3/8" half nickel and half brass **AL MC MINNOW**, and the 3-1/2" **MCKNIGHT NO. 4** that had five different light reflecting planes. (PG-2)

ALASKA TACKLE COMPANY
SEATTLE, WASHINGTON

You might wonder how this company got its name, being located at 203 White Building and later 4619 37th Avenue S. W., both in Seattle, Washington. It's because Allan R. Seaton was from Juneau, Alaska, and he was the designer of the swivel hook system used on these early, late-1940's **ALASKAN PLUGS**. He was awarded Patent No. 2,561,144 on July 17, 1951, for that swivel hook system he designed in 1948. He also had an earlier patent issued on March 19, 1942, No. 2,275,869. The lures were made of polished hollow brass in a torpedo shape with a slanted and cupped nose. The scarcer model is the one hooker, but both are pictured. The two-belly hook models were 5-1/2" long, and the one-hook models were 4-1/2" long. Both two-piece white cardboard lure boxes were the same, except for the different street addresses in the lower left corners of the covers. (PG-3,43)

ALBIN TACKLE COMPANY
TACOMA & SPOKANE, WASHINGTON

The principle production by this company was the **ALBIN SPINNER**, in 2-3/4" and 3-1/4" sizes, shaped like a modern bow hunter's big game four-bladed arrowhead. The lures were first patented by John R. Bingham on December 4, 1923, under Patent No. 1,476,139. Albin Abrahams moved the company at a later date to Spokane, Washington. He had used his first name in founding his Albin Lure Company. He slightly modified the Bingham patent in production of his later version of the lure that resembles today's modern hunting arrowhead. He named the lure the ALBIN SPINNER and made the lure's larger plate of copper and the top, smaller plate of aluminum, and these flashing, alternating colors helped attract fish. The diamond-shaped blades had opposite-facing twists at the tail to make the lure revolve. Patent No. 1,804,391 was awarded to Albin Abrahams on May 12, 1931. (PG-4)

ALLEN TACKLE COMPANY
SEATTLE, WASHINGTON

In 1935, Percy H. Allen, of Seattle, Washington, produced a 2-1/4 and 3-1/2" metal salmon spoon he called the **LIMPER**. The Ohio Pflueger Company introduced their version of the spoon at around the same time. However, it was Allen who invented and patented the lure under Patent No. 2,058,121 granted on October 20, 1936. The Pflueger Company purchased the rights to the Limper lure shortly after the patent was issued. (PG-4)

B. K. MANUFACTURING COMPANY
PORTLAND, OREGON

In the late 1940's, the B. K. Manufacturing Company, located at 8333 S. E. 13th Street in Portland, Oregon, made metal trolling spoons and spinners for trout and salmon fishing in both salt and fresh waters. The pictured example is a 2-1/8", highly polished, egg-shaped brass spinner blade mounted on a shaft with two glass red bead spacer-bearings. The white card had red print and indicated on the back, "We guarantee the workmanship and materials in this spoon to be of the highest quality."

S. E. BACON
BACON BROS. FISH LURE COMPANY
SEATTLE, WASHINGTON

In 1938, Sydney E. Bacon and his brother introduced a salmon lure that really was different from the others. The only wooden part of the lure was the fish-shaped head, which, from a top view, was teardrop-shaped and, from a side view, had a typical salmon plug notched mouth. The eyes were glass, and the line tie was channeled through to the hook heavy cord (some had Snell tied hooks). The back of the head was slotted, and the body of the lure was cut in the shape of a fish out of a rubber-leather compound which was marine cemented in the back of the head slot. The cord (or Snell) to the line tie had two single hooks tied to it, and the cord was held up to the belly by a metal clip near the tail. When a fish struck the lure, there was no pressure put on the lure itself, as the hooks pulled away and the cord was on a direct line to the nose line tie. Sydney E. Bacon received Patent No. 2,183,059 for this lure on December 12, 1939.

In 1933, Al Sisco, working out of Loraine, Ohio, patented a lure called the Shure-Bite Minnow that had a hard plastic head and a flexible rubberized body. A few years later, in 1938, Charles D. Lovelace patented a Breathing Minnow in San Antonio, Texas. That 3" hard plastic head minnow had a hollow silk cloth body that filled with water via a nose port that gave the appearance of a breathing, swimming action. This same era lure by the Bacon Brothers, working out of 137 North 83rd Street in Seattle, Washington, was a very similar lure that they called **THE MINNOW THAT SWIMS**.

The lure was sold in a red two-piece cardboard lure box with white print on the cover. The Bacon Brother's minnow is very rare, especially fully intact (like the one pictured) as the bodies usually deteriorated over the years. Because of the rarity of this lure in nice condition, the lure in box (like the one pictured) will trade in the $500 to $600 range.

Pictures are courtesy of the Roscoe Plikerd collection. (PG-4,5)

BARDON-GREAVES COMPANY
SEATTLE, WASHINGTON

In 1928, Donis M. Bardon formed the Bardon-Greaves partnership in Seattle, Washington, and made at least one salmon spoon, the 5-1/2" **BARCO SPOON**. The teardrop-shaped spoon had a dimple in the center and a spoon-cupped-shaped area at the tail. Patent No. 1,938,653 was awarded to Donis M. Bardon on December 12, 1933. (PG-5)

EDDIE BAUER SPORTING GOODS
SEATTLE, WASHINGTON

Eddie Bauer (1899 - 1986) started his Sporting Goods Company at 519 Union Street in Seattle, Washington, sometime in the later 1920's. In addition to distributing salmon plugs for other lure makers, he developed his own line of wooden salmon plugs called the **BAUER PRECISION TESTED PLUGS**. Bauer was very particular about all of his plugs being cut the same way on lathes and properly balanced; in fact, he guaranteed, "Every item we sell will give you complete satisfaction or you may return it for a full refund." Bauer also sold his plugs under the trade name **PROVEN KILLER**. His two-piece cardboard lure box had the print in the upper left corner, "It's all in the head." In the center of the box was the outline of a salmon with "BAUER" printed in the belly and "PRECISION" printed in the mouth and

"TESTED" on the tail. In 1936, Eddie Bauer made a 5" torpedo-shaped spoon, named simply, the **BAUER BAIT**, with a bent-down, squared tail. (PG-5)

BUZZ FLIES
SEATTLE, WASHINGTON

I'm picturing a 4"-overall-long streamer salmon fly that was given the name **KANDLEFISH KATE** that was tied by "Buzz" Fiorini of Seattle, Washington. This carded fly may look like just another salmon fly, but, when you learn of the history behind it and the man who tied it, you will realize that this is a special fly of significance.

Sebastian "Buzz" Fiorini has been an avid outdoors enthusiast in the Washington area all of his life. One of his outdoor passions in his younger years was skiing, and, in 1947, he and his wife, Julie, founded the Fiorini Ski School in Seattle, Washington, that provided top-notch ski instructions and even transportation from the school to the slopes. Buzz Fiorini was also an avid fisherman, particularly a fly rod fisherman, and he has won many awards in that area. He was also a popular fishing guide, was his own skilled pilot, and, later on, was a significant rod builder.

Buzz had worked for a few years at the Orvis Company, and, in 1950, he founded the famous Fenwick Rod Company. In 1960, he opened Fiorini Sports at 2686 N. E. 49th Street in Seattle, Washington.

You would think that Buzz Fiorini, in his better 70 years of age by the year 2000, would be willing to slow down and retire, but that was not so. In that year, he formed a partnership with another famous rod and line maker, Bill McGuire, and, together, they founded the B & B Enterprise Company at 1240 Center Street in

Rock Island, Washington, where they specialized in rods and other equipment for handicapped or partially disabled fishermen. The picture of the two men with this story is from the year 2000, with Buzz Fiorini on the left and his new partner Bill McGuire on the right, in their new B & B Enterprise store.

So now you know why I consider the Kandlefish Kate salmon streamer fly a fly of significance.

Part of this history and the pictures are courtesy of writer Dave Graybill. (PG-5,6)

The carded Kandlefish by Buzz Fiorini trades in the $20 to $35 range.

CANADIAN BAIT COMPANY
WINNIPEG, MANITOBA, CANADA

I should point out that there was no connection between the late-1940's and early-1950's Canadian Bait Company of Manitoba and the other one in Minneapolis, Minnesota. The Canada Company made a lure that resembled the "Williams Wabbler", a 2-3/4" spoon called the **WHALEBACK**. They also made a teardrop-shaped **DEVIL BAIT**, a 3" oval-shaped **WIZZARD**, and a 1-1/2" pointed-nose "Dardevle" type called the **CANADIAN BAIT**.

CHESTER BAIT COMPANY
VANCOUVER, BRITISH COLUMBIA, CANADA

In 1934, Frank Reginald Chester developed a different idea for a salmon spoon. The lure consisted of two flat planes of sheet metal cut in a rounded bathtub shape. The front half of one plane had the side bent up at an angle towards the rear of the spoon. The second plane also had a bent-up side covering half the length of the spoon angled from the rear towards the front of the spoon, but to the opposite side. These two sides of the lure were then soldered together, giving the lure both two light reflecting planes and also a spinning action caused by the two raised flanges. Frank R. Chester was awarded Patent No. 2,017,486 for his **CHESTER SPOON** on October 15, 1935. (PG-6)

CHIX FISH LURE COMPANY
SEATTLE, WASHINGTON

William Slepica filed for a patent on July 28, 1939, and was granted Patent No. 1,239,404 on April 22, 1941, for his lure made by Chix Lures Company. **CHIX** lure had a forehead line tie fixed to a wire passing at a downward angle through the lure to the tail treble hook. Along the way, it also was secured to a swivel through an access belly hole for that treble hook. The nose of the lure was double notched to a center point like on a railroad snow plow. The three-arm and screw-held round nose dive lip may have been made for this lure by Heddon. In any event, it was just like the dive lip used on Heddon's "Vamp". The lure had hand-painted gills and an unusual dot-finish scale pattern. The Chix lure had painted eyes with indent irises and raised center pupils and was made in a total of one-and-a-half dozen different body colors. Later, on November 22, 1948, William Slepica filed for another patent on a typical salmon plug, and patent No. 2,497,473 was granted to him on February 14, 1950. This CHIX lure had swiveled hooks and pressed eyes with indented irises and raised pupils, and a tail belly screw to secure the tail hook system. The lure box was two-piece red cardboard with a jumping fish on the left about to engulf a CHIX plug and print, "SALMON-MUSKIES Chix Swiveled Fishing Lures." The company, located at 2637 West 87th Street in Seattle, Washington, also sold their lures in a similar white box that basically had the same print and picture on the top of the box cover. (PG-6,7)

CLINK SALMON PLUGS
SEDRO WOOLLEY, WASHINGTON

The 5" and 5-3/4" **CLINK** wooden salmon plug was a little different from the norm. It had the typical slanted face but had an oval-shaped metal deflector plate secured by a screw and the line tie. This metal piece covered the slanted face and extended slightly both above the head and below the chin. The eyes were unpainted concave washers with center holes for the pupils. The lure had a metal pointed cone piece fixed to the tail for balance. The Clink had the typical cord-held treble hooks on the belly, but also had the addition of four red cords dangling from the belly to simulate a blood trail. Some of these lures had the red cords installed in the tails. Ray Clink started making his plugs at the end of World War II, in 1946, out of Sedro Woolley, Washington. He applied for a patent in that year, and Patent No. 2,515,591 was issued to him on July 18, 1950. (PG-7)

CORDELL & SEGER
RENTON, WASHINGTON

In 1930, John U. Cordell formed the Cordell & Seger partnership in Renton, Washington, and produced at least one salmon spoon, the 3-1/4" long **C & S JIGGER SPOON**. The long oval-shaped spoon was twisted into a mild S-shape front to back and had curled-down sides. John Cordell was awarded Patent No. 1,924,350 for his spoon on August 29, 1933. (PG-7)

E. A. DAHLQUIST
LONG BEACH, CALIFORNIA

In 1926 they developed the **DAHLQUIST**

TROUT SPINNER that was somewhat unique in design. The spinner blade was made from a thin and pliable piece of sheet metal and cut in an overall-arrowhead shape with the wing tips curled in opposite directions. The spinner was designed to glide through the water with ease with a rapid rotation. The spinner blade had fish-attracting serrations on the surface, simulating fish scales and a multitude of glass red spacer bearings that were arranged to also help give extra thrust. The blade had an elongated elliptical slot cut in the center for the wire through shaft to hold up to seven red glass beads inside of this window, as well as the beads at both the front and tail of this blade. The Trout Spinner was designed to be cast or trolled as a fishing lure with a hook attached or without a hook as a forward attracter with a trailing live bait, fly, or lure. Ernest A. Dahlquist was awarded Patent No. 1,627,637 on May 10, 1927, for this spinner blade design. (PG-7)

DANDY-GLO TACKLE COMPANY
SEATTLE, WASHINGTON

The 1970's Dandy-Glo Tackle Company, of Seattle, Washington, made a 5", hollow plastic, semi-transparent plug called the **DANDY-GLO 5**. The lure had the traditional slanted-face salmon-plug shape with a dimpled, convex face. The head screwed off for the insertion of a light bulb and batteries to make this a light-emitting lure for night and dark-water salmon fishing. The lure is pictured in a solid green color. (PG-9)

LES DAVIS FISHING TACKLE COMPANY
DAVE DAVIS
TOCOMA, WASHINGTON

Lester M. Davis and David Davis, with separate companies, were in the business, in Tacoma, Washington, of making casting and trolling trout and salmon spoons and spinners for over 35 years from 1930 to well into the 1980's, when the Les Davis Tackle Company was sold to Luhr Jensen. I believe Les Davis' first patent was on April 28, 1931, under Patent No. 1,803,056, for his **SILVER DART**.

Les Davis, the father of Dave Davis, developed, or at least manufactured and sold, over a dozen different metal lures in his years. His early productions included **EDIZ HOOK**, **JACK-O-DIAMONDS**, **SLIM JIM TROLL**, SILVER DART, and the **WITCH DOCTOR**. In later years, he produced the famous **HOT ROD**, **BIG FRANK**, **RIPPLE**, **POINT DEFIANCE**, **SCALELITE WOBBLER**, and the hard plastic **CUT PLUG**.

The 2"-long (3-5/8" with hook) **PT. DEFIANCE SPOON** is pictured on its card. The spoon had the unique ability to be fished with cut bait that would not kill the action of the spoon.

Lester Davis took the famous 1935-patented **TRIPLE TEASER**, invented by William J. Eggleston, and redesigned it slightly. If you compare the Walla Walla, Washington, Eggleston Patent No. 1,991,142 to the Les Davis Patent No. 3,146,542 granted on September 1, 1964, you will see that the only difference was in the tail. Davis made the lure in a 1-1/8" Triple Teaser size and in a 1-1/2" Big Triple Teaser size.

Dave Davis made most of his lures in the 1950's and 1960's. They included the **SALMON SPINNER**, **INDIANA SPINNER**, and a **HEART SPOON**.

Les Davis made several sizes of pearl wobblers, and I have pictured a 2" **LES DAVIS PEARL WOBBLER** on a tan card with blue trim.

One of the later lures made by Les Davis was introduced in 1958. This was his 3-3/8"-long **CANADIAN WONDER** trolling and casting spoon that was issued Patent No. 2,855,735 in late October of 1958.

The plastic, no-head **DAVIS CUT PLUG** was introduced in 1950 and was invented by Clifford M. Burns from Tacoma, Washington, who received Patent No. 2,642,695 for the lure on June 23, 1953.

One of the more unusual salmon trolling dodgers distributed by Les Davis was the 6-1/2"-overall-long, teardrop-shaped **ARON DODGER**. This flat, metal, forward-trolling dodger had an internal window holding an in-line heart-shaped spinner. Each rotation of this internal blade caused whatever lure that was being trolled to jerk forward erratically. (PG-9,56)

DEE-GEE LURES
AIKI BEACH, WASHINGTON

Dee-Gee Lures made salmon lures very much like the many others out of the small coastal town of Aiki Beach near Seattle, Washington, in the late 1940's and early 1950's. The thing that was different about these early Bead Chain "J-Plug" types was that, I believe, this company was the first, or one of the first, to make a quality plastic salmon plug. The company lined the nose line tie hole, which was direct to the swiveled belly hook location, with brass for extra protection. Pictured is one of their 6"-long, red-and-white-swirl-marbled plastic plugs. The lure had indented yellow painted irises with small black center pupils and was imprinted on the belly, "**DEE-GEE**...PAT PEND." (PG-9)

DEVITO'S LURES
SOLDOTNA, ALASKA

Alaska is another of about six states that are not well represented in these books, due to the fact that they just did not have that many lure makers in their history at any time. So, although

DeVito's Lures, out of Box 317, Soldotna, Alaska, is a relatively modern company, I am going to cover them.

Pictured is the 1970's and 1980's **DEVITO CO-NOOK SALMON LURE**. The cork-body lure was 6-1/4" long overall. Parts of it were made from lure productions of the Worden Company of Washington. Worden invented the "Spinning Moth" and developed it in 1934 but renamed it the "Spin-N-Glo" in more modern times. The Co-Nook lure consist of a round, in-line, 5/8" cork ball up front, followed by a plastic red spacer-bearing and a 1-1/4", cork, teardrop-shaped body with rubber wings, and finally a large 5/0 single salmon hook dressed in a shredded plastic skirt. DeVito was a famous Alaskan fishing guide for the Kenai Peninsula salmon and used the current Yakima Bait Company (the old Worden Company) Spin-N-Glo and their Lil' Corky in tandem with a large shredded plastic tail skirt to form his Co-Nook Salmon Lure. The lure was sold in a plastic sack with a white card with blue print giving "use" instructions and company name and location. The instructions read, "Fish just off the current, but DO NOT fish the slack water. Fish close to the bottom as possible...use a swivel...especially effective when used with a gob of roe" (roe are salmon eggs). (PG-9)

ALLEN DIVINE
PORT ANGELES, WASHINGTON

Allen Divine, working out of Port Angeles, Washington, filed for a patent on March 27, 1942, and Patent No. 2,338,577 was awarded to him on January 4. 1944, for his **DEVINE PLUG**. The plug can be easily identified and not confused with other salmon lures of that era by the notched side grooves and ridges cut on both sides of the lure. These cuts started one-third of the way back from the nose and ran to within one-third of the rest of the distance to the tail. (PG-10)

E & O MANUFACTURING COMPANY
OLYMPIA, WASHINGTON

I believe that the E & O Manufacturing Company, located in Olympia, Washington, only made salmon spoons for two years: 1930 and 1931. Their lures included the 2-3/4" **STEWART KING**, the 3-1/4" **KING SPOON**, the 5" **KING MAC**, a copy of the McMahone Spoon, and the 5-1/4" **HUSKY KING**. The pictured example, Husky King, shows the unique design of the Husky line of spoons. This brass spoon was 1-1/4" wide at the nose and 1-5/8" wide at the tail and had bent, pyramid-shaped tabs at both the nose and tail. The front tab was bent out for the barrel swivel line tie, and the rear tab was bent in for the single large tail hook. This lure was stamped at the nose, "HUSKY KING…Pat. Pend." Two other lures that were all made very similar to the "Andy Reekers Spoon" were the 4" **KING DANDY**, the No. 4 **KING TROLLING SPOON**, and the 3-1/4" **KING**. (PG-10)

ERICKSON LABORATORIES
SEATTLE, WASHINGTON

TRADEWINDS, INC.
TACOMA, WASHINGTON

In 1949, Charles E. Erickson, out of Seattle, Washington, introduced **THE FISH PLUG**, also known as the **SPIN-IN HERRY**. The intro, two-piece, green cardboard box had a silhouette picture of a fish on the cover with "THE FISH PLUG" printed therein. The cover also said, "By ERICKSON Laboratories, Seattle, Wash." The box indicated that the lure was made in four sizes. However, eventually the lure was made in the six sizes: 1-1/2", 2-1/2", 3", 4", 4-1/2", and 5" long. Just prior to these lures being made

by the Tradewinds Company, Erickson Labs was selling them out of a red, one-piece cardboard box with a plastic cover and a blue catalog insert indicating that the Spin-in Herry was made in only three sizes by this time (the pictured example is 5" long). By the 1950's, the lures were manufactured for Erickson by Tradewinds, Inc., out of P.O. Box 1191, Tacoma, Washington.

The lures were designed to be trolled or back cast for varieties of salmon and trout. The Spin-in Herry, a plastic lure, was made most commonly in the sizes of 4-1/2" and 4" long in a bowed-transverse configuration. This curved bait fish simulation had a tiny hole in the head just below and back of the eye and another hole near the tail. A heavy fishing line was pushed through the front hole and knotted so it would not pull through. The line was then tied to a swivel and passed through the tail hole and tied to a treble hook. The tie point to the swivel was key to the lure's spinning action; it was at a point so that the lure would ride at an angle, head forward, and sideways to the fisherman. In this manner, the lure would spin and dart about like the action of a crippled bait fish. See the drawing furnished with the patent.

Lure colors were mostly in natural Herring browns, gold, and silver bait fish colors, but the lures were also made in bright colors, such as the pictured red-flash scale. The TRADEWINDS, INC., one-piece, red cardboard lure box had a plastic cover and yellow print that said "Spin-in Herry" and "TRADEWINDS INC." on the bottom of the box, there was an illustration of the five different hook-up combinations that the lure could be rigged with, along with two varied actions.

By the time Tradewinds was making the lures, the Spin-in Herry was made in six sizes and had pressed, indent eyes with painted gold irises and large center black pupils.

Charles E. Erickson invented the lure in 1949

and was awarded Patent No. 2,595,191 on April 29, 1952.

Sometime in the 1950's, the Tradewinds Company produced a spinner-prop version of the Spin-in Herry, that, I believe, they just name the **SPINNING MINNOW**. The plastic lure had the same body curvature, but it was equipped with floppy-bow tie props fore and aft. It is pictured with this story in green back with perch scale.

In late 1950 or early 1951, the Tradewinds Company introduced a plastic lure in four sizes called the **ZIMMY PLASTIC PLUG**. The cupped-nose, slanted-face Zimmy was offered in colors of yellow flash, silver flash, red glow, blue flash, brass flash, and pearl pink. The four sizes for the semi-transparent plug with the foil-colored inserts were 3", 4", 5", and 6" long. The Zimmy was a strong lure designed to go to depths of 300 feet with weights and withstand a 150-pound pull-weight tested by hydraulic pressure. A copy of a 1952 ad is pictured along with the two-piece cardboard box for the 3" size lure. The company also made a smaller size and differently rigged version of the Spin-In Herry that they named the **SPIN-IN MINNY**. That lure is pictured in the 3" size with its one-piece, plastic-cover, green cardboard box. Picture of that lure with box is courtesy of the Dan Basore collection.

In the early 1960's, Tradewinds started reproducing the "Twin Minnow" as their **SPIN-IN GOONY** and selling it in a clear plastic tube with a red cap.

The 2" plastic lure was invented by Floyd D. "Slim" Sweeney in 1943 under Patent No. 2,402,853. He made the lures in Fresno, California, until he passed away in 1956. His company was then purchased by George Wildrick, who moved the company to Elmira, New York, as the Twin Minnow Bait Company. I have pictured the California Sweeney boxed Twin Minnow on the right alongside the Spin-In Goony for comparison purposes. (PG-10-12)

Boxed Tradewinds Spin-in Herry lures trade in the $15 to $20 range; however, the early Erickson intro-boxed lures trade higher, in the $35 range and up. The Spin-In Goony in tube trades in the $5 to $10 range.

REX FIELDS
COURTENAY, BRITISH COLUMBIA, CANADA

Rex Fields made traditionally shaped, 5"-long salmon plugs in the late 1970's and into the 1980's. His plastic lure had a direct nose line tie through-body special clip to the lure's only single hook under the chin. The lure was sold in a clear plastic sack with a stapled-on ID card, giving the address as Box 3392, Courtenay, British Columbia. (PG-13)

FRUMENTO FISHING TACKLE WORKS
VICTORIA, BRITISH COLUMBIA, CANADA

This company got underway just at the close of World War II, in 1946. They made up-slanted-nose wooden salmon plugs in the 3" to 7" range for approximately seven years. Their two-piece cardboard lure box was white with red print that simply said, "USE NEW **TILLICUM PLUG**."

POP GEER LURES
TACOMA, WASHINGTON

Pop Geer Lures was a post-war late-1940's and early-1950's lure maker. They specialized in trolling spoon and "cowbell" types of trolling attractors. Such an example would be the **POP GEER TROUT TROLL**, a series of half-moon-shaped blades rigged in tandem. The company also made the 2-1/4"

MONTREAL SPINNER, which was teardrop-shaped with three red glass bead spacers and a single hook, and the **NEW IDEA SPINNER**, which was rigged on a bead chain with an in-line Colorado spinner blade.

GRIZZLY FISHING TACKLE
VANCOUVER, BRITISH COLUMBIA, CANADA & GRIZZLY, WASHINGTON

The Grizzly TM "fine fishing tackle", out of P. O. Box 649, Vancouver, Washington, is another relatively young company. One of their trademarks was a picture of a Grizzly Bear with a salmon in its paw next to a stream. The company was in the exclusive manufacture of salmon and trout lures. The pictured example, called the **CANADIAN PLUG**, is a quality plastic lure with a sturdy hook system. The 3-3/4" plug had the traditional salmon plug shape made by several dozen different companies in Washington and Oregon, except it had a better patented hook hanger system than most. There was a flat, rectangular-oval-shaped metal piece that was one piece for both the line tie and the hook hanger, so there was never a danger of hook pullout. Furthermore, the hook was connected by a strong swivel, which helped prevent the fish from gaining leverage during the fight. Grizzle Tackle lures were packaged in bubble-topped cards that were brown with the trademark grizzly bear on the sides. The lure was fashioned after an earlier patent by a Seattle, Washington, man. Wallace A. Sleness received Patent No. 2,587,658 for this plug on March 4, 1952.

The company also made several metal baits, including the famous **ANDY REEKER SPOONS** and the **SIDE WINDER SPOONS**. Jim Maxwell designed a little plastic lure with a long nose dive lip designed for steelhead fishing called the **LIL'GUY** that was sold on a gray bubble-topped card.

It was the Jim Maxwell Manufacturing Company that produced many of the metal baits sold by Grizzly, such as the pictured carded, 4-3/4" and 5-1/4" ANDY REEKERS TROLLING SPOON. Andrew Reekers started producing several sizes of his ANDY REEKERS SPOONS in the mid 1930's, and, except for the war years, he made them into the 1950's. The flat, narrow spoon had a bent-up rounded tail with a single hook fixed to the top with a split ring and often had a plastic attractor attached as well. Reekers, who was from Portland, Oregon, was awarded Patent No. 2 132,760 for his spoon on October 11, 1938.

Another lure, a metal spoon with four red plastic bead in lays that ran down the center of the lure was called the **SCULPIN SOUNDER**. It was made for fishing most western species, such as lake trout, Coho, Chinook, steelhead, and browns. (PG-3)

WILLIAM A. HANSEN
GIG HARBOR, WASHINGTON

William Hansen made and sold lures in a company with his name spelled differently than what appeared on his patent, HANSON LURES. His Hanson Fish Lure Company was located at Route 3 Box 3557, which was located at North 215, 300 feet East on Highway 99 (today Aurora Avenue) in Gig Harbor, Washington. He also sold lures for a longer time out of Edmonds, Washington. He filed for one of his patents on June 15, 1950, and Patent No. 2,572,616 was granted to him on October 23, 1951, for his **BILL'S ACTION PLUG**, a banana-shaped, hump-back lure also using a heavy cord from line tie to the hooks. He also made salmon plugs in the traditional pointed-tail torpedo shapes with slanted faces.

His earliest box was a two-piece tannish-white cardboard box that read, "TRUE ACTION

PLUG," and had a picture of straight swimming salmon facing right. His later two-piece box was yellow and also read, "TRUE ACTION PLUG," but added, "Equipped with Mustad Hooks." This box pictured a jumping salmon facing left.

There is some confusion with the name Hansen (Hanson) in Washington salmon plugs. On April 1, 1947, Oswald A. Hansen filed for a patent on a salmon plug, and Patent No. 2,549,463 was issued to him and a man named Leland E. Cook on April 17, 1951. I always thought that he sold as the Hanson & Son Fish Lure Company on 65th Street in Seattle, Washington, using an all-green, two-piece cardboard box with black print. However, the box cover print read, "The True Action Plug," and how could both companies get away with that? Also, the spelling on this box was "Hanson", not "Hansen", as on the patent. So, what I have written here on William and Oswald Hansen (Hanson) may not be correct at all; time will tell. Both company names and all of the boxes may be from the one William A. Hansen. (PG-13)

HARRIS FISH LURES
SEATTLE, WASHINGTON

Another post-war, 1946 start-up company was Harris Fish Lures, located at 2317 West 70th Street in Seattle, Washington. Pictured is a 4", glass-eyed plug with a slant nose. It had a barrel swivel attached to a heavy cord that passed down through the slanted nose to two tied belly treble hooks. Another red head with white model is pictured that was 5" long and had zinc metal inserted eyes and the ball swivel line tie. (PG-14)

H. W. HEITMILLER
SEATTLE, WASHINGTON

In 1928, using the initials of his first and last name, Heitmiller introduced his 1-3/4" **H & H SPOON** that had five light-reflecting surfaces. His best known lure, however, was his 3-1/2" **DEW-DAD**. The Dew-Dad had some of the appearances of the Buck Perry "Spoonplug" with raised sides and a general incline to the tail. The lure had a bent-down nose lip, and the eyes were two indented, unpainted eye rings. Pictured are the later larger sizes of the Dew-Dad, at 7-1/2" and 8" long, one in nickel and one in brass finish. These larger sizes were made in two metal pieces, one had a rounded, down-turned head as a dive plane, that then tapered back to the tail. To this piece, there was riveted a second metal piece that was egg shaped with folded-up side wings. From a side view, this gave the lure the overall Buck Perry "Spoon Plug" look.

ADOLPH R. HENDRY
PORTLAND, OREGON

I don't know how effective they were because of the lack of the "smell" factor, but, in any event, a Portland, Oregon, man made plastic imitation salmon egg lures in the mid 1950's. He made two styles. One was just a 2" globe of apparent salmon eggs with a line tie wire through to the tail treble. Another version was somewhat made in a frog shape with a globe of eggs for the main body and four round, flat shaped disks on each of the hind leg wires. This lure was 3-7/8" long overall with the front in-line spinner and the trailing tail treble hook. Adolph R. Hendry was awarded Patent No. 2,860,440 on November 18, 1958, for his **SALMON EGG LURE** idea. (PG-14)

HERRING MAGIC, INC.
SEATTLE, WASHINGTON

Herring Magic, of 4010 36th Avenue W.,

Seattle, Washington, started production of a salmon fishing system called the **HERRING MAGIC** in 1946. They developed a unique trademark of a king salmon in a jumping position wearing a crown on its head. The caption that circled this caricature said, "For His Majesty-The King," and then had the letters "H M" printed underneath. The two-piece, oil-yellow and sea-blue cardboard box also had a picture of a jumping king salmon on the cover with a fisherman in a boat fighting the fish in the background. The side of the box read, "The Frantic Swimming Actionizer...It's 'Red Hot' Wherever Big Fish Eat little Ones." The other side of the box said, "True 'Crippled Minnow' Swimming Action... Better Than Live Minnows At Their best." The clear plastic head of the Herring Magic had a molded dive lip and a system for holding a herring in place for casting or trolling. The device was made in five sizes designed to hold herring from 4" long up to 8" long. The bottom of the box showed a picture of the correct size herring in actual size to be used with that size lure. Box papers said, "Be sure you have the right minnow; too large will overload, too small will not stabilize." Myron C. Miller of Seattle designed and patented the Herring Magic on February 15, 1949, under Patent No. 2,461,755. He filed for an improved plastic nosepiece on April 22, 1946, and Design Patent No. D155,307 was granted on September 20, 1949.

Herring Magic was not the only company selling this lure in this same era. The Miller-patented lure was also being marketed by the Seattle-based Martin Fish Lure Company as the "Hotter 'N Ell" lure.

The two pictured examples are size two, for 5" herring, and size three, for 6" herring. (PG-15)

E. G. HOLTZCLAW
PORTLAND, OREGON

In 1931, Earl G. Holtzclaw, out of Portland, Oregon, started production of a lake trout and salmon spinner. The **HOLTZCLAW SPINNING LURE** consisted of a unique, 3-1/2", Colorado-shaped spinner blade mounted on a loop-clip for the addition of a hook of the fisherman's choice. The spinner blade had a leaf-like pattern with a stem line down the center and ten sets of raised veins and grooves emanating from each side of the center stem that were angled slightly towards the rear. These multiple reflective surfaces produced an infinite number of intersection beams of light to aid in attracting fish. Earl Holtzclaw finished his brass blade in copper plating with a second nickel plating on top of the copper. He then polished off the nickel plate on one side of the blade, leaving a finished product of half nickel and half copper. Patent No. 1,862,893 was awarded to Holtzclaw on June 14, 1932, for his spinning lure. (PG-15)

HOOK BROS. FISH LURE COMPANY
SEATTLE, WASHINGTON

A post-war-1930's salmon plug maker was the Hook Bros. Fish Lure Company that was first located at 5653 32 Ave., S. W. in Seattle, Washington, and later 1713 Harbor Ave., S. W., Seattle, Washington. They made a salmon plug in the traditional style, except for a dimpled area on the belly under the large glass inserted eyes. Two of the 5" wooden plugs are pictured, one white with red gills and another white with red gills with red eye blush and tail trim. The lure was sold in a neat two-piece cardboard box with a picture of two men fishing in a rowboat in the lower part of the cover with one fighting a salmon. The cover read, "This Plug is Action Tested and Guaranteed." Most of the **HOOK BROS. PLUGS** were rigged for a rear hook pull-a-way tied to the front hook that was through-body secured directly to the nose line tie. However, some had a line tie wire-through system that was direct to the belly and tail-rigged treble hooks. (PG-16-17)

HOT SPOT FISHING, LTD.
VICTORIA, BRITISH COLUMBIA, CANADA

The late-1960's and 1970's Hot Spot Fishing, located at 1150 Tattersall Drive in Victoria, British Columbia, Canada, made a plastic salmon planer type of lure called the **HOT SPOT-APEX**, in the sizes of 4-1/2" and 5-1/2" long. The flat, plastic, fish-shaped lure was made with a molded curve and was designed to be fished in the same manner as the Tradewinds "Spinnin-in Herry" lure. They were sold without hooks in a dozen-count, yellow, two-piece cardboard dealer box. There were directions on how to rig with direct hooks to the lures or with trailing flies. (PG-15)

JOHNSON TACKLE COMPANY
SEATTLE, WASHINGTON

Roy Johnson and his tackle company, located in Seattle, Washington, made metal salmon lures from around 1931 to well after World War II, although, I don't believe, he was in actual production during the war. One of his earliest lures was his **ROY'S BELL SPINNER**. This 6"-overall-long spinning lure consisted of two large red glass bead spacer-bearings with an arrowhead-shaped spinner blade in between that had flared-out leg-wings at the tail, each bent in a different direction. This lure was designed and patented by Bertie D. Bell on January 16, 1934, under Patent No. 1,943,283.

Other Johnson lures from the 1930's included the **ROY'S ACE, ROY'S WOW, ROY'S DODGER**, and the **FISHING FOOL**. From the 1940's, the company produced the **ROY'S CANDLE FISH, MAHATMA SPOON**, and the **MICKEY SPOON**.

In the mid 1970's, Roy's son, Ray Johnson, got into the lure-making business in Salt Lake City, Utah, with his molded rubber "Real Minnow Lures" made in four sizes. (PG-16)

A. E. JONES
HOQUIAM, WASHINGTON

Hoquiam, Washington, is located at the back end of Gray's Harbor due west of Olympia. There, in 1947, just after World War II, Aron E. Jones entered the salmon lure-making business. His first lure was the 3-7/8" **ARON SALMON TROLLER**. This flat, stainless steel, fish-shaped trolling spoon had two joints with door-like hinges and a large split-ring single tail hook. The eye of the lure was just a drilled hole, which also was the location for the split-ring line tie.

In the late summer of 1947, Jones developed his 6-1/2"-long **ARON DODGER**, a forward trolling attractor for a trailing fly or bait for salmon fishing. The main-body teardrop-shaped trolling device had a heart-shaped spinning center blade with the wings curled in opposite directions. One of the unique features of this salmon dodger was a coiled spring-operated lever at the tail of this trolling attractor. With each revolution of the heart spinner, the arm would cock and then snap forward, giving the trolled fly, or lure, a jerk each time for extra attraction.

Aron E. Jones used his first name in naming each of these salmon fishing productions. He received Patent No. 2,521,852 for his Aron Dodger on September 12, 1950. In later years, this Dodger was also distributed by the Les Davis Company. Both the lure and the dodger are pictured with this story along with a copy of the patent. (PG-18)

Both the Aron Lure and the Aron Dodger are rare today, and each trades in the $25 to $35 range.

JOSEPH KLIEN

Joseph Klien filed for a patent on December 5, 1946, and Patent No. 2,516,468 was granted to him for his **ARLINGTON PLUG** on July 25, 1950. This lure had a special flat bar line tie extended in a channel within the body to the axis pin that passed through the side of the lure. This pin, as well as another near the tail, held a special swivel to the lure's two single hooks. With this system, the fisherman had a better chance of not losing his fish during the fight. (PG-19)

NED P. KRILICH

Ned P. Krilich filed for a patent on December 6, 1947, and Patent No. 2,565,660 was granted to him on August 28, 1951, for his **KRILICH KILLER PLUG**. This had the traditional salmon plug body but a slightly different hardware system. It consisted of a line tie double-twisted wire-through body to a large ring under the chin that then held the two treble hooks with a clip release and heavy cord system found on most western salmon plugs. The 4"-, 5"-, and 6"-long wooden plugs were always white in color with red faces, had no eyes, and were sold, out of Tacoma, Washington, in plastic sacks with cardboard inserts. The Krilich Killer was referred to by area salmon fishermen as the "Blind Plug", I guess because of its color and the fact that it had no eyes. (PG-19)

EDWARD LIPSETT, LTD.
(ALSO VICTORIA & PRINCE RUPERT)
VANCOUVER, BRITISH COLUMBIA, CANADA

Although records indicate that the Edward Lipsett, Ltd. dates to 1890, their salmon lure production dates to the 1940's out of 68 Water Street in Vancouver, British Columbia. They also had locations in Victoria and Prince Rupert, British Columbia, Canada, producing wooden salmon plugs. Pictured with its black, two-piece cardboard box with silver-white print is the 6"-long **STRIPED SEA KING**. The box had the trademark symbol in the center of the cover of a jumping salmon with the word "SEEKING". Also pictured is a 7"-long blue and white **SEA KING** wooden plug with a wire through from the line tie directly to the double shank belly hook. The lure had large, glass eyes with yellow irises and sometimes was rigged with two double hooks, as seen in the 6" red head with white model. (PG-20)

J. LLOYD TACKLE
SEATTLE, WASHINGTON

In 1930, Jack Lloyd, working out of Seattle, Washington, made a couple of metal salmon spoons: the **HERRING FLASH** and the **SHOE HORN**. The lure that made him famous, however, was his wooden **WATER WITCH**. The lure had glass eyes with a painted eye socket around the perimeter and a washboard-shaped metal dive lip. The lure had two holes drilled through the sides, one near the head just behind the eyes and the other near the tail. A heavy cord was passed through each hole and was tied to individual treble hooks. Most lures are found with a wire piece fixed to the top of the nose line tie. The lure is pictured in the 4" size, painted red with a black checker-scale pattern on the back. (PG-20)

LYMAN LURES
KELOWNA, BRITISH COLOMBIA, CANADA

Lyman Lures was actually a trade name for the L. R. Dooley Manufacturing Company out of Route 4, Kelowna, British Columbia, Canada. He made a wooden, slanted-nose salmon plug in sizes from 1-1/4" to 5-1/4" long. The painted-eye and indent-plastic-inserted-eye lures had swiveled belly hook hangers or direct line tie cord tie hooks and were offered in some bright colors, such as the yellow belly silver scale back with red spots and the yellow with green eye shadow and tail trim models pictured. The 1950's lures were first sold in hinged plastic boxes with card ID inserts, and, in later years, the lures were sold on plastic bubble-topped red and yellow cards. (PG-21-22)

MAGARD TACKLE COMPANY
WASHINGTON SPOON & BAIT
SEATTLE, WASHINGTON

Starting just after the war, in 1946, out of 5030 California Ave., Seattle, Washington, Roy Magard produced his **SPARX-PLUG**. His early, one-piece, flip-cover cardboard box was white with red print. His lures followed the same basic design of most other Pacific Northwest salmon plugs, except his did have pressed, indent, center bump eyes and cup and swivel belly hooks. Magard's second two-piece cardboard box style was light purple in color, and his third box was a two-piece dark blue cardboard that had brilliant red print, "SPARX-PLUG". The last Magard's cardboard box was one-piece flip cover in white with red print. (PG-22)

MARINE APPLIANCE
MANUFACTURING COMPANY
SEATTLE, WASHINGTON

Starting in 1929, the Marine Appliance Manufacturing Company, working out of 119 West Denny Way Seattle, Washington, introduced their trade name **SIBERIAN** lure line. These were all made with scent pockets built into the spoons with fine mesh-screen pock-

ets that would dispense whatever scent the fishermen would choose to place inside. The pictured example is the 4-1/2" **SIBERIAN WOBBLER**. Other metal lures included the 2-3/4" **SIBERIAN BASS SPINNER**, the 4" **SIBERIAN CHAMPION**, and the little 1-1/2" **SIBERIAN TROUT SPINNER**. These productions are quite rare today and trade higher than most salmon spoons, reaching the $50 and higher range.

All of the lures made by this company were invented and patented by Jules Catarau. He also made some wooden versions on his own that were "Bass-Oreno" in shape. These two lures were given the names **JIGGER**, at 4" long, and **LITTLE JIGGER**, at 3" long. He did patent one lure, the **UNIVERSAL FISH-GRAPPLER**, which was the only non-scent-pocket lure that the Marine Appliance Company made. That patent No. was 1,921,657 that was issued on August 13, 1935.

See the more detailed story on the Marine Appliance Company elsewhere in these books.

The close-up picture of the 4-1/2" Siberian Wobbler is courtesy of the Walter Geib collection. (PG-8)

All Siberian lures are rare today and trade in the $50 range or better, and the very rare wooden Catarau plugs trade at the $100 level.

MARINE SPECIALTIES
MANUFACTURING COMPANY
SEATTLE, WASHINGTON

Harry W. McMahon received Patent No. 1,136,475 for his **MCMAHAN SPOON** back on April 20, 1915. A number of western salmon lure companies produced these spoons. Undoubtedly the biggest company doing so for over 35 years was the Pacific Marine Supply Company of 1223

Western Avenue in Seattle. Actually, after World War II, these spoons were made for them by the Marine Specialties Manufacturing Company, located at the same address. They were the manufacturer and Pacific Marine the distributor. The spoons were made in the sizes as follows: 1-1/4" long with little size four hooks, 1-5/8", 2", 2-1/8", 3-1/8", 4", and big 4-7/8" long with 2/0 size hooks. The spoons were made in 50/50 finishes of brass and silver, bronze and silver, and bronze and brass and painted herring scale. (PG-23)

MARTIN FISH LURE COMPANY
SEATTLE, WASHINGTON

There were a number of metal baits made by the 2121 Second Avenue, Seattle, Washington, Martin Fish Lure Company from the 1920's through the 1940's. One of the first was the 1924-introduced 4" brass **CROWG** that was developed by Frank S. Tucker, who was awarded Patent No. 1,706,906 for his lure on March 26, 1929. Shortly after that, the company produced the brass **MAPEL SPOON**, made in two styles of 3-3/4" egg-shaped or 4" hourglass-shaped with a twist in the middle. George Maple was awarded Patent No. 1,692,674 for these lures on November 20, 1928. The **CAMANO SPOON** was a 2-1/2" lure with a raised center rib at the head, followed by a depressed cupped area from the center of the lure to the tail. There were two sizes, 1-3/4" and 2-1/4" long, of the elongated oval-shaped **MARTIN WOBBLER**. The **CANDLE FISH** was a 3"-long, narrow, smelt-shaped lure that received Patent No. 1,852,620 on April 5, 1932. The owner and founder of this company, Joseph H. Martin, developed most of the company's lures and patented several, such as his **KACHMOR**, a peanut-shaped spoon with four raised back ribs that reflected light in many different directions, for which he received Patent

No. 1,846,130 on January 23, 1932. Some of his other lures included the **HUTTON**, the **PEARL WOBBLER**, and the **HOOD SPORT**, an elongated teardrop-shaped lure. No doubt, the best known lure made by the Martin Fish Lure Company was the **HOTTER 'N ELL**. The transparent hood and harness assembly gave irresistible wounded minnow action to live or fresh dead bait. In the water, the plastic invisible hood had spring-loaded sharp wires on the sides of the head. The fisherman could slide the head of his favorite minnow bait in the hood and push the retaining side wires into the minnow's body, which held the minnow snuggly in place via the side springs. The Hotter 'N Ell was made in at least two sizes of 2" and 1-1/2", and the long molded-nose slanted dive face would take the harness deep at all speeds. The two-piece white cardboard lure box had a blue label on the cover that had a picture of a salmon about to eat a rigged minnow. The box cover read, "Crystal clear allows full view of bait in action...It's the HOTTEST of the HOT lures." The Hotter 'N Ell received Patent No. 2,461,755 on February 15, 1949, and Design Patent No. D155,307 on September 20, 1949, for the special dive lip, both patents awarded to Myron C. Miller for his 1944 invention.

During the late 1940's, the Miller lure was also distributed by another Seattle company. Their name for the lure was the **HERRING MAGIC**. The two-piece yellow and water-blue box cover had a picture of a jumping salmon with a boat trolling in the background. The right corner of the box read, "WORKS MIRACLES WITH MINNOWS."

The company trademark was of a martin (the animal) standing over a dead salmon at the water's edge. Of course, the most famous of the Martin lures was the wooden, glass-eyed **MARTIN SALMON PLUG**. Joseph H. Martin received Patent No. 2,110,382 on March 8, 1938, for this lure. It was made in several sizes, from 3" long up to a large 7" size. The lure had a unique system to keep the fish from leveraging himself free of the hooks during the fight. The line tie wire extended down through the nose to under the chin. There was a cord on the smaller size and a wire cable on the larger size that was tied to the end and passed through the front treble hook eye to the tail and then was tied to the eye of the trailing treble hook. There were two clips located at both ends of the lure that held the cord. These hooks then pulled away from the clips at the strike of a fish, leaving the fish to fight directly with the line tie system. The pictured examples in the 7" size show the two types of cable holders used by the company. The company made this lure in smaller sizes of 1-1/2" and 1-3/4", called **TROUT PLUGS**, with glass eyes and fixed double belly hooks.

Other wooden plug type lures were the 3-1/4" **WESTERN BASS PLUG**, the 3-1/4" **MARTIN BASS PLUG**, the three-hook 3-1/2" **INJURED MINNOW**, and the 3-1/2" **MARTIN TAD**. The latter had the same pullout hook and cord rig system described on the larger, slant notch nosed MARTIN SALMON PLUG.

Another Martin production that is very scarce is the 3" wooden **MARTIN FLATIE**. This lure (pictured in red scale) had a secure hook system with the rear tail treble hook (on a fish-strike) pulling away attached to a cord on a direct line tie to the front treble and the through-the-nose line tie. The lure is also pictured in red head with gold scale, but some fisherman has painted the hooks and hook tie cord in pink for extra attraction. Some of the smaller plugs were each sold in a red, two-piece cardboard box with a white label and the picture of a fish on the cover. One of the early two-piece cardboard boxes was white with red trim and a picture of a salmon on the cover in red print. The cover had the caption, "FISHING LURES OF PROVEN QUALITY FOR FRESH OR SALT WATER FISHING."

Two of the rarest Martin salmon plugs are the yellow with red trim **MARTIN TADPOLE** (26th set of pictures) and the rainbow color Rush Tango Type (27th set of pictures).

The Martin Fish Lure Company ceased all lure production in 1970. (PG-23-27)

MASON FISH LURE COMPANY
SEATTLE, WASHINGTON

Many collectors of northwestern salmon plugs consider the Tacoma, Washington, "SCHROEDER'S WASHINGTON WONDER PLUG" to be the top-of-the-line collectible salmon plug. The 5-3/16"-long, two-jointed plug was patented on February 9, 1937, under Patent No. 2,069,972, awarded to Fred H. Schroeder. I, however, do not agree, as I feel the later **MASON DELUXE LURE** had greater beauty and, for sure, more utility value as a salmon plug.

Roland G. Mason was awarded Patent No. 2,616,205 on July 28, 1948 for his deluxe lure. The 5"-long lure had everything: removable hooks, a sliding adjustable belly weight, an adjustable sleeve at the head, nose swiveled line tie, and, the "biggy", rubber snubber held hooks. The swivel-axis nose line tie always kept the lure in the correct running position. The adjustable sleeve at the head and the adjustable shark-tooth-shaped lead belly keel and weight controlled both depth and trolling speed. Tension kept the belly weight in place, but, by sliding the weight forward in its 2-7/8" belly slot, the lure went deeper and could be trolled slower. By sliding it backwards, the fisherman would fish shallower and with a faster troll. The hooks were held by split rings for quick change if necessary, and the split rings were attached to rubber internal snubbers. These strong, but stretchy snubbers eliminated split plugs, pulled hooks, broken fishing line, and fish throwing the hooks. The lure had 1/2"-

diameter, metal, convex shaped eyes inserted in drilled sockets in the wooden body, and the eyes were painted bright yellow with center black pupils. The eyes had red rings painted around the sockets and a red painted gill next to each. The lure is pictured (courtesy of the Dan Basore collection) in dark green back blending into green-yellow scale, then blending into a pupil-silver scale, then blending into an all-white belly. The lure box was just as neat, with a lure picture on the cover and all of the important features of the lure pointed out. (PG-28)

The boxed "New! Amazing Mason De Luxe" lure trades in the $200 to $250 range, but I have seen the boxed lure trade higher years ago.

JAMES D. MAXWELL
VANCOUVER, WASHINGTON

In 1973, James D. Maxwell made plastic imitation salmon egg cluster lures in two styles. The 1-3/8" body was made in a pink cluster with a wire through from line tie to a treble hook, or it was mounted on a No. 2 long shank hook with two split-tied tufts of deer hair mounted on the front of the hook shank as an added attractor. Maxwell received Design Patent No. D237,612 for his plastic eggs on November 11, 1975. The lure's card gave the address as, "Box 649, Vancouver, Washington". (PG-29)

AUSTIN O. MIDDLEMISS
PORTLAND, OREGON

Austin O. Middlemiss, of Portland, Oregon, filed for his first patent on November 7, 1938, and Patent No. 2,189,958 was granted to him on February 13, 1940, for his **MIDDLEMISS PLUG**. This plug had the traditional body shape but a little different hardware system. There was

a flat, metal bar doubled over forming an eye for the cord to be tied to for the clip-release tied hooks. The clips were two spring wires driven in to the wooden body separately but close together, forming a pressure grip on the cord until a fish struck the lure, pulling the hooks free from the clips. The front bar that I mentioned had a bent-over tab that rested against the lure's face so that it could not be pulled back through and also served as the line tie.

Around the same time Middlemiss developed an **AUTOMATIC HOOK LURE**. The 4"-long spoon had a slightly up-turned nose and mouse-type ears turned up at the tail. The spoon had a fixed single hook at the tail held by a split ring, which also acted as the trigger for the spring-activated lure. Triggered, this larger hook would slap the salmon in the side of the head for a secure hookup. The spoon had a long spring on the wire line tie shank. At the tail, this wire was fixed to the larger spring hook eye that was in a hinged axis. The fisherman would pull this hook barb around forward and lock it into a notch in the line tie shank. When a fish struck and put pull pressure on the lure, the spring hook was released from this notch and swung around for the kill. Patent No. 2,087,955 was granted to Austin O. Middlemiss on July 27, 1937, for this spoon. (PG-29)

MILLER MANUFACTURING COMPANY
SAN FRANCISCO, CALIFORNIA

Although George W. Miller made metal salmon spoons and was from Everett, Washington, he did the actual manufacture of the lures in San Francisco, California. His best known lure was the **DIAMOND FLASH WOBBLER** made in several sizes. The spoon had nine different diamond-shaped, light-reflecting surfaces that bounced light back in every direction to attract fish. The spoon also had a half-figure-eight twist front to back, giving the spoon an extra wobbling erratic action on the troll or retrieve. Patent No. 1,770,003 was awarded to George W. Miller on July 8, 1930, for the Diamond Flash Wobbler. Miller made his lures from 1928 to around 1931. He made another spoon simply called the **MILLER SPOON**. (PG-30)

MINSER TACKLE COMPANY
SEATTLE & CHINOOK, WASHINGTON

In the 1920's, 1930's, and 1940's, there was a vast and prolific introduction of western salmon lures, especially right after World War II. The Minser Tackle Company was started by William D. Minser with his wooden salmon plugs in the mid 1930's, first out of Seattle, Washington. One of his early patents was applied for on July 12, 1939, and Patent No. 2,236,353 was awarded to him on March 25, 1941. This patent was for a typical notched and slant-nosed wooden salmon plug with pull-away hooks. This lure had a drilled channel from the nose to the front treble hook location. There was a bead chain direct line tie to this front belly hook. Like many other western salmon plugs of that era, this plug had a strong cord tied from the front hook to the tail treble and secured to the belly by two quick-release clips. This allowed the fisherman to fight his salmon with the fish having less leverage to throw the hooks and also prevented any danger of hook pullout.

One of Minser's early boxes was a one-piece flip cover that was half white and half blue with yellow trim. A little later, the two-piece cardboard lure box was orange tinted with white labels with the print reading, "MINSER TACKLE COMPANY...Lucky Louie Plugs... Seattle, Washington." The "209 Aurora Avenue, Seattle, Washington" address two-piece cardboard boxes were both green with white labels and orange with white labels. Later, in the early

1940's, out of Chinook, Washington, Minser developed a blue label on white cardboard box and then a beautiful and colorful two-piece cardboard box for his salmon plugs. The sea-blue color box had a picture of a leaping salmon on the cover with white print, "**LUCKY LOUIE** by Bill Minser". The side of the box read, "Minser Sinkers - Minser Rod Holders...Minser Tackle Co., Chinook, Wash." I believe that, over time, Minser used five, and maybe six, different box styles. The early box is pictured with a yellow plug with red trim. The later box is pictured along with a picture of a 5-1/2" pink and white Lucky Louie salmon plug.

His later salmon plug designs, however, were not unique, but followed the traditional body shape of the salmon plugs made by over two dozen Oregon and Washington lure makers. Far less common is the Minser 2" **MOON FISH**. The Moon Fish was nearly an exact copy of the Floyd D. "Slim" Sweeney-developed "Twin Minnow", made first in Fresno, California, and later by the George W. Wildrick-owned Twin-Minnow Bait Company in Elmira, New York. Sweeney developed the original Twin Minnow in 1939 and was awarded Patent No. 2,220,133 for it on November 5, 1940. The Moon Fish by Minser is pictured in yellow with red spots and pressed, embossed eyes. The lure was sold in a clear plastic tube with a red cap and card insert.

The regular shaped salmon plug with a different take, was the **WEE LUCKY LOUIE SHOVELNOSE SALMON PLUG**, which basically just had a metal nose plate added to it.

The last lure ever patented by Minser was on June 18, 1968, under Patent No. 3,388,495, for a two-piece lure that slide up the line tie wire when a fish struck the lure, leaving just the hook in the fish.

In the early 1970's, I believe under new ownership, the Minser Tackle Company was located in Port Angeles, Washington. They made the

Lucky Louie lures there in plastic. One of their productions out of that address was the little 1-7/8" semi-transparent **TROUT LOUIE**. The lure, sold in a plastic box, had a line tie bead chain that passed directly though the lure to the belly treble hook. Pictured is a pink-with-white-trim 4" **TINY LUCKY LOUIE** in a yellow one-piece cardboard box with plastic cover.

Floyd De C. "Slim" Sweeney from California would have been very surprised to see how many different lure companies made his famous 1930's "Twin Minnow". Minser Tackle became the seventh company to make these little 2"-long plastic minnow imitations. Minser Tackle made the lures in the late 1960's and called their version the TROUT LOUIE and sold it on a yellow color card within a plastic sack with ID print on the back of the package. (PG-30-32)

The early Seattle, Washington, Lucky Louie boxed plugs are scarce and trade at $50 or higher. The very common boxed Minser Lucky Louie Salmon plugs, out of Chinook, Washington, seldom trade higher than the $20 to $25 range, and the little Moon Fish is in the same trade range or higher. The much later plastic model in box made in Port Angeles trades in the $10 range or less.

JOHN E. NELSON
SEATTLE, WASHINGTON

John E. Nelson filed for a patent on December 21, 1939, and Patent No. 2,290,702 was awarded to him on July 21, 1942, more for his hook attaching system than his plug. This strong, continuous wire harness system started with an end clip under the nose of the wooden lure, passed up through a channel to form a round line tie, then doubled back down the channel and bent back along the belly to a tail clip, formed a loop for

the tail hook, double backed along the belly with a dip for the second belly hook, and then locked into the first clip described – one continuous secure wire system. This system also allowed the fisherman to make a quick and easy change of hooks if he so desired. The lure box was a one-piece, green, flip-cover cardboard box with the trademark, "NELSON WILD ACTION LURE," printed on the cover, with the letter "L" in "Lure" both large and sweeping up over the top of the word "Action". Nelson Plugs was located at 314 Second Ave., So., Seattle, Washington. Their 6" red head with white plug is pictured with box. (PG-33)

WILMER "BILL" NORTHRUP
GARDNER-REEDSPORT, OREGON

Wilmer Bill Northrup (1890 - 1970) preferred to go by his middle name most of the time. Since he did not sell his lures in boxes, I can't say for sure what city he worked out of. However, we do know that he worked out of the Gardiner - Reedsport area, along the central Pacific coastline of Oregon. There was a herring-like bait fish called the pilchard that came into the Umpqua River to spawn that was a favored food fish of both stripers and salmon. Bill Northrup attempted to copy that bait fish with rubber and then foam lures, but they did not work well, so he switched to carving the lures out of cedar wood. His wooden striper and salmon lure production started around 1948 and lasted to around 1961.

His first lure had a pointed nose, a curved head, and either tack or painted eyes. He then moved on to a wider lure body and a glass eye. His lures, made in the sizes of 4" long to a giant 12" long, are pretty distinctive. The lure had a forked tail, flared out cheeks, and then a four-way slanted head that came to a squared-tipped nose. The most prevalent colors were a blue back with a silver belly for salmon fishing and a yellow or black lure for striper fishing, especially at night. The line tie was a barrel swivel that was inserted halfway in a nose hole and was directly linked to the front treble hook. The front hook then had a tied cord that went to a second hook, a tail pull-away clip treble hook. Thus, a hooked fish did not have the advantage of two hooks in the lure to gain leverage. He called his lure **WILMER'S NO FOOLIN**. All Northrup lures are very scarce, but the most common size found is 6", with the 4", 7-1/2", and other sizes being very rare. Note that the No Foolin lure had a small metal inserted dorsal back fin and that there was a carved gill mark line. Pictured are an all yellow 6" lure and a white 6" lure with a red side stripe. Also pictured is the rare size 7-1/2" No Foolin lure in black back with silver. Note that this larger size, and all other larger sizes of the No Foolin, had a forked tail with a wider spread and a higher-thicker through forehead. I have been told that "Wilmer" Northrup's lures were sold in plastic sacks with stapled-on ID cards, but I have yet to find any collector who has this packaging system.

Bill Northrup was born in Hanfield, California, on March 5, 1890, so in the 1950's Bill made an attempt to sell his lures in Sacramento, California, with little success. Consequently, most of his lures were only sold regionally in the Gardiner, Oregon, area. In the 1950's, Bill Northrup took on a partner, a Thomas Wayne Kaylor. Wayne Kaylor brought some new money into the lure venture and put up the money to apply for a patent. Patent No. 2,999,331 was issued to Willmer Bill Northrup and Thomas Wayne Kaylor on September 12, 1961. In the early 1960's, Bill's health was failing, so he retired to Coquille, Oregon, to live with his son, where he passed away in 1970.

Pictures and much of this history are courtesy of the Doug Ramey collection. (PG-34)

The 6" size lures trade in the $300 range, but the other sizes trade higher, in the $450 to $550 range.

L. E. OLSEN MANUFACTURING COMPANY, INC.
BELLINGHAM, WASHINGTON

Another post-war 1940's company, L. E. Olsen Manufacturing Company, Inc., out of 1908 Monroe Street, Bellingham, Washington, produced the smaller sizes of salmon plugs. Pictured is a tan color two-piece cardboard box with a jumping salmon on the cover and the caption, "FISH LURES FOR SALT OR FRESH WATERS." The 3" yellow scale **OLSEN SALMON PLUG** had indent embossed pressed painted eyes. In 1944, Olsen introduced his **CANDLE FISH PLUG** that was designed to be trolled behind a Herring Dodger. The 3" lure was designed by Olsen with the assistance of Verne Hawley, a Lummi Island salmon fishing guide. Some Olsen salmon plugs had the split leather tail pork rind type trailers inserted in the tails. (PG-35)

PACIFIC ARROW MANUFACTURING COMPANY
SEATTLE, WASHINGTON

Just as World War II was drawing to a close in 1946, the Pacific Arrow Manufacturing Company, of 237 Yale Ave., North, Seattle, Washington, started production of their **ARROW LAMINATED SPOONS**. The lures were made in three sizes of 2-1/2", 4-3/4", and 5-1/2" long, which is the size pictured. The lure was transparent, except for an actual lamented color picture of a minnow, or young salmon, in the center of the lure, visible from both sides. The lure's clear portion was in the shape of a McMahon Spoon with a slight curve at the nose and a sharper curve at the tail that was also cupped. The spoon was equipped with a soldered ring barrel swivel at the nose and a soldered ring salmon type single hook at the tail. The pictured example is 4-3/4" long with a molded-in picture of a smolt (a young salmon). The lures had been invented before the war by a Hansville, Washington, man in 1940. Archibald S. Kincaid was awarded Design Patent No. D124,722 for the lures on January 21, 1941. (PG-35)

PACIFIC MARINE COMPANY
SEATTLE, WASHINGTON

Actually, there is no connection between these two companies other than the fact that the lures they made are remarkably similar and were made in the same city. The Pacific Marine Company and the Marine Specialty Company, both located in Seattle, Washington, made very similar lures, as will be discussed. First, there were the several sizes, between 3-1/2" and 5", of the brass **MCMAHON SPOONS** made by Pacific Marine Company starting in 1914. This salmon spoon had a dimpled, pyramid-shaped area at the nose and another at the tail, but the pressed-in areas were facing opposite directions to give the spoons more erratic action. Harry W. McMahon received Patent No. 1,136,475 for his lures on April 20, 1915.

Another lure by Pacific Marine was the **FEY SPOON** in two sizes: 2-1/4" for bass and the 4" for salmon. This lure was also made from a single piece of sheet metal with a flat arrow-, or boat-, shaped head and with spaced pointed arms at the tail. In between these two arms was a tongue-shaped piece that was humped, or con-cave-shaped, and this piece held the lure's soldered ring single tail hook. This later spoon was awarded Patent No. 1,123,717 on January 5, 1915, granted to George W. Fey. Both lures were made for salmon fishing.

Six years later, the Marine Specialty Company, also of Seattle, Washington, introduced their salmon **HANSEN TROLLING SPOON**. These brass spoons were made in the same approximate sizes and similar shapes as the McMahon Spoons. These spoons also had lateral water-reaction surfaces at either end of the lure, but the tail of the Hansen was a round dimple, and the head was a raised center rib with depressed areas on either side of the rib. For the same reasons, these two reaction surfaces faced in opposite directions. Joseph Hansen received Patent No. 1,450,546 on April 3, 1923.

Departing from this lure style, the company produced the **SEBENIUS TROLLING SPOON**. This 3-3/4" salmon spoon really had a wild swing action and was cigar shaped with a fat, pointed nose taper and a narrow, pointed tail taper. The head of the lure had a cut and pushed-through rectangular tab to which the line tie was fixed. With the line tie set back from the nose, this gave the lure leverage in the water for wild erratic turns, dips, and darting actions. John A. Sebenius was awarded Patent No. 1,309,966 for this lure on July 15, 1919.

A rather large 5" fish-shaped spoon was made called the **APEX COD JIGGER** that had two large single hooks rigged at the tail and a tornado-type spinner blade at the nose. (PG-36,57)

GEORGE HENRY PATTERSON
SEATTLE, WASHINGTON

George Henry Patterson filed for a patent on January 20, 1947, and Patent No. 2,547,279 was granted to him on April 3, 1951, for his **PATTERSON PLUG**. This wooden lure had a down-slanted face instead of the traditional up-slanted face. This plug incorporated a novel arrangement, whereby the two single hooks were mounted on the plug accessible to the striking fish. When taken by the fish, the hooks were pulled completely free from the plug, held on cord a short distance from the plug, with a far less chance of the fish throwing the hooks. The cord was equal in length to each hook, but, depending on which hook caught the fish, that hook slid further back from the lure, pulling the other hook out of the way up near the tail. See the drawing in the patent. (PG-37)

PERFECT ACTION FISHING PLUGS
SANDWICK, BRITISH COLUMBIA, CANADA

Another post-war wooden salmon plug maker from British Columbia was Perfect Action Fishing Plugs. They really didn't make a plug any different from the other north west coast salmon plug makers. Their two-piece white cardboard lure box had blue print that gave the company name and address. (PG-37)

LOYD PETER'S FLY SHOP
PORT ANGELES, WASHINGTON

In the late 1940's and early 1950's, the Loyd Peter's Fly Shop, located at 1902 West View Drive in port Angeles, Washington, produced a large, 4-1/2"-long, tied hair salmon fly for trolling behind a flasher or dodger. The **MACDONALD'S SECRET WEAPON** was designed by Hector Macdonald, who owned MacDonald's Boat House on the shores of the Strait of Juan de Fuca. (PG-23)

POINT WILSON COMPANY
PORT TOWNSHED, WASHINGTON

There were at least a dozen western salmon lure makers that made **CANDLEFISH LURES** representing sand eels, some in wood, some in plastic, and others in metal, or lead. One of the more modern 1970's lure makers was the Point Wilson Company that was located in Port Townshed, Washington. Pictured are their trademark **DART CANDLEFISH** lures in the three sizes of 1-1/2 ounce and 2-1/4 and 3-1/2 ounces on cards.

QUY-L-UR-E LURE COMPANY
LECTROLURE COMPANY, INC.
STOCKTON, CALIFORNIA

An unusual name for an unusual lure, the patented 1950's **QUY-L-UR-E** was a metal lure with the spoon twisted both vertically and horizontally. Both the company name and the lure name are a play on the inventor's last name Quyle and the word lure. Martin E. Quyle was awarded Patent No. 2,711,049 for his spoons on June 21, 1955, from an October 25, 1952, applied for patent. The spoons were made from a fly rod trout size at 1-1/4", long up to the large 4-1/2" salmon casting or trolling size, with 2-1/4" and 3-1/4" sizes in between. The larger sizes were almost always finished in nickel plate; however, the smaller size is usually painted in white with red spots, frog spot, black with yellow spots, or red with white spots. The company trademark that appears on the backs of the spoons was a Chinook Salmon with the name "QUY-L-UR-E" printed inside of it.

The company also made a very similar double-horizontal, S-shaped twist spoon, almost in a spiral shape. The lure, the **WRIGHT SPINOBBLER**, was named after the inventor. It was usually finished in half highly polish nickel plate and the other vertical half in copper. However, although a rare color, the 3-3/8"-long spoons were sometimes painted red and white in the lower half. On May 13, 1956, Martin Quyle was awarded Patent No. 2,834,143 for a lure that was so close to the South Bend "Super Duper" that he was advised not to manufacture it. So, he modified it to a 2-1/4" lure that could almost pass as a South Bend "Trix-Oreno". His lure was different, however.

The South Bend lure was two metal parts screwed or rived together. Quyle's lure was all one-piece metal and had a barrel swivel attached directly to the long shank single hook that ran along the back of the lure tipped with a small Colorado blade spinner. See the comparative picture with three South Bend lures at the top and the Quyle below.

By the way, the South Bend "Trix-Oreno" lure was invented by an Alabama man. William M. Jordon was issued Patent No. 1833,581 on November 24, 1931, for that lure.

Later, in the 1960's, Martin Quyle developed a 2-1/2" metal **QUYLE SPOON** that was manufactured by the Electrolure Company also located in Stockton, California. (PG-37-39)

All lures by this company are very scarce and trade in the $10 to $15 range, but the little 1-1/4" QUY-L-UR-ES are rare and trade as high as $25

ANDREW REEKERS
PORTLAND, OREGON

In the early 1920's, out of Portland, Oregon, Andrew Reekers developed two types of **REEKERS TROLLING SPOONS**. One was an oval-shaped spinner blade mounted on a wire shaft that had an interchangeable spinner blade feature. The blade had a clevis fixed to a rotary member between two fixed collars with a sliding sleeve so the fisherman could easily remove and substitute different spinner blades. The more Common Reekers Trolling Spoon was rounded at the nose with a gradual expansion in width to the tail. The tail area had a slight up curve and a rounded, raised back ring area at the tail that gave the spoon a different distinct action. Andrew Reekers was awarded patents for these

two: Patent No. 1,467,116 on September 4, 1923, and Patent No. 1471,280 on October 16, 1923. (PG-40,45)

RED SHANK GAFF HOOK COMPANY
SEATTLE, WASHINGTON

The mid-1930's Red Shank Gaff Hook Company, working out of Seattle, Washington, made 3-1/4" and 4" oval-shaped spoons called the **RED SHANK SPOONS**. The lures are distinctive and easy to ID, as they had seven indented lines running the vertical lengths of the spoons. The brass spoons were half nickel plated front to back and one half painted red over the brass. However, it is rare to find one with all of the red paint still on it, if any, leaving just the brass underlay finish that had originally been painted.

SAM E. ROBBINS & FRANK L. LARSON
SEATTLE, WASHINGTON

Sam E. Robbins, and Frank L. Larson filed for their patent on December 18, 1944, and they received Patent No. 2,459,288 on January 18, 1949, for the **ROBBINS-LARSON PLUG**. The only thing different about this plug was that a folded-over bar served as the clip for the front treble hook, and it was connected to a cord to the rear treble hook and slid down the cord when a fish was caught. Most western salmon plugs anchored the cord to the front via the line tie, but this one was anchored in the rear. (PG-40)

DORA ROSEGARD
SEATTLE, WASHINGTON

Dora Rosegard filed for a patent on March 13, 1944 and was awarded Patent No. 2,373,417 on April 10, 1945. This is one of very few examples where a woman designed and patented a lure.

Offhand, I can only think of a couple others: the rare Van Dyke, Michigan, "Groove Head" was patented by Josephine M. Cole and the famous "Spinno Minno" was patented by Violet Van Buren. The **ROSEGARD PLUG**, made by a company of the same name, had the traditional body shape but utilized a double cord from the hooks strung through a swivel at the head. The water resistance of the retrieve or troll kept the lure pulled back with the hooks held tight to the belly in recessed holes. However, when a fish struck the lure, there was enough slack in the line behind the line tie swivel to allow the hooks to fall back away from the lure itself. The Rosegard was made in four sizes: 4", 5", 6", and 7" long. There were ten colors: yellow head with aluminum, pearl pink, red head with white, white with red gills, white with silver scale, blue backs, yellow shiner scale, red head with yellow, yellow with red gills, and black scale. The Rosegard, "The Salmon Plug That Has Everything," is pictured with one of its box styles, an all black box with white print. The Rosegard was made at 6602 28th Ave., N.W., Seattle, Washington. Also pictured is a copy of a 1950 advertising poster. (PG-41)

JOHN H. SAARELA
SEATTLE, WASHINGTON

John H. Saarela filed for a patent on June 1, 1938, and Patent No.2,165,071 was granted to him on July 4, 1939, for his **NIF-T-PLUG**. This plug was rigged entirely different from other era salmon plugs. The cord line tie went through the nose line tie eye and up over the back in a cut groove, down through a tail eye and the eye of the tail treble hook trough a clip holder, and up to the under-the-chin large single hook held by another clip, with that hook facing backwards. When a fish caught the rear treble hook, it pulled free, and the cord passed around the lure through all of the eyes, causing the plug to reverse itself, gaffing the hooked salmon again in the side of the head or throat with that large back-facing hook. At first, Saarela sold his salmon plugs as "JOHN H. SAARELA…NIF-T Fishing Tackle, 1330 Boren Avenue, Seattle. Wa." The box also had large print, "QUALITY SALMON PLUG," on the cover. Later, however, the two-piece, gold-color cardboard boxes carried the makers name as, "SULAK AND WALKER PRODUCTS," out of 310 N. W. Industrial Building, Seattle, Washington. (PG-41)

CHUCK SCATES
PORTLAND, OREGON

Even though the hard, plastic salmon lures made by Chuck Scates are relatively young compared to other salmon lure makers, his late-1950's and early-1960's lures are quite scarce. Pictured is a 5-1/2" **CHUCK'S SPECIAL** that is a curved, fish shaped with a forked fish tail. The lure was painted red head and tail with a white glowing phosphorescent center. Scates made a sturdy hook system with a line tie wire through to the belly treble that continued on to the tail treble, then up through the lure to the back with a 1/4" bend, and then back down through the lure again to the tail treble. A 5-1/4", second plastic lure is pictured in red and white with a single Siwash hook that sat in a pullout clip and was secured by a swivel and through-body line tie wire belly, and the plug-body was then out of the way of the hooked fish. (PG-42)

OTTO SCHECHTERLE

Otto Schechterle filed for a patent on September 25, 1940, and Patent No. 2,256,173 was granted to him for his **SCHECHTERLE PLUG** on September 16, 1941. The major difference with this plug was that the cord was tied to an external swivel, then passed through the eye of a snap (a male and female snap, like found on many clothing articles today) that was mounted on the face of the lure. The cord then passed through a chin cut notch, was tied to a front belly hook, then to a rear belly hook, and ended tied to a deep tail screw eye. When a fish was hooked, the nose snap popped free, and all of the hooks ended up at the tail, free from the lure.

FRED H. SCHROEDER
TACOMA, WASHINGTON

Fred H. Schroeder filed for a patent on May 16, 1934, and was awarded Patent No. 2,069,972 on February 9, 1937, for his **SCHROEDER'S WASHINGTON WONDER PLUG**. This 5-3/16", wooden, double-jointed plug is, without a doubt, the more sought after of all salmon plus of that era. It frequently trades in the $100 to $150 range. The glass-eyed lure had heavy-duty screw-eye-held hooks at the tail and in the middle section. The lure was finished in five color options: white with red gills and eye shadow, Allen Stripey, shiner scale, silver scale with green flitter, and white with red eyes and tail. The rather plain, white, two-piece cardboard lure box had, on the cover, black print for the word "SCHROEDER'S" and following blue print for, "WASHINGTON WONDER LURE...2012 So. KAY STREET, TACOMA, WASH." (PG-42)

The lure is very scarce, but the box is outright rare, trading, empty, in the $200 to $250 range, making the combo a $400 to $500 value in trade.

ALLAN R. SEATON
SEATTLE, WASHINGTON

Allan R. Seaton, out of Seattle, Washington, received Patent No. 2,275,869 on March 10, 1942, for his **SEATON SALMON PLUG**. The only major difference in this plug from others was the belly hook release system. This consisted of two U staples placed in the belly at a bent-down angle towards the rear. A single spring wire was designed to lay just over the edge of the bottom of the U-clip, which formed an oval-shaped window that held the treble hook eye inside. A cord was tied to a front treble hook and a rear treble hook and then to a deep-set screw eye at the tail. When a salmon took the lure, both hooks pulled free from the front cord clips.

Seaton also developed the hollow, metal, fixed-hook **ALASKA PLUG** that was made by the Alaska Tackle Company out of 4619 37th Ave., in Seattle. That is covered earlier in this segment on Pacific Northwest Salmon plugs. (PG-43)

SEATTLE FISHING LURE COMPANY
SEATTLE, WASHINGTON

The 1940's Seattle Fishing Lure Company was located at 1668 W. Florida Street in Seattle, Washington. Their two-piece, orange cardboard lure box had a jumping salmon in the center of the cover and the print, "THE SEATTLE PLUG GETS THE FISH." The 5"-long, no-eyed wooden plug had a cord line tie to a fixed screw eye under the chin. The cord holding two treble hooks was then sandwiched in between a set of two double screw eyes that were spring steel and pinched the cord in place until a fish pulled the cord and hooks loose. The hooked fish was then only secured by the cord tied to the front screw eye. The lure had a slanted nose and a dimple in the bottom of the neck that continued as an indentation halfway up both sides of the neck of the lure. The lure is pictured in red head with white with its box. (PG-43)

SEDCO MANUFACTURING COMPANY
SEATTLE, WASHINGTON

In the 1950's, the Sedco Company, out of P. O. Box 3903, 1016 First Avenue South, Seattle, Washington, produced a hollow, transparent plastic salmon plug called the **LURE-LITE**. The 6"-long electrically illuminated fish lure was in the shape of the traditional salmon plug, like those made of wood by the Martin Company and others. This lure, after unscrewing the head from the body, used a standard AA battery and a #222 battery lamp made by Westinghouse, General Electric, or Burgess. The lure had a slanted, reinforced plastic nose with a hollow tube opening set at an angle to the nose. Through this channel, the fisherman passed a "bead chain" attached to the line tie with a split-ring treble hook at the other end. The LURE-LITE was sold in a one-piece, yellow cardboard box with burgundy print and a slide-on all-around plastic cover. In addition to the lure name and maker's address, there was a picture of the head of an opened-mouth salmon about to eat the lure on the side of the box. (PG-44)

ROY SELF
SEATTLE, WASHINGTON

In the 1930's, Roy Self made several sizes of his **BROKEN THERMOS REFLECTOR SPOONS**. These spoons, made in the 2-1/4" to 3-1/4" range, were first plated in highly polished nickel finish and then painted in red. The red was then polished off in ten to twelve irregular shapes in a pattern resembling what the broken glass would be from a thermos bottle. He made smaller 1-1/4" sizes of these spoons named the **MIRRORED TROUT SPOONS**. Roy Self lures were sold on individual cards. (PG-44,45)

SILVER HORDE FISHING SUPPLIES, INC.
SILVER HORDE SPORTS PLUGS
LYNNWOOD, WASHINGTON

In the mid 1960's, the Silver Horde companies made several metal salmon lures. Examples were the 2-1/2" **CANADIAN # 6 SPOON**, the 5-1/4"-long, narrow **CANADIAN NEEDLE FISH**, a 3" **EGG WOBBLER**, and a 2-3/4" **CANADIAN WOBBLER** that was basically round with six different light-reflecting surfaces.

In the 1970's and 1980's, **SILVER HORDE** salmon plugs were made at P. O. Box 150 in Lynnwood, Washington, and sold there as well by distributor Silver Horde Sports Plugs out of Cowichan Station, British Columbia in Canada. Unlike most other salmon plugs, these were made of plastic in the traditional salmon plug shape. The bead chain line tie to the single belly hook system was loose and fitted through an angled hole in the plug (like on a J-plug) when the fisherman was ready to fish it. The Silver Horde was made in sizes of 3-1/2" long to 6-1/2" long, but there were other models as well. The **LITTLE JOE** was only 3" long, followed by **BIG JOE**, **TATOOSH**, and the 5-1/2" **ACE HI**.

The company also made several metal salmon lures from 3" long to 6-1/2" long, and they included the **CANADIAN SILVER HORDE SPOON, CANADIAN LOU PACK SPOON, WOBBLERS, SILVER HORDE** EGG WOBBLERS, and the **CANADIAN PALLISTER WOBBLER**.

Plugs and spoons are pictured from ad posters. (PG-45)

SOUND METAL PRODUCTS COMPANY
TACOMA, WASHINGTON

The 6", hollow, metal **CARR BAIT** was introduced in 1948 by the Sound Metal Products

Company out of Tacoma, Washington. The torpedo-shaped lure, designed by L. E. Carr, had a sleek general fish shape with a flattened tail.

SPOOFER LURES COMPANY
LOS ANGELES, CALIFORNIA

The long, all-cast-metal **SPOOFER** was introduced in early 1953 in several sizes. The largest size (pictured) was chrome plated and weighed a full 2 ounces and was 5-1/4" long for the spoon and 7" long overall. The lure had a long, spoon-like nose and a washboard tail that consisted of three rows of diamond-like reflective surfaces. The lures were made primarily for coastal saltwater fishing.

The company also made a very similar looking 6-1/2" heavy metal bait called the **MONSTER**. The front half of the lure was pointed and had a smooth surface finish. The last half of the lure had the same washboard tail that consisted of several rows of diamond-shaped light-reflecting surfaces, just like the Spoofer.

The two company productions were the invention of John L. Perkins, who was awarded Patent No. 2,736,125 for the Spoofer on February 28, 1956. (PG-46)

STAR FISH LURE COMPANY
SEATTLE, WASHINGTON

The late-1940's, early-1950's Star Fish Lure Company, out of 462 North 34th Street, Seattle 3, Washington, made a 6-1/4"-long **STAR SALMON PLUG** that was a complete departure from the typical salmon lures of that era. The very rare plug had a slanted nose that ended squared off at the front. The line tie was through the nose to a heavy cord under the belly and was tied to two treble hooks and also held a pinched-on large split shot for weight. The lure had a humped forehead and a curved-down back to the tail holding a double-screw-eye-hinged tongue-tip-shaped wooden tail piece. The early lures had painted eyes and the later ones pressed, indent painted eyes. The lures were painted in only two known colors: red head with white with red and white tail or red head with orange with a white and orange tail. The lures were packaged in two-piece cardboard boxes.

Pictures of lure with box are courtesy of the Dick Ellis collection. (PG-46,47)

The very rare Star Salmon Plug is another high-end trader, reaching the $275 to $300 level in box. The box alone is valued by western salmon collectors in the $150 to $200 range.

TACOMA BAIT COMPANY
TACOMA, WASHINGTON

The late-1930's Tacoma Bait Company made spoons and spinners for trout and salmon fishing. The pictured carded example, **TACOMA TROUT BAIT**, measured 6-3/4" long overall. The lure was very flexible with two interconnected in-line wire shafts with swivels in between. The lure had two copper Colorado spinner blades and eight green glass bead spacer-bearings. The lure was mounted on white card with red print. (PG-59)

TILLICUM COMPANY
VICTORIA, BRITISH COLUMBIA, CANADA

The late-1940's and early-1950's Tillicum Company, located at 899 Esquimatt Road in Victoria, British Columbia, made both traditional wooden salmon plugs and flatie types in the 3-1/2" to 5" range. They sold their lure in a two-piece white cardboard box with a red border on the cover and red print, "THE NEW TILLICUM PLUG." (PG-59)

TOMIC LURES
BRITISH, COLUMBIA, CANADA

Tomic Lures, Box 550 Sooke, British Columbia, Canada, made plastic-body salmon plugs in the 1970's and 1980's. The lure had an internal metal harness with a loop for the line tie and a direct link to the belly and tail hooks, with another loop for these two treble hooks. The pictured six-pack of 4" to 6" **TOMIC PLUGS** is in its cardboard six-compartment box with a solid blue cover and ID stamped on the box end. The lure was also sold on a carded bubble-top package showing their trademark in the upper left corner of a red, opened-mouth salmon head about to eat the letter "T" in Tomic. (PG-48,53)

These are on the low end of trade values in salmon lures.

FLOYD TUCKER COMPANY
GIG HARBOR, WASHINGTON

DAROLD TALLEY COMPANY
TACOMA, WASHINGTON

ELLIS E. WHITE
PORTLAND, OREGON

One of the longest-running salmon plugs ever made was the wooden, and later plastic, lures invented by Ellis E. White of Portland, Oregon. He received patent No. 2,225,676 (pictured) on December 24, 1940, and another Patent No. 2,547,103 on April 3, 1951. He made the lures in wood up until World War II, and then Floyd Tucker continued to make them after the war in wood. Tucker gave the lures the new name Mac's Squid, but I am unable to tell you how he arrived at that name. In the 1960's, Darold Talley acquired the rights and made the lures in plastic, as did a still later company, Mehler Tackle, making this a 1939 to 1970's produced lure.

The 4" **MAC'S SQUID** salmon plug was continued in wood after the war by the Floyd Tucker Company in Gig Harbor, Washington. The lure is pictured painted all white with a red, oval, slightly-cupped face. The lure's two treble hooks were each secured by a single screw through the eye of a quality swivel so that the hooks had a 360-degree swing-arch to aid in keeping a fish on, once hooked. The fisherman had a choice of two line tie spots on the face of the lure to change "point of tow", creating two different actions in the water. The two-piece cardboard lure box had a jumping salmon on the cover with the plug in its mouth and read MAC'S SQUID in blue print and "SALMON PLUG" in red print.

In the mid 1960's, the Darold Talley Company, of 11164 Gravelly Lake Drive S. W. in Tacoma, Washington, purchased the rights to this lure. Talley switched from making the lure in wood to plastic, but, otherwise, the no-eyed lure was the same, except it had just the one line tie location on the nose. Talley even used old stock Tucker boxes to sell his lures.

The two Tucker brothers designed a number of western type lures, some of which were patented, that were made by several companies in Washington and Oregon. By the 1970's, another company was making these lures, still in plastic, but in some wild and flashy color patterns. That was the Mehler Tackle Company, located at P.O. Box 1465, Sandpoint, Idaho. (PG-49)

FRANK S. TUCKER
SEATTLE, WASHINGTON

In addition to having his own company, the half dozen or more metal lures designed and patented by Frank S. Tucker, of Seattle, Washington, were made by several other western lure makers for trout and salmon fishing. No doubt, none of his spoons was copied by more manufactures than was his **FST SPOON** (F.S.T. stands for Frank

S. Tucker in this lure's name). Tucker received patent No 1,706,906 on March 26, 1929, for this 1924-developed spoon.

Tucker received another patent, No. 1,938,266, for another spoon on December 5, 1933. This 5" spoon had a cupped area at the tail facing up and another cupped area at the nose facing down. This 4-1/2"-long **FREAK SPOON** was another lure introduced and patented by Tucker and later made by several other companies. The Freak Spoon was also made by the Shoff Company, in Kent, Washington, and by Gibbs in Canada. (PG-49)

VALEZ LURES
SEATTLE, WASHINGTON

Valez Lures, out of 1167 Mercer Street in Seattle, Washington, made wooden salmon plugs very much like the many others in the 1930's. (PG-59)

VANDES & DITLEFSEN FISH SPOONS
WASHINGTON

Two rare, metal, fish-shaped spoons, made in Washington in the early 1930's and later 1940's, are covered here in one story. The 3-1/2"-long **MOORE'S SUPER CATCH** was the earlier spoon made in 1931 by Ditlefsen Machine Works out of Seattle, Washington. The 2-1/4" **VANDES SPOON** was made in 1946 by the Vandes Lure Company located in Tacoma, Washington. The Vandes Spoon is pictured, but both lures were very similar in appearance. (PG-58)

WALLACE INDUSTRIES
SEATTLE, WASHINGTON

Wallace A. Sleness filed for a patent on March 14, 1949, and Patent No. 2,587,658 was granted to him on March 4, 1952, for this **WALLACE HIGHLINER** plug. The line tie was fixed to a special clip passing through the body at a backwards angle to the front belly hook. The rear hook was secured by a deep eye screw. Wallace A. Sleness had been in production for a time before the war, and then started again after the war.

I believe the boxed lure that I'm picturing with this story is his early, pre-war box. It's yellow with a white paste-on label reading, "Mfg. by WALLACE INDUSTRIES...66 Marion Street Seattle 1, Washington." Over time, Wallace Industries developed four different two-piece cardboard boxes in which his lures were sold, all pictured with this story.

One of the company's more interesting lures was the 6"-long **HIGHLINER PINK NEEDLE** that had a flat, metal, through-body bar from line tie to belly treble hook (pictured). (PG-50,51)

WASHINGTON SPOON & BAIT COMPANY
SEATTLE, WASHINGTON

Harry Crow started the Washington Spoon & Bait Company in 1925 and was in business at least up to the start of World War II. His early productions were the **SEATTLE**, which was not a lure but a trolling flasher attractor. He made a smaller version that was called the **SEATTLE JR.**, but this 3" production was a lure with a single tail hook. A couple of years later, he made another flasher attractor called the **OTTO'S SPECIAL** along with a little 1-3/4" trout lure called the **OTTO'S SPECIAL SPINNER** that was a Colorado spinner blade on a shaft with three red glass beads and a single hook. The company made a set of trolling "cowbells" called the **HARDY BOYLE TROLL**. A lure designed and patented by Harry Crow was his 2-3/4" **CROW'S NUAXION** that was a pointed-nose, egg-shaped spoon that had six different light-reflecting surfaces. (PG-59)

V. S. WATERS
SEATTLE, WASHINGTON

In 1935, Vance Sylvian Waters developed a lure that might as well be called the "Coast-to-Coast Lure" because it was intended for west coast salmon fishing but also became a popular east coast striper bass lure. The actual name was the **WATERS' SWIMMER**. It had a hollow channel down the inside with raised wavy sides. The stainless steel fish-shaped spoon was 6-3/4" long and measured 1-3/8" across the shoulders with 1"-high sides. The lure had a 3-1/2"-long brass bar that was held by four brass rivets on the inside of the spoon. This bar not only held the lure's belly treble hook, but it also provided two optional line tie locations. The rare Swimmer is shown from both side and top inside views. For comparison, I'm picturing the 6-1/2" Water's Swimmer (bottom of picture) with the 6-1/2" Adjustable Action Russelure (top of picture) made in Los Angeles in the early 1950's. Note the remarkable similarities. The lure trades in the $35 to $45 range.

Vance Sylvan Waters' earliest lure was his 4-1/2"-long **WATER'S WOBBLER**, for which he received Patent No. 1,681,316 on August 21, 1928. This stainless steel minnow-shaped lure had a heart-shaped tail piece soldered to the tail that acted as a stabilizer and a dive plane. Most lures had the dive plane at the nose, but this one, located at the tail gave the lure an irregular swimming action like that of a wounded minnow.

I have pictured the V. S. Waters Patent and the lure for that patent, the Waters' Wobbler. However, I am unable to locate my picture of the Swimmer and the comparison pictures of the Swimmer with the Muskie size Russelure. So, I'm picturing the Muskie size of the Russelure to give you the idea of the Swimmer, as the two lures were almost identical, except for the belly hook arrangement. (PG-52)

JOHN E. WEBB
SEATTLE, WASHINGTON

John E. Webb filed for a patent on March 14, 1950, and Patent No. 2,670,559 was awarded on March 2, 1954, to Webb for his **ZIMMY PLUG**. This more modern, Seattle, Washington, plug was made of plastic with a metal interior plate holding the line tie and two belly trebles. There were two hollow, transparent bodies fixed to the sides of this plate with colored body inserts placed inside at the time of assembly.

ELLIS E. WHITE
PORTLAND, OREGON

Ellis E. White, of Portland, Oregon, was awarded two patents, the first on December 24, 1940, No. 2,225,676, and the second on April 3, 1951. Some of his early patented lures each used a cord from line tie to either one or two single hooks, and others used small link chains. His second lure patent called for a release clip for the front treble hook. The cord line tie was first tied to a fixed, strong, rear-end screw eye and then passed through the eye of the front hook that was held to the clip by a round ring. The cord then passed back through the tail eye screw and was tied off to the tail treble. When a fish pulled the front hook free, with this doubled-over cord, the hooks all slid to the rear on a now extended line some distance behind the lure for a more efficient fight with the fish.

After World War II, the Floyd Tucker Company, of Gig Harbor, Washington, was manufacturing the White's Salmon Plug as the **MAC'S SQUID**. Tucker invented a number on salmon lures himself, many of them made of metal. The Tucker Mac's Squid two-piece cardboard box had a jumping salmon on the right side of the cover and "MAC'S SQUID" in blue and white double line print and "SALMON PLUG" in red print.

By the mid 1960's, the Darold Talley Company, out of 11164 Gravelly Lake Drive S. W. in Tacoma, Washington, had purchased the rights to the lure and was making the original wooden plugs in plastic. He used Tucker's old stock lure boxes until the supply ran out. The pictured example is 4" long in all white with a red face and the face print "Made In USA." The lure had two screw-held belly hooks secured by swivels that allowed the hooks to both rotate and swing in a 360-degree circle.

Still later, these plastic lures were made in wild, flashy colors by the Mehler Tackle Company located at P. O. Box 1465, Sandpoint, Idaho. This makes the original 1939 Ellis White's lure one of the longest manufactured salmon plugs ever, from 1939 to the mid 1970's. (PG-49)

WITTMANN LURES
TUCSON, ARIZONA

In 1949, Joseph J. Wittmann, Jr. started his Wittmann Lure Company out of 4637 East 14th St., in Tucson, Arizona. He produced a series of 2-1/2" to 4" all-metal **WITTMANN SALMON LURES**. Each lure was shaped like a woman's long fingernail with the head end open-ended in an oval/teardrop shape. The open end had a center metal flange soldered in place with three line tie options at the front and with a 1"-long wire clip holding the lure's treble hook at the other end. The bottom line tie option was for surface fishing, the middle hole would take the lure down two to six feet, and the top line tie was for deep diving. The larger 4" size had a split-ring tail treble hook, as well as a wire extension treble hook on the belly. Lure colors were red head with white, white with black spots, red head with yellow, orange with red spots, and green with yellow and black spots. Pictured are two lures

in the 2-1/2" size in white with black spots and red head with yellow, both having slight bump-raised, molded-in eyes with large black pupils surrounded by yellow. The lures were sold in one-piece cardboard boxes with plastic covers. Wittmann, Jr. filed for a patent on these lures on December 23, 1953, and Patent No. 2,736,124 was granted to him on February 28, 1956.

In the summer of 1958 the company introduced the **Z-RAY** lure. This little 1/8-ounce 1-3/8"-long (the size pictured) metal lure had a side twist and a bent-down tail that imparted a wild, erratic retrieve action. The lures, made primarily for stream trout fishing, were also made in other sizes. They were sold on red and yellow bubble-topped cards with a P. O. Box 12701, Tucson, Arizona, address. The example shown is gold with red spots, and the card indicated that the Z-Ray had "Proven Results - Terrific Action." Wittmann was awarded Patent No. 2,945,317 for his Z-Ray lure on July 19, 1960, from an application date of November 7, 1958. The Z-Ray was made in a saltwater version that was 5-3/4" long called the **BIG SEA Z**. (PG-53,54)

Wittmann Salmon Lures are rather scarce and trade in the $20 to $35 range. The carded Z-Ray lures, however, seldom trade above the $5 level.

WILL'S TACKLE MANUFACTURING COMPANY
SEATTLE, WASHINGTON

In the mid 1960's, Willis Korf formed his small Willis Tackle Company, located at 5214 Ballard Avenue N. W. in Seattle, Washington. Korf was the inventor of the famous cork **CHERRY BOBBER SPINNER** made for steelhead fishing. Pictured are three of his steelhead and salmon **SAMMY SPECIAL** spinning lures on their card. The card had a picture of the

Cherry Bobber at the top and a picture of Willis Korf, himself, holding a pair of steelhead trout caught on his lure in October of 1964. (PG-54)

WRIGHT TACKLE COMPANY
SEATTLE, WASHINGTON

The post-war-1940's Wright Tackle Company, out of Seattle, Washington, only made one lure that I know of, but it was a unique one. The Wright **SPINOBBLER** was made in the three sizes: 3-3/8", 4", and 4-1/2" long. The lure was double curved into a worm-like S shape and made of brass. The spoons were usually finished in vertical half polished brass and half nickel plate, but, on some, the tails of the spoons were painted at slants in half white and half red. In addition to the unusual shape described, the spoon was slightly cupped at the head in one direction and cupped at the tail in the opposite direction, which resulted in the lure spinning and wobbling at the same time, thus, the name SPINOBBLER. This lure was also made by the QUY-L-UR-E Lure Company, out of Stockton, California, in the 1950's.

EDWARD YEO
ROLLING BAY, WASHINGTON

As far as I know, Edward Yeo only made one salmon lure. It was a 5"-long **YEO**, introduced in 1932 out of Rolling Bay, Washington. The rounded-nose, carrot-shaped lure had a unique tail section. It was V'ed towards the tail from the center of the spoon, and a second V-shaped metal piece was soldered to the main lure body. One side of the lure had two half-circle holes but not drilled through both sections. The other side had six such holes in ascending sizes, front to back, along the outer edges of the spoon, but they were only drilled in the one section, not

through both. The purpose of all of this was to give added weight to the rear and to prevent the lure from revolving, as the lure was meant to be a higher speed trolling spoon that would swim in a vertical position without revolving or wobbling. Edward Yeo was awarded patent No. 1,956,783 for his YEO spoon on May 1, 1934.

Yeo also made and sold a spoon invented by Joseph Hansen, who received Patent No. 1,450,546 on April 3, 1923, for his **HANSEN TROLLING SPOON**.

GROUP PICTURE OF WEST COAST METAL LURES

Starting from the top left, the Canadian Spoon (with the center hole), Minneapolis, Minnesota, trades in the $5 range, sometimes higher for the larger sizes. The next several lures covered trade in the $10 to $20 range; they include all of the **KEWELL-STUART SPOONS** pictured in the rest of row one and all of row two. The next four large spoons are two **SUPERIOR SPOONS** and two **McMAHONE SPOONS** by Pacific Marine, as well as the middle three spoons in the second row; these spoons trade in the $5 and up range. Last in this row is the 1960's Les Davis **HOT ROD**, $3. The first spoon in row two is the **SUPER DIAMOND**, made in the 1910s by the Evans Manufacturing Company of both Seattle and Vancouver; trading in the $20 range. The first lure in row three is the very rare 4" **BUBBLE-TROLL** by Les Davis in 1934 Tacoma, Washington, that can reach $50. Next, the 2-1/4" **DAVIS HEART SPOON** is by 1930's Dave Davis; trading at $25. Next is the **EGG WOBBLER** by the Silver Horde Co. of Lynnwood, Washington, 1958; trading in the $10 range. The next four hammered-finish lures are by Les Davis; three **WOBBLERS** and a double pointed **JACK-O-DIAMOND**; trade at $10 to

$15 each. Bottom row: Glen Evans **DARDEVLE SPOON**; 1978; only trades at $3. The Les Davis 1-3/4" hammered brass **RED EYE TROUT** and a 2-3/4" **RED EYE WIGGLER**; trade between $15 to $20 each. The hollow brass plug is by Linquist Bros. of Windsor & Tecumseh, Ontario; 1950's **CANADIAN WIGGLER** trades up to $10 and higher in box; Next, the very rare VANDES SPOON by 1946 Vandes Lure Co., Tacoma, Washington; trades up to $50. Next are two scarce **VIBROLITE SPOONS** by the 1940's Northwest Silversmith Co. of Portland, Oregon; $15 each. Directly above them is a Les Davis 1934 SILVER DART; scarce; will reach the $20 level. The ear-shaped copper-bladed spoon is a very rare **AMENT PORK RIND WIGGLER**, patented in 1966 by Weston H. Ament of the Ament-Douglas Manufacturing Company of San Bruno, California; trades at the $35 level. Last is a scent-pocket lure called the **SIBERIAN WOBBLER** by the early 1930's Marine Appliance Manufacturing Company of Seattle, Washington; can reach $25.

Due to the vast number of sets of pictures that are utilized to cover all of these companies, I have put a caption with each one listing the companies and/or lures pictured in that particular set. Also at the end of each of these sub-stories, the picture group (PG) number is indicated in parentheses. I recently discovered a large envelope of pictures that I overlooked, so these pictures may not be in alphabetical order after set 54.

Picture set #55 is of lure patents that correspond with stories covered here.

#56. Les Davis lures: Pearl Wobblers, Cut Plugs, Canadian Wobblers, Witch Doctor, and others.

#57. Western metals that are all covered in the text. Note the V. S. Waters SWIMMER LURE that is very similar to the muskie size of the California RUSSELURE.

#58. On the left, the rare Marine Appliance SIBERIAN WOBBLER, and, below, two Al McKnight lures. On the right are two very rare HEITMILLER SPOONS by H. W. Heitmiller that are similar to the Buck Perry Spoonplugs, and, below, the 1946 VANDES SPOON fish-shaped spoons. The others are Pop Gear, Tucker's F.S.T., and Roy Self.

#59. It includes a beautiful rainbow finish TILLICOM PLUG from British Columbia, Canada. Below are two Jack Lloyd WATER WITCH lures. On the right are three Northwest Silversmith Spinning lures. Finally, there are a Roy Self MIRRORED LURE and a 1930's Tacoma Trout Bait.

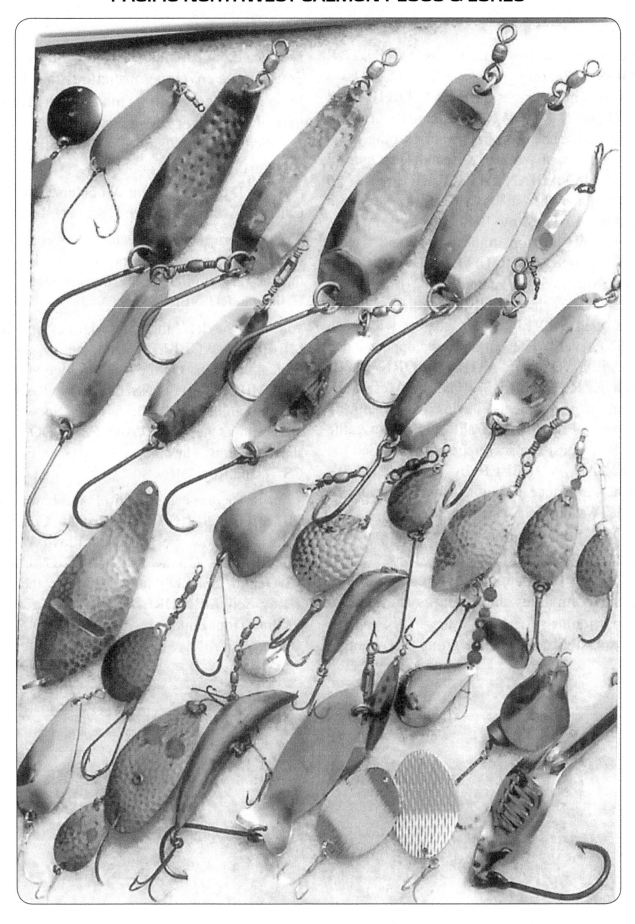

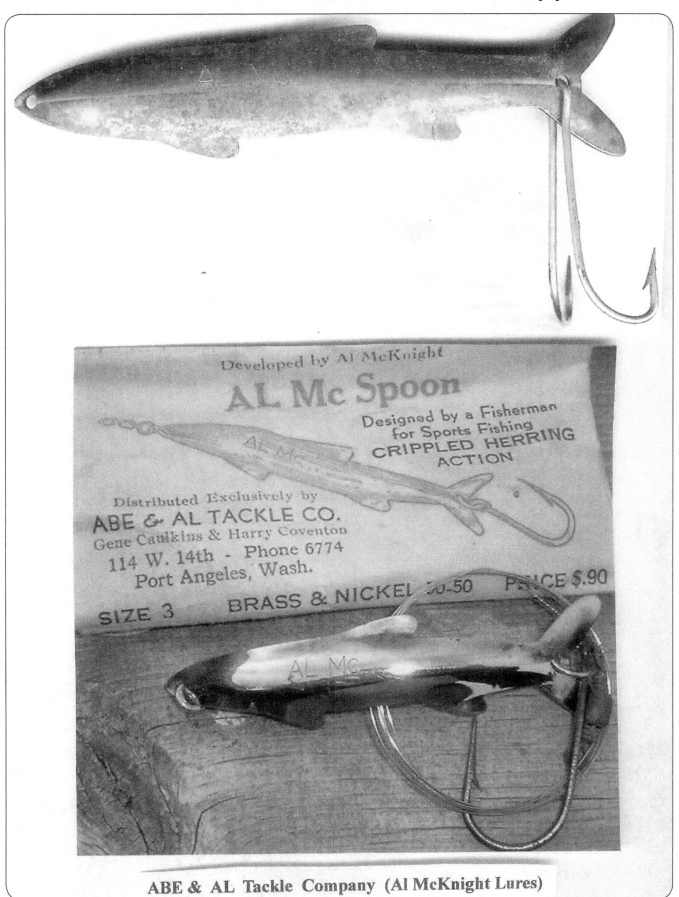

ABE & AL Tackle Company (Al McKnight Lures)

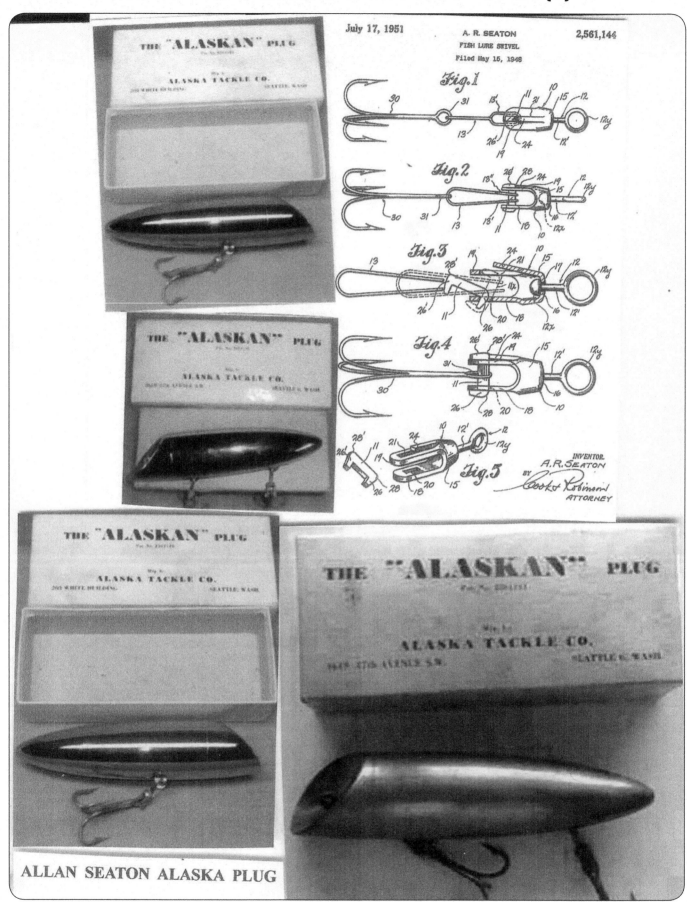

ALLAN SEATON ALASKA PLUG

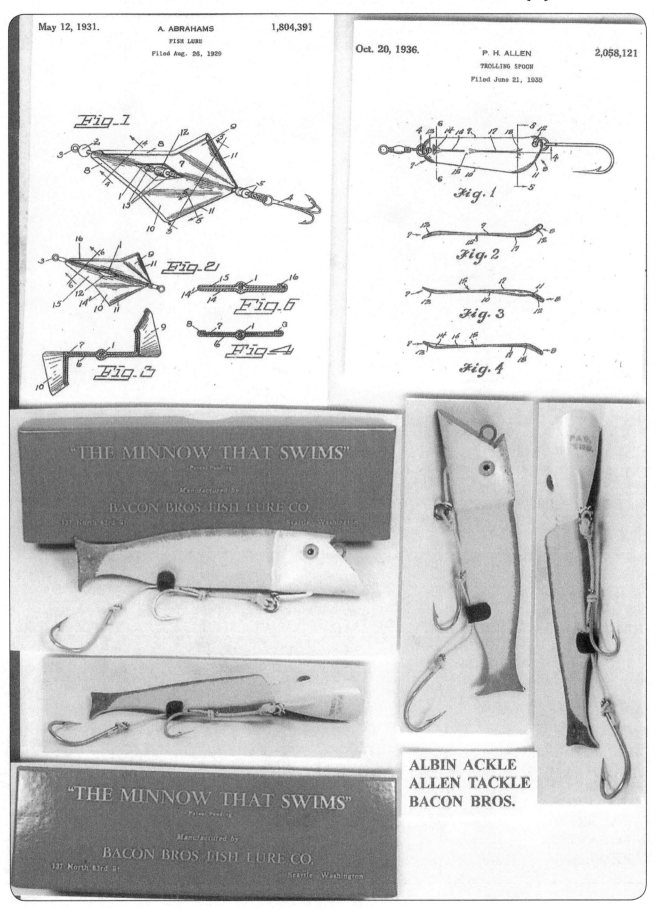

ALBIN ACKLE
ALLEN TACKLE
BACON BROS.

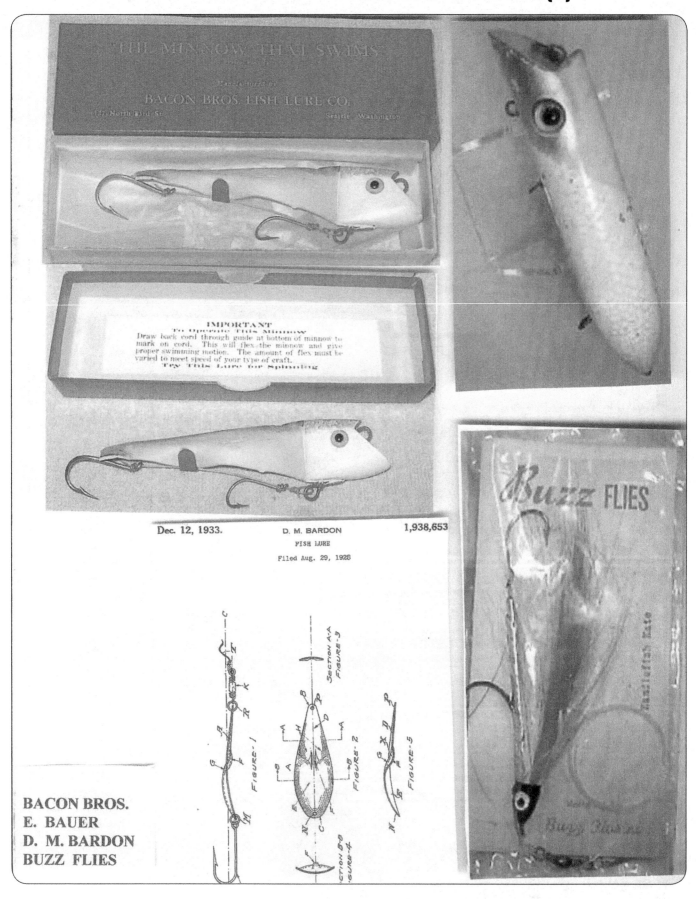

THE MINNOW THAT SWIMS

BACON BROS. FISH LURE CO.

117 North 82nd St.　　　Seattle, Washington

IMPORTANT
To Operate This Minnow
Draw back cord through guide at bottom of minnow to mark on cord. This will flex the minnow and give proper swimming motion. The amount of flex must be varied to meet speed of your type of craft.
Try This Lure for Spinning

Dec. 12, 1933.   D. M. BARDON   1,938,653

FISH LURE

Filed Aug. 29, 1928

BACON BROS.
E. BAUER
D. M. BARDON
BUZZ FLIES

Buzz FLIES

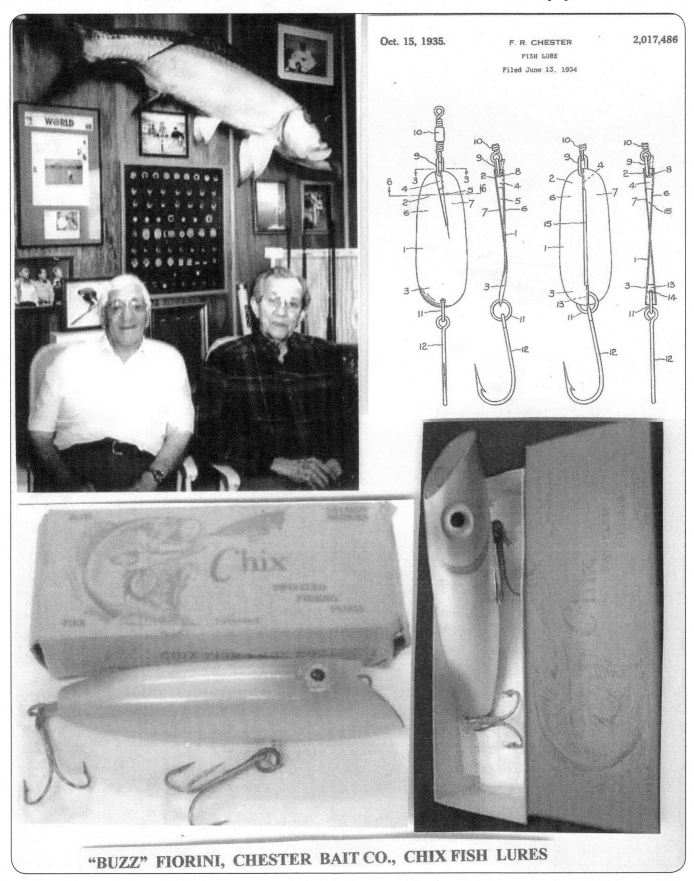

Oct. 15, 1935.

F. R. CHESTER
FISH LURE
Filed June 13, 1934

2,017,486

"BUZZ" FIORINI, CHESTER BAIT CO., CHIX FISH LURES

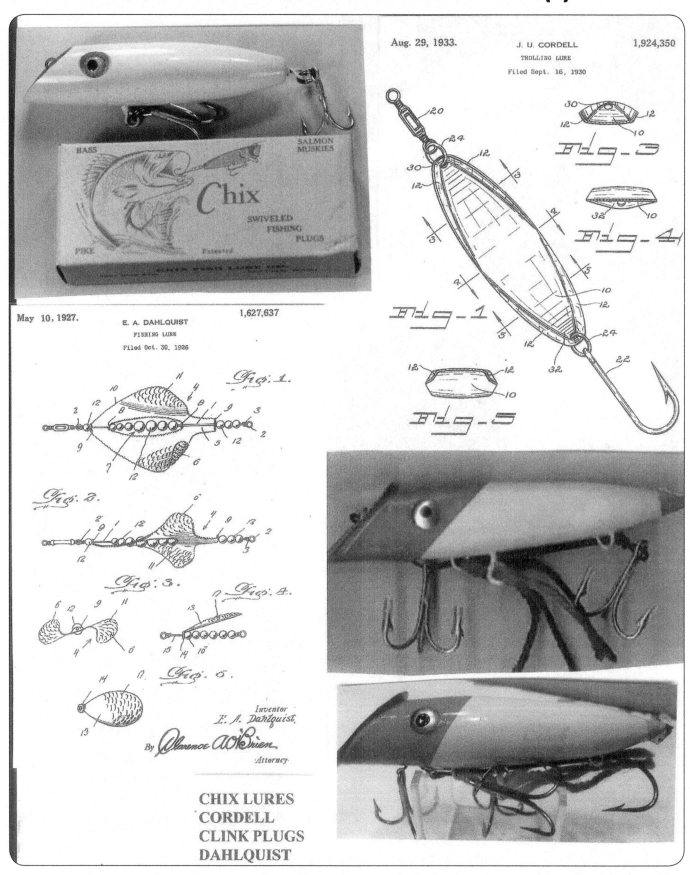

CHIX LURES
CORDELL
CLINK PLUGS
DAHLQUIST

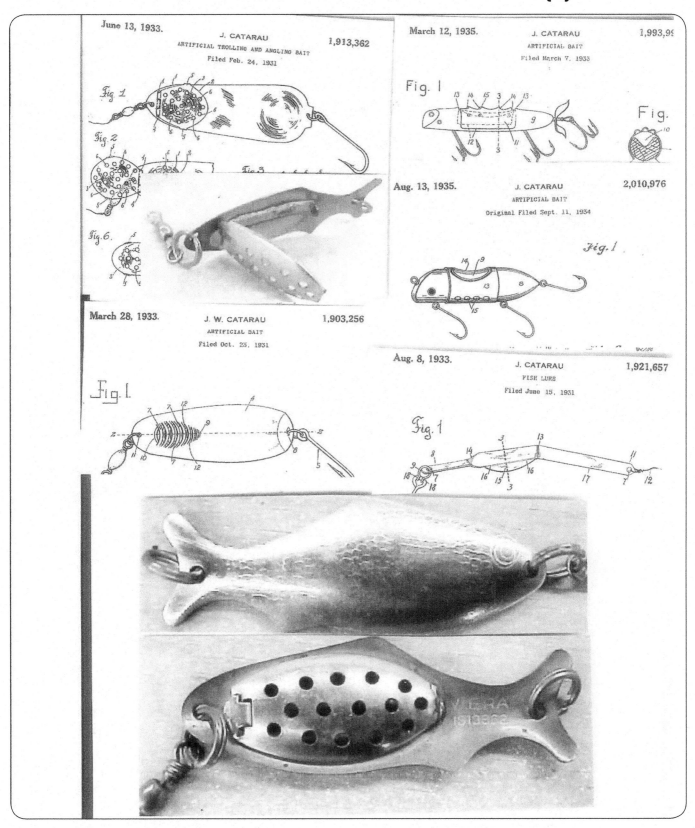

June 13, 1933.

J. CATARAU

ARTIFICIAL TROLLING AND ANGLING BAIT

Filed Feb. 24, 1931

1,913,362

Fig. 1

Fig. 2

Fig. 3

Fig. 6

March 28, 1933.

J. W. CATARAU

ARTIFICIAL BAIT

Filed Oct. 23, 1931

1,903,256

Fig. 1

March 12, 1935.

J. CATARAU

ARTIFICIAL BAIT

Filed March 7, 1933

1,993,99

Fig. 1

Fig.

Aug. 13, 1935.

J. CATARAU

ARTIFICIAL BAIT

Original Filed Sept. 11, 1934

2,010,976

Fig. 1

Aug. 8, 1933.

J. CATARAU

FISH LURE

Filed June 15, 1931

1,921,657

Fig. 1

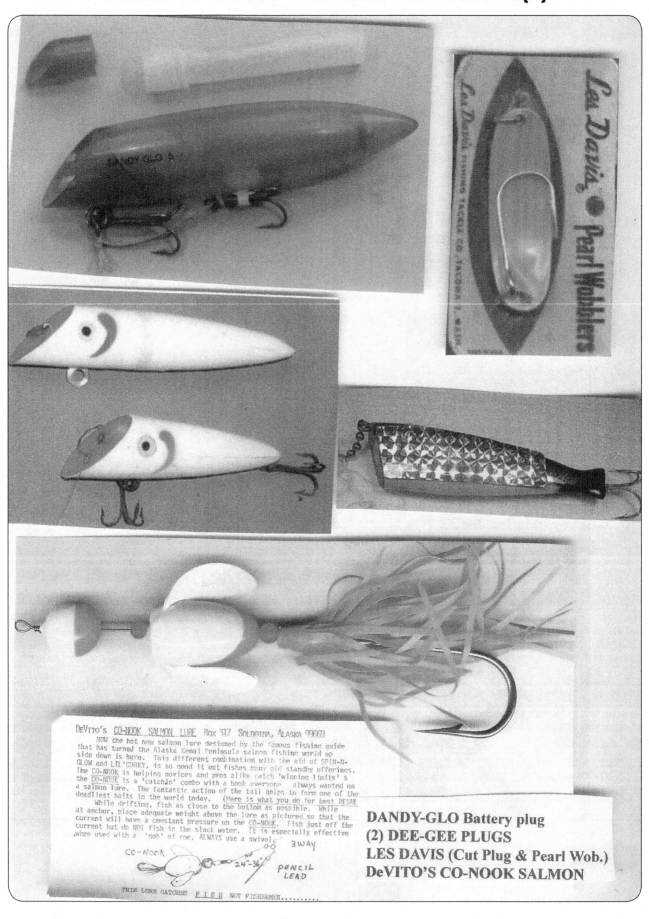

DeVito's CO-NOOK SALMON LURE Box 317 Soldotna, Alaska 99669
    NOW the hot new salmon lure designed by the famous fishing guide that has turned the Alaska Kenai Peninsula salmon fishing world up side down is here. This different combination with the aid of SPIN-N-GLOW and LIL'CORKY, is so good it out fishes many old standby offerings. The CO-NOOK is helping novices and pros alike catch 'winning limits' & the CO-NOOK is a 'catchin' combo with a hook everyone always wanted on a salmon lure. The fantastic action of the tail helps to form one of the deadliest baits in the world today.   (Here is what you do for best RESUL
    While drifting, fish as close to the bottom as possible. While at anchor, place adequate weight above the lure as pictured so that the current will have a constant pressure on the CO-NOOK. Fish just off the current but do NOT fish in the slack water. It is especially effective when used with a 'gob' of roe. ALWAYS use a swivel.
                                                                3 WAY
    CO-NOOK
                                                         24"-36"   PENCIL
                                                                    LEAD
    THIS LURE CATCHES F I S H NOT FISHERMEN..........

DANDY-GLO Battery plug
(2) DEE-GEE PLUGS
LES DAVIS (Cut Plug & Pearl Wob.)
DeVITO'S CO-NOOK SALMON

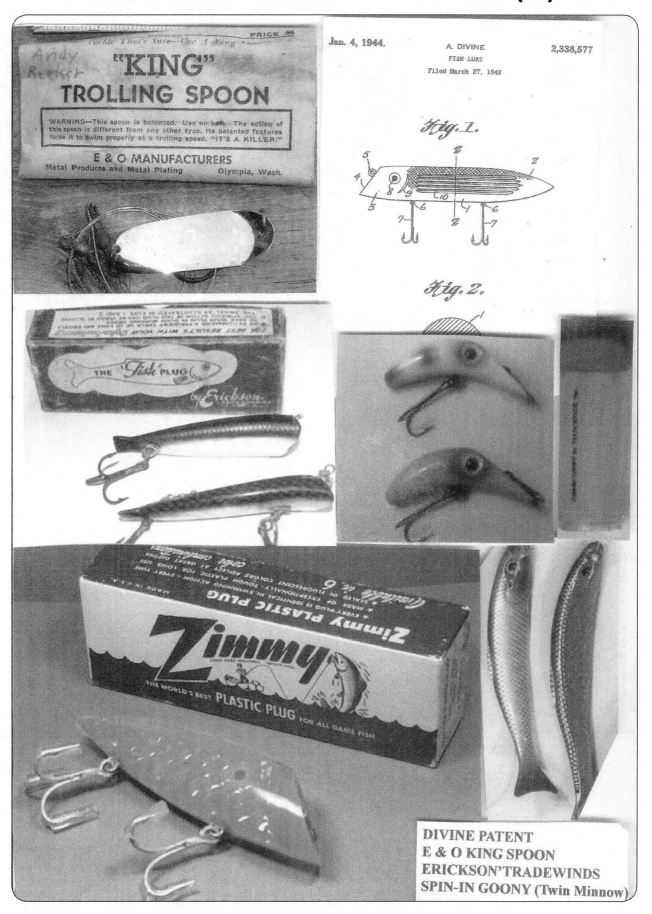

**DIVINE PATENT
E & O KING SPOON
ERICKSON'TRADEWINDS
SPIN-IN GOONY (Twin Minnow)**

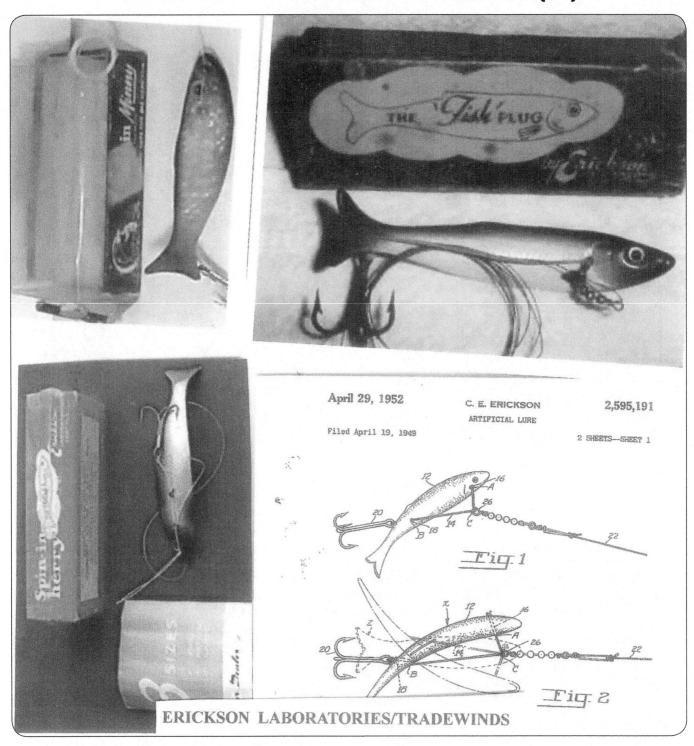

April 29, 1952

C. E. ERICKSON

2,595,191

ARTIFICIAL LURE

Filed April 19, 1949

2 SHEETS—SHEET 1

Fig. 1

Fig. 2

ERICKSON LABORATORIES/TRADEWINDS

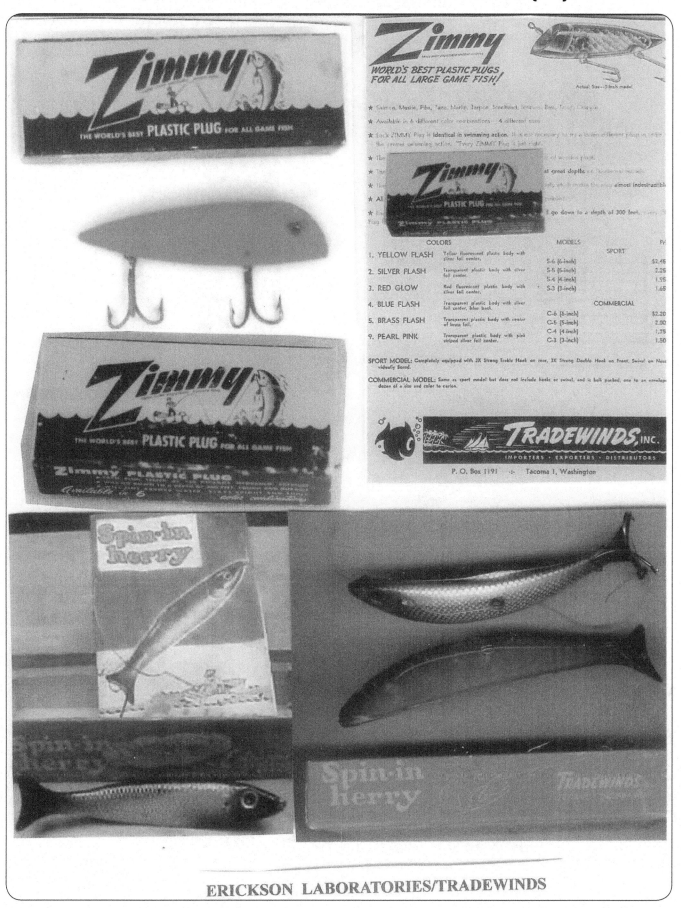

ERICKSON LABORATORIES/TRADEWINDS

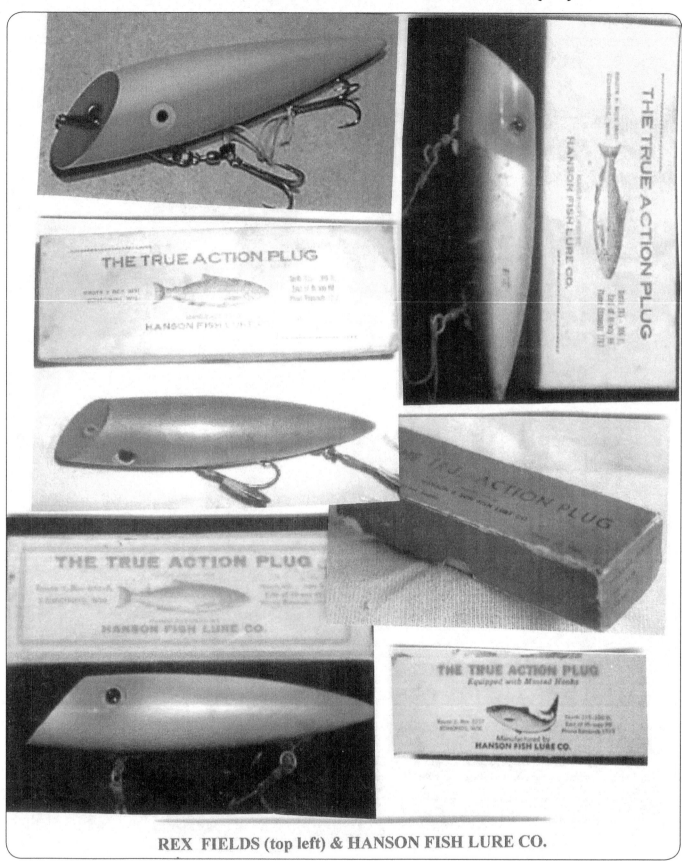

REX FIELDS (top left) & HANSON FISH LURE CO.

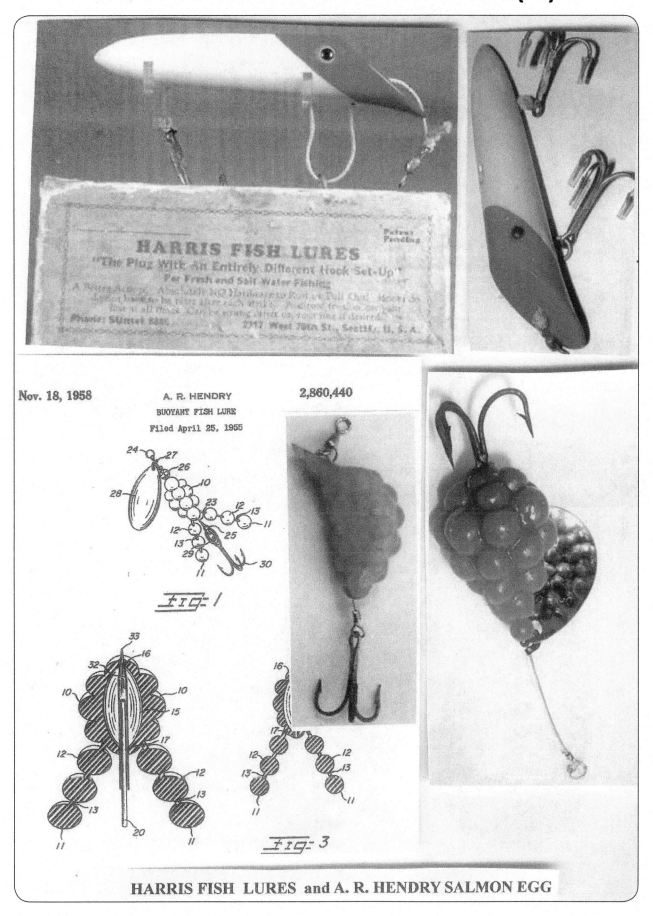

HARRIS FISH LURES and A. R. HENDRY SALMON EGG

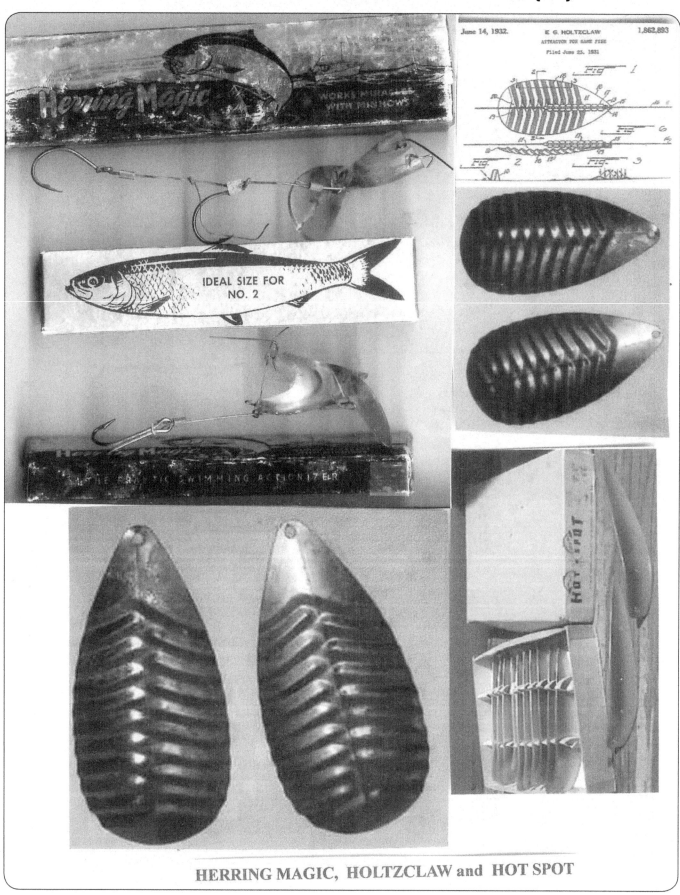

HERRING MAGIC, HOLTZCLAW and HOT SPOT

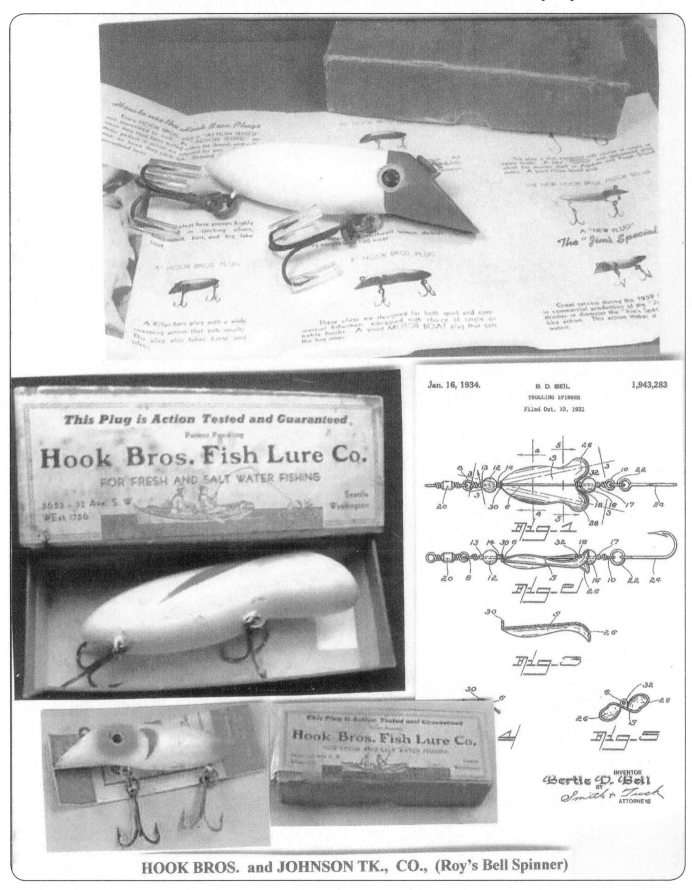

HOOK BROS. and JOHNSON TK., CO., (Roy's Bell Spinner)

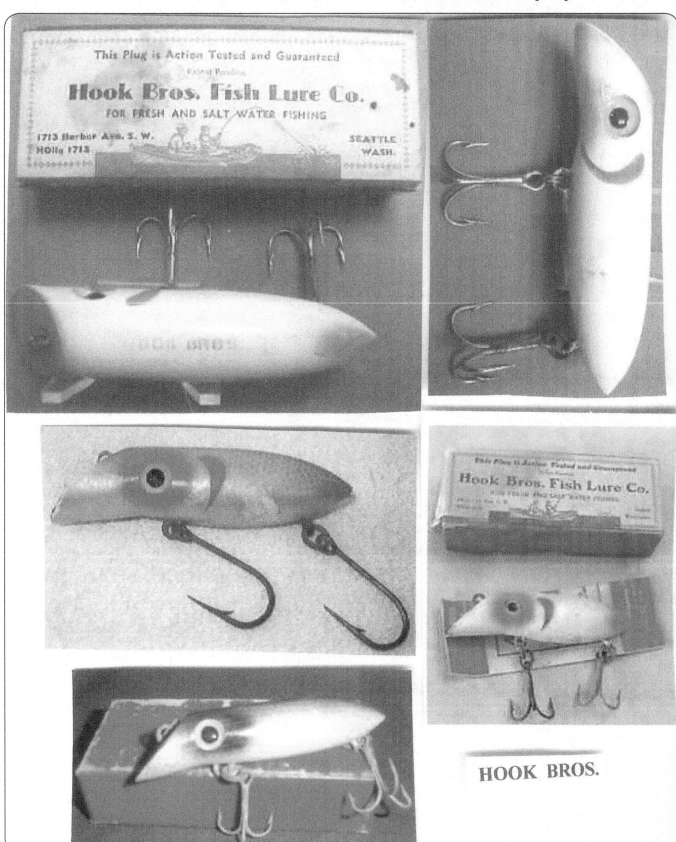

HOOK BROS.

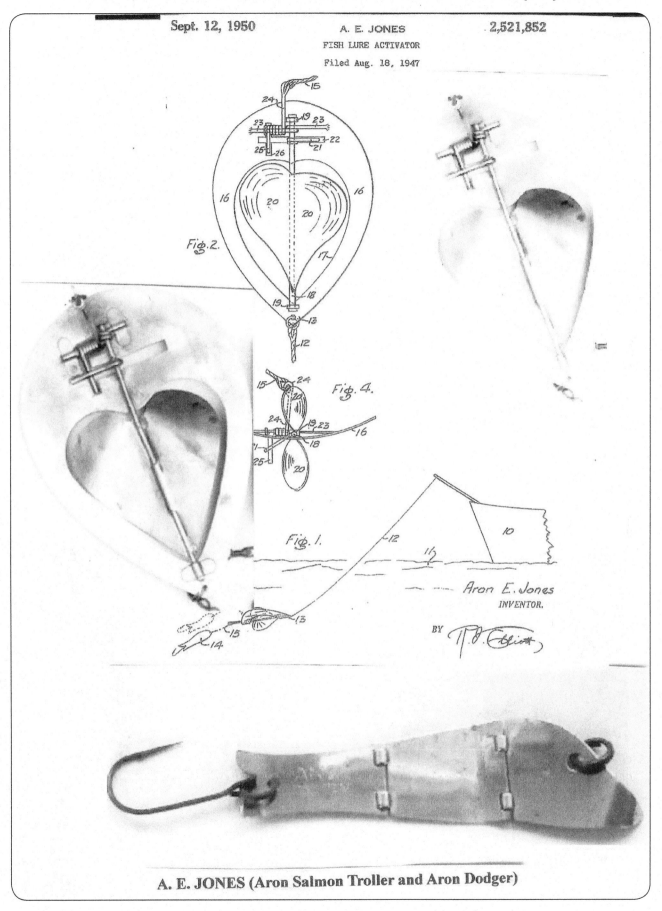

Sept. 12, 1950

A. E. JONES

2,521,852

FISH LURE ACTIVATOR

Filed Aug. 18, 1947

Fig.2.

Fig. 4.

Fig. 1.

Aron E. Jones
INVENTOR.

BY

A. E. JONES (Aron Salmon Troller and Aron Dodger)

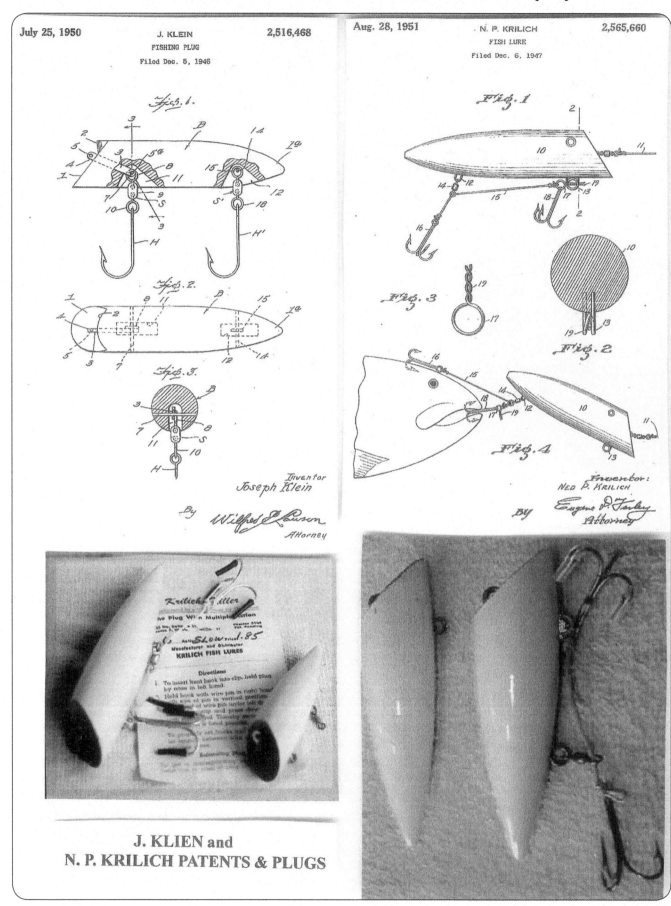

July 25, 1950   J. KLEIN   2,516,468

FISHING PLUG

Filed Dec. 5, 1946

Fig. 1.

Fig. 2.

Fig. 3.

Inventor

Joseph Klein

By Wilfred Lawson

Attorney

Aug. 28, 1951   N. P. KRILICH   2,565,660

FISH LURE

Filed Dec. 6, 1947

Fig. 1.

Fig. 3.

Fig. 2.

Fig. 4.

Inventor:

NED P. KRILICH

By Eugene D. Farley

Attorney

J. KLIEN and
N. P. KRILICH PATENTS & PLUGS

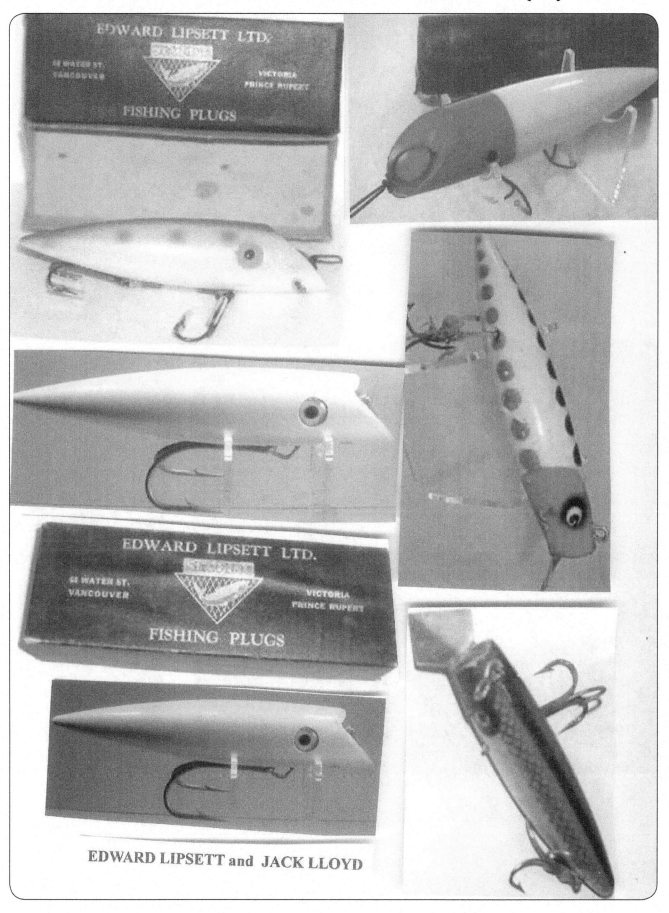

EDWARD LIPSETT and JACK LLOYD

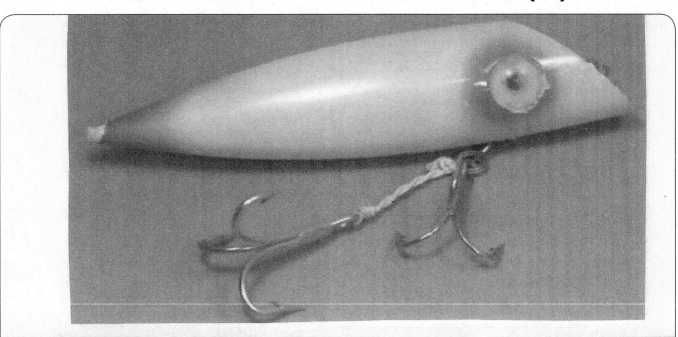

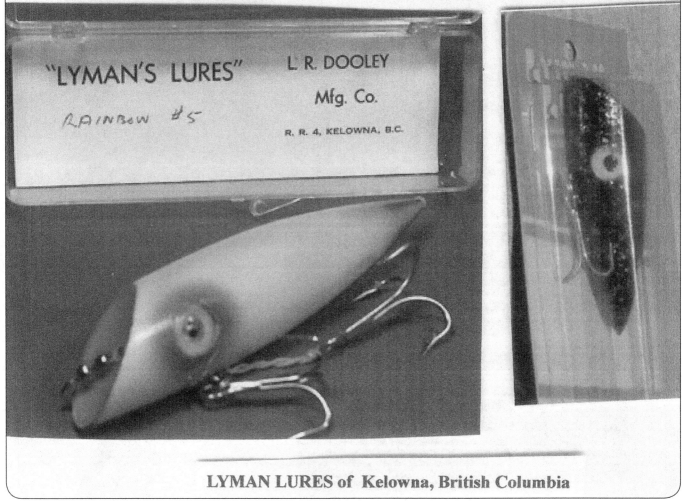

LYMAN LURES of Kelowna, British Columbia

(2) More LYMAN's and MAGARD SparX-PLUGS

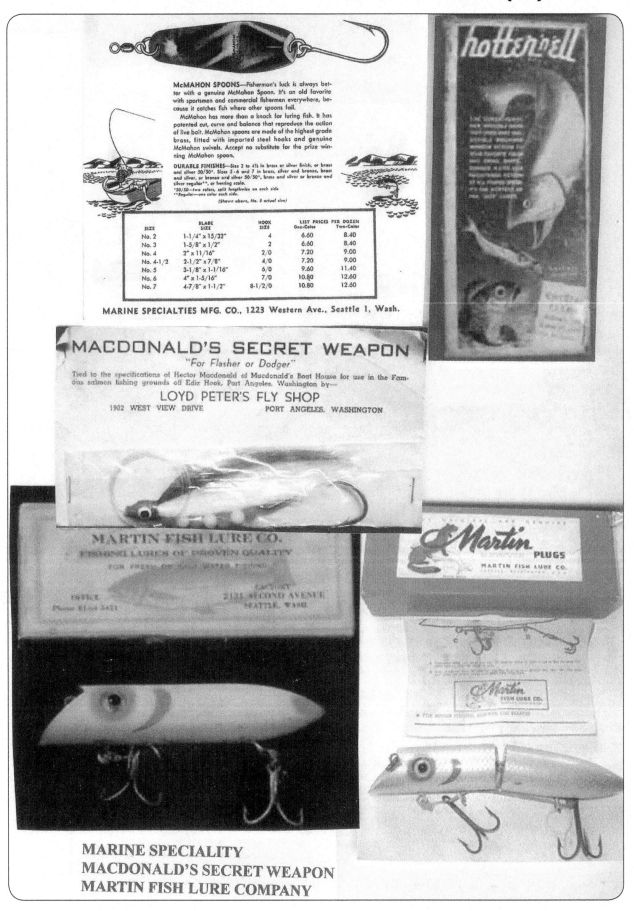

McMAHON SPOONS—Fisherman's luck is always better with a genuine McMahon Spoon. It's an old favorite with sportsmen and commercial fishermen everywhere, because it catches fish where other spoons fail.

McMahon has more than a knack for luring fish. It has patented cut, curve and balance that reproduce the action of live bait. McMahon spoons are made of the highest grade brass, fitted with imported steel hooks and genuine McMahon swivels. Accept no substitute for the prize winning McMahon spoon.

DURABLE FINISHES—Size 2 to 4½ in brass or silver finish, or brass and silver 50/50*. Sizes 5-6 and 7 in brass, silver and bronze, brass and silver, or bronze and silver 50/50*, brass and silver or bronze and silver regular**, or herring scale.
*50/50—two colors, split lengthwise on each side.
**Regular—one color each side.
(Shown above, No. 5 actual size)

SIZE	BLADE SIZE	HOOK SIZE	LIST PRICES PER DOZEN One-Color	Two-Color
No. 2	1-1/4" x 15/32"	4	6.60	8.40
No. 3	1-5/8" x 1/2"	2	6.60	8.40
No. 4	2" x 11/16"	2/0	7.20	9.00
No. 4-1/2	2-1/2" x 7/8"	4/0	7.20	9.00
No. 5	3-1/8" x 1-1/16"	6/0	9.60	11.40
No. 6	4" x 1-5/16"	7/0	10.80	12.60
No. 7	4-7/8" x 1-1/2"	8-1/2/0	10.80	12.60

MARINE SPECIALTIES MFG. CO., 1223 Western Ave., Seattle 1, Wash.

MACDONALD'S SECRET WEAPON
"For Flasher or Dodger"
Tied to the specifications of Hector Macdonald at Macdonald's Boat House for use in the Famous salmon fishing grounds off Ediz Hook, Port Angeles, Washington by—

LOYD PETER'S FLY SHOP
1902 WEST VIEW DRIVE   PORT ANGELES, WASHINGTON

MARINE SPECIALITY
MACDONALD'S SECRET WEAPON
MARTIN FISH LURE COMPANY

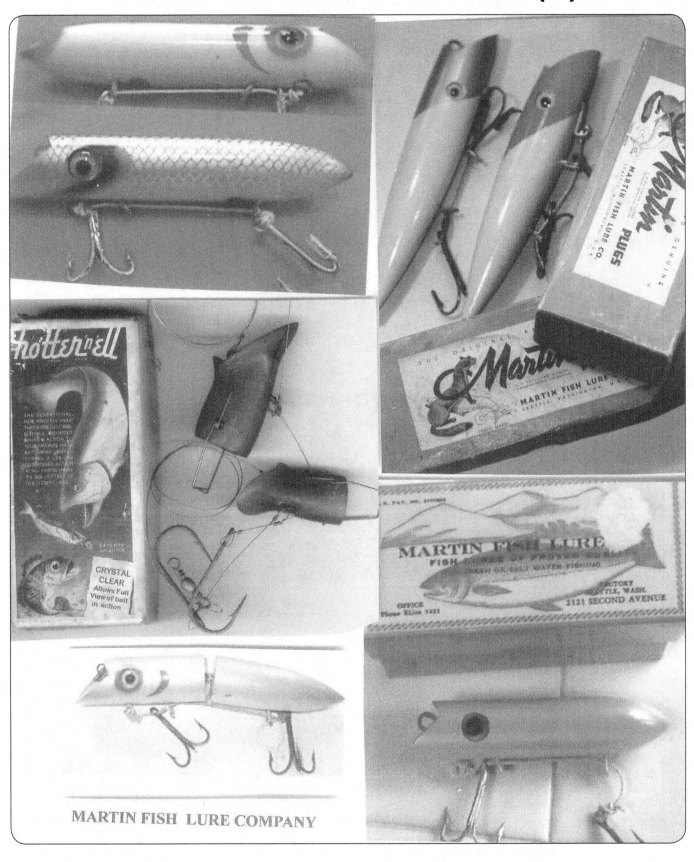

MARTIN FISH LURE COMPANY

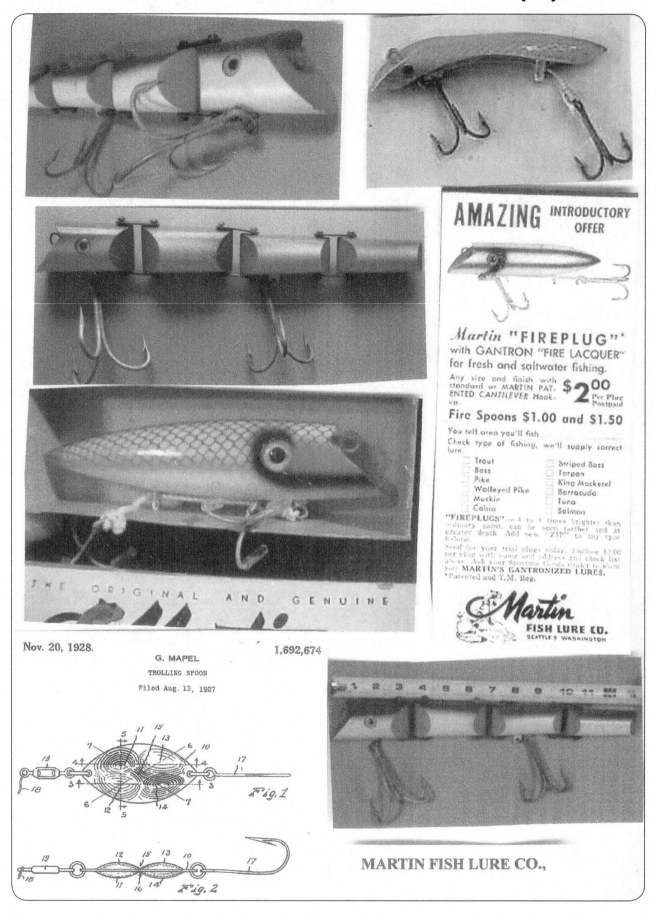

Nov. 20, 1928.   1,692,674

G. MAPEL

TROLLING SPOON

Filed Aug. 13, 1927

MARTIN FISH LURE CO.,

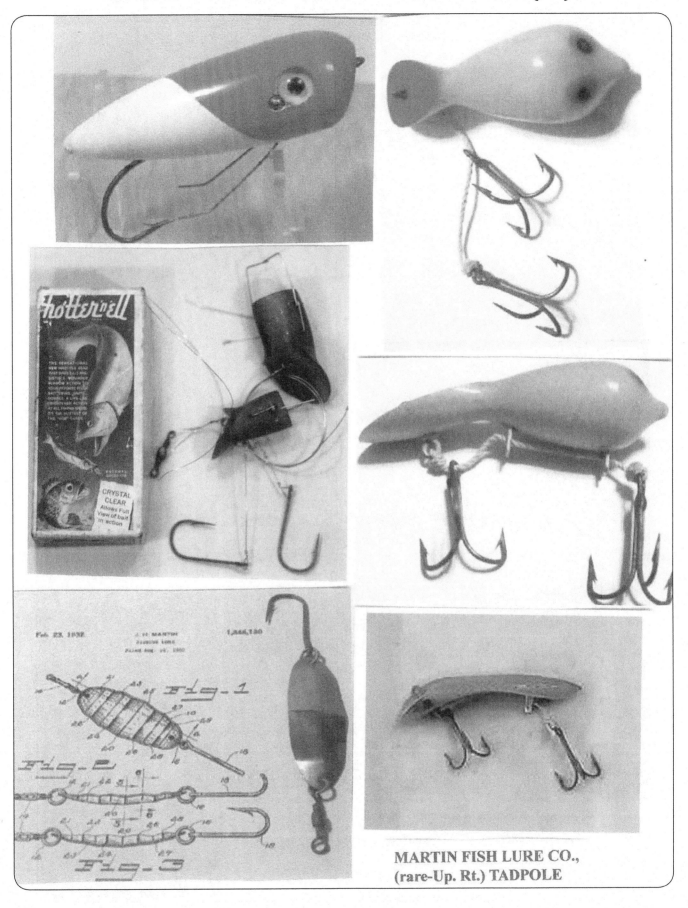

MARTIN FISH LURE CO.,
(rare-Up. Rt.) TADPOLE

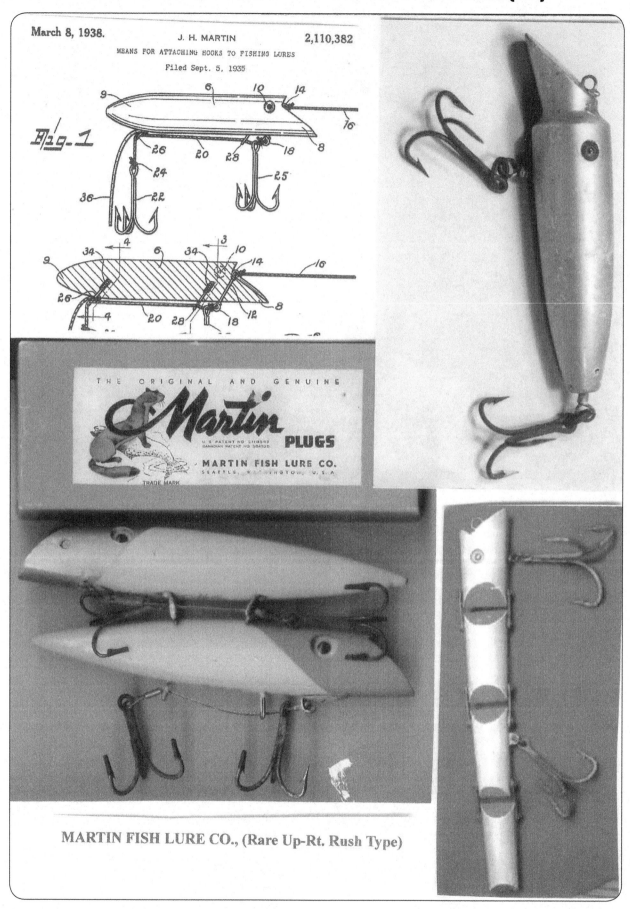

March 8, 1938.   J. H. MARTIN   2,110,382

MEANS FOR ATTACHING HOOKS TO FISHING LURES

Filed Sept. 5, 1935

THE ORIGINAL AND GENUINE

Martin PLUGS

U. S. PATENT NO 2110382
CANADIAN PATENT NO 384520

MARTIN FISH LURE CO.
SEATTLE, WASHINGTON, U.S.A.

TRADE MARK

MARTIN FISH LURE CO., (Rare Up-Rt. Rush Type)

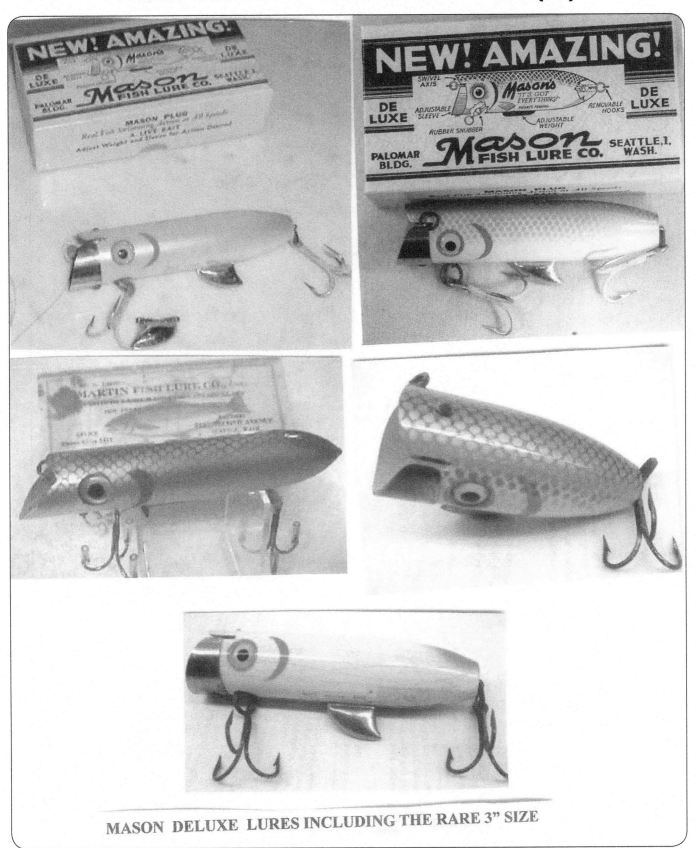

MASON DELUXE LURES INCLUDING THE RARE 3" SIZE

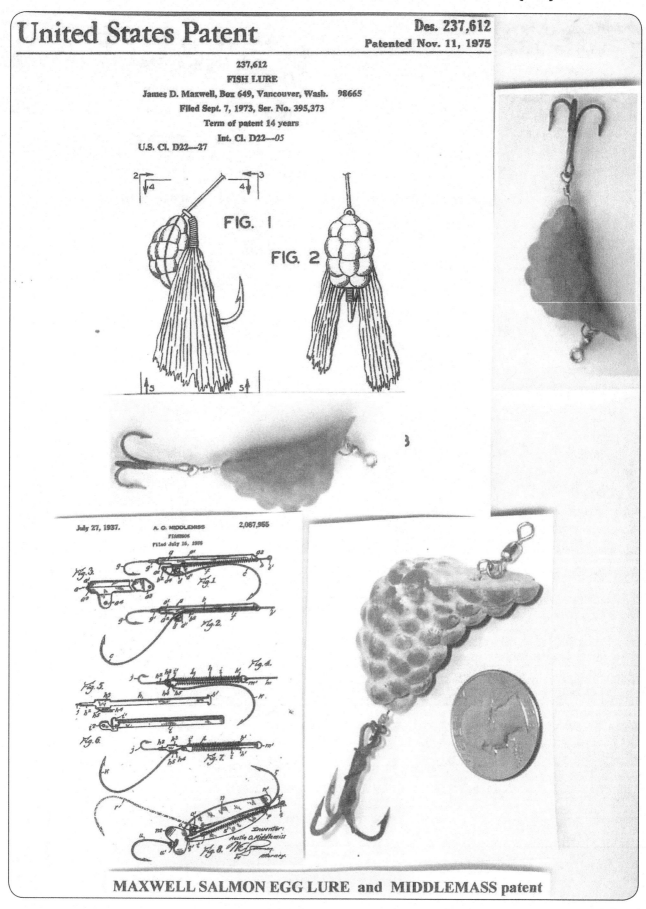

United States Patent

Des. 237,612
Patented Nov. 11, 1975

237,612
FISH LURE
James D. Maxwell, Box 649, Vancouver, Wash. 98665
Filed Sept. 7, 1973, Ser. No. 395,373
Term of patent 14 years
Int. Cl. D22—05
U.S. Cl. D22—27

FIG. 1

FIG. 2

July 27, 1937.   A. O. MIDDLEMISS   2,087,955
FISH HOOK
Filed July 15, 1936

MAXWELL SALMON EGG LURE and MIDDLEMASS patent

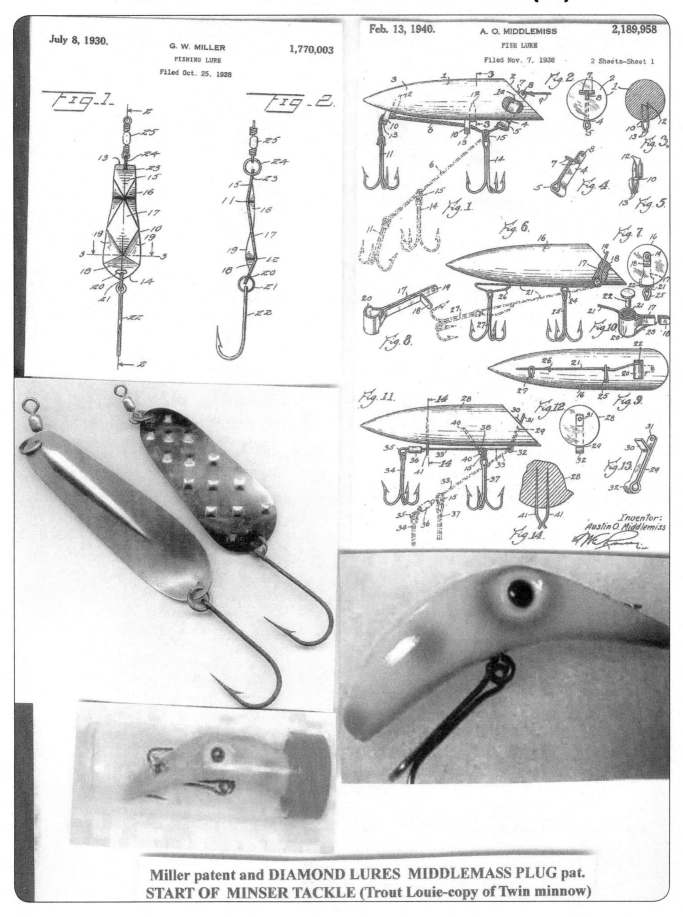

Miller patent and DIAMOND LURES MIDDLEMASS PLUG pat.
START OF MINSER TACKLE (Trout Louie-copy of Twin minnow)

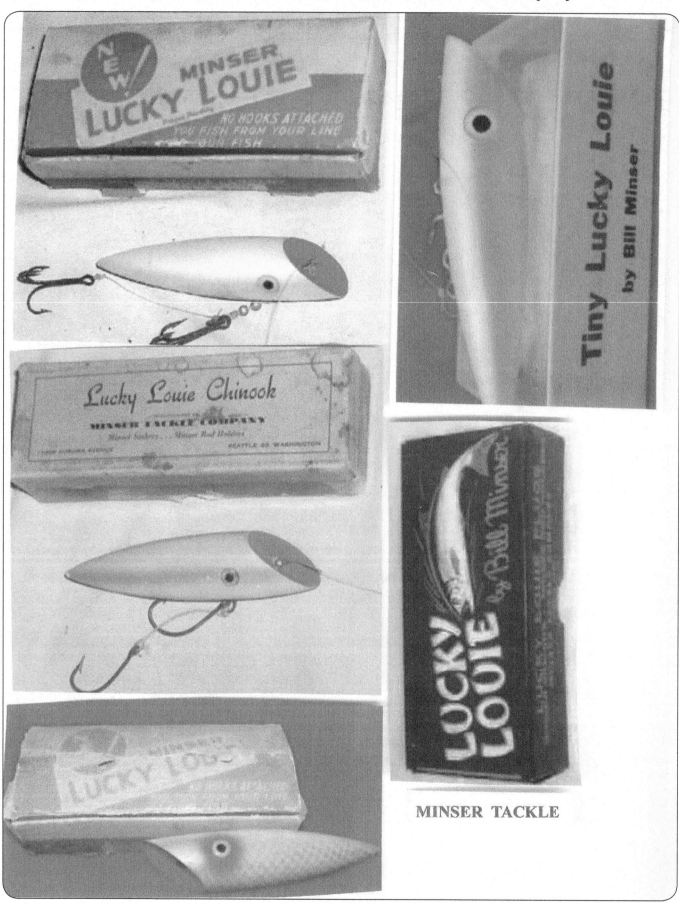

MINSER TACKLE

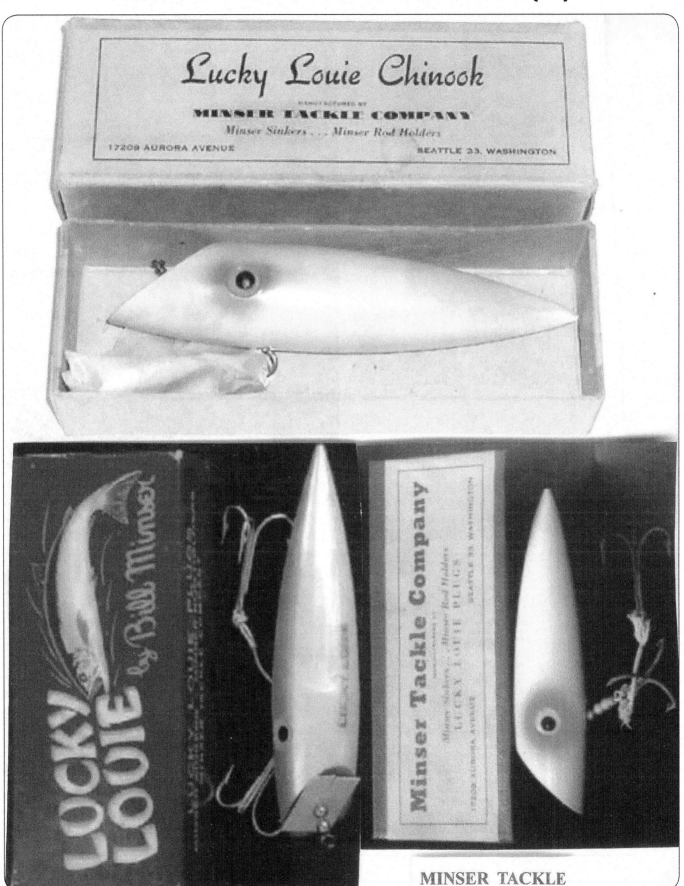

MINSER TACKLE

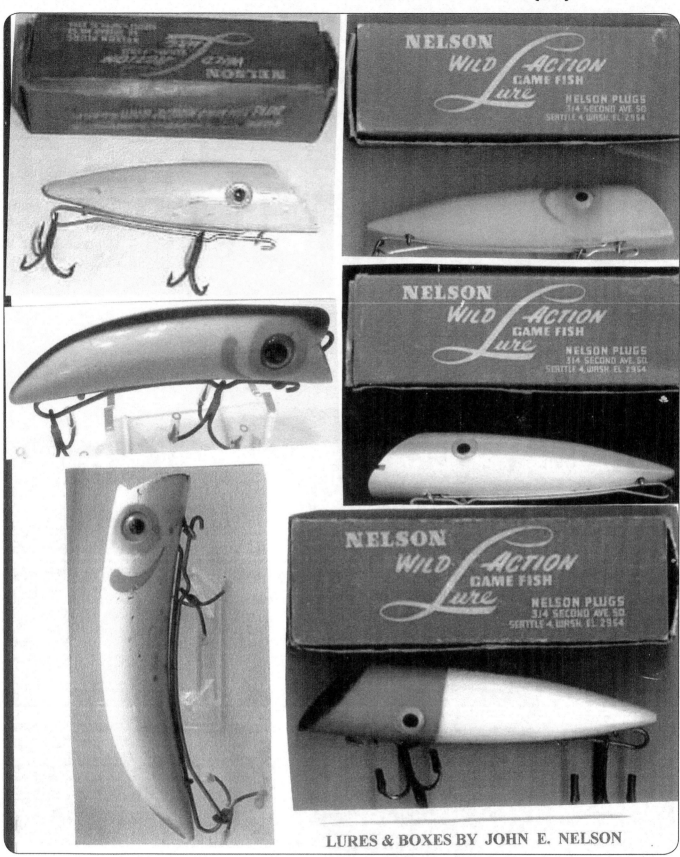

LURES & BOXES BY JOHN E. NELSON

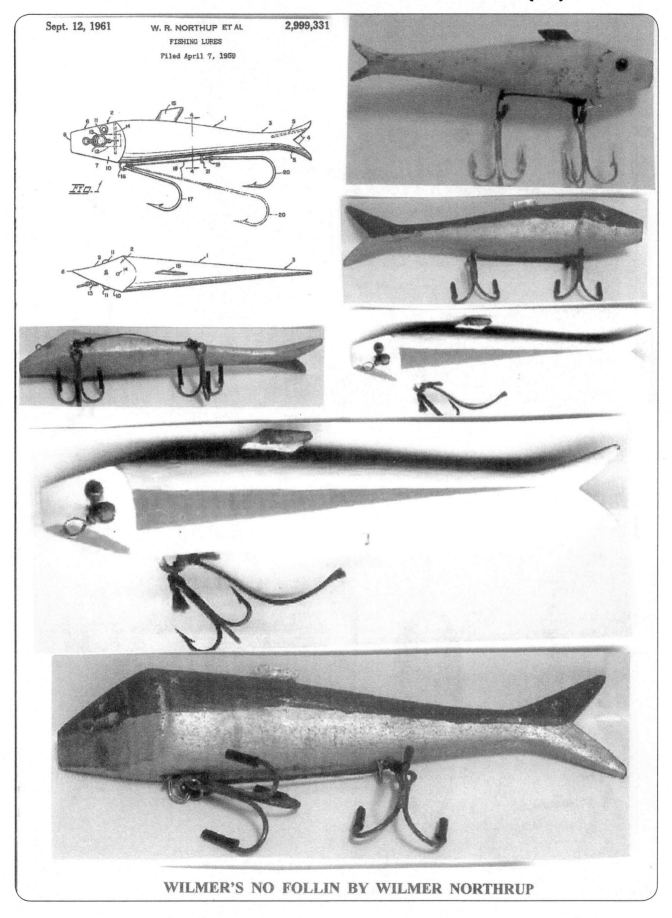

Sept. 12, 1961   W. R. NORTHUP ET AL   2,999,331

FISHING LURES

Filed April 7, 1959

WILMER'S NO FOLLIN BY WILMER NORTHRUP

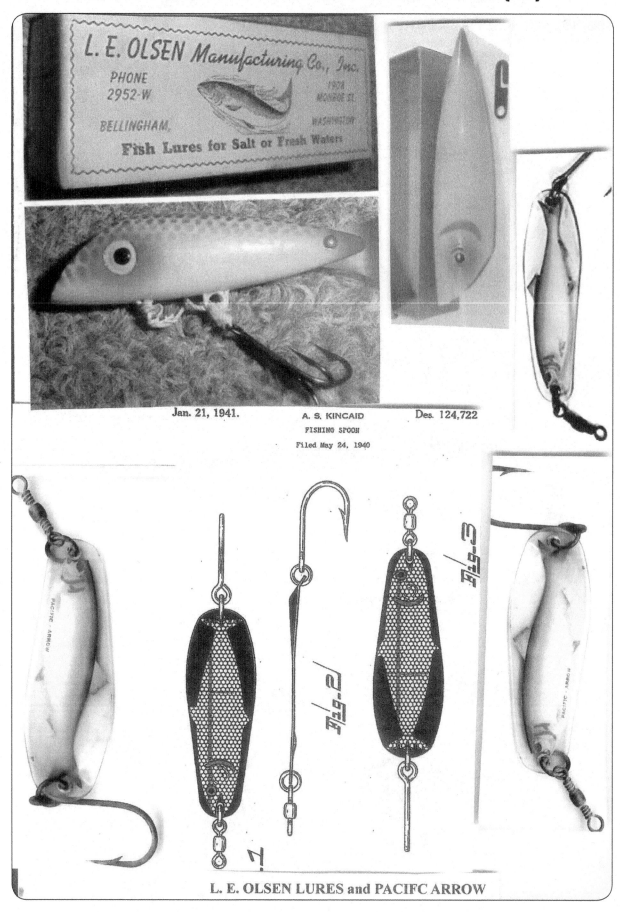

Jan. 21, 1941.

A. S. KINCAID

Des. 124,722

FISHING SPOON

Filed May 24, 1940

L. E. OLSEN LURES and PACIFC ARROW

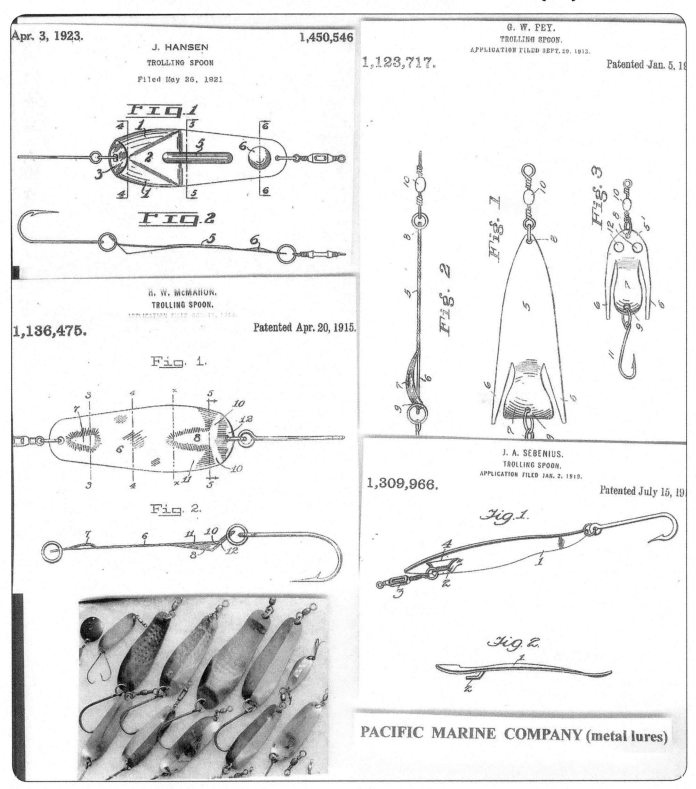

Apr. 3, 1923.

J. HANSEN

TROLLING SPOON

Filed May 26, 1921

1,450,546

Fig.1

Fig.2

H. W. McMAHON.

TROLLING SPOON.

APPLICATION FILED OCT. 19, 1913.

1,136,475.

Patented Apr. 20, 1915.

Fig. 1.

Fig. 2.

G. W. FEY.

TROLLING SPOON.

APPLICATION FILED SEPT. 29, 1913.

1,123,717.

Patented Jan. 5, 19

Fig. 1

Fig. 2

Fig. 3

J. A. SEBENIUS.

TROLLING SPOON.

APPLICATION FILED JAN. 2, 1919.

1,309,966.

Patented July 15, 19

Fig.1.

Fig. 2.

PACIFIC MARINE COMPANY (metal lures)

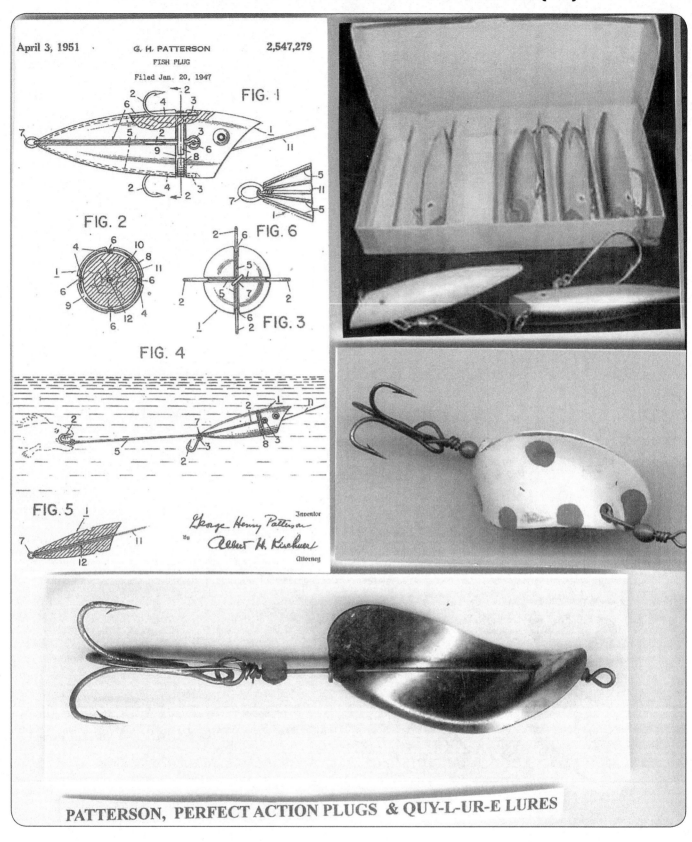

PATTERSON, PERFECT ACTION PLUGS & QUY-L-UR-E LURES

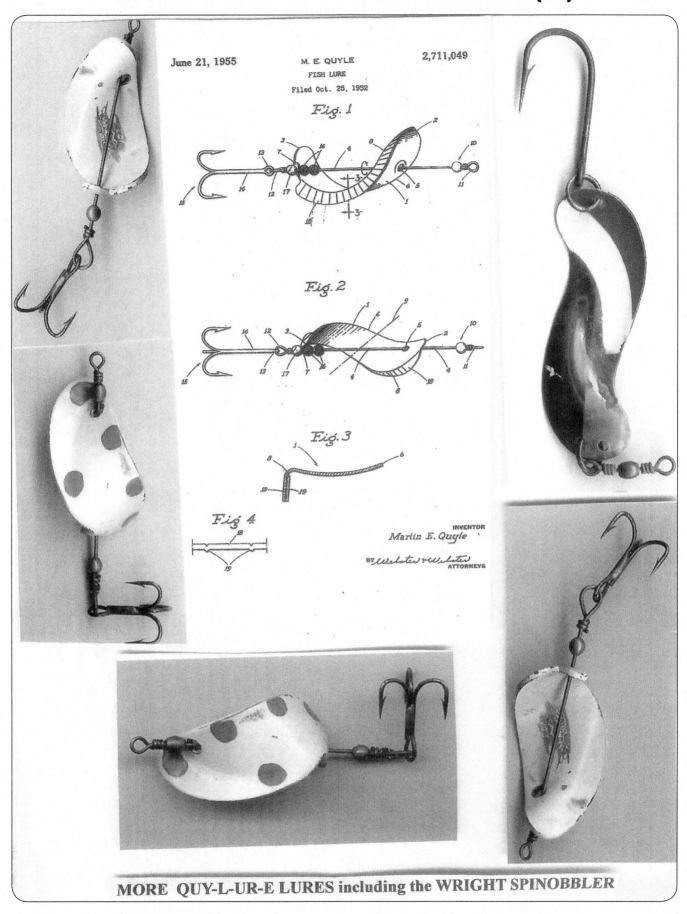

June 21, 1955

M. E. QUYLE
FISH LURE
Filed Oct. 25, 1952

2,711,049

Fig. 1

Fig. 2

Fig. 3

Fig 4

INVENTOR
Martin E. Quyle

BY Webster & Webster
ATTORNEYS

MORE QUY-L-UR-E LURES including the WRIGHT SPINOBBLER

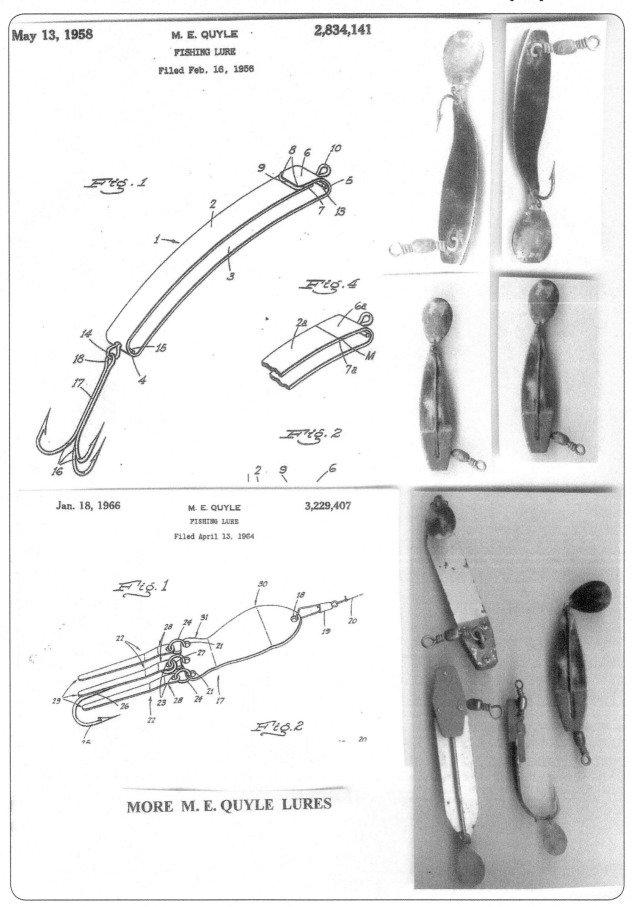

May 13, 1958
M. E. QUYLE
2,834,141
FISHING LURE
Filed Feb. 16, 1956

Fig.1

Fig.4

Fig.2

Jan. 18, 1966
M. E. QUYLE
3,229,407
FISHING LURE
Filed April 13, 1964

Fig.1

Fig.2

MORE M. E. QUYLE LURES

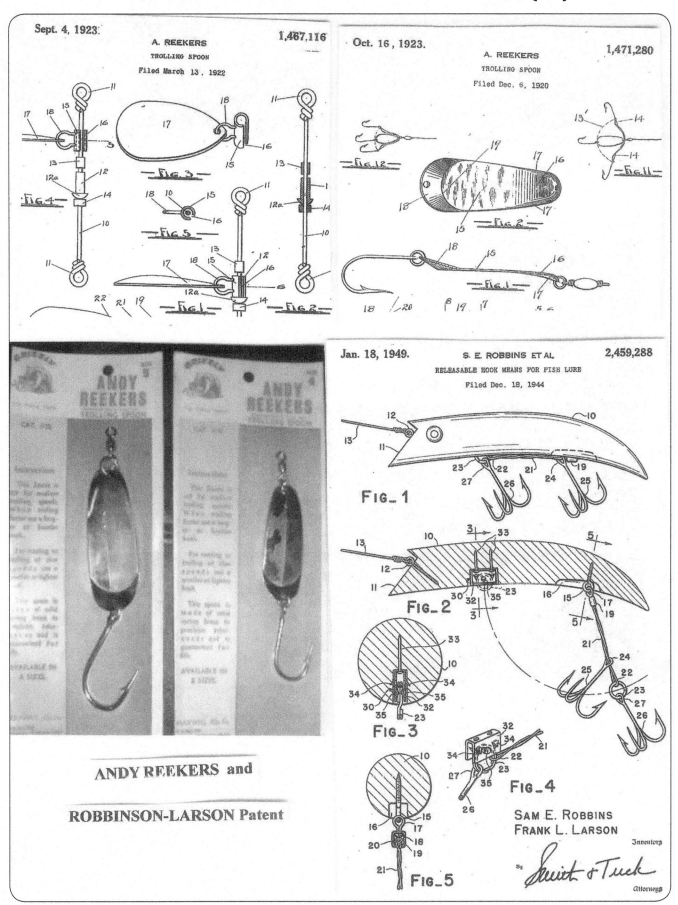

ANDY REEKERS and

ROBBINSON-LARSON Patent

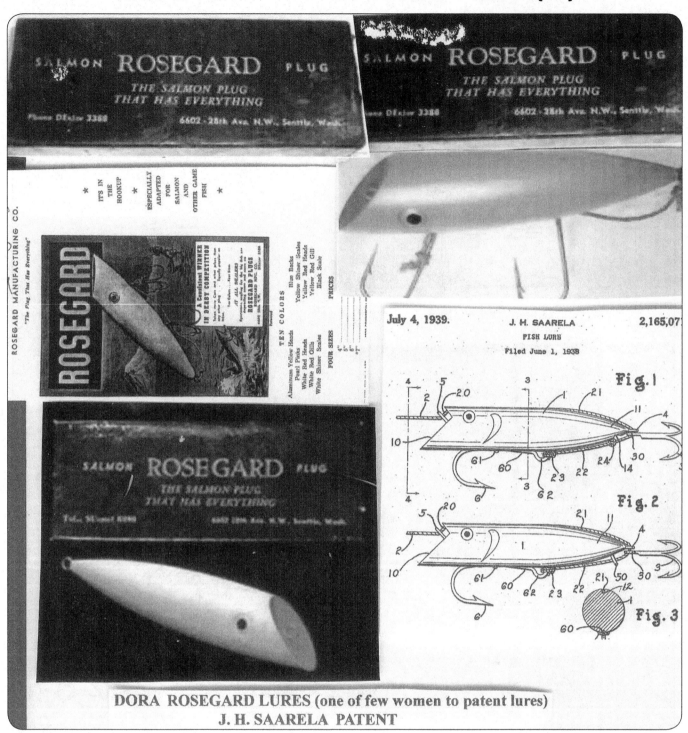

DORA ROSEGARD LURES (one of few women to patent lures)
J. H. SAARELA PATENT

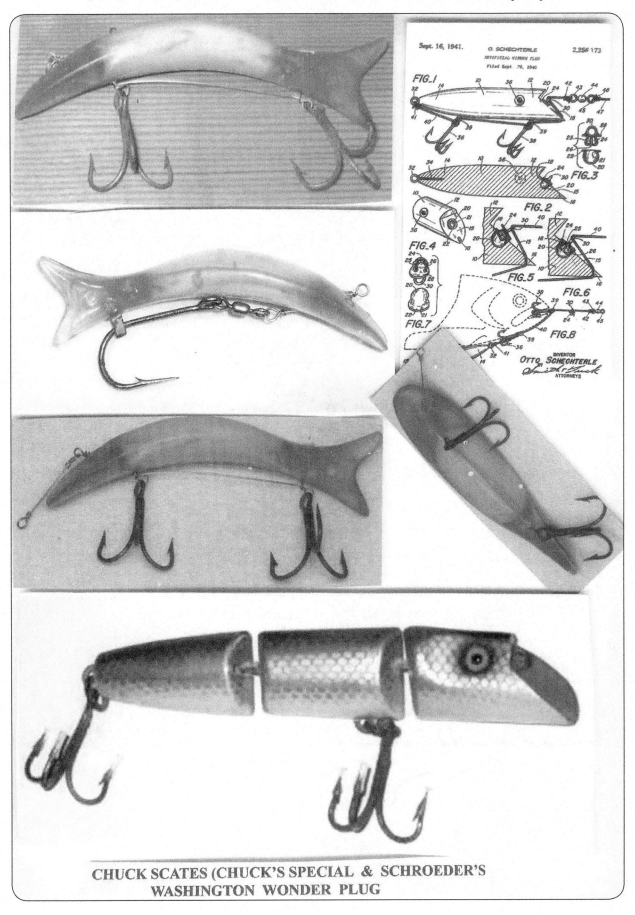

CHUCK SCATES (CHUCK'S SPECIAL & SCHROEDER'S
WASHINGTON WONDER PLUG

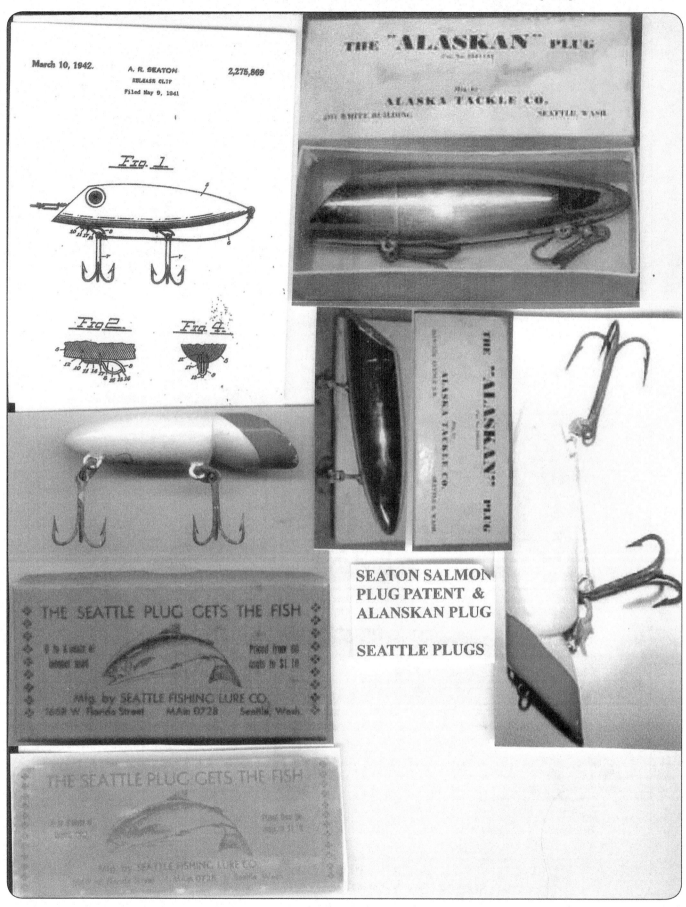

March 10, 1942.   A. R. SEATON   2,275,869
RELEASE CLIP
Filed May 9, 1941

Fig. 1.

Fig. 2.   Fig. 4.

THE "ALASKAN" PLUG

Made by
ALASKA TACKLE CO.
SEATTLE, WASH.

THE "ALASKAN" PLUG

SEATON SALMON
PLUG PATENT &
ALANSKAN PLUG

SEATTLE PLUGS

THE SEATTLE PLUG GETS THE FISH

Mfg. by SEATTLE FISHING LURE CO.

THE SEATTLE PLUG GETS THE FISH

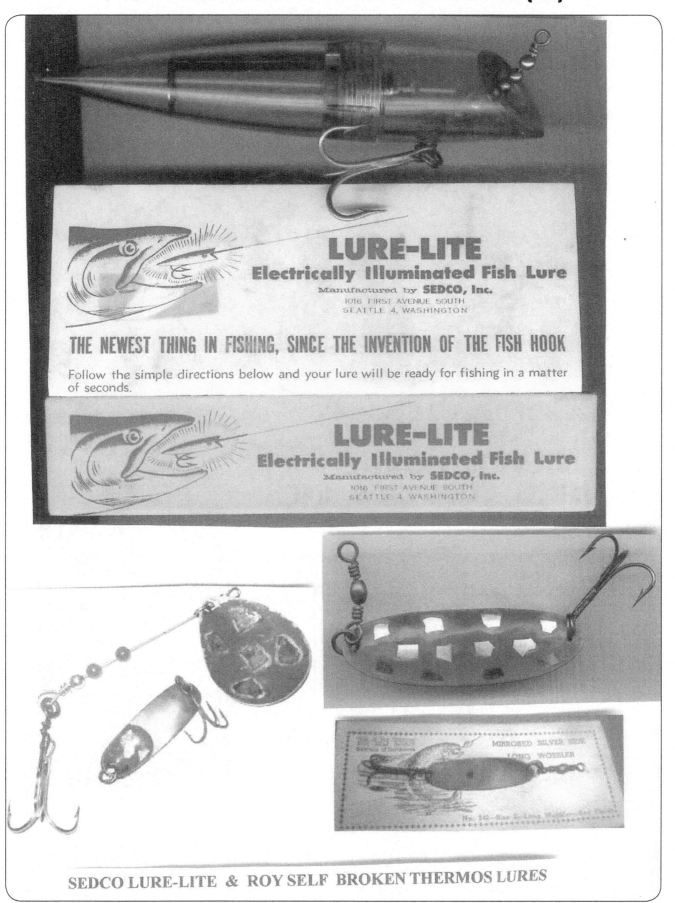

SEDCO LURE-LITE & ROY SELF BROKEN THERMOS LURES

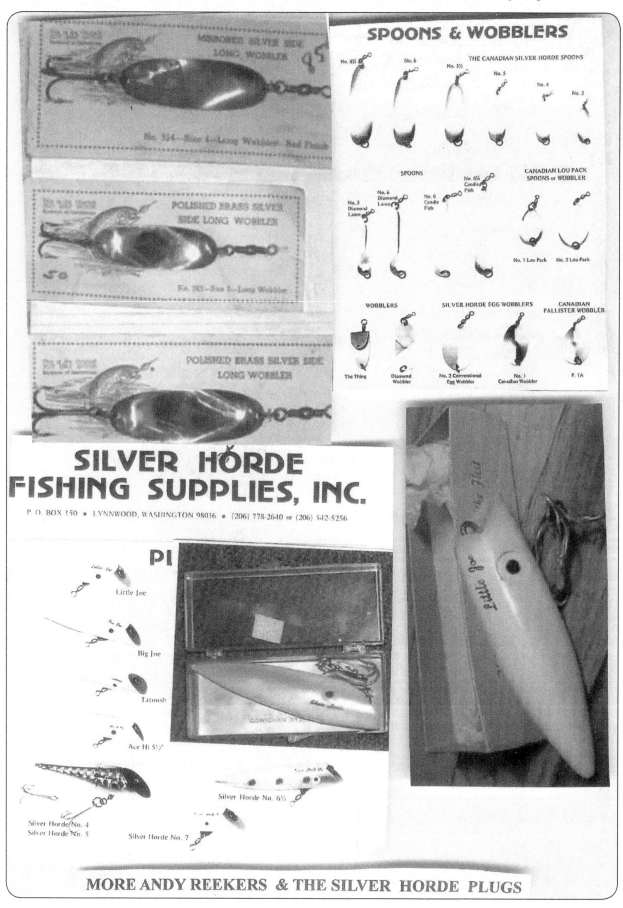

SILVER HORDE
FISHING SUPPLIES, INC.

P. O. BOX 150 • LYNNWOOD, WASHINGTON 98036 • (206) 778-2640 or (206) 542-5256

MORE ANDY REEKERS & THE SILVER HORDE PLUGS

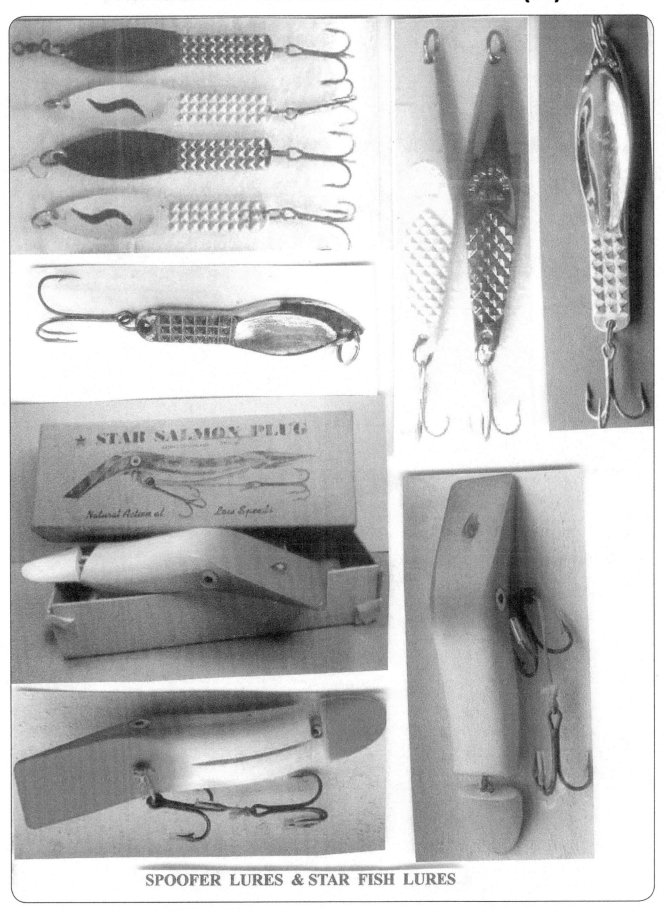

SPOOFER LURES & STAR FISH LURES

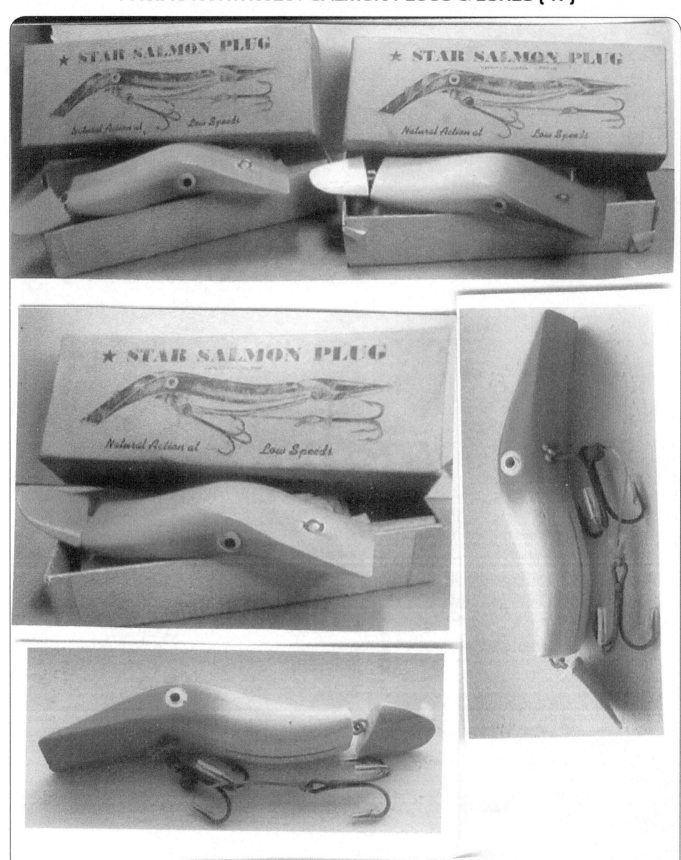

MORE (RARE) STAR FISH LURES

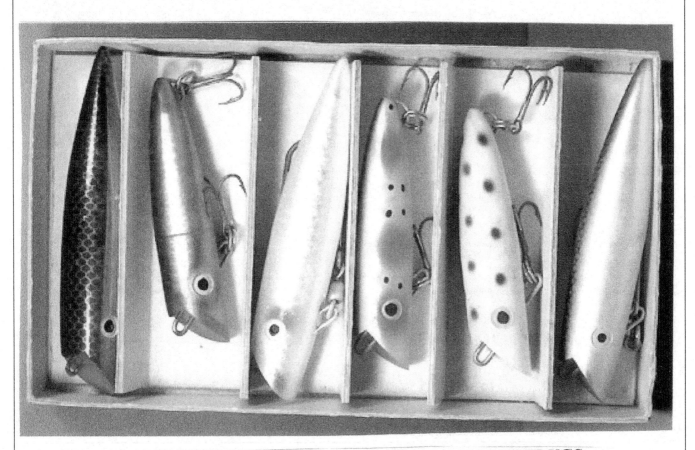

THESE ARE THE MORE MODERN PLASTIC SALMON PLUGS MADE BY TOMIC LURES OUT OF SOOKE, BRITISH COLUMBIA, CANADA. THEY ARE PICTURED IN A 6-PACK OF 4" TO 6" SIZE.

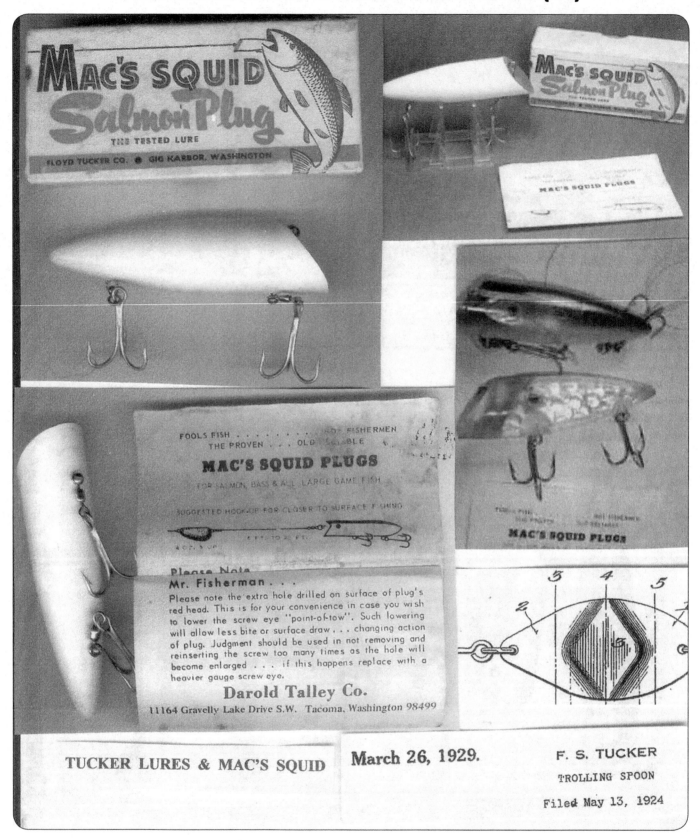

MAC'S SQUID *Salmon Plug*

THE TESTED LURE

FLOYD TUCKER CO. ● GIG HARBOR, WASHINGTON

MAC'S SQUID FLUGS

FOOLS FISH . . . . FISHERMEN
THE PROVEN . . . OLD . . . . . BLE

MAC'S SQUID PLUGS

FOR SALMON, BASS & ALL LARGE GAME FISH

SUGGESTED HOOK-UP FOR CLOSER TO SURFACE FISHING

Please Note
Mr. Fisherman . . .

Please note the extra hole drilled on surface of plug's red head. This is for your convenience in case you wish to lower the screw eye "point-of-tow". Such lowering will allow less bite or surface draw . . . changing action of plug. Judgment should be used in not removing and reinserting the screw too many times as the hole will become enlarged . . . if this happens replace with a heavier gauge screw eye.

Darold Talley Co.
11164 Gravelly Lake Drive S.W. Tacoma, Washington 98499

TUCKER LURES & MAC'S SQUID

March 26, 1929.

F. S. TUCKER

TROLLING SPOON

Filed May 13, 1924

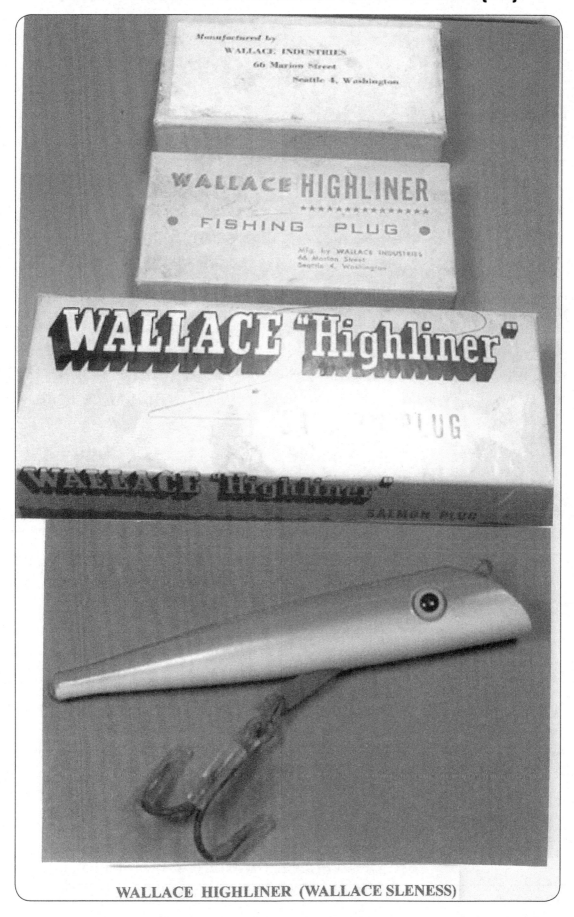

WALLACE HIGHLINER (WALLACE SLENESS)

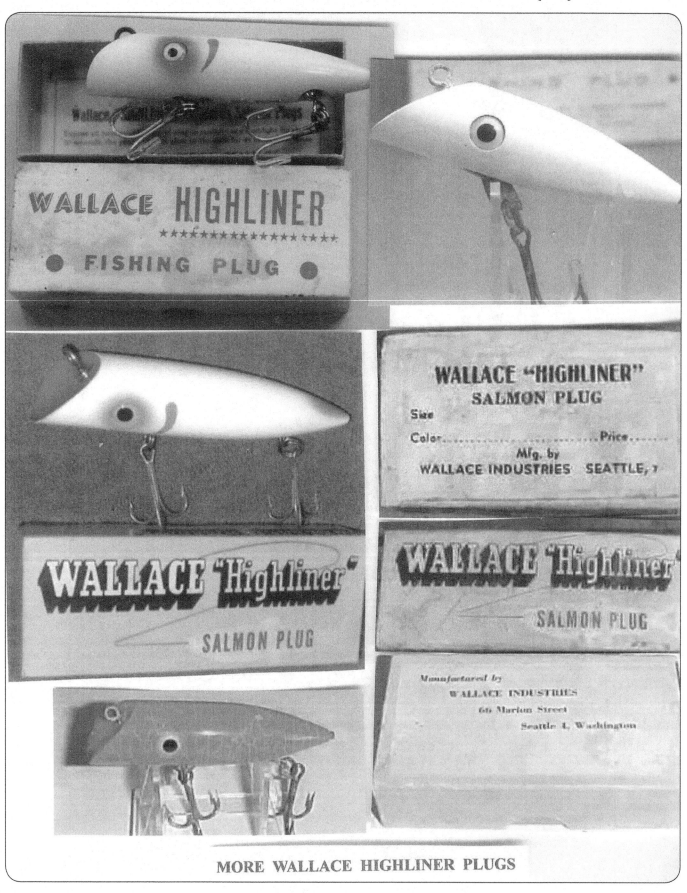

MORE WALLACE HIGHLINER PLUGS

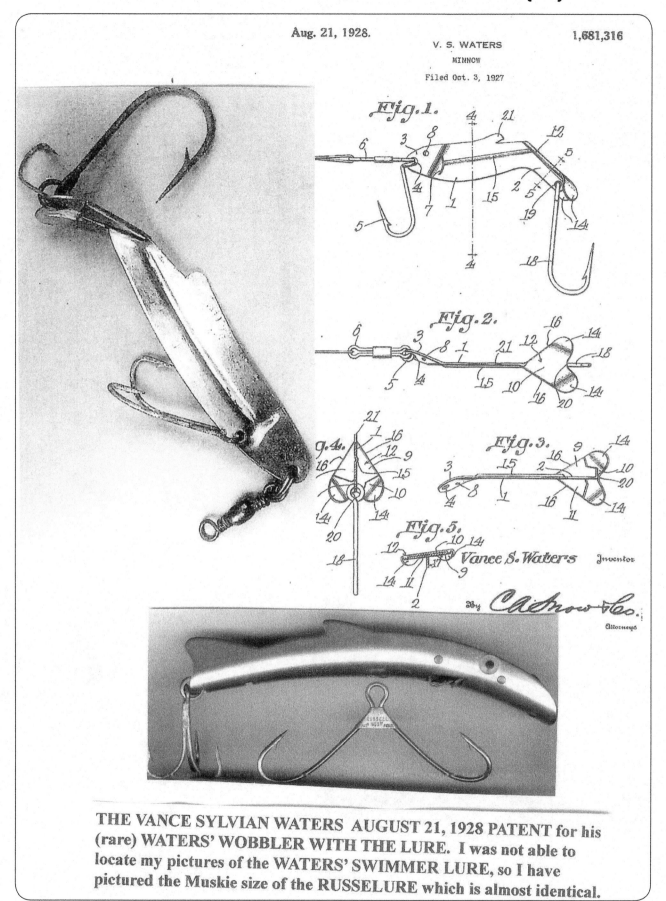

Aug. 21, 1928.

V. S. WATERS

MINNOW

Filed Oct. 3, 1927

1,681,316

Fig.1.

Fig.2.

Fig.4.

Fig.3.

Fig.5.

Vance S. Waters   Inventor

By *C. A. Snow & Co.*

Attorneys

THE VANCE SYLVIAN WATERS AUGUST 21, 1928 PATENT for his (rare) WATERS' WOBBLER WITH THE LURE. I was not able to locate my pictures of the WATERS' SWIMMER LURE, so I have pictured the Muskie size of the RUSSELURE which is almost identical.

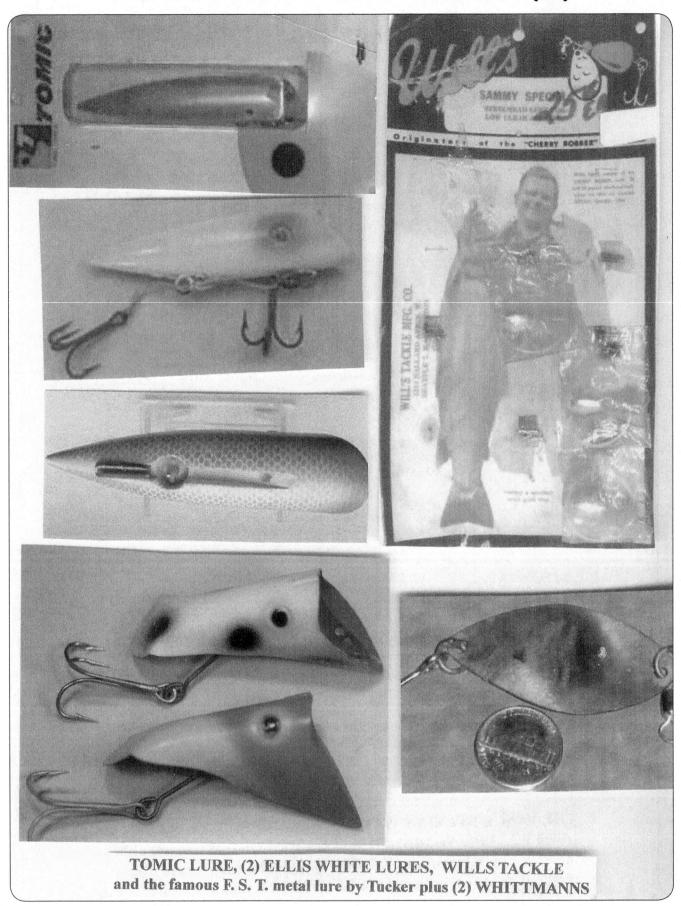

TOMIC LURE, (2) ELLIS WHITE LURES, WILLS TACKLE
and the famous F. S. T. metal lure by Tucker plus (2) WHITTMANNS

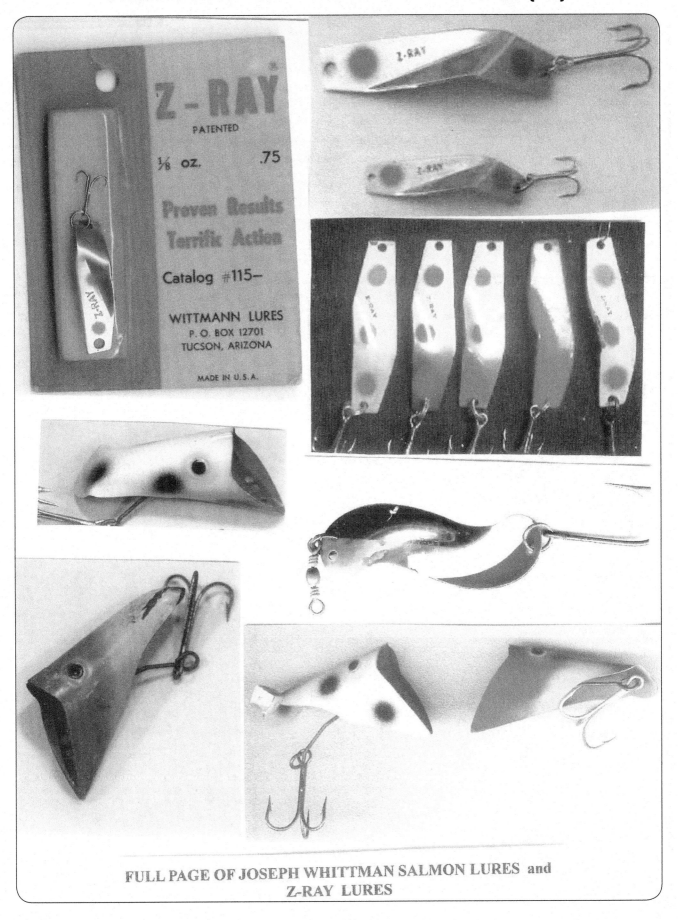

FULL PAGE OF JOSEPH WHITTMAN SALMON LURES and
Z-RAY LURES

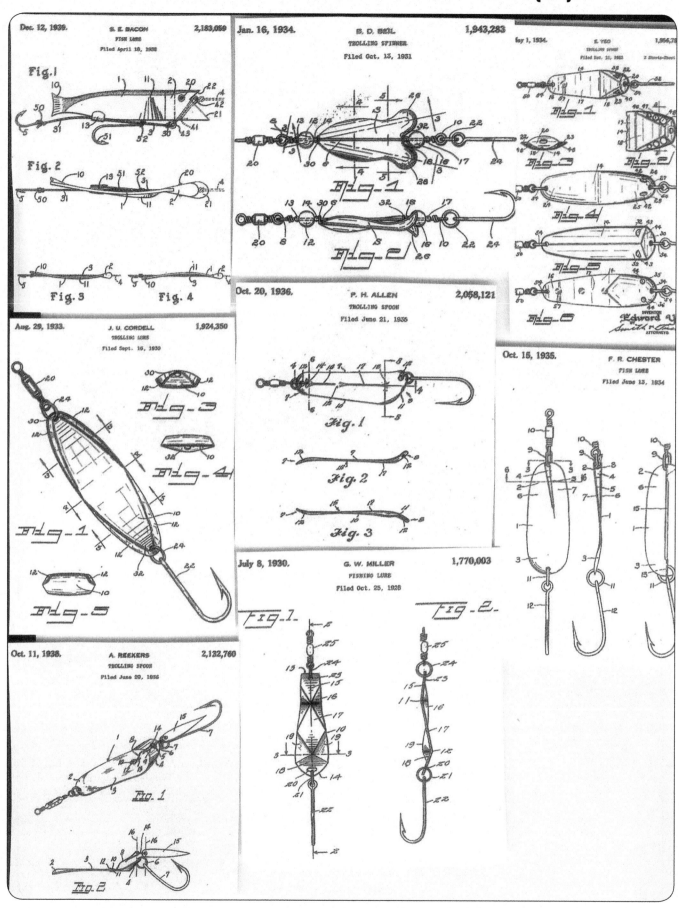

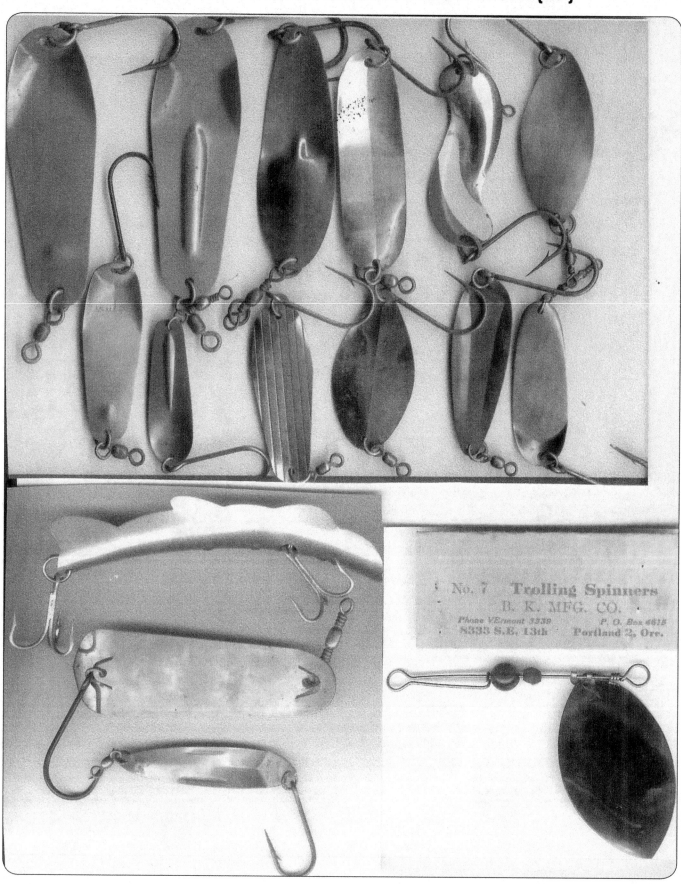

No. 7   Trolling Spinners
B. K. MFG. CO.
Phone VErmont 3339   P. O. Box 4615
8393 S.E. 13th   Portland 2, Ore.

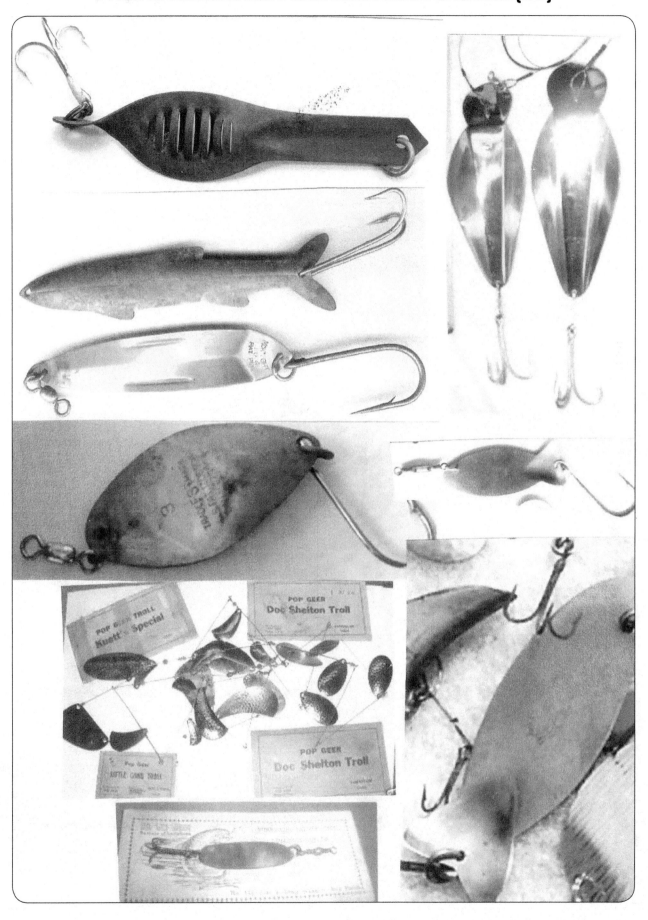

PAGE, GROVER

NEW ALBANY, INDIANA

On March 15, 1932 Grover Page, of New Albany, Indiana, was awarded Patent No. 1,849,434 for his wooden frog lure. That specific lure was never manufactured as to the patent design. However, in 1936 or 1937, Page made a few minor design changes and produced two models of his **PAGE FROG**. The smaller frog had a 2-1/2" wooden body with a heart-shaped dive lip for medium-depth running. This frog had a slightly taller frog-like back hump than the larger 2-3/4" model. Designed to be a deep runner, the larger frog had a wide-shovel-like dive lip. Both frogs were made with a shallow recessed-cup eye socket, into which Page inserted round wooden balls and marine glued in place for the frogs' eyes. These frog-like hump eyes were then painted with yellow irises and black pupils. At the tail of the frog were two wooden peg-nipples, which were designed to hold flexible rubber hind legs (unfortunately, the rubber legs are missing from both lures in the picture). The frogs were then hand painted by Page in natural green frog spot patterns. The metal piece for the tail treble hook was exactly like the original patent called for; it was connected to a wire that ran along the belly to the nose line tie. The metal plate was held by two screws and two staples that held the wire flush to the belly. The lure had a belly counter sunk-recess into which the eye screw for the belly treble fit. This hook was further secured by the line tie wire described, passing through the eye of the hook.

The lures were family produced in limited numbers and are quite rare. The Page Frogs were sold locally in Indiana, and, to my knowledge, a lure box was never developed. Trading starts at $75.

Lure picture courtesy of the (late) Art Hansen collection.

In the group picture, the Page Frogs are on the left. On the right, there is a rare 3-1/2" wooden CLAFLIN MUSKIE FROG made by Bert Claflin from the Land O' Lakes area of Wisconsin in the early 1950's; trading is $75 and up. Bert Claflin was a noted musky fisherman, sometime guide, and writer from Chicago. His book Muskie Fishing, published in 1948, is a popular collectible. Claflin is best known for his famous MUSKRAT PLUGS. Trading for these plugs and his book is at the $75 range and up. Read the full Claflin story elsewhere in these books. The yellow spotted frog, lower right, is the smaller fly rod 1"-body-size MIKESELL FROG made in Chetek, Wisconsin, in the 1960's by Freeman Mikesell; trading is $35 to $45.

March 15, 1932.　　　　G. PAGE　　　　1,849,434

ARTIFICIAL BAIT

Filed April 3, 1931

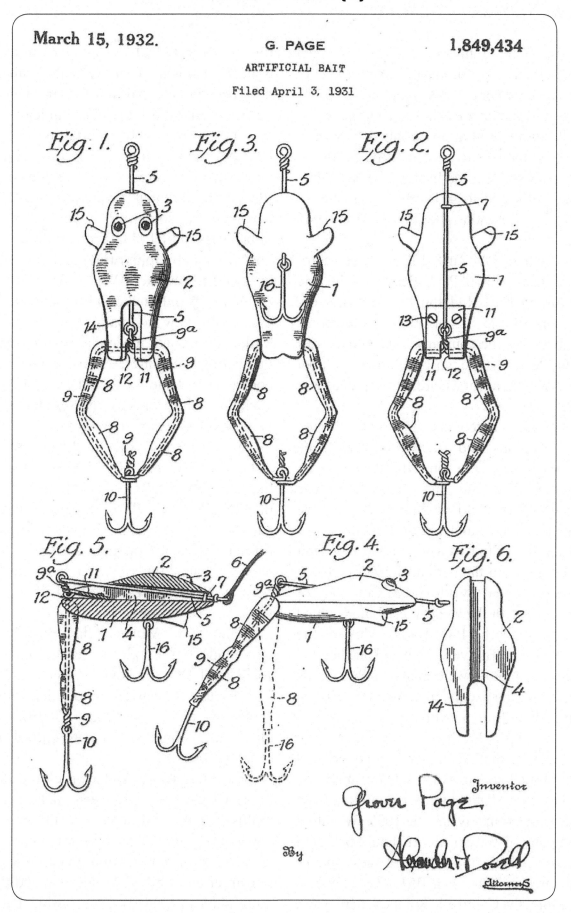

Inventor

Grover Page

By

Attorneys

PAL TOOL COMPANY
MINNEAPOLIS, MINNESOTA

A man named John Eric Anderson formed a tool company in Minneapolis in 1932 to 1933 in the basement of his home at 5512 27th Avenue South and later established a larger company building in 1934 at 507 South 4th Street in Minneapolis that was to become PAL Tools. In 1937, they moved to 2300 East 31st Street. They were later relocated to 4411 Hiawatha Ave. in Minneapolis, Minnesota, after the war from 1946 and after.

I believe that "PAL" in Pal Tools was an acronym for the last names of Per L. Pearson, John Eric Anderson, and Karl Rudolph "Ruddy" Larson, all members of the organization. Anderson's wife, Agnes, was the company's secretary. Karl Larson proved to be the most important member of the partnership as far as lure development was concerned.

Larson had an ingenious mind for developing lures. He designed and patented the Centipede Spinner, what was to become the Paul Bunyan Minnow, the Twirl Bug, the Elecro Lure, The Body-Action lures sold by Lloyds & Co., the Paul Bunyan Dodger, and the weedless hooks for the Weed Splitter Plug, as well as all Larson Bait Company lures. In the period of 1935 to 1938, all of the lures sold by Lloyds & Company of Chicago, except for the Hungry Jack and Lighted Pirate, were made by PAL Tools. Most of the lures sold by Paul Bunyan, after Larson founded the company in 1939, were made by PAL Tools dies that Larson had acquired as he left Pal Tools and formed Paul Bunyan with his silent financial partners, the Clarity brothers.

I'm not sure that the "Lady Bug Diver" and the "Ole Olsen" spoons were actually made by Larson, however. These lures were imports from the Bates Bait Company and the 100% Weedless Bait Company of Wisconsin. It should be noted that PAL was also selling some of these manufactured lures in their own PAL TOOL boxes. With one lure, the Centipede Spinner, there was a

fourth company that was involved in its production. That was the Century Bait Company, but I have been unable to develop their relationship to Pal Tools with this lure. This duplication in sales may be the reason for the falling out between Pal Tools and the Lloyds Company, but I don't know that for sure. After the greater portion (the Larson lure making die portion) of Pal Tool Company was sold in 1939, the owners remained in business until 1943. From 1943 to 1965, Pal Tool was run by John Eric Anderson and then by his son, Eric Wallace "Wally" Anderson.

In the meantime, John Eric Anderson formed a separate, new company, Minneapolis Plastic Molders, Inc., and made plastic lure bodies for a number of companies. On a contract basis, lure bodies were made for Lazy Daisy, the Rockland Tackle Co., Inc., of Suffern, New Jersey, and the Falls Bait Company of Wisconsin.

The Rockland Tackle "LI'L ARTY " and "ROCKY SR." and "ROCKY JR." were exactly like the Falls Bait Co. "FISH' N FOOL" and the "INCH MINNOWS", except for lure names, because they were all made under contract by the former Pal Tool Company for these two companies. Later, the Harrison Industries inc., of Vernon, New Jersey, made the Li'l Arty and the Rocky Sr. & Jr. lures.

The new Minneapolis Plastic Molders also made lots of plastic reel parts for Lloyd Johnson of Denison-Johnson Reels of Mankato, Minnesota, the inventor of the closed-face spinning reel. (After Charlie Denison died, the company became known only as Johnson Reels.)

In 1965, Wally Anderson closed down Pal Tool, which had only been making dies and molds for the Minneapolis Plastic Molders anyway. He merged the two companies, and they went on to big production, opening new plants in Carver and LeRoy, Minnesota, and then later a big plant in Fredrick, Wisconsin. During this time, they made parts for "pots and pans" manufactures in Wisconsin: West Bend Company, Mirro-Aluminum, and Volrath, Inc. Other customers included Speed Queen IBM and Litton Industries.

In 1995, Wally Anderson sold the old Minneapolis Plastic Molders Company to the Lakeland Tool & Engineering Company, and they are still in business today.

After Karl Larson left Pal Tools in 1939, he founded and became the owner of the Paul Bunyan Company as a corporation. The official Articles of Incorporation were signed at 12:20 P. M. on June 6, 1939, with Karl "Ruddy" Larson as owner and brothers Morgan "Bill" Clarity and M. E. Clarity as silent financial partners. "Silent" they were, having nothing to do with the management of the company and seldom even showing up at the plant, according to plant foreman, Ewan Chowen. Chowen (pronounced Cowen) was the second person to be hired by the new Paul Bunyan Company. He is still alive today, in his late 80's, living in Minnetonka, Minnesota.

Many of the lures produced by Paul Bunyan were only made in part in Minneapolis, with many of the lure parts being made elsewhere and then shipped in for assembly and painting. The following is a list of some of the important Karl Rudolph "Ruddy" Larson lure patents:

RUBY-EYE SPOON, Filed July 24, 1939, granted October 31, 1939, under Design Patent No. D117,378;

ELECTRO-LURE, Filed March 23, 1938, granted February 20, 1940, under Patent No. 2,190,791;

DODGER, Filed September 16, 1938, granted December 27, 1938, under Design patent No. D112,681;

PAUL BUNYAN MINNOW, Filed September 16, 1938, and July 24, 1939, granted January 16, 1949, and March 11, 1941, under Patent Numbers 2,187,609 and 2,234,439;

CENTIPEDE, Filed December 2, 1938, granted July 5, 1938, under Patent No. 2,123,150;

PAUL BUNYAN WEAVER, Filed June 22, 1945, granted April 11, 1950, under Patent No. 2,503,620;

As creative a mind as Karl Larson had in the many lures he invented, his social skills were just as lacking. He was a very difficult man to get along with, according to his partners and employees. He was a heavy drinker and was frequently arrested for beating his wife. After he and his wife retired and moved to Florida, both died as a result of a murder-suicide at the hands of Larson.

We owe a great deal of thanks for much of this history from an interview with Eric Wallace "Wally" Anderson of Frederic, Wisconsin.

I'm not going into any more details or providing pictures of Pal Tool lures, Lloyds & Company Lures, or Paul Bunyan lures, as they are covered elsewhere in these books. I will show copies of many of the Karl R Larson patents, however.

July 5, 1938.

K. R. LARSON ET AL

SPINNER

Filed Dec. 2, 1935

2,123,150

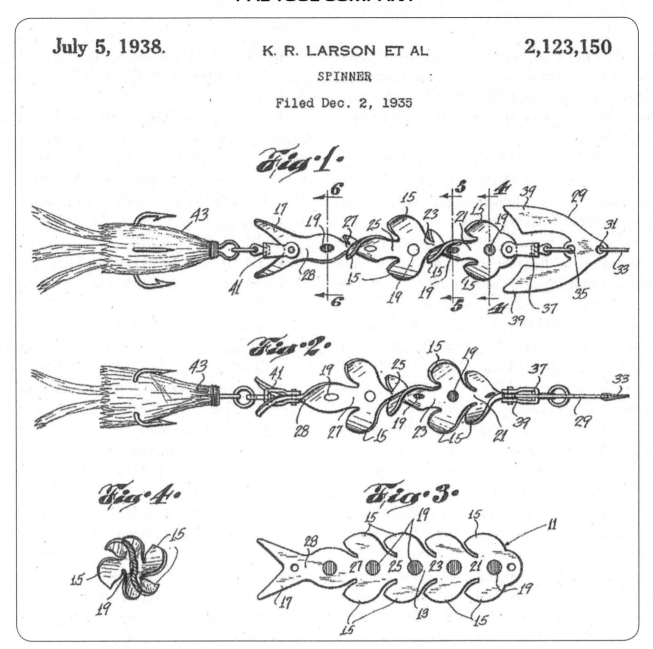

Fig. 1.

Fig. 2.

Fig. 4.

Fig. 3.

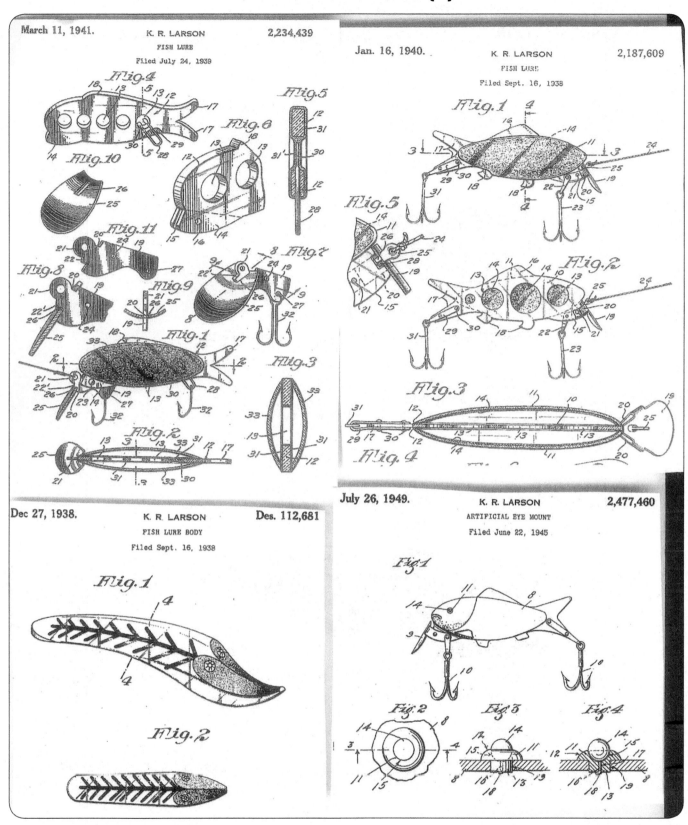

March 11, 1941.   K. R. LARSON   2,234,439
FISH LURE
Filed July 24, 1939

Jan. 16, 1940.   K. R. LARSON   2,187,609
FISH LURE
Filed Sept. 16, 1938

Dec 27, 1938.   K. R. LARSON   Des. 112,681
FISH LURE BODY
Filed Sept. 16, 1938

July 26, 1949.   K. R. LARSON   2,477,460
ARTIFICIAL EYE MOUNT
Filed June 22, 1945

Oct. 31, 1939.

K. R. LARSON

FISH LURE

Filed July 24, 1939

Des. 117,378

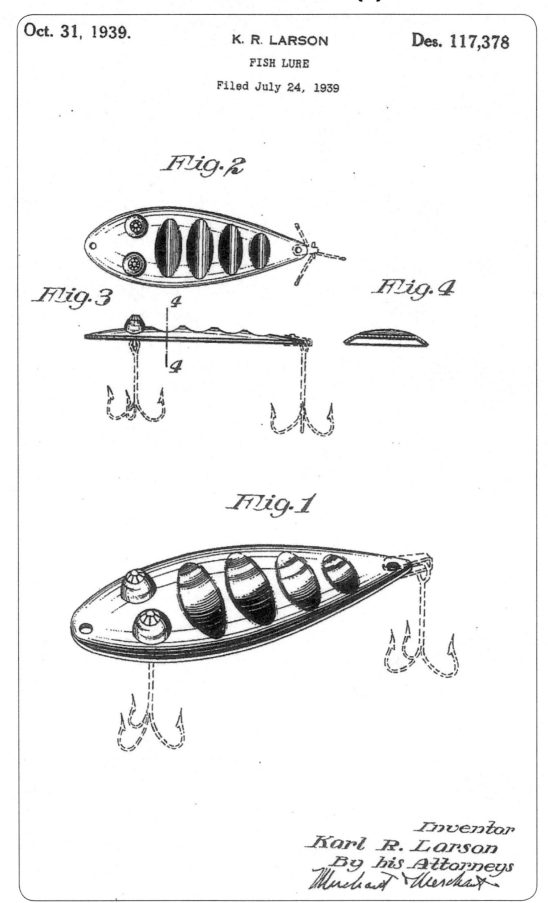

Fig.2

Fig.3

Fig.4

Fig.1

Inventor
Karl R. Larson
By his Attorneys

April 11, 1950   K. R. LARSON   2,503,620

BASE FOR ARTIFICIAL FISH BAITS

Filed June 22, 1945   2 Sheets—Sheet 1

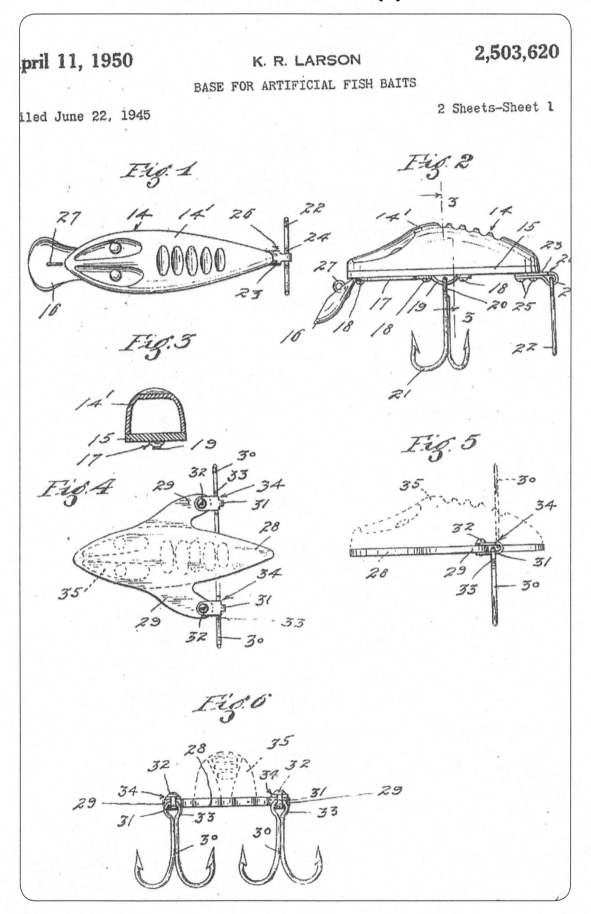

Feb. 20, 1940.　　　K. R. LARSON　　　2,190,791

ILLUMINATED BAIT

Filed March 23, 1938

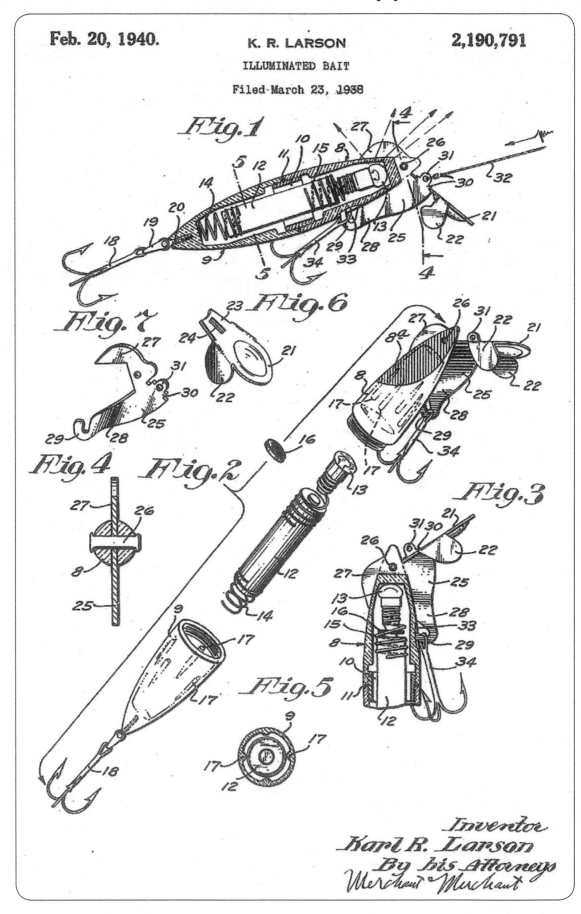

Fig.1

Fig.7　*Fig.6*

Fig.4　*Fig.2*　*Fig.3*

Fig.5

Inventor
Karl R. Larson
By his Attorneys
Merchant Merchant

PALM SPORTING GOODS COMPANY
METAIRIE, LOUISIANA

The Palm Sporting Goods Company was started in the early 1960's at 328 Carrollton Street in Metairie, Louisiana, but, by the mid 1960s, they became incorporated and moved to 5605 Rickey Street, still in the same city. I only know of just the one lure that they made, the 2-1/2" plastic **MITTY MIKE**. The lure, made in the same general shape of many of the Texas-made Doug English, Bingo, and Hump lures, is pictured in the most common color of red head with white with silver flitter and with large red spots and small green spots. The lure was sold in a clear plastic hinged box with an ID card insert. The card had the statement, "100% Balanced Lure... Real Life Action...Just Cast & Retrieve."

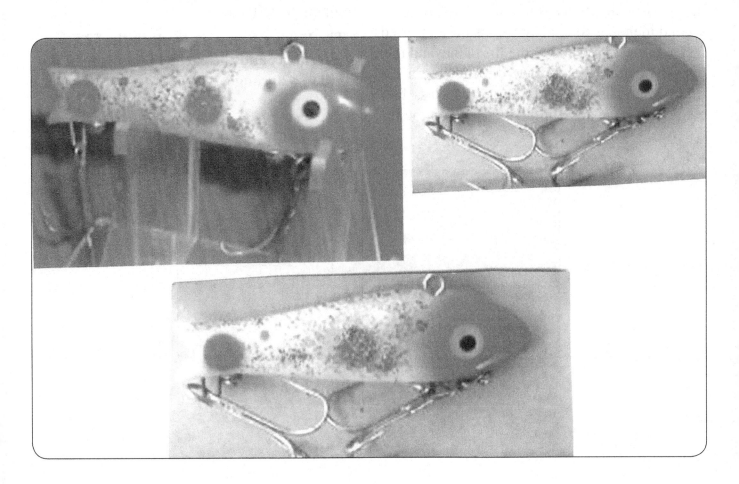

PALMER SPINNERS & FLIES
PASADENA, CALIFORNIA

In the early 1930's and into the late 1930's, a husband and wife team by the names of Ray M. and Lea G. Palmer of Pasadena, California, made spinner baits and tied flies. Their **PALMER CONE SPINNER** was unique for its time. The lure was 4-1/4" long overall from box swivel to tail treble hook. The lure consisted of two cone-shaped hollow lure bodies that had a flared skirt at the rear with the tips forming a prop, each bent in different directions as to cause a rotation. A second identical cone body had its nose inserted inside of the flared end of the first cone, and this body rotated in the opposite direction from the first cone. The lure had a large red glass faceted bead at the apex of the first cone on the in-line wire spinner shaft and a series of four glass spacer-bearing beads at the rear. The couple was awarded Patent No. 1,897,529 for this lure on February 14, 1933.

Pictured with this story is an overall 1"-long **PALMER GRASSHOPPER** that had a 7/8" quill and feather tied fly on a No. 4 hook.

The Palmer lures were sold on white cards that each had a picture of a jumping rainbow trout on the left side.

The Palmer Spinners trade in the $25 to $35 range, and the carded flies trade in the $10 to $20 range.

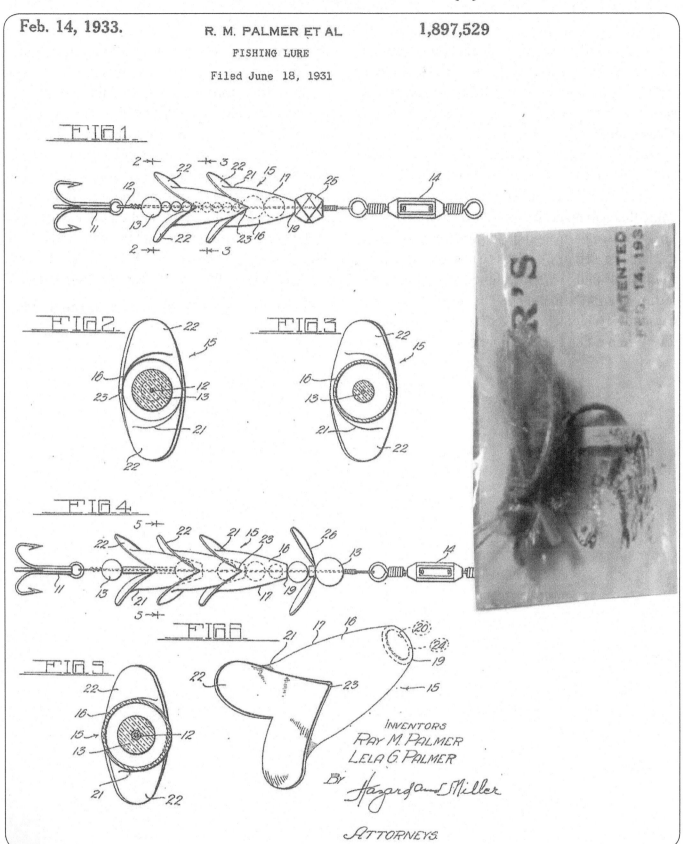

Feb. 14, 1933.   R. M. PALMER ET AL   1,897,529

FISHING LURE

Filed June 18, 1931

INVENTORS
RAY M. PALMER
LELA G. PALMER

By Hazard and Miller

ATTORNEYS.

PARA-LURE COMPANY
NEWARK, NEW JERSEY

In 1946, Roy Schaffer invented a simple lure that he named the **PARA-LURE** and formed his Para-Lure Company at 117 Roseville Avenue in Newark, New Jersey. A year later, he moved to 368 Sixth Avenue, still in Newark. He developed the sales logo, "LAND THE ONE THAT GOT AWAY FROM SOMBODY ELSE."

The Para-Lure consisted of a plastic parachute that had no hooks and had a stretch of heavy Snell passing through to a jig-headed, single-feather-dressed hook. This feathered jig was the catch lure, and it was designed to be trolled or retrieved approximately 18" behind the collapsed parachute, which also served as a forward attractor. When a fish took the lure and pulled against the parachute, creating drag, the chute opened, creating even more drag and making it difficult for the fish to throw the hook. This also allowed the fisherman to use lighter weight fishing tackle and a lighter test line. The lure was sold on a plastic-covered card with a blue-color print silhouette of the parachute being trolled backwards in a closed position trailing the jig. Below that was a drawing of a large hooked tuna swimming in the opposite direction with the parachute open. The bottom of the card said, "FOR BIGGER FISH ON LIGHTER TACKLE TRY PARA-LURE."

The carded Para-Lure trades in the $10 to $15 range.

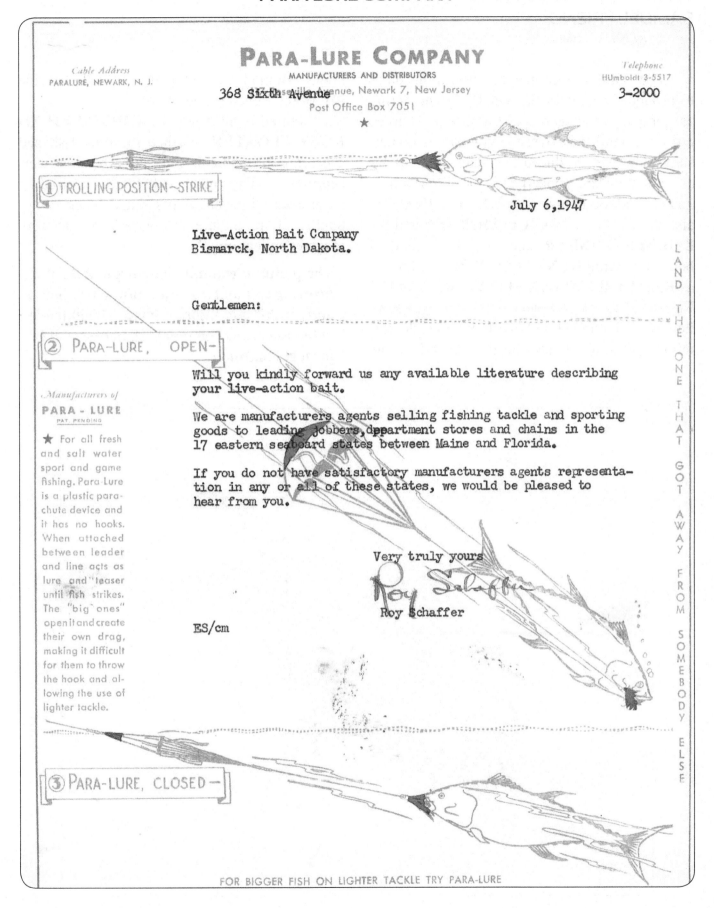

PARA-LURE COMPANY

MANUFACTURERS AND DISTRIBUTORS

368 Sixth Avenue, Newark 7, New Jersey

Post Office Box 7051

★

Cable Address
PARALURE, NEWARK, N. J.

Telephone
HUmboldt 3-5517
3-2000

① TROLLING POSITION ~ STRIKE

July 6, 1947

Live-Action Bait Company
Bismarck, North Dakota.

Gentlemen:

② PARA-LURE, OPEN—

Manufacturers of
PARA - LURE
PAT. PENDING

★ For all fresh and salt water sport and game fishing. Para-Lure is a plastic parachute device and it has no hooks. When attached between leader and line acts as lure and "teaser" until fish strikes. The "big ones" open it and create their own drag, making it difficult for them to throw the hook and allowing the use of lighter tackle.

Will you kindly forward us any available literature describing your live-action bait.

We are manufacturers agents selling fishing tackle and sporting goods to leading jobbers, department stores and chains in the 17 eastern seaboard states between Maine and Florida.

If you do not have satisfactory manufacturers agents representation in any or all of these states, we would be pleased to hear from you.

Very truly yours

Roy Schaffer

Roy Schaffer

ES/cm

③ PARA-LURE, CLOSED —

LAND THE ONE THAT GOT AWAY FROM SOMEBODY ELSE

FOR BIGGER FISH ON LIGHTER TACKLE TRY PARA-LURE

PARDEE, F. A., & COMPANY
SAMUEL FRIEND
KENT, OHIO

The Pardee lure-making operation dates to around 1900, with Samuel H. Friend acting as company manager. In 1906, when Pardee retired, Friend took over the company's ownership. The two produced two main lures as far as collectors are concerned: the 4", wooden, fish-shaped, double-spinner **KENT MINNOW**, also known as the **MANCO MINNOW** and the **DOUBLE SPINNER**; and the 2-1/4" wooden-body, 4"-overall **KENT FLOATER**, also known as **KENT CHAMPION FLOATER**, **MANCO FLOATING FROG**, and other names. Both lures were equipped with the box-hub style aluminum props and twist wire-through side treble hooks. Both glass-eyed lures eventually became part of the Pflueger line of lures.

Pictured is an original **PARDEE-FRIEND KENT FLOATER** that had the funnel-shaped T-bearing props with red glass bead spacer-bearings. The lure had large, protruding glass eyes with yellow irises and black center pupils. Lure picture is courtesy of the Tom Jacomet collection.

The pictured example had original dark brown paint and an aluminum-color belly, and, in this condition, it has a $3,000 trade value but would be much higher were it in perfect condition.

PARDON HOOK COMPANY
OWENSBORO, KENTUCKY

At the turn of the twentieth century, in 1900, a man named Frank H. Pardon established a small company in Owensboro, Kentucky, and produced a 3"-long lever-action bait hook that he named the **KINGFISHER FISH HOOK**. If you will take a close look at the first model of this hook, it had a loop in the shank that held the smaller bait hook. The longer hook had a lead ball weight at the normal line tie end for balance, and this pendulum type hook would swing into action when a fish took the bait on the smaller hook, causing the longer hook to snag him a second time. This hook was given Patent No. 668,658 on February 26, 1901, awarded to Frank H. Pardon.

A couple of years later, Pardon redesigned and made it an automatic spring hook. This hook, in the same length, was designed so that when a fish pulled down on the baited hook, the upper, longer hook would spring down, hooking the fish in the side of the head for a sure catch every time. Advertising of the day said, "The Kingfisher Fish Hook hangs perpendicular in the water...

and safely lands fish that would otherwise get away from a common hook." The price in those days was just $0.15 each, or twelve for $1.00. Pardon received a second Patent No. 740,775 on October 6, 1903, for this improved hook system. This one is actually more common than the fist hook, but a third design is the rarest.

The third hook designed, which Pardon called his Pendent Hook, had a spring wire affair holding the bait hook to the shaft of the longer swing hook. The bait hook was fixed to a metal rod that passed through the eye of the swing hook, and a fish taking the bait caused the longer hook to arc, or collapse, into the fish.

The first model is shown in the first picture. All pictures of the hooks and advertising are courtesy of the Matt Wickham collection.

The trade values are approximately in the $75 to $100 range for the first model, $25 to $50 higher for the second model, and $200 to $250 for the rarest, third model.

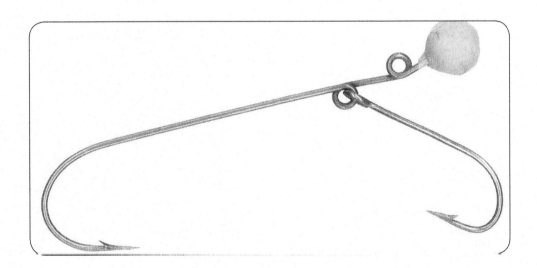

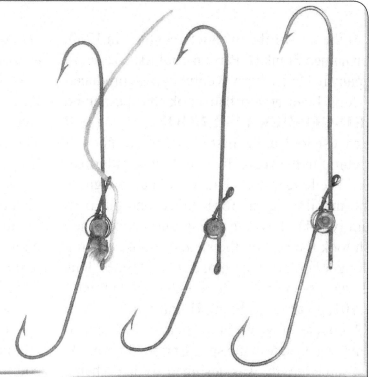

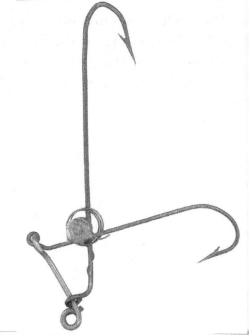

Specialty Price List No. 9.

A word to customers. In connection with our Fish Bait we handle a few other specialties for fishermen, and when making up your order, we would be pleased to have you include any of these you may need. We handle nothing but the very best grade of goods, and everything we sell is guaranteed to give perfect satisfaction or money refunded. Send us a trial order and you will be well pleased, and know where to get your money's worth when you want anything in fishing tackle.

How to send money. Postal money orders are the safest way to send remittances. They cost but little and there is no chance for loss. If you cannot purchase a money order at your post office, send money by registered letter, or any way that is safe and convenient. Postage stamps accepted for small amounts, which may be sent safely in an ordinary letter. (One Cent Stamps Preferred.)

We pay the postage. Everything shown in this price list, sent by Parcel Post, Prepaid, and we guarantee safe delivery of goods. Make up your order now while you think of it. Be sure to always write your name and address plainly, so there will be no delay in filling your orders. No foreign stamps will be accepted.

The "Kingfisher" Hook
Makes Every Bite A Catch.

This is an automatic spring hook and is so constructed that when a fish gives the slightest pull on the bait the upper hook reaches down and gets a hold that lands him, every time. It hangs perpendicular in the water, so that the upper hook is entirely out of the way and does not interfere with the fish when taking the bait. The upper hook is larger and longer than the lower one, and gets a deep, sure hold on the fish that saves him. Many fish are safely landed with the Kingfisher where a common hook would have let them get away.

Nothing is more discouraging or disappointing, than to get a shallow hold on a fine large fish and have him splash back into the water just as you are about to land him. That luck never happens when you are using the Kingfisher—he is sure YOUR MEAT whenever he gives it a "yank."

This wonderful hook is automatic in action, and should it fail to catch the fish the first time he touches the bait, it quickly resets itself and is ready for him again; and just as sure as he gives the least pull on the bait he will be your fish, for there is no chance for him to get away after he is once hooked on a Kingfisher. If you want to catch every fish that "monkeys" around your bait use the Kingfisher Hook.

Made in 3 sizes—No.1 for small fish, No.2 for medium, and No.3 for larger fish.

Price Each 15 cts. 2 for 25 cts. 12 for $1.00
A Complete Set of the Three Sizes for 35cts.

Agents wanted. Send $1.00 for a dozen and you will be surprised how fast they sell. Guaranteed to give perfect satisfaction or your money refunded. Try a dozen.

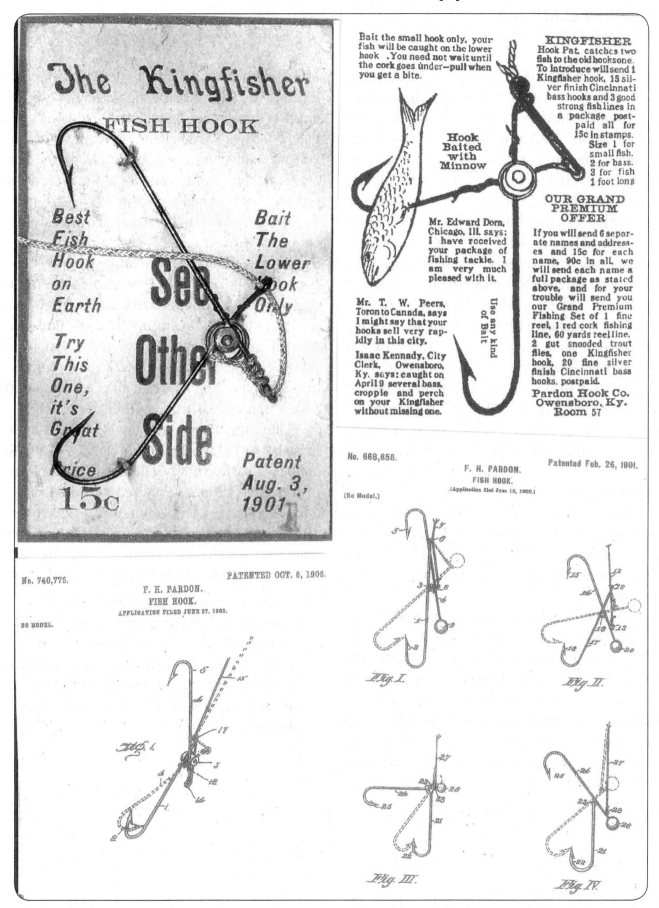

The Kingfisher
FISH HOOK

Best Fish Hook on Earth

Bait The Lower Hook Only

See Other Side

Try This One, it's Great Price

15c

Patent Aug. 3, 1901

Bait the small hook only, your fish will be caught on the lower hook. You need not wait until the cork goes under—pull when you get a bite.

KINGFISHER

Hook Pat. catches two fish to the old hooks one. To introduce will send 1 Kingfisher hook, 15 silver finish Cincinnati bass hooks and 3 good strong fish lines in a package post-paid all for 15c in stamps. Size 1 for small fish. 2 for bass. 3 for fish 1 foot long

Hook Baited with Minnow

Mr. Edward Dorn, Chicago, Ill. says: I have received your package of fishing tackle. I am very much pleased with it.

Mr. T. W. Peers, Toronto Canada, says I might say that your hooks sell very rapidly in this city.

Isaac Kennady, City Clerk, Owensboro, Ky. says: caught on April 9 several bass, croppie and perch on your Kingfisher without missing one.

Use any kind of Bait

OUR GRAND PREMIUM OFFER

If you will send 6 separate names and addresses and 15c for each name, 90c in all, we will send each name a full package as stated above, and for your trouble will send you our Grand Premium Fishing Set of 1 fine reel, 1 red cork fishing line, 60 yards reel line, 2 gut snooded trout flies, one Kingfisher hook, 20 fine silver finish Cincinnati bass hooks, postpaid.

Pardon Hook Co. Owensboro, Ky. Room 57

No. 740,775.   PATENTED OCT. 6, 1903.

F. H. PARDON.
FISH HOOK.
APPLICATION FILED JUNE 27, 1902.

NO MODEL.

Fig. 1.

No. 668,658.   Patented Feb. 26, 1901.

F. H. PARDON.
FISH HOOK.
(Application filed June 13, 1900.)

(No Model.)

Fig. I.   Fig. II.

Fig. III.   Fig. IV.

PARK MANUFACTING COMPANY
FRANK DELLERMAN
CINCINNATI, OHIO

The **JAKE'S BAIT** is much older than most collectors realize, having first been introduced with a lead body in 1928 by the lure's inventor, Frank Dellerman, of Cincinnati, Ohio. (Actually, the lure got its name from an uncle of Dellerman's, named Jake, who helped him get started with financial backing.) The first lure had the same basic shape as the later one made of steel, but it was solid molded lead with a screw-held hook dressed with feathers. I believe that, when Dellerman switched to having the lures machine stamped out of steel after World War II, was when he contracted with the Park Manufacturing Company to stamp the bodies. The post-war 1940's Park Manufacturing Company, of 7511 Griffin Drive in Cincinnati, had their name and address for the "JAKE'S BAIT" on a cardboard box that read, "JAKE'S BAIT...Has the right action," in blue print on the cover.

The elongated-oval-shaped lures were made in a casting size at 3/8 oz and 1-3/4" long and spinning size at 1/4 oz. and 1-5/8" long. However, in 1960 Dellerman introduced this lure in a smaller, JAKE'S FLYWEIGHT, size but this is rare, as he discontinued making that size around 1962.

Some boxed lures had an optional plastic forked tail piece. It was suggested that pork rind could also be added instead of the plastic tail piece. The bait worked equally well retrieved slow or fast, shallow or deep. The lure had a raised center beneath the screw holding the single fixed hook and was perfectly balanced with or without the optional tail piece or pork rind. Box papers claimed, "A trial will convince you."

The lure was usually painted in dark colors, such as black, and had a single fixed hook with a tuft of black deer hair. Cataloged colors were black, brown, red, green, silver, white, and yellow with contrasting bucktails of the same colors. The plain, white two-piece cardboard box for this lure had blue print.

After 1969, under new ownership, the company moved to 227 Burkhart Ave., still in Cincinnati. Frank Dellerman had sold his company to Don Tuthil in 1969, and Tuthil ran the company at that address until 1978. After Tuthil sold the company again in 1978, the lures were sold in plastic hinged boxes with card inserts giving the then address of 3726 Lonsdale, still in Cincinnati. I believe that all production of the Jake's Bait ceased around 1985.

I have mentioned the name Richard Walton in these books before. He is undoubtedly one of this country's earliest lure collectors, having started in the early 1900's. Pictured with this story is a letter addressed to Walton, dated December 8, 1955, signed by Frank Dellerman. Included with that letter were two company advertising pages, pictured courtesy of the Dan Basore collection.

Cardboard boxed "Jake's" Bait trades in the $15 to $20 range and plastic boxed lure under $10. The exceptions are the original lead body Jake's Bait and the rare Flyweight size that will trade higher, at over $50, especially with knowledgeable collectors.

PARK MFG. CO.
7511 GRIFFIN DRIVE   Cincinnati 16, Ohio
Zone 3?

December 8, 1955.

Rcd.- Dec. 12, 1955 -

Mr. R. Walton
2301 Franklin St. North
Wilmington, Delaware.

Dear Mr. Walton:

We appreciate very much your very nice letter in regard to our Jake's Baits.

Yes! we make the Jake's Bait and enclosed is descriptive folder which gives full and complete information on the casting size. You will note the price is 98¢ per bait, the weight 3/8 oz and the colors are as listed.

We also now make Jake's Bait in the spinning size. It is similar to the casting size except that in the spinning size an eyelet is used instead of the set screw that is used in the casting size.   The price on the spinning size is 75¢ per bait, the weight 1/4 oz. and the colors are the same as the casting size.

We can well imagine that in your 46 years of plug casting you have had some very enjoyable times and we like to think that our Jake's Bait was part and parcel of some of these good catches, as evidenced by the large perch you have caught on our Bait.   The Jake's Bait is very effective with perch, as well as all game fish.

We will be very glad to fill your order for whatever number of Jake's Baits you want in either size.   If check is sent with order, we pay the postage, which also saves the rather high COD cost.

We again want to tell you how much we appreciated receiving your letter.

Very truly yours

PARK MFG. COMPANY

Frank Dellerman

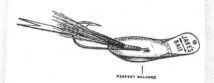

JAKE'S BAIT

FOR ALL GAME FISHING

FOR
ALL
GAME
FISHING

A Trial Will Convince You

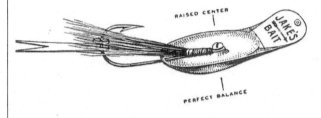

JAKE'S BAIT

HAS
THE
RIGHT
ACTION

MADE BY

THE PARK MANUFACTURING CO.
7511 GRIFFIN DRIVE   CINCINNATI 37, OHIO

MANUFACTURED BY

THE PARK MANUFACTURING CO.
7511 GRIFFIN DRIVE   CINCINNATI 37, OHIO

JAKE'S BAIT HAS THE RIGHT ACTION

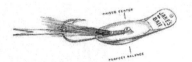

A raised center beneath set screw gives it perfect balance, can be used in the shallowest or deepest water, retaining a swimming motion until completely stopped.

This permits the angler to retrieve his bait fast or slow without affecting its action.

Bait Casters Find This Lure To Their Liking And Give it First Choice

JAKE'S BAIT HAS THE RIGHT ACTION

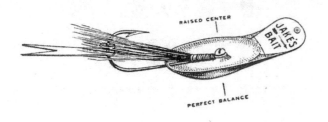

RAISED CENTER

JAKE'S BAIT

PERFECT BALANCE

A raised center beneath set screw gives it perfect balance, can be used in the shallowest or deepest water, retaining a swimming motion until completely stopped.

This permits the angler to retrieve his bait fast or slow without affecting its action.

Bait Casters Find This Lure To Their Liking And Give it First Choice

JAKE'S BAIT is made up in the following standard colors:

BLACK............with black buck tail
BLACK............with white feather tail
BROWN............with brown feather tail
RED.................with white feather tail
GREEN ....with ~~either black buck or~~ white feather tail
SILVER............with red head, with black buck tail
WHITE............with red head, with black buck tail
YELLOW.........with black buck tail
ALL WHITE....with white feather tail
SILVER ...... with white feather tail

JAKE'S BAITS are packed one dozen baits per carton, boxed individually.

You can have your choice of baits in all one color per box, or box can be assorted in any manner you prefer.

Rec'd Dec. 12, 1955

Retail Price - 98c per Bait on Casting size - 3/8 oz
75¢ " " " Spinning " 1/4 oz

ON YOUR NEXT FISHING TRIP TRY — JAKE'S BAIT

PARKER, H. G., & SON
BATTLE CREEK, MICHIGAN

Battle Creek, Michigan, the cereal capital, was also the home of a very rare **AEROPLANE BAIT**. I have been a collector for over 46 years and have only seen one of these lures "alive and in person". The bomb-shaped wooden body was painted white and had a unique harness system. The spring wire harness formed a rectangle around the lure, holding two in-line polished brass U spinners with tube and bead bearings, and then formed a wire wrap for two side treble hooks. The lure had a screw-eye-held nose box-swivel and a screw-eye tail treble. A 1910 ad listed the lure at $0.75 by H. G. Parker & Son, Dept. C, Battle Creek, Michigan. Sorry, buy my pictures of this rare Aeroplane Bait were lost when my basement was flooded during Wisconsin's heavy rains.

The Aeroplane Bait is very rare and is infrequently traded, so there are no established trade values at this time.

PARKER DISTRIBUTORS
NEW ROCHELLE, NEW YORK

The Parker Distributors Company, of 40 Industrial Place in New Rochelle, New York, were distributors of all kinds of outdoor sporting equipment, especially fishing tackle. Although they were not as old as many of the other distributors covered in these books, they were at least in business for over twenty years. Catalogs, like the 1966 Fishing Catalog pictured, are collectible.

Trade values on Parker catalogs vary by vintage, from $5 to $15.

PARKER LURE COMPANY
AMARILLO, TEXAS

In 1956, Ewell E. Parker, Jr. started production of his little, jointed, 2"-long plastic **EWELURE**. Working out of his home at 3545 Barclay in Amarillo, Texas, Parker made his semi-transparent lures. From a side view, the head of the lure was shaped like the GI canteen that I carried in Korea, and the tail was a thick-through forked fish tail. The joint-hinge was two eye screws linked together. The lures had painted yellow irises, as seen in the pictured example in brown and yellow scale (yellow perch). Other colors were red head with white, shad, green perch, black rib, and black back. By 1958, Ewell Parker, Jr. had moved his operation to 821 Florida Street still in Amarillo, but he had added new colors of crappie, white perch, yellow perch with white belly, black perch, and black perch with yellow belly. The lure was patented on January 28, 1958, under Patent No. 2,821,043. It was sold in a clear plastic hinged box with a white card insert with blue print.

The lure pictured with its original box card is courtesy of the Dan Basore collection.

The rather scarce Ewelure trades in the $25 to $35 range.

Jan. 28, 1958

E. E. PARKER, JR

2,821,043

FISH LURE

Filed Oct. 5, 1956

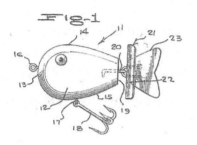

Fig-1

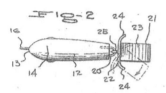

Fig-2

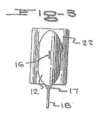

Fig-3

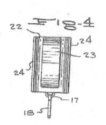

Fig-4

INVENTOR.

EWELL E. PARKER JR.

BY

McMorrow, Berman & Davidson
ATTORNEYS

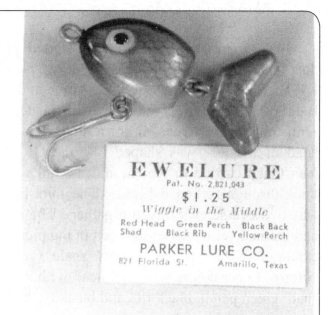

EWELURE
Pat. No. 2,821,043
$1.25
Wiggle in the Middle

Red Head   Green Perch   Black Back
Shad   Black Rib   Yellow Perch

PARKER LURE CO.
821 Florida St.   Amarillo, Texas

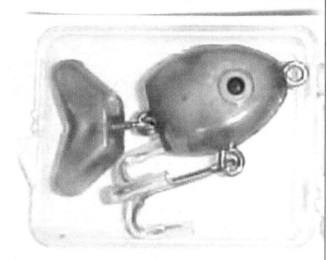

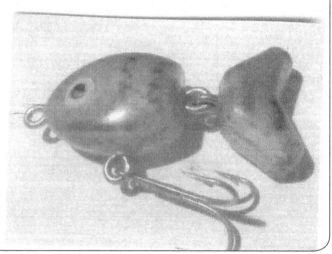

Recd.
Aug. 9, '58.

EWELURE

Patent No. 2,821,043

3/8 Oz.

$1.25

Wiggle in the Middle

● A new lure with enticing tail wiggle that begins in the middle, where the fish's does.

● The Ewelure catches fish at all depths; a fast retrieve runs shallow, and a slow retrieve runs very deep.

● The tail wiggles all the time even while the Ewelure sinks, and catches fish anywhere, anytime.

FIVE COLORS

RED HEAD   GREEN PERCH   BLACK BACK
SHAD   BLACK RIB   YELLOW PERCH

YELLOW PERCH
YELLOW BELLY   WHITE PERCH   CRAPPIE   BLACK PERCH   BLACK PERCH
YELLOW BELLY

Parker Lure Co.

821 FLORIDA STREET   AMARILLO, TEXAS

PARKER LURES
NEW YORK, NEW YORK

Not much is known about this 1930's lure company. The 4-1/4" nickel-plated spoon with a large single tail hook was stamped "**PARKER**". The lure had two 3-1/2" tapered nose-tip flanges, one each soldered to the top and bottom, which gave the lure its spinning, wobbling action. The lure was very similar to the shorter 2-1/4"

"Mackerel Spinner" that was distributed by the New York Spinning Unlimited Company earlier.

Lure picture is courtesy of the Steve O'Hern collection.

The Parker spoon trades in the $5 to $10 range.

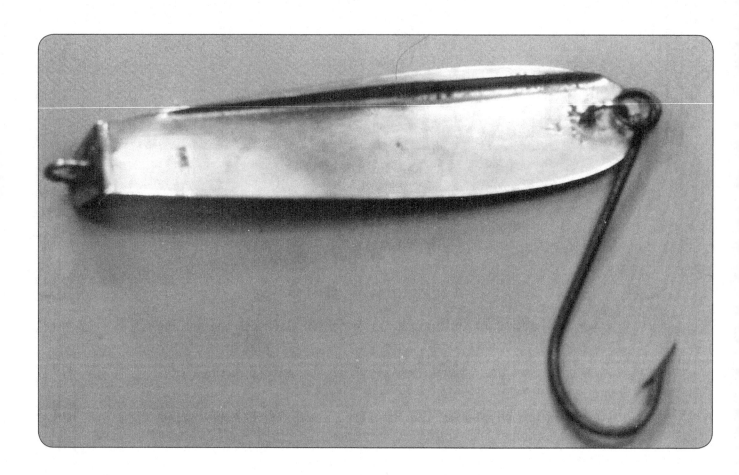

PARSE, EUGENE
WAUPACA, WISCONSIN

In the 1950's, Eugene Parse, working out of Waupaca, Wisconsin, developed a 2-1/2"-long bait hook he named the **COBRA HOOK**, "THE HOOK THAT SNAPS BACK". It was designed to be baited at one end on a single hook. The fishing line was tied off at that end but was looped back through another eye at the double hook opposite end. The hook was hinged so that when a fish took the bait, the line caused the other set of hooks to swing, or "SNAP", around and strike the fish in the mouth or head again for a secure catch. The scarce hook is pictured (courtesy of the Dan Basore collection) with its instructional papers.

The Parse Cobra Bait Hook trades in the $10 to $15 range.

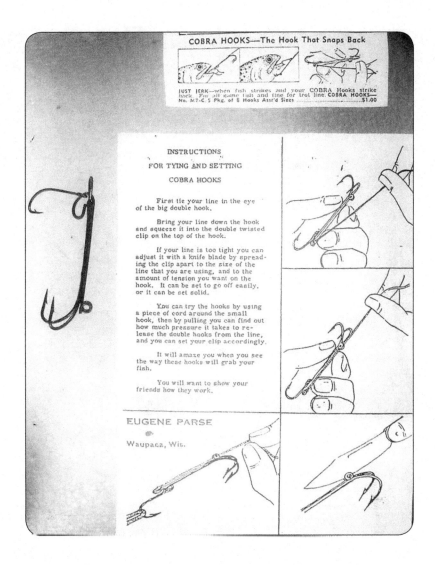

PARSE, EUGENE (2)

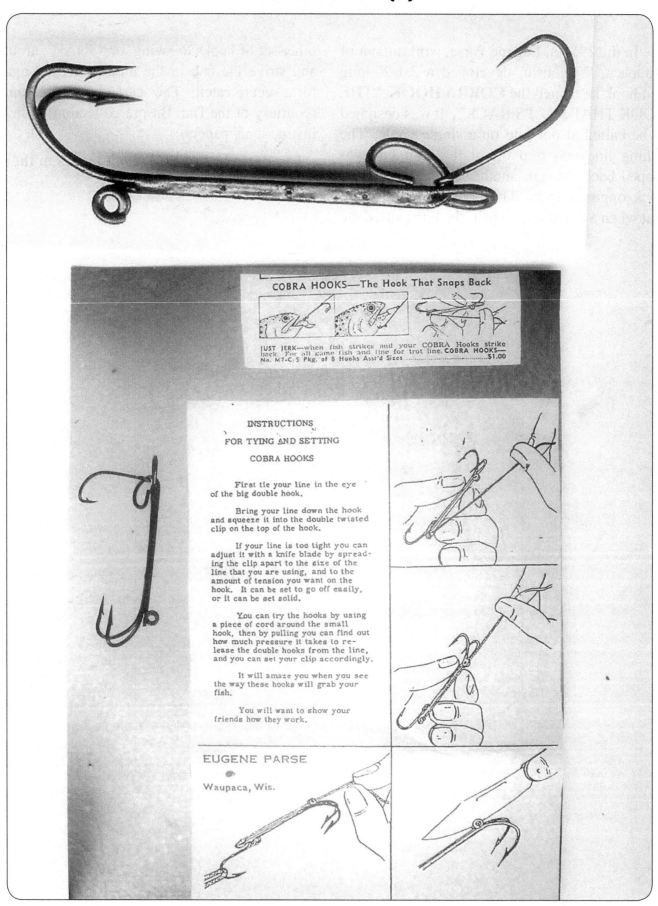

COBRA HOOKS—The Hook That Snaps Back

JUST JERK—when fish strikes and your COBRA Hooks strike back. For all game fish and fine for trot line. COBRA HOOKS— No. M7-C/5 Pkg. of 8 Hooks Ass'd Sizes $1.00

INSTRUCTIONS

FOR TYING AND SETTING

COBRA HOOKS

First tie your line in the eye of the big double hook.

Bring your line down the hook and squeeze it into the double twisted clip on the top of the hook.

If your line is too tight you can adjust it with a knife blade by spreading the clip apart to the size of the line that you are using, and to the amount of tension you want on the hook. It can be set to go off easily, or it can be set solid.

You can try the hooks by using a piece of cord around the small hook, then by pulling you can find out how much pressure it takes to release the double hooks from the line, and you can set your clip accordingly.

It will amaze you when you see the way these hooks will grab your fish.

You will want to show your friends how they work.

EUGENE PARSE

Waupaca, Wis.

PARTTI, ALBIN (IMPORTED BY)
DULUTH, MINNESOTA

The 2-5/8" brass, nickel-plated **PUIJO** spoon was made in Finland and imported by Albin Partti in the late 1940's. The lure was distributed in a rather plain two-piece cardboard box that said, "Made in Finland," and had a paste-on label for distributor ID.

A much neater plastic lure imported by Partti was the 3-1/2"-long **RAVAGEUR**. This double-jointed fish-shaped lure with painted eyes is pictured in a beautiful red and silver scale pattern. The two-piece cardboard box had a blue-green label over a yellow box with a drawing in white in the lower right corner of the cover of a pike with the lure in its mouth.

The company trade mark was PM in a circle formed by white arrowheads.

Another early 1950's import from Sweden was the **DRAGET SPOON**, which was a tear-drop-shaped spoon with a scale finish on the bottom half and three red center line dots. The 3-1/8" lure had a split-ring-held treble hook with a little red plastic tail flasher attached as well. There was not much to the lure, but the two-piece yellow cardboard lure box was somewhat neat with a cartoon drawing of a wide-eyed smiling fish on the cover with the trade name "FISK DRAG".

Three other lures, the **LAS-95**, the **LAS-DRAGET**, and the 3" **LYS-DRAGET**, by this Swedish company are pictured.

The 3-1/4" **WEEDLESS FISH DRAG** was a beautiful, gold-plated spoon with intricate fish scales layered on its back. On the underside, there were two rivets that held a spring housing unit that held the lure's single hook point up against a notch in the lure until a fish compressed it for the catch. Some of these are luminous, glow in the dark lures. The yellow boxed lure picture is courtesy of the Dan Basore collection.

Another import from Finland was the unique **NILS MASTER MOUSE**, pictured in yellow with black back trim and all white eyes, as well as in other colors. The red plastic lip on this lure was reversed, as it was meant to be a surface jumping lure, not a diver.

Another Niles Master lure was the **SNAKE HEAD**, a 3-1/8"-long plastic lure with an under-the-chin clear dive lip and a flared-wing-like head. It is pictured in yellow with blue back with black V-markings.

Boxed Puijo lures trade in the $15 to $20 range. Boxed Ravageur lures trade higher, at over $35 and up. Boxed Fisk Drag (Dragnet) trades in the $15 to $20 range. The Nils Master Mouse and Snake Head trade in the $10 to $15 range.

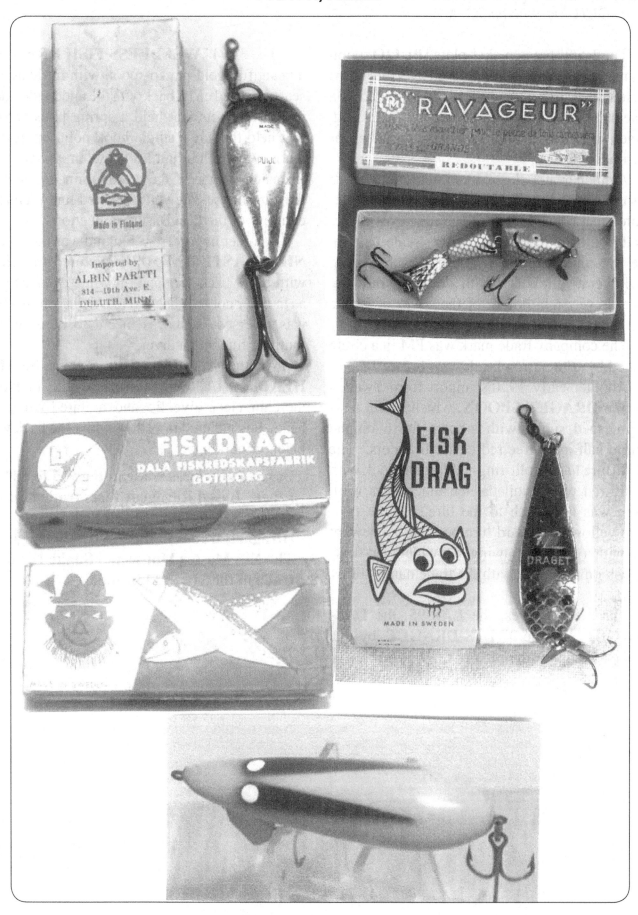

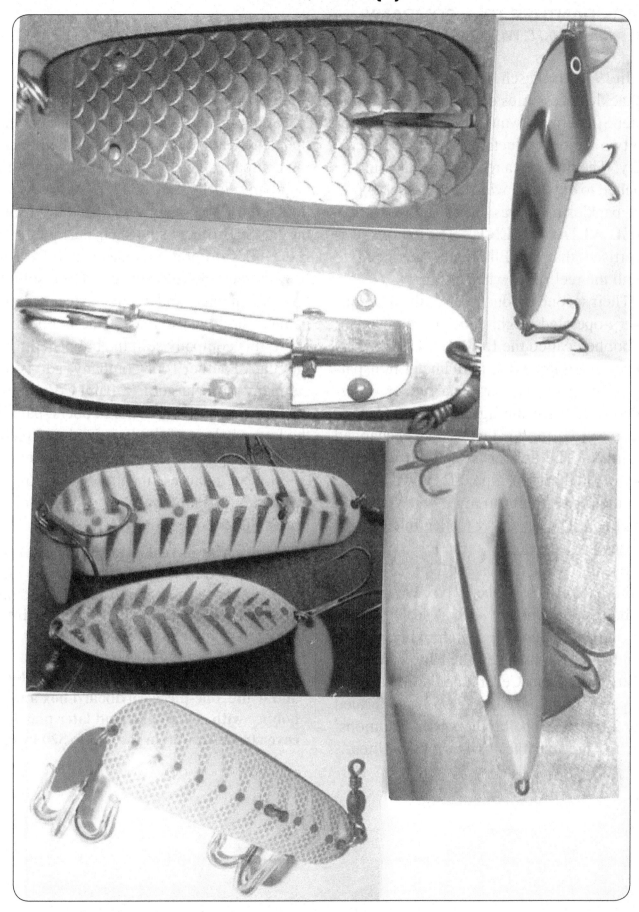

PASCH BROTHERS
BLACK PANTHER TOOL COMPANY
MILWAUKEE, WISCONSIN

In 1946, the Pasch Brothers formed a fishing tackle accessories company at 229 North Water Street in Milwaukee, Wisconsin. They had two major productions that are collected today. The first was a reel brake that could be attached to any level wind casting reel to prevent backlash. It was called the **MARGIS REEL ATTACHMENT**. The Margis was advertised that it "Eliminates the need to thumb the reel spool when casting."

Their second production was their famous battery-operated, light-emitting night fishing bobber, called the **BOB-ER-LITE**. This bobber had a large 2-1/4"-diameter transparent plastic bulb that sat on a rubber water-sealed fixture for the light bulb and battery. Over the years, the box for this bobber changed six times. The bobber is pictured with this story in the third box type. If you wish to see the other boxes, refer to my 1999 Wisconsin lures book, The History & Collectible Fishing Tackle of Wisconsin.

By the way, the patent No. 2,746,633 on the later Pasch bobber's box was not for the bobber but for the special sealed eyelet to control the on-off switch when a fish would bite. It was designed by a William E. Simmons from Cedar Rapids, Iowa, with the patent applied for in 1952 and issued May 22, 1956. The brothers used Simmons' idea to improve the "[when] Fish Bites… Bobber Lites" aspect of the bobber when night fishing.

Sometime along the way, the brothers opened a divisional sales and manufacturing company, the Bob-Er Lite Manufacturing Company, located at 3313 Douglas Avenue in Racine, Wisconsin. In the later 1950's, the Pasch Brothers sold their business to the E-Z Paint Corporation, located at 4051 South Iowa Street in Milwaukee. They sold the bobbers in blue and white boxes, but they painted the lower halves of the bobbers red. Later, this company sold the bobbers through the Black Panther Tool Company, a divisional company of the larger E-Z Paint Corporation, who continued to make the bobbers, painting the lower halves of the bulbs red and picturing a black panther on each of the boxes.

Bobber pictures in third Pasch box and the first E-Z Paint box are courtesy of the Travis Slater collection.

The rare Margis reel brake in box trades in the $100 range. The boxed Bob-Er-Lite bobbers trade from $35 to $50, depending on the age of the box, with the blue print first, red topped box second, the third (pictured), then the blue print paste-on label, and so on. The black panther, blue and white, one-piece cardboard box and bobber with cellophane, and later plastic, cover trades lower, in the $15 to $20 range.

PAT'S FISHING TACKLES
SHEBOYGAN, WISCONSIN

In 1950, Robert Patterson, using the first three letters of his last name, founded Pat's Fishing Tackles out of P. O. Box 164, Sheboygan, Wisconsin. His company specialized in both fine domestic and imported smaller spinning lures. I'm showing a picture of nine spoons and spinners that he sold out of Sheboygan that were imported from Germany from 1950 through the later 1950's. An <u>Outdoor Life</u> October 1956 ad on page 170 read, "HOW DOES IT LOOK TO THE FISH? There are two ways to design a fishing bait. One way is to make it attractive to the fisherman. The other way is to make it attractive to the fish. We believe that the best way to make steady customers and friends is to offer a line of baits that gets a man something to carry home to eat for dinner."

Pat's Fishing Tackles sold their lures on cardboard wood-grain-color dealer cards that had green trim and print. These dealer display boards, in lots of one dozen lures, contained different colors of the same lure on some boards, or offered an assortment of different lures, usually in the metal bait line. The bottom of the dealer board had a green section with a white silhouette of a smiling fisherman in a rowboat and the caption, "Plastic Skirt Defies Weeds!...A Product of PATS FISHING TACKLES."

One of Pat's more unique domestic lures was the **SUPER SPIN-NIK**, a 2-3/8"-long, plastic, top-water lure. This 1/4-oz., fat-torpedo-shaped lure had a round, bullet-shaped nose that was smaller in diameter than the wider main body. The lure had an exhaust-pipe-type tail extension holding the treble hook that was equipped with the red finger-spread weedguards that were common on lures made in the 1950's. The lure had a double-blade nose prop and a convex washer facing a concave washer for bearings and for the screw-eye line tie. By 1959, according to an ad (pictured) from that year, Pats Fishing Tackle Company renamed the Spin-Nik to the **SPUTNIK**.

Another Pat's lure was the 1-7/8" **SUPER DIVE-MINNOW** that had a slot in the nose holding a hammer-finished dive lip. The lure had the same reinforced exhaust-pipe tail extension for the tail hook and a one-piece, surfaced-rigged belly treble. The lure did not have the plastic finger guard weedguards but did have a plastic red sleeve on the hook shanks. The lure is pictured in green scale with red chin blush and decal eyes with half-moon pupils.

Another production that was made in both a pan fish size and a bass and pike size was the **BUMBLE SPINNER**. The spinner consisted of a large plastic red bead for the head, a large prop representing the wings, and a coiled wire for the body, all mounted on a wire shaft with tail treble hook and made to look like a bumble bee. The lures were sold in plastic sacks on an orange-topped dealer display board that had a cartoon drawing of a flying bumble bee and the caption, "The BIG catch is on BUMBLE SPINNER with built in action.

Individually, Pat's Fishing metal lures trade only in the $5 range, and the Spin-Nik and Dive-Minnow lures in the $10 to $15 range, but full dealer boards will top the $65 to $75 range. Boards that are not full should be adjusted downward in value accordingly. Dealer Boards of Bumble Spinners trade in the $15 to $20 range.

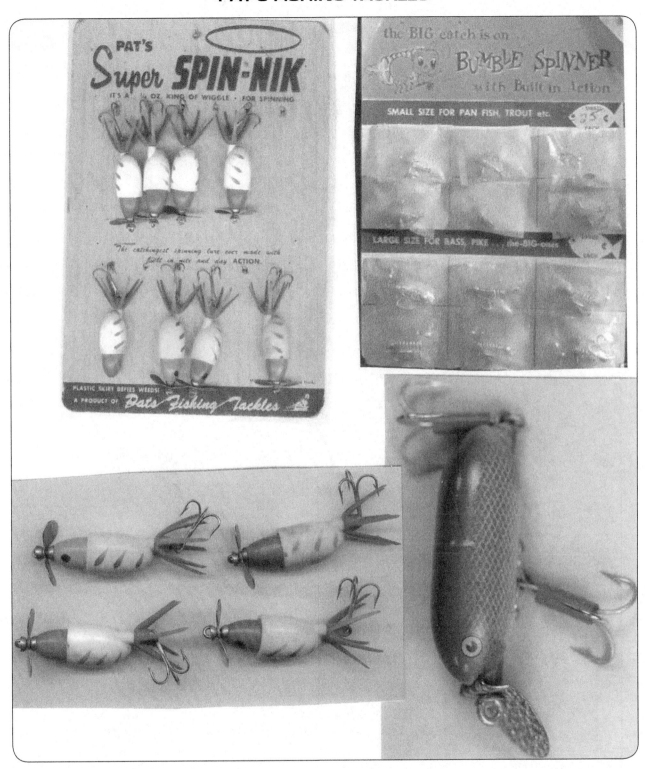

FINEST IMPORTED ARTIFICIAL BAITS
MADE IN GERMANY

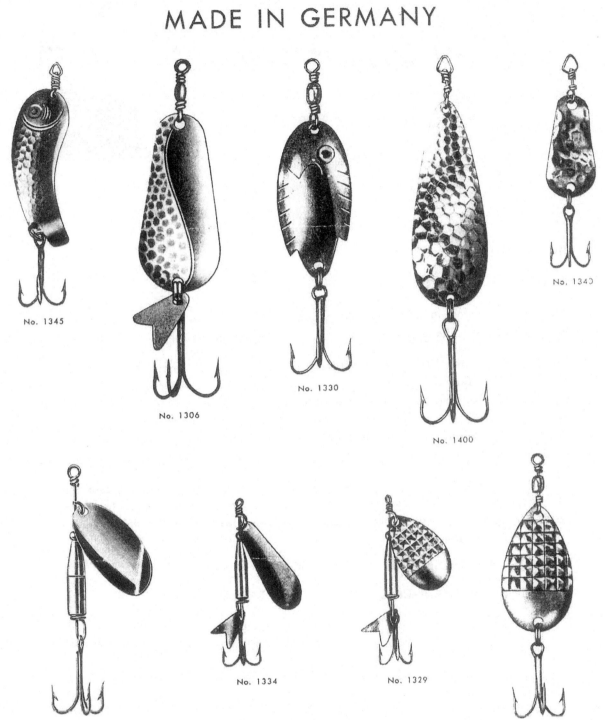

No. 1345

No. 1306

No. 1330

No. 1400

No. 1340

No. 1335

No. 1334

No. 1329

No. 1304

PAT'S FISHING TACKLES
P. O. BOX 164
SHEBOYGAN, WISCONSIN

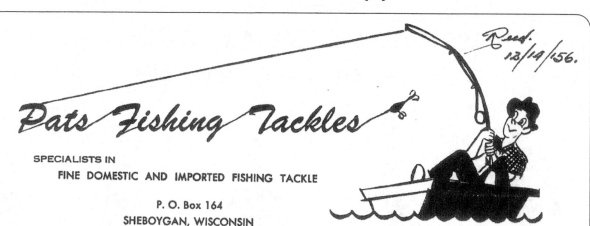

Recd. 12/14/'56.

Pats Fishing Tackles

SPECIALISTS IN
FINE DOMESTIC AND IMPORTED FISHING TACKLE

P. O. Box 164
SHEBOYGAN, WISCONSIN

Dear Fishermen:

HOW does it look to the fish?

There are two ways to design a fishing bait. One way is to make it attractive to the fishermen. The other way is make it attractive to the fish.

We believe that the best way to make steady customers and friends is to offer a line of baits that get a man something to carry home to eat for dinner. Our imported baits are worked out by experienced designers and thoroughly tried and tested by veteran anglers under the toughest fishing conditions to make sure you get just what you want in the maximum of thrills and fishing pleasure plus the maximum of fishing results. They are the best baits you can possibly buy at any price.

WE HAVE ALWAYS PREFERRED QUALITY. Let us sell fine grade merchandise that we may gain your confidence as a customer and keep our reputation. Herein are listed fine quality materials, fairly priced, fully guaranteed to give satisfaction. It is our earnest desire to render you efficient and reliable service.

BAITS ARE OUR BUSINESS BUT THEY'RE ALSO OUR HOBBY.

ORDER NOW, MONEY BACK IF YOU ARE NOT SATISFIED.

PAT'S FISHING TACKLES

Robert Patterson

note — classified ad —
Outdoor Life
Oct. '56
page 170.

PATENT ENGINEER'S, INC.
MILWAUKEE, WISCONSIN

In 1938, a Milwaukee man named Wagner received a patent for a fish and frog harness rig. The metal **WAGNER'S FISH AND FROG HARNESS** had a front hook to secure the head of the bait and an unlocking skewer that could be passed through the body of the bait of choice that also would hold a tail hook of choice. There was an adjustable wire ring that could be secured around the body of the bait. The harness two-piece white cardboard box was neat, with green trim and a caricature of a musky about to engulf a minnow rigged in the harness. The company address was 229 E. Wisconsin Ave., Milwaukee.

The rare boxed Wagner's Harness trades in the $30 to $35 range.

PATRICK, T. A.
DETROIT, MICHIGAN

I will make just brief mention of **THE EYE** lure because it is most often found in the fly rod size. However, Thomas A. Patrick also made The Eye in a spinning size on a 1-1/2" # 4 hook and sold it on a white card. Patrick was awarded Design Patent No. D169,326 for his lure on April 14, 1953.

A similar lure was designed by Harold Lipman, of Kansas City, Missouri, in 1950. His lure was called "Lippy's BIG EYE" by Lipman Lures, Inc., of 2528 Dodier Street, St Louis, Missouri.

The Michigan carded "The Eye" lure trades in the $5 and higher range.

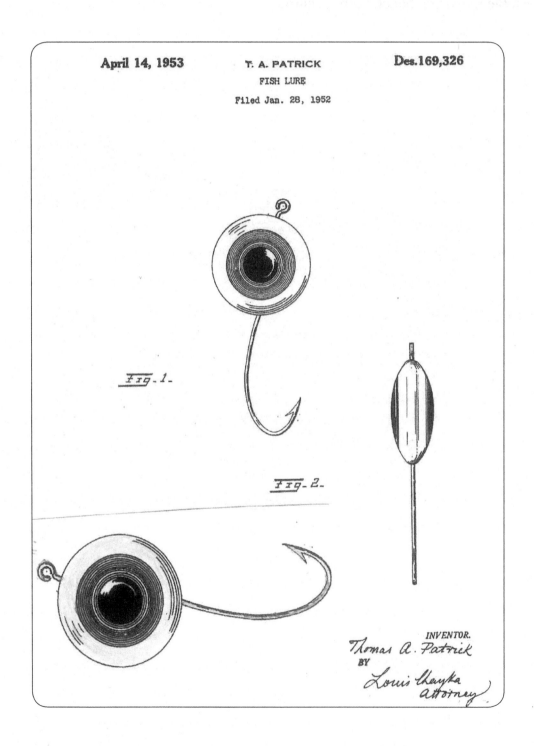

April 14, 1953   T. A. PATRICK   Des.169,326

FISH LURE

Filed Jan. 28, 1952

Fig.1.

Fig.2.

INVENTOR.
Thomas A. Patrick
BY
Louis Chayka
attorney

PATTERSON, CHARLIE
FORT MEYERS, FLORIDA

Charlie Patterson (1912 - 2006) was an avid smallmouth bass and musky fisherman and was also a prolific lure maker in the lures he designed to catch those two species of fish. His wooden lures date to the 1950's and 1960's and include over two-dozen different lure designs in the 1-7/8" smallmouth sizes up to the 7-1/2" musky sizes. The first picture is of Charlie Patterson on the left with his life-long fishing buddy, Ward "Rusty" Reed, on the right.

In the first lure picture, I'm showing you the **PATTERSON FLAPTAIL** that measured 4-1/2" long for just the wooden body, but reached 6-1/2" long with the extended trailing flap tail, and that does not include the 3-3/4" wire nose line tie. The lure had painted eyes and recycled Heddon two-piece flap hardware for the belly trebles and was finished in a dark green with spotted frog.

The lure underneath that musky lure was the 1-7/8" (2-5/8" overall) **PATTERSON SMALL MOUTH DIVER**. This lure also had painted eyes, a 1-1/4"-long rounded-tip dive lip, and converse cup and screw-eye hardware for the belly treble.

Patterson's no-rust brass dive lip was always held by a treble hook eye screw and two other tiny screws. The dive lips were made in a rounded tip, pointed tip, or heart-shaped tip, and each has a 1-1/2" wire line tie extension.

The first set of lure pictures also shows the belly view of the Flaptail and the 7-1/4" jointed and unique wooden **PATTERSON GLOBE**. This colorful red-headed lure had the metal wing-props inserted in the head and had a special rudder on the belly of the second section to prevent it from turning. In addition to this stabilizer-rudder, the lure had a belly balance-weight.

The second set of lure pictures shows typical **PATTERSON MUSKY BANANA** and **MUSKY MINNOW** lures in the 6-1/4" to 7-1/2" range.

The third set of lure pictures depicts all of Patterson's lure types and color patterns.

Lure pictures are courtesy of the Ward "Rusty" Reed collection.

Patterson lures trade in the $30 to $75 range today.

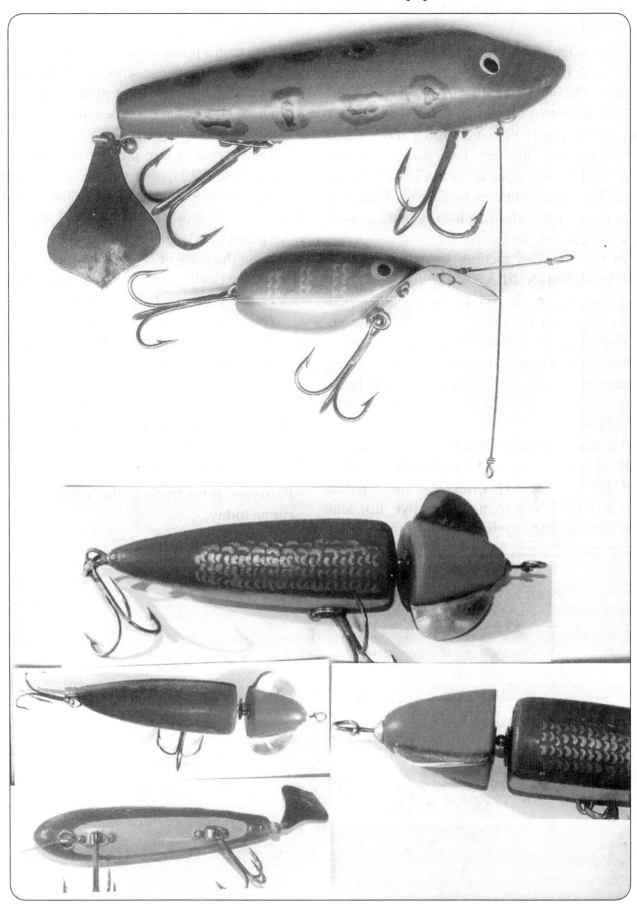

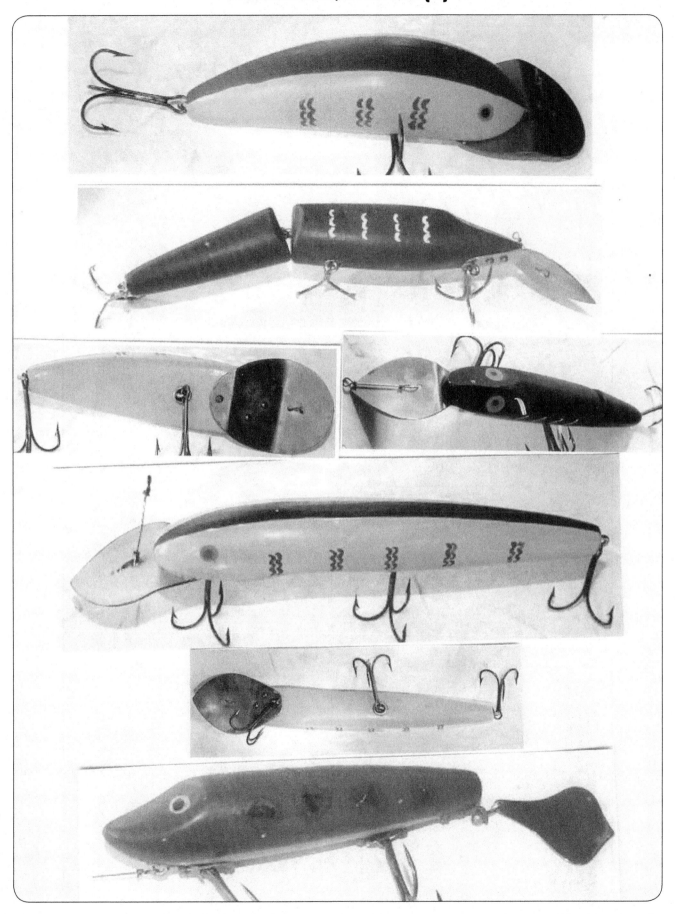

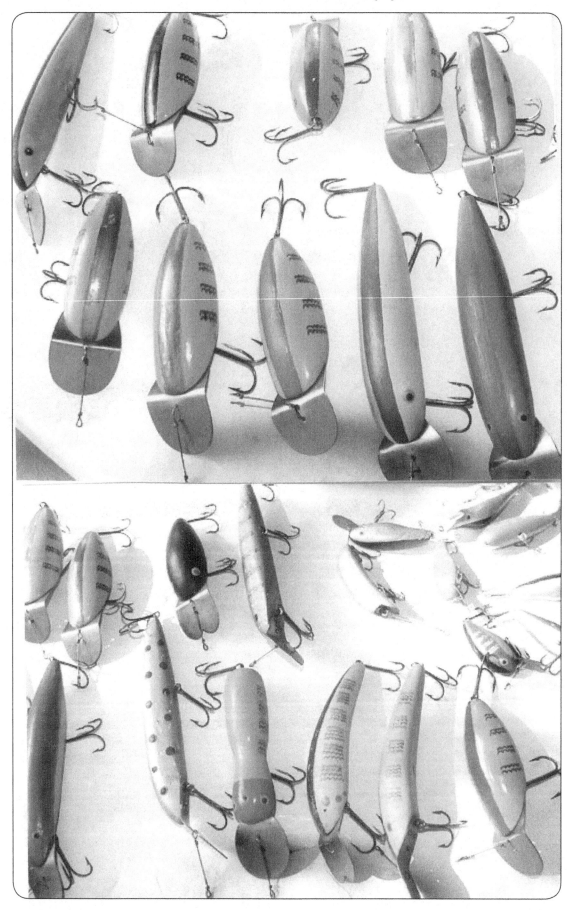

INDEX

C

D

E

F

G

H

N

Ned P. Krilich, 301
New Idea Spinner, 297
Nif-T-Plug, 312
Night Crawler, 275
Nils Master Mouse, 413
North & South Coast Minnows, 1
North American Production Co., 4
North American Tackle Co., 7
North Coast Minnow, 1
Northern Bait, 10
Northern Minnow, 16
Northern Specialties Co., 12
Northern Specialty Co., 13
Northern Tackle Co. (IL & WI), 19
Northern Tackle Co. (Ontario), 16
Northern Waters Bait Co., 24
Northern Wisconsin Bucktail
    Musky Lure Makers, 25
Northport Industries, Inc., 26
Northport Nailer Spoon, 26
Northway Products, 28
Northwest Silversmiths Co., 29
Northwest Specialty Mfg. Co., 33
Northwest Tackle Mfg., Ltd., 34
Northwood Tackle Co., 35
Norviel, Tim, 38
Norwich Florida Corp., 39
Norwich Shrimp Lure No. 600, 39
Nova Spinner Bait, 40
Nova Tackle Co., 40
Novelty Lure Co., 45
Novelty Plug Shop, 51
Noweed Bait Co., 52
Noweed, 52

Nungesser 4 in 1 Troller, 54
Nungesser Shad Killer Spoons, 54
Nungesser Shad Killer, 54
Nungesser, R.E.-Troller Bait Co., 54
Nuvalu Minnow USA Co., 57
Nuvalu, 57
Nyglo Products, 59
Nylure Bait Co., 61
Nylures, 61

O

O.K. Bait Co., Not Inc., 63
O.K. Machine Co., 67
O.M. Bait Co., 68
Oberlin Bait Cage, 75
Oberlin Bait Canteen, 75
Oberlin Canteen, Inc., 75
Obie Tackle Co., 77
O'Brien Artificial Minnow, 70
O'Brien, Richard F., 70
OB's Tackle Co., 77
Ocean City 350 Spin Cast Reel, 79
Ocean City Mfg. Co., 79
Oceanic Tackle Shop, 81
Odon Bait Co., 83
Ogene Co., 85
Ogilvy, 93
Ogilvy, Robert, Co., 93
Ohio Outdoor Products, 94
Oil Capitol Electronics Corp., 95
Ojie Bait & Tackle Co., The, 96
Ojie, 96
OK Crab, 67
OK Reel, 67
Okelite Single Blade, 98

P

Red Fin Minnow, 239
Red Shank Gaff Hook Co., 311
Red Shank Spoons, 311
Red Wing Blackbird, 265
Reekers Trolling Spoons, 311
Reelslick Caster's Kit, 222
Rex Fields, 296
Rip-Jack, 81
Ripple Tail, 253
Ripple, 293
Rivalure, 274
Robbins-Larson Plug, 311
Rolling Plug Baits, 159
Rosegard Plug, 312
Roy Self, 314
Royal Coachman, 165
Roy's Ace, 300
Roy's Bell Spinner, 300
Roy's Candle Fish, 300
Roy's Dodger, 300
Roy's Wow, 300
Rubber Frog, 277
Ruby-Eye Spoon, 385

S

S.E. Bacon, 290
Salmon Egg Lure, 298
Salmon Plug Lures, 114
Salmon Spinner, 293
Saltwater Lippy, 274
Salt-Water Walkie Talkie, 275
Sam E. Robbins & Frank L.
    Larson, 311
Sam-Bo, 45
Sammy Special, 319

Samuel Friend, 396
Scalelite Wobbler, 293
Schechterle Plug, 312
Schroeder's Washington Wonder
    Plug, 313
Sculpin Sounder, 297
Sea King, 301
Seaton Salmon Plug, 313
Seattle Fishing Lure Co., 313
Seattle Jr., 317
Seattle, 317
Sebenius Trolling Spoon, 309
Sedco Mfg. Co., 314
Seiter Spoon, 52
Shawnee Spinning Lure, 180
Sheik Metal Minnow, The, 242
Shinner, 274
Shinners Hartford Minnow Float, 127
Shoe Horn, 301
Siberian Bass Spinner, 302
Siberian Champion, 302
Siberian Trout Spinner, 302
Siberian Wobbler, 302 & 321
Siberian, 302
Side Winder Spoons, 297
Silver Dart, 29 & 293
Silver Horde Egg Wobblers, 314
Silver Horde Fishing Supplies,
    Spoons, 314
Silver Horde Sports Plugs, 314
Silver Horde, 314
Silver Minnow Streamer, 165
Slim Jim Troll, 293
Slippery Slim, 196
Slow Fall Jigs, 98
Smallmouth Bass with Frog, 114

Wright Tackle Co., 320
W-V Mfg. Co., 45

Y

Yellowknife, 233
Yeo, 320

Z

Zani, 79
Zardeen, 184
Ziggy Jointed Fish, 211
Zimmy Plastic Plug, 296
Zimmy Plug, 318
Z-Ray, 319

CPSIA information can be obtained
at www.ICGtesting.com
Printed in the USA
LVOW03s2152301016

510941LV00005B/259/P

9 781425 152468